Contents

Preface

The two volumes of this book are intended mainly, though not exclusively, for students enrolled on a Business Education Council National (Certificate or Diploma) level course, and studying the Common Core double module (3 and 4) entitled "The Organisation in its Environment".

This book attempts to make clear the environmental and organisational scenes that students will face in their everyday life. Each scene provides a framework which will guide students to understand and appreciate their role within their own organisation and their local environment, and make them aware of other organisations operating in the United Kingdom and international environment.

Material presented provides students with specific knowledge about demographic, economic, legal, political and social disciplines which, when brought together, will help students to analyse and solve problems associated with their work. In applying this knowledge students will become effective contributory members of the organisation that employs them.

In producing the book we have attempted to provide complete coverage of the 'general' and 'learning' objectives specified by the Business Education Council. Sometimes we may have gone beyond what was required, but if we did it was done to make life easier for the student. There would be less need to look up the meaning of words or facts in other books. In general, the book aims to be sufficiently self-contained.

We wish to take this opportunity to express our deep appreciation to our colleagues for their encouragement and help. We also owe a debt of gratitude to authors and students, both past and present, whose influence on our thinking is reflected in the book.

To those who very kindly gave us permission to reproduce some of their copyright material we gratefully acknowledge their co-operation.

We are especially grateful to the Director of Publishing of Her Majesty's Stationery Office for giving us permission to use Crown material; material that is vital to understanding our environment.

Finally, to our immediate families we would like to express our gratitude. Their patience and sympathy smoothed the way to bringing this book into print.

Norbert L. Paulus

The Organisation in its Environment

Volume 1

Editor:
Norbert L. Paulus, B.Sc.(Econ.)
Senior Lecturer in Economics
West Bromwich College of Commerce and Technology

Contributors:
David M. Lee, LL.B. Cert. Ed.
Anthony P. Nisbett, B.A., Dip.Ed.
Gerald G. Paulus, B.A.(Econ.)

POLYTECH PUBLISHERS LTD STOCKPORT

First published in 1979

Set in 10 pt Times series by
Bury Phototypesetting Limited, Peel Mills, Bury, Lancashire
and printed in Great Britain by
Ashworths Print Services, Peel Mills, Bury, Lancashire

Chapter 1

Organisation and Environment

Learning objectives:
At the end of your study of this chapter you should:
1. be able to define the terms organisation and environment.
2. understand, basically, why organisations are important to individuals.
3. be aware of the increased attention being given to the study of organisations.
4. recognise the forces that operate in the environment.
5. understand that organisations have an impact on their environment, *and* the environment on organisations.
6. be aware that organisations and the environment are subject to change and must be considered as dynamic subjects.

Organisation

Organisation is a term that has been defined in many ways by many people. Dictionaries give several meanings but the one most acceptable for our study is that it is "a body of persons organised for some end or work".

Organisations have existed for centuries but it was not until the turn of the 20th century that vast amounts of literature appeared on the subject. Since that time they have been studied from different points of view and, as a result, there *now* exist different schools of thought.

The classical school has its roots mainly in the early years of the 20th century dating from the investigations and reports of Frederick W. Taylor (1856-1915) — the 'father of scientific management'. He and other writers[1] associated with the school were involved in studying almost exclusively various sections of formal organisation (where the efforts of people in an organisation are arranged to achieve greater effort than they would if they were unorganised) in the field of business. Their movement was to get away from the 'rule of thumb' methods and move towards 'rule by measurement'.

The school started from the narrow concept of the division of labour applied primarily at the production level, such as time and method studies of basic physical activities, and widened to include every person in the organisation and some of the following organisation situations: span of control, chain of command, delegation of authority and responsibility, line and staff, functional management. Thus, this school concentrated on the formal anatomy of the organisation; informal human activities were not studied.

1. Notably Henri Fayol (1908), Mooney and Reiley (1931), and in the U.K.: E. T. Elbourne (1914) and E. F. L. Brech (1957).

A new school developed. They accepted the classical school concepts of formal human action but introduced into the formal organisation the informal actions of individuals and groups, such as cliques and intra-organisational rivalry.

The start of the new school, called the 'human relations school' or 'neo-classical school', is associated with the studies made by Elton Mayo and colleagues at the Hawthorne works of the Western Electric Company in Chicago, Illinois, U.S.A. which were carried out between 1927 and 1932.

The most recent school, 'the modern school', studies and analyzes and organisation as a system. The idea is to identify the basic factors that exist in the organisation, noting the qualities attributed to each factor separately and how each factor is linked to other factors and their attributes. Each system has its own sub-systems, and yet each system is viewed as a sub-system of some larger system. For example, the U.K. can be studied as a system. It is a sub-system of the world system, and at the same time it has its own sub-system such as its own economic system, social system and political system. Each of these have their own sub-systems. A system, therefore cannot be treated as being completely independent of other systems — an organisation cannot be treated as being independent of other organisations.

The modern school claims that the only meaningful way to study an organisation is to study it as a system.

The above schools of thought are linked to the growing importance of organisations. Several centuries ago the people of the U.K. lived in isolated communities and the number of organisations they came into contact with were few. As the decades passed communities became less isolated and more and more individuals were moving into the cities. The break-down of people being self-sufficing (requiring nothing from outside, independent) encouraged the growth of organisations (economic, political and social organisations) to meet their needs. People came into contact with various organisations more often. A continuation of people becoming more dependent on others encouraged the growth of organisations in number, size and activities. Because they played a more important role in the lives of people it became more important to study and analyze them. Organisations became more complex and so did studies relating to them.

Why are organisations important? A simple answer is that they are important because a considerable part of each individual's life is involved with them. Children spend a large part of their lives in school organisations and youth organisations. Workers normally spend one-quarter of their weekly hours and more than one-third of their weekly waking hours in work organisations. After work they become involved in other organisations such as sports, leisure, educational, retail. It is difficult to view the life of individuals without organisations and conversely to view organisations without individuals. Each is important to the other.

Another important relationship is that which takes placed between an organisation and its environment.

Environment

The term environment refers to the aggregate of surrounding things, conditions or influences. For our purposes we take it to mean the total of all the forces that exist outside the control of the organisation.

These forces or factors are normally grouped under broad headings such as economic, natural, political, social and technological. They impinge on the operations of the organisation to varying degrees depending upon the type of organisation and whether they closely surround or are at a distance from the organisation's operations.

Exhibit 1.1

ENVIRONMENT AND FORCES IN THE ENVIRONMENT
HAVING AN IMPACT ON U.K. ORGANISATION

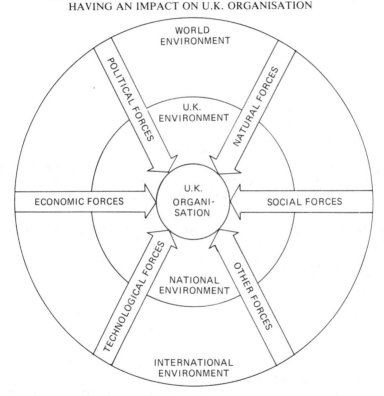

The exhibit clearly shows that the environment can broadly be classified as the 'national environment' and 'international or world environment'. The national environment closely circles the organisation that operates within its boundary and we would expect, normally, that the forces within this environment would have a greater impact on the organisation than the forces that are exerted in the international environment farther out from the organisation.

The reverse situation also occurs. The previous information in Exhibit 1.1 remains the same except for the direction of the arrows — they should point in the opposite direction. In other words the organisation influences its environment by its activities. Naturally the impact that an organisation has on its environment will depend on its field of operations (economic, social, etc.) and whether its activities takes it outside the local and national boundary.

The point being made is that an organisation does not operate in a vacuum. Each has activities that take it outside the organisation. It purchases goods and services from other organisations (national and perhaps international) and makes its goods and services available to the community. Thus, an organisation is part of a market, a community, and a nation — it is part of its environment. Because this is so it establishes relationships with individuals and organisations outside its circle. It must, therefore, influence the forces in its environment just as the environmental forces outside its circle must influence the organisation's activities.

How big an impact does the environment have on an organisation? This is difficult to gauge because organisations do not react to their environment in the same way. Some may not be aware of the fact that the environment is in a continuous, although not necessarily noticeable, state of change. They, as a result, may stagnate, decline or die. Other organisations are very much aware of this fact and are constantly searching for the phenomena (remarkable things that impress the observer as being extraordinary) that may be potentials for environmental change. These extraordinary events may be any one of many social, economic, technological and political changes. Organisations, if they respond to the change, are likely to grow because being aware of environmental changes makes it easier for an organisation to be successful.

The positive or negative impact that environmental change has on an organisation will depend upon:

1. whether the environmental changes are favourable or unfavourable to the present activities of the organisation,

2. whether the organisation is aware of the changes, and

3. whether the organisation, once aware of the changes, is stimulated by the environmental phenomena and responds by planning and initiating action to meet the changes.

In an attempt to explain environmental change it is, perhaps, best to provide a set of examples under each environmental force area using actual changes that have taken place in the U.K. over recent years. Only a few, of many, examples have been provided to given an idea of environmental change.

In the environmental force area 'population' some noticeable changes have been:

1. increasing numbers in the population,

2. changing shape of the population — bulges,

3. increase, absolute and relative, of the number of older persons, and

4. a steady decline in births each year since 1964 (to 1977).

In the 'economics' scene, the following changes have been noted:

1. increase in foreign competition,

2. rising labour costs,

3. decline in the number of small, and an increase in the number of large, organisations, and

4. increase in the number of unemployed.

'Social' changes that have occurred:

1. growth of suburban area,

2. movement towards equality of the sexes,

3. raising of school leaving age and general tendency for students to stay in education for longer periods, and

4. more leisure time.

The 'political' environmental force area changes:

1. increase in public sector expenditures,

2. action to bring about equality of the sexes,

3. active participation in the European Economic Community, and

4. tendency to swing towards direct controls — a movement away from free enterprise.

'Technologically' the changes that have taken place might be noted as:

1. acceleration in the use of new materials,

2. increased attention to research for new forms of power,

3. increased costs of research and development, and

4. improvement of motor-way system.

These changes, and many other not listed, represent a complex of shifts in the environment. From an organisation's point of view they must consider the sum of all the changes that occur outside their control. To do this it is necessary to consider each change in depth because a change in one factor is likely to influence changes in other factors in the same environmental force area as well as others. The following example, shown in Exhibit 1.2, is an attempt to give a simplified version of the likely influences one environmental change has on other factors in the environment.

The exhibit uses a 'population' factor that did change from 1964 up to 1977, that is to say, the steady decline in the number of births over this period of time. The changes that take place as a result of this change is shown for the short period of time (now and in the near future) and those that occur later on in time, but *all* likely changes are not shown. Also not shown are the chain reactions that take place — the original change influences other factors and these in turn influence changes in other factors. For example, the decline in the number of births is likely to influence the size of the labour force (a decline in numbers) and this in turn, assuming the demand for labour has not changed, is likely to influence the age at which students leave school, the age of retirement, the number of women working, and wages paid. Each of these will influence other factors and cause them to change — and so the story goes.

Exhibit 1.2

AN EXAMPLE OF AN ENVIRONMENTAL FACTOR THAT
HAS CHANGED AND ITS LIKELY INFLUENCE ON OTHER
ENVIRONMENTAL FACTORS

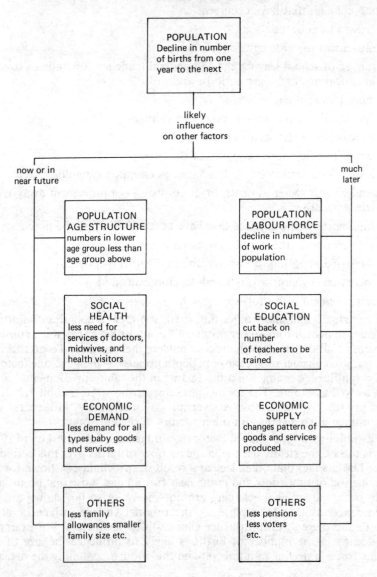

As stated before environmental changes bring about changes in organisations within the nation, and the nation itself. The nation, in our case the U.K., has changed over time as its sub-systems (economic, social, political, etc.) changed, moving from a free enterprise position towards a planned system.

In the later 1970's the U.K. has what is called a 'mixed' economy, and this forms the national environment of which U.K. organisations are part. It therefore becomes essential to explain the main features and underlying principles of the 'mixed economy'.

Assignments

1. Define the terms 'environment' and 'organisation' then briefly discuss the environmental forces that impinge on the operations of organisations.

2. "An organisation does not operate in a vacuum". Explain.

3. In what ways are organisations important to individuals, and individuals important to organisations?

4. Consider, in depth, the likely impact that will occur in the near future and later in time from an increase in the number of births over the next few years.

Chapter 2

Mixed Economy

Learning objectives:

At the end of your study of this chapter you should be:

1. aware of the basics relating to extreme economic systems.
2. able to explain the main features of the 'mixed' economy as exemplified by the United Kingdom.
3. capable of explaining the underlying principles of the 'mixed' economy as exemplified by the United Kingdom.

The world's population, in 1974 it was estimated to be almost 4,000,000,000, has unlimited wants, but, on the other hand, the means to supply all these wants is limited. Each country in the world faces this relationship. It is this problem of scarcity of the means that creates economic and social problems domestically and internationally.

Internationally, groups of nations have set-up a variety of institutions, such as the International Monetary Fund, the International Bank for Reconstruction and Development, the European Economic Community, and others to smooth the relationship.

Domestically, each economy has set-up its own system.[1] That is to say, the people within each nation create their own customs, ethics, and habits, and these are expressed through their form of government and the laws their government creates. The economic system of any country must be viewed through the institutions which tend to organise the relationships between unlimited wants and limited means.

Each country, whatever their state of development (developed or underdeveloped) and whatever their form of government (absolute monarchy, dictatorship, democratic, socialistic, etc.) must attempt to answer three basic supply questions, namely:

1. What goods and services should be produced, or not produced? For goods and services that will be produced it is necessary to decide on the quantities of each and the cost to society in producing those commodities rather than others. In economics this concept is referred to as 'opportunity cost' or, as it is sometimes called 'the trade off'.

2. How shall these goods and services be produced? Decisions will have to be made about the organisation of production for each good and service; the methods of production, the amount of materials, and the number of persons.

1. There are many types of systems operating in a country at a point in time, such as political systems, religious systems, social systems, etc.. Each has interacting influences on the others.

3. For whom shall the goods be produced? Here, decisions have to be made about their distribution. How much to the various sectors that make up aggregate or total demand of the nation: how much to consumers, to businesses, to the government, and to foreigners? Decisions will have to be made on the proportion that will go to consumption and capital goods markets.

The first question involves the student in understanding something about the concept of 'trade off' which requires some knowledge about production possibility curves, opportunity cost and diminishing returns.

The second question requires knowledge about input-output relationships, and optimum (the most favourable) combination of the factors of production and the cost associated with factors.

The third question requires knowledge on income and wealth distribution, taxation, subsidies, Acts of Parliament, and many other factors that operate in the decision making process.

All questions require knowledge about the factors associated with supply and demand and the relationships between them.

In attempting to solve these three specific allocative situations we find that each country has its own system of making decisions. It is impossible to study all systems in the world, or even one country, for example the United Kingdom, and completely understand its economic system. It is difficult because economic systems are dynamic; changing over even short periods of time. Before studying the economic system of the United Kingdom it is necessary to have an understanding of two extreme theoretical economic systems.

Extreme Economic Systems

At one extreme we have a society which provides the individual with the freedom and incentive to follow his own interest. The individual leads in organising, planning and operating economic activity, and it is through this self interest situation that the well being of the rest of the community is enhanced. This type of economic system is referred to as a 'free enterprise' system or, it might be called a 'capitalist' system. It is guided, as Adam Smith[2] said, by an 'invisible hand'. It is a system in which private enterprise flourishes and public enterprise does not exist. No country in the world has this *pure* system, although the United States is claimed to be nearest to it.

At the other extreme it is the community, rather than the individual, which leads the economy in making the decisions to answer the three basic questions posed earlier. The individual, one might say, works for the community's interest; not his own self interest. This type of economic system is referred to as a 'planned' system. Other names have been appended, such as 'command' system, 'full communism' system, and 'pure socialistic' system. In this system public enterprise dominates economic activity and private enterprise does not exist. In the real world this *pure*

2. "The Wealth of Nations", Adam Smith, published in 1776.

system does not exist. Soviet Russia, a socialist country (but not pure socialist), is considered to come closest to this extreme.

Exhibit 2.1 is an attempt to consolidate names and features that are normally associated with these extreme economic systems.

Exhibit 2.1

EXTREME
ECONOMIC SYSTEMS

PLANNED SYSTEM	FREE ENTERPRISE SYSTEM
Other names:	Other names:
Full Communism	Capitalist
Pure Socialist	Laissez-faire
Command	
Some associated terms:	Some associated terms:
State sovereignty	Consumer sovereignty
Public ownership	Private ownership
Public enterprise	Private enterprise
Collectivism	Individualism
Bureaucracy (red tape)	Freedom of choice
Community welfare	Individual welfare
Public or community interest	Self interest
Planned control	Price mechanism control
Visible hand (personal	Invisible hand (impersonal
institutions)	institutions)

Mixture of the two extreme systems

It can be briefly stated that all countries in the world have economic systems that come somewhere between the two extremes; they have a mixture of both systems. Some countries approximate to the self interest concept and others the community interest concept. These economic systems are given the title 'mixed economy'.

To help us understand more about a mixed economic system it is necessary to highlight some important facts about the extreme *pure* systems, but first a note relating to all systems.

All systems — vital questions

If one can satisfactorily answer the following questions it becomes possible to state the type of economic system a country has. The questions are:

1. Ownership. Who owns the factors of production?

2. Decisions. Who decides how the factors of production will be employed? This requires answers to the three questions at the beginning of the chapter.

3. Control. What control mechanisms are used to ensure decisions are put into operation?

Now we can look at the various systems, starting with the *pure* systems and then the 'mixed economy'; using the United Kingdom for our investigation.

Free Enterprise System

In the free enterprise system we find:

1. The ownership of the factors of production is private. Owners are *free* to use their factors in order to maximise their welfare .... in their own self interest.

2. Decisions are *freely* made by individuals or groups of individuals .... in their own self interest.

3. The controlling mechanisms which ensures decisions are carried out is the price mechanism. This mechanism also resolves decisions that are in conflict in the market. Markets, too, are *free* from outside control, for example, by the state. It is in this type of market that the 'invisible hand' operates.

The free enterprise system, as can be seen, is based on freedom, on self interest, and on the price mechanism operating in the markets. There are many markets (labour market, capital market, market for good X, market for service Y, etc.) and each market is an impersonal institution.

In each market there are many buyers and sellers, and each buyer and seller is interested in maximising their own welfare. Each buyer will try to maximise his welfare by 'buying cheap' and each seller will attempt to maximise his profits by 'selling dear'. The buyer or consumer, however, is considered to be sovereign because the profits made by producers depend on the price paid by consumers.

The price that consumers are willing to pay to satisfy their wants shows their eagerness to purchase. High prices communicate to the producers that buyers are very eager to purchase a commodity, and low prices communicate to producers that consumers are less eager to purchase. It stands to reason that producers will find it more profitable to allocate the resources at their disposal to high price rather than low price commodities.

Producers (sellers) are guided by the profit motive and it is assumed that it is in their interest to maximise profits. Profit provides a guide to the most effective use of the factors of production. When profits (the difference between total revenue and total cost) are negative or nil, producers will stop their production lines, or they will continue producing only if their cost of employing the factors has fallen. Owners of factors are unlikely to lower the price for their use (sell dear is their motto) and so are likely to move to another line of production, producing for some other market, where returns are higher .... it being in their interest to do so. If our producer stops his production line, as noted above, he, like the other factors, will seek a new market which satisfies his self interest as indicated by higher profits. If such a profitable market is found he will take his resources and allocate them to the new production line.

Thus, the market mechanism (price mechanism operating in a free market) determines the allocation of resources. The signal that establishes the relationship between demand (consumers) and supply (producers) is the price in the market.

In the end, however, it is the eagerness or lack of eagerness of consumers which guide the economy in using scarce resources to satisfy wants that are greater than others and carrying out the consumer-producer relationship in the most efficient way.

The question now arises as to the role of government. The government plays a passive role in the free enterprise system, and does this by following a policy of 'laissez-faire'. The dictionary defines this as 'government abstention from interference with individual action, especially in commerce'. In other words, the government should not interfere with the economic sphere.

Laissez faire can be better understood by referring to the writing of Adam Smith (so called father of Economics) and John Stuart Mill.

Adam Smith (1776) tended to exalt competition, individual rights and laissez-faire. He claimed that every man, as long as he does not violate the laws of justice, is left perfectly free to pursue his own interest his own way. He said the sovereign (government) has only three duties of great importance. These were:

1. the duty of protecting the society from the violence and invasion of other independent societies;

2. the duty of protecting, so far as possible, every member of the society from the injustice or oppression of every other member of it, or the duty of establishing an exact administration of justice; and

3. the duty of creating and maintaining certain public works and certain public institutions which it can never be for the interest of any individual, or small number of individuals, to erect and maintain; because the profit could never repay the expense to any individual, or small number of individuals.

John Stuart Mill ("Principles of Political Economy" 1848) claimed that the proponents of laissez-faire laid down the motion that the provinces of the government should be limited to the protection of persons and property against force and fraud. Laissez-faire, from Mill's point of view, should be the general practice; every departure from it, unless required by some great good, is a certain evil.

Thus, the role of the government, in the free enterprise economy, is to leave the economics of the community to individual action.

Advantages and Disadvantages

The economist's task is not to make judgements of one system being better than another. His task is to take the details supplied and present information so others can make judgements, such as the politician or managing director. With this in mind, some advantages and disadvantages will be noted which will enable students to make their own judgements. Importance should not be attached to the number of points made nor should more importance be given to those mentioned first.

Advantages

1. Individuals, singly or in groups, have freedom to choose how they will use their resources.

2. Resources will be used to produce goods and services for which there is great demand, and, conversely, they will not be wasted when there is nil or little demand.

3. The economy runs itself and therefore there is no need for government interference in the market, for example: taxes and subsidies.

4. Competition is stimulated. Entrepreneurs are encouraged to explore new methods of production, invest in new machinery, etc., thus reducing costs and maximising profits.

5. Price competition will decide the methods of production. Efficient producers will succeed and inefficient producers will go out of business.

6. The best possible allocation of all factors of production is ensured. Each factor can be used in a variety of ways but the system ensures each is used to create maximum benefits.

7. Consumers (not producers, nor government) are sovereign. It is the consumer who communicates to producers what to produce.

8. Ownership and control of resources is 'private' and not 'public'.

9. There is a tendency for all available productive resources to be kept fully employed. This arises from forces generated in the economy which encourages producers to decide, freely, how to allocate resources, coupled with the profit motive.

10. The individiual plays the leading role. All economic activity (how it is organised, planned and decisions put into operation) is determined by individuals.

Disadvantages

1. Experience has shown that competition leads to improvements in producing and distributing commodities, and this tends to create imperfections in the market. Market imperfections can be to the detriment of the consumer (exploited) and employees (oppressed).

2. The free market mechanism will not prevent productive resources going to consumer demand which attract those resources even when that production, for example, drugs, may be against the interest of the individual and society in general.

3. Production tends to be directed towards those with the most money. In other words, scarce resources would be towards 'luxury' markets rather than 'necessity' markets. This favours the rich at the expense of the poor, and this does not maximise the satisfaction of all individuals.

4. The system is unlikely to produce socially desirable community goods, such as public parks, public roads, hospitals, schools, etc..

5. The system does not ensure that the output of the community is distributed equally among its members. Equality would tend to maximise the satisfaction of all individuals.

6. The individual, singly or in groups, in pursuing their own self interest cannot maximise the well-being of the community. Such things as pollution of water and air with poisonous matter is detrimental to the community. So to is the felling of trees without consideration for replacement or conservation, and the eroding of land by overworking it is detrimental to the community.

7. Resources may be used efficiently now but inefficiently over time.

8. The sum of individual choice, it is argued, will not bring about efficiency in the use of the scarce factors of production. Nor is it accepted that the system will provide full employment of labour continuously; technological advances often being labour-saving machines.

9. The system is not perfect. Imperfections may arise because producers will make mutually beneficial agreements. Movements towards monopolies keep prices high and wages low.

10. The system can not operate satisfactorily when conditions are abnormal, such as wars and depressions. Hence the government must come to the rescue; planning must come from the centre in order to adjust to these conditions.

It should be noted that the free enterprise system advantages are normally associated to 'perfect' situations (normal conditions, perfect competition, economic man) whereas the disadvantages are usually centred around the idea that the real world is 'imperfect', and imperfections can only be controlled by central planning.

Planned System

The 'pure' planned or full communism system has a totalitarian philosophy which puts the state in full command. The state owns and manages property. The state controls and directs economic activities.

In this system we find the following:

1. The state owns the means of production. Individuals cannot own resources such as land and machinery. Individuals do not have the freedom to choose their own occupations because the state directs them to their specific places of work. The state owns and operates industry; industries associated with the land, manufacturing and services. The means of production belong to the whole of society.

2. Decisions are made by the state in the interest of the community. The decisions to provide for the common welfare takes place in a single centre which is completely centralised. Commands always move from the top to the bottom, and never the reverse.

3. The controlling mechanism that ensures decisions are made comes from the single centre. This centre issues directives commanding or ordering individuals to specific places of work, directing how the land will be used, and what methods of production will be employed. Consumption is assigned to various sectors according to a state determined programme. In short, the state controls decisions and guides the economy with a 'perfectly visible hand'.

It can be seen from the above that the state is sovereign. It dictates the what, when, and where of production and distribution. The plans that are formulated and the directives issued are based on the common interest of the community. Supposedly there must be common agreement, or single mindedness, amongst the population about their common welfare and production priorities. These must be conveyed to the single centralised organisation at the top to ensure scarce means are channelled into the correct economic activities. The state plans; planning is the essential feature in this system and must cover 100 per cent of all economic activity. State control must be 100 per cent.

The concepts of the free enterprise system such as private ownership, individual freedom, profit motive and maxmisation, and the price mechanism cannot exist in the planned economic system. The state plans everything and all plans are carried out by government orders. It has been claimed that this system of planning necessarily implies cultural uniformity and political dictatorship. In this totalitarian state (a centralised form of government that permits no rival loyalties or parties, or a state where the ruling body does not recognise nor tolerate parties of different opinions) it is the state that controls all economic activity and therefore controls the means for all wants. In fact no economy has ever existed which has been controlled and organised by the state as indicated above.

Advantages and disadvantages associated with the pure planned economy are as follows:

Advantages
1. The community (not individuals) plans, organises and controls all economic activity. It is carried out to maximise common welfare rather than individual welfare.
2. Economic problems are solved by a personal institution, the state, and not by an impersonal institution such as the market.
3. Workers work for society and therefore are not exploited by other individuals seeking their own self interest. In other words, the exploitation of man by man is abolished.
4. The state owns the tools and resources of production. Private ownership does not exist.
5. There is no private monopoly and all its associated social evils, for example, misallocation of resources and redistribution of income in favour of the monopolist and shareholders at the expense of workers in the monopolistic industry, and consumers.

6. The state allocates resources in order to achieve the state's objectives which will reflect some order of social priorities.

7. Poverty does not exist because the state ensures there is a more equitable distribution of goods and services than that possible in the free enterprise system.

8. Planning by the state, with full information and full command, should be able to smooth out the 'trade cycle'. It is generally agreed that the free enterprise system is less able and less likely to do this compared to the central economic planning by the state.

9. Planned economic societies can provide goods and services which are socially desirable such as education and health facilities. These, normally, would not be available to low income earners in a free enterprise economy.

10. Uncertainty, risk and the concept of profit maximisation, along with business methods associated with free enterprise businesses, such as advertising, branding, etc., are removed.

Disadvantages

1. A centralised authority cannot plan for the entire community. Too much information is required and too many personnel would be required to examine the vast amount of information.

2. Bureaucracy (excessive formalism, red tape) prevails, and this creates inevitable delays and the possibility of corruption.

3. The individual may not own land, forests, mines, businesses, houses, etc.. All things are state property.

4. Consumers cannot choose. Only the state can choose how scarce resources will be allocated.

5. Individual freedom is undermined. Individuals are not free to choose where they live or work, nor are they free to bargain in their own self interest. They are shunted from areas of lesser needs to areas of greater needs without due consideration for their family.

6. Production is completely controlled by the state through its centralised ministries. This requires all production units to refer everything to the centre for decisions. Wasted time creates inefficiencies.

7. Production quotas are set and are, normally, based on physical quantities. To reach these quotas workers create waste. In other words they find ways of reaching the quota without adding to the benefit of the community. The important thing is to reach the quota, not how the work should be carried out.

8. Consumers must accept goods which are not, necessarily, of good quality. Nor do they have the choice of choosing from many styles. The planned system is not a market oriented system.

9. Each member of the work force is an employee of the state. Each is given a strict set of rules and regulations which *must* be followed. If not, severe penalties are administered.

10. There is no way of testing whether decisions are in the best interest of the community.

The question whether a planned economy is better than a free enterprise economy, or vice versa, must depend on which system makes better use of its scarce resources in satisfying the unlimited wants of its population. Seeing that no country in the world has either of these 'pure' systems, it becomes important to investigate the type of system they do have .... the mixed economy.

Mixed Economy

As previously stated, the mixed economy is a mixture of features inherent in the free enterprise and planned systems. There is a mixture of ownership, decision making and controls.

At the present time, the latter 1970s, every country in the world has a mixed economy. They have different mixtures yet they all, more or less, have the same economic objectives, namely,

1. maintaining a high and stable level of employment,

2. maintaining reasonable stability of the internal purchasing power of money, and

3. achieving a steady growth of the economy and improving the standard of living for members of its society.

In addition to these internal economic objectives, many countries also have external economic objectives, such as,

4. contributing to the economic development of the world, and

5. strengthening the ability of the country to finance its trade with the rest of the world.

Alongside these economic objectives a nation may have other goals, such as maintaining a strong and up-to-date fighting force, providing an adequate welfare system, and establishing stronger political institutions. Economic objectives and non-economic goals are trying to be achieved in the face of satisfying unlimited wants with limited means. Hence, it is impossible to view economic arrangements in any society solely from the economic point of view. It is necessary to know the effects that economic arrangements have on other spheres (moral, political, psychological, social and even religious) and vice versa. All spheres should be taken into account when discussing and investigating the type of mixed economy a country has.

The term 'mixed economy' is somewhat ambiguous. All countries, including the United Kingdom, have a mixed economy, but the mixture in the United Kingdom is different from that of the United States and Soviet Russia. Different labels have been given to various mixtures. However, the least objectionable of all titles, for any mixture, is simply 'mixed economy'.

Economic systems are dynamic; they are constantly being modified. At one point of time the mixture may be to the right on the mixture scale (refer to exhibit 2.1), then towards the left and later back to the right. A study of the history of the various countries making up the United Kingdom would support this statement. In fact, even over very short periods of time, conclusions reached about the mixture of a country may be no longer valid because of some recent change in that society, such as a war, industrial or technological revolution, political revolution, an election, depression, recession, or even less dramatic, but nevertheless a change, a recent legal enactment.

Economic systems develop and change because the attitudes, desires and ideals of the population change. On the other hand, changes can be traced to philosophies expounded by individuals, for example, Adam Smith and his exaltation for 'laissez faire' or Karl Marx and Friedrich Engels writings on 'communism'. The pattern of behaviour, customs, institutions and thoughts that exist at any one time can be changed by man. Economic systems are dynamic, not static.

United Kingdom — A Mixed Economy

The United Kingdom is a mixed economy. In this economy we find the following:

1. Ownership. Ownership of land is both private and public. Some businesses are owned by the state (public enterprise) and many are owned by individuals or groups of individuals (private enterprise). Some businesses are a mixture of private and public ownership (mixed enterprise).

2. Decisions. In some areas decisions are freely made by individuals or groups of individuals, such as businessmen selecting their labour force or workers freely deciding where they will live or work. On the other hand the state makes decisions in the public interest, about roads, hospitals, schools, etc.. Other decisions may be a mixture of individual freedom as long as they stay within certain minimums and maximums ordered by the state.

3. Control. The price mechanism operates fairly freely in some markets but is hindered by government intervention in others. On the other hand, the state may issue directives and commands to certain sectors of the community (nationalised industries, local authorities, businesses that violate the monopoly laws, etc.). Also, the state, through taxation and subsidies, may harm certain industrial sectors whereas other sectors may be assisted.

Basically, the above mentioned points exist in the United Kingdom economy. Perhaps further consideration of certain features, mainly since the end of the second world war, may highlight the idea of 'mixture' and help us to understand the type of mixed economy we live in. In order to keep time in perspective a time diagram showing the political party in power is provided. This information is shown in Exhibit 2.2.

Exhibit 2.2

POLITICAL PARTIES IN POWER

POLITICAL PARTY IN POWER	APPROXIMATE YEARS IN POWER	STARTED	PERIODS OF TIME (showing election months)	ENDED
Coalition		1939		July 1945
Labour	6 and ¼	July 1945	(March 1950)	Oct 1951
Conservative	13	Oct 1951	(May 1955) (Oct 1959)	Oct 1964
Labour	5 and ⅔	Oct 1964	(April 1966)	June 1970
Conservative	3 and ⅔	June 1970		Feb 1974
Labour	5 and ¼	Feb 1974	(Oct 1974)	May 1979
Conservative		May 1979		

Ownership

Public ownership is not, solely, a post World War II phenomena. Public corporations existed before 1945, for example:

1908 Port of London Authority

1919 Forestry Commission

1926 British Broadcasting Corporation

1927 Central Electricity Board

1933 London Passenger Transport Board.

War years are periods of time that a country begins planning for peace. These years are also times when central planning grows as there is need for the state to rescue the economy from a severe abnormal situation; an abnormality that the price mechanism can not handle satisfactorily. It was during the second world war that the Beveridge Report[3] was published. The Report stated that there existed in the United Kingdom five giant evils, namely; disease, idleness, ignorance, squalor and want. It was pointed out that society owed its members the basics of a good living, as much as was economically and socially possible. It was deemed necessary to remove these evils by improving the health of the community, by creating employment, by improving education, by providing better housing conditions, and by providing the minimum support to individuals so that they could acquire the necessities of life. To these ends, legislation was introduced and many properties were moved into state ownership. For example, The National Health Services Act 1946 transferred nearly all hospitals from voluntary organisations and local authorities ownership to central government ownership.

In 1945 the Labour Party was voted into power. Labour policies were geared to the principle of public ownership in certain sectors of the community. On the other hand, it should be noted that the Conservative Party tend to encourage private ownership. When parliamentary power changes hands, legislation swings ownership back and forth from one type of mixture to another.

---

3. "Report on Social Insurance and Allied Services", Cmd 6404, HMSO, 1942.

In 1945, therefore, there was an immediate introduction of a substantial programme in favour of public ownership. Legislation was introduced to nationalise certain industries considered vital to community welfare, such as coal, electricity, transportation and steel.

The Bank of England Act 1946 was first in priority. The Bank, a privately owned and controlled organisation for more than 250 years, was considered to be the key by which the government could control the entire financial structure of the economy. The Act changed The Bank from a privately owned organisation to public ownership; a movement that brings the mixture closer to the planned system.

The second step was to nationalise the coal industry (1946). The Government declared that coal was so vital to the British economy that ownership should not be left in the hands of private businesses. Other reasons were given (prices too high, out dated methods of production, seams at lower levels not being operated, etc.) but the end result was the transfer of ownership from private to public.

Electricity (1948) and gas (1949) soon followed. The production and distribution sides of these industries were transferred from private to public ownership because it was considered wrong that these private industries should compete with the publicly owned coal industry. Other reasons were given, for example, there were too many high cost small plants and they were operating inefficiently.

Transportation, which covered nearly all inland transportation, was nationalised in 1947. Air transportation was excluded as this area was already owned by the public.[4] Private ownership was mainly private but included some local authority undertakings. Ownership was transferred to central government control. Along with change in ownership of railways, steamships and long distance road haulage vehicles went the ownership of hotels and houses which were owned by the private firms that were taken over. Considerable changes have taken place in transportation; in 1953 the Conservative Government partially denationalised road haulage but found difficulty in selling assets back to private ownership. In 1968 the Labour Government took over road passenger services.

Steel, like transportation, also became a special case. In 1949 the state took over the ownership of private steel firms, except for small firms and firms in the fabrication sector of the industry. In 1953, under the Conservative Government, steel was denationalised. In 1967, the Labour party was in power and steel was renationalised. The pendulum of ownership of steel goes from private to public to private to public; the mixture moving back and forth along the mixed economy scale according to which political party is in power.

Another consideration in the ownership discussion is that of The Local Employment Act 1972 which consolidated, with certain exceptions, the

4.   The state, in 1939, amalgamated two subsidised companies (Imperial Airways and British Airways) to form a public corporation, British Overseas Airways Corporation. Immediately after the war, 1947, British European Airways became public ownership.

Local Employment Acts 1960-1971. This Act enabled the Secretary of State to acquire land and buildings and to build factories for rent or sale in the development and intermediate areas. This is just another example of a trend towards public ownership.

In 1977, the Labour Government introduced the Aircraft and Shipbuilding Industries Act. The Act provided for the vesting of securities of certain companies in the manufacture of aircraft and guided weapons (4 firms were listed), and in the shipbuilding and allied industries[5] (19 plus 8 firms were listed) to special corporations called British Aerospace and British Shipbuilding. These public corporations were to become the owners of 31 companies, all of which were, once, privately owned.

Ownership can be viewed from other areas, for example in the construction and ownership of new houses; central and local authorities versus private ownership. In the eleven year span from 1946 to 1956 inclusive the total number of new houses was 2,250,287. Of this total the government (mainly local authorities) built and owned 1,628,303 (72.4 per cent) and private ownership the remainder.[6]

The Conservative Party are of the opinion that "Most people want to become home-owners. Yet we devote the overwhelming majority of our resources to public rented housing."[7]

On the other hand, ownership by central government can be considered by noting their portfolio of shares held in quoted ordinary shares. The public sector owned shares having 2½ per cent of total market value at 31 December, 1973. That is to say that the public sector's share of private enterprise's quoted ordinary market value of £40,520,000,000 amounted to approximately £1,020,000,000.[8] Private ownership, however, was still very large.

Lastly, private ownership of business organisations still forms a considerable part of the United Kingdom economy. It is difficult to obtain accurate and up-to-date information, but it is safe to say that there are well over 500,000 enterprises[9] that are privately owned.

Decisions

Decision relate to the basic supply questions posed at the beginning of the chapter. Individuals, in declaring their eagerness to purchase goods and

5. The vesting date for shipbuilding was 1 July 1977.

6. Calculated from Housing Returns for England and Wales, Cmnd 155, 1957 p4.

7. "The Right Approach" — 'A statement of Conservative aims' by Conservative Central Office, Oct 1976, p50.

8. Economic Progress Report, No. 83, February 1977. Prepared by the Information Division of the Treasury, page 2, from article entitled 'Profits in British Industry'.

9. Enterprise, according to Census of Production Report 1968, means one or more establishments under common ownership or control. An enterprise consists of a single establishment, more than one establishment owned by the same firm or a number of establishments owned by a parent company and its subsidiary companies.

services and the necessary supply decisions made to satisfy them are, normally, made freely with no or little government interference. The state does not usually dictate to individuals which goods and services they must purchase with their incomes. However, some goods are recognised not be be in the self interest of individuals, such as drugs, and so the government tends to control decisions made on their production and sale.

Businessmen also tend to be free in deciding how they will put their money to work, and how they distribute their profits. They, normally, have maximum freedom in deciding what they will produce, their methods of production, and how they will combine the factors in producing. However, there are times that the government does tend to interfere. For example, a Price Commission was established by the Counter-Inflation Act 1973. This Commission was given powers to restrict any prices or charges for the sale of goods or the performance of services in the course of business. The Commission was given new powers under The Price Commission Act 1977; price increases may be restricted. In fact, the Commission has the power to freeze prices for up to 12 months. Thus, decisions by the private sector in setting prices may be cancelled or not allowed to take place. It can be seen, that the state may interfere with individual or business decisions that create conflict between the interest of the public and the interest of the individual.

Another example of government interfering in the decision making of businessmen is in their recruitment, training and promotion of personnel. An Act in 1975 made it unlawful for employers to discriminate in opportunities in these areas either on grounds of sex or on grounds of marriage. The Equal Pay Act 1970, fully implemented by 29 December 1975, created equality for women in terms of pay. No longer is it possible for businessmen to pay women at a cheaper rate than men for similar work.

Recent restrictions on pay awards and dividend payments force business decisions to remain within the upper limits set by the state. Businessmen are still free to make wage settlements and dividends below the upper limits but are not free to go beyond the levels indicated by the government.

Even the decision made by individuals where to locate a new house may be restricted. Local planning may decide that it is not in the interest of the local community to have, say, 40 new houses erected in their area. Or, central government may curtail the building of new houses if they are to be erected in a 'green belt' area. Businessmen, too, may not locate factories in certain areas because they violate local or central government plans. Even when companies are located in one area and wish to expand their plant by say, 25,000 square feet, they must seek an 'industrial development certificate' from a government department. The government may tell them that they cannot expand their plant alongside the old one but must, if they wish to expand, locate their new plant in a Development Area. The freedom of decision is still left with the businessman; accept the government decision or decide not to expand.

This idea that private business decision are no longer strictly private is not restricted solely to recent times. For example, the Factory Act of 1833 applied to the employment of children in textile mills. The Act stated that the employment of young children below the age of nine, in these mills, was prohibited. This was legally stated in 1819 but was not put into practice. This Act, also, lowered the number of hours worked by young children over the age of nine. Further, to ensure state decisions were being obeyed, the Act established 'factory inspectors'. The most recent Act relating to the safety and health of workers at work was in 1974.

Alongside individual and business decisions there are those made by the government on behalf of the community. These cover many areas which are considered to be, essentially, national problems, such as the protection of green belts, land reclamation, building of 'new towns', restrictive trade practices, drainage, education, health, and of course, those associated with the nationalised industries.

Decision making in the United Kingdom is, like ownership, a mixture of decisions that one would find in the free enterprise and planned systems. More will be learned about decision making when considering the next area of investigation — control.

Control

In the United Kingdom the controlling mechanism, to ensure decisions are carried out, is a combination of market forces operating through the price mechanism and the rules and regulations laid down by the government.

In the mixed economy one can envisage three possible situations.

1. Price mechanism controls decisions and there is no government intereference.

2. Price mechanism operates but there is state interference.

3. Government controls economic activity without the use of the price mechanism.

The price mechanism refers to prices that operate in individual markets, and links consumers demands with producers supplies. Hence, it would be necessary to investigate every market to establish whether it operated under situation 1, 2 or 3 as noted above. If interference did take place it may operate on the demand side, or supply side, or on price. The interference may be direct (fixing a price, rationing goods, etc.) or indirect (taxation, subsidies, etc.).

There are many goods and services markets. Just to mention a few, to give an idea of the vastness of market operations and investigations, we have markets for different foods (milk, bread, eggs, etc.); for different manufactured goods (tables, refrigerators, televisions, etc.); for services (hairdressing, banking, insurance, etc.). We have labour markets, money markets, retail markets, investment markets, etc.. Each market would require investigation to give a complete answer to this area of control.

The government intervenes directly in markets when it acts as a producer of goods, such as coal or steel; or as a seller of services, such as air flights or railway journeys; or as a provider of services such as education or health.

On the demand side the government operate as the sole demander of goods, such as the Post Office as a buyer of telephone exchanges; or as one of many buyers, for example, in the purchase of furniture for hospitals and schools. On occasion the government may intervene directly when it has calculated that, as a producer of a good, it has paid abnormal prices. The state may then command the private enterprise supplier to return, from its abnormal profits, a substantial sum of money. This has been done on at least two occasions: Ferranti and Roche Laboratories. As long as the state operates in any market, whether it be as a supplier or purchaser, it interferes, simply by its size if in no other way.

We cannot investigate all areas of control. We can consider certain individual situations in this chapter, and others will arise as we progress through various chapters of the book. Before citing individual cases it is perhaps best to make note of government interference in more general terms.

An overall indicator of government interference is obtained, but not accurately, by noting the claim the government has on national supply. To start off with it is claimed that government demand for national supply, during the second world war, was approximately 50 per cent. Taking figures from 'National Income and Expenditure' tables, it has been calculated that government demand, over recent years, was as follows:[10]

$$1966 \ldots\ldots\ldots\ldots\ldots\ldots 18.2 \text{ per cent}$$
$$1977 \ldots\ldots\ldots\ldots\ldots\ldots 20.0 \text{ per cent}$$

This indicates the government's control over national supply is increasing but it is still a long way from the war time situation.

The next general consideration was to look at the general government (includes local authorities) intereference through taxation on income and expenditure (including rates) as a percentage of the 'gross national product'.[11] Other receipts from television licences, etc. are not included.

The figures obtained are as follows:

$$1966 \ldots\ldots\ldots\ldots\ldots\ldots 29.8 \text{ per cent}$$
$$1976 \ldots\ldots\ldots\ldots\ldots\ldots 32.1 \text{ per cent}$$

Next, to look at total government receipts, from all sources, and the percentage of these in relation to the 'gross national product':

$$1966 \ldots\ldots\ldots\ldots\ldots\ldots 43.2 \text{ per cent}$$
$$1976 \ldots\ldots\ldots\ldots\ldots\ldots 53.1 \text{ per cent}$$

These last two sets of figures[12] also show, like government demand, an upward movement of government interference and control in the economy.

10. Calculations based on figures obtained from National Income and Expenditure blue book, 1966-1976, published by HMSO for the Central Statistical Office. Table on page 3 and 67. Demand was based on government expenditure on goods and services plus non trading capital consumption, government's gross domestic fixed capital formation and increase in value of stocks.

11. For definition refer to chapter on National Income.

12. Based on figures from table 9.1 in 'National Income and Expenditure' blue book 1966-1976.

Another way to look at government interefernce in general terms is to consider the degree of control exerted by comparing terms associated with the 'stick and carrot' approach. The stick is a form of control that forces decisions to be carried out (compulsive measures), and the carrot entices decisions to be carried out along specified directions laid down by the government. (inducive measures). Exhibit 2.3 establishes these situations.

Exhibit 2.3

ACHIEVING OBJECTIVES BY STICK AND CARROT MEASURES

OBJECTIVES (desired by the government)	STICK MEASURES (measures that interfere with the price mechanism)	CARROT MEASURES (measures introduced to guide the price mechanism)
to increase the consumption of a commodity (example: milk)	*fix* a maximum price below the existing price	*subsidise* consumers or producers
to lower the price of a commodity (example: tea)	*order* firms to lower the price	*subsidise* producers
to remove inequality in the distribution of a commodity (example: sugar)	*ration* the commodity	*subsidise* sector failing to get its share
to change interest rates in attempt to stimulate investment	*fix* a maximum rate	*allow* market to operate freely (in open market)
to build new factories in specified areas	*compel* them to locate as government directs	*subsidise* by providing special allowances on buildings, machinery, etc.
to lower wage claims to keep inflation in check	*establish* a maximum level not to be exceeded (example: 10% and no higher). When violated, fine and/or imprison decision makers.	lower *tax* burden of wage earners (example: lower tax band or increase personal allowances to off-set against tax)
to protect an industry from foreign competition (example: U.K. car industry)	*fix* import quotas	*tax,* heavily, the commodity as it enters the country

It can be seen from the exhibit that compulsive measures (fix, order, compel, etc.) force individuals and firms to carry out decisions made by the government. On the other hand, inducive measures (subsidies, taxes, allowances, etc.), introduced by the government, allows individuals and firms freedom in making their decisions, but offers then incentives to decide according to the desires of the government. Both measures steer the economy towards the 'planned economy' but compulsive measures are more immediate and more certain in reaching that position farther to the left (as shown in exhibit 2.1).

At the present time, as we enter the 1980's, the measures introduced by the government appear to be more 'inducive' rather than 'compulsive' but there are signs that compulsive measures, at least under the Labour Government, have been used more than before (except during the wars). Both measures indicate that controls in the United Kingdom are 'mixed'.

Now, to look at some isolated situations.

An example of strong government interference in a market took place towards the latter part of February 1978. The Price Commission informed the major tea blenders (Brooke Bond-Oxo, Co-operative, Tetley-Lyons, Typhoo) that an investigation by the Price Commission indicated they were making a very handsome profit at the housewife's expense (27 pence per quarter) and thay they should, voluntarily, lower their prices by five pence. The big tea blending companies refused to carry out the price reduction. On Friday, 24th February, the Price Minister Roy Hattersley, interviewed on television, stated the blenders will reduce their prices even it it was necessary for him to obtain a statutory order.

Another type of interference with business activities has been in the field of cigarette advertising. Firms, must state on their cigarette packages and advertisement (newspapers, magazines, etc.) the following: "H.M. Government Health Department's Warning: cigarettes can seriously damage your health". A directive that must be carried out if cigarettes are to be sold in the United Kingdom.

In the area of wage negotiations the government has interfered, off and on, with union and employer discussions. For example, the Labour Government instituted a guide, for one year commencing August 1977, that wage settlements should not exceed ten per cent. Both sides of industry were allowed to settle these matters freely. However, when settlements exceeded the guide line the Government placed the names of the firms on a special government 'blacklist'.[13] One of the first companies to violate the guide line was warned that the Government would take away their 'Export Credit Guarantee' facilities. Others were warned that they could lose valuable Government contracts. In fact, the Government inserted a new clause in contracts made between the Government and firms which stated that the contract would be broken if a firm went beyond the ten per cent level. The Attorney General claimed that the guide line was essential for the national economic well-being that inflation should be controlled.

Certain business practices, such as exclusive dealings and deferred rebates, which tend to restrict competition, and others which remove competition and thus lead towards monopoly situations have been interfered with by the government. The Monopolies and Restrictive Practices (Inquiry and Control) Act of 1948 defined a legal monopoly as a situation where the firm's market share was one-third. This figure was changed to one-fourth by The Fair Trading Act 1973. This latter Act broadly strengthened and improved the effectiveness of existing controls over restrictive practices and monopoly. Mergers were kept under review; when proposed mergers exceded the monopoly level, and were considered to be against the public interest, the government could halt the merger. An excellent example of the government dictating to firms that they were not free to merge took place

---

13. Refer to article in The Times, February 7, 1978 page 11 "Attorney General explains policy on blacklist firms". This is a report on a case in the Court of Appeal the previous day.

towards the end of the 1960s. The proposed merger of Barclays, Lloyds and Martins (all clearing banks)[14] was referred to the Monopolies Commission. The merger was declared to be against the public interest. As a result, Barclays and Martins merged but Lloyds remained independent.

Ownership, Decisions and Controls

Each area investigated (ownership, decisions and controls) shows the United Kingdom has a 'mixed economy'. However, a thorough investigation of each area is needed to ascertain whether the mixture is more towards the planned or free enterprise system. Whatever the mixture, it has been claimed that it does not have, nor has it had, the correct balance to ensure that the economy is able to reach the major internal economic objectives of maintaining a high and stable level of employment, maintaining a reasonable stability of the internal purchasing power of money, and achieving steady growth of the economy and improving the standard of living of the population.

Assignments

1. Briefly discuss the features that are normally associated with a 'free enterprise' system, and then explain the role of government in this type of society.

2. In terms of 'ownership' the United Kingdom can be defined as a 'mixed economy' that tends to favour the 'free enterprise' system rather than the 'planned' system. Define these three terms. What features does one expect to see in the planned system?

3. Which economic system would you prefer to live in — free enterprise or planned? Explain why.

4. In the free enterprise system it is claimed that the 'consumer is sovereign'. Explain why they say this.

5. Compare and contrast the free enterprise system with that of the command system.

6. Write a letter to a friend in the United States of America explaining the likely changes you expect from a change in government control — say from Labour to Conservative.

---

14. On Feb. 8, 1968 the proposed merger was announced for the £350m combination to create the fourth largest bank in the world. On July 9th, 1968 the Monopolies Commission rejected the merger by 6 votes to 4.

Chapter 3

Governing the U.K. mixed economy

Learning objectives:
At the end of your study of this chapter you should be able to:

1. describe the structure and functioning of the major institutions of local and central Government

2. summarise the main aspects of legislation, its interpretation and enforcement

3. describe the major domestic influences affecting Government policies, with special reference to:
   a) the Treasury
   b) the activities of other Government departments
   c) pressure groups
   d) political parties
   e) the media

4. summarise the activities of public sector administration

5. describe the major quasi-judicial and quasi-governmental bodies and compare the function of the former with that of the judiciary.

Major Institutions

The British system of government can be described as a *UNITARY* system, which is different from the *FEDERAL* system of the U.S.A. In a UNITARY system there is *one* central source of authority and power (or SOVEREIGNTY). This source is Parliament in Britain. There is no separate system of regions or "states" as can be found in the U.S.A. Of course, we do have a system of local government in Britain, but the local authorities have been created by Parliament. In the U.S.A. and other FEDERAL systems there is a 2 tier system of government; the Federal or Central Government has certain defined powers, whilst the 50 individual states which, together make up the United States of America have their own powers of government.

Unlike the United States of America which has a written constitution which sets out the distribution of governmental powers for the nation, Britain does not have such a written constitution. The British system of government has developed over the course of time.

Constitutional sources include statutes, common law and conventions, which are important rules of the constitution. Unlike statutes, however, they are not enforceable in a court of law. An example of a constitutional statute is the Representation of the People Act 1969 which allows people to vote at 18 years. An important convention is the one which provides that the Prime Minister should be the leader of the party with most seats in the House of Commons. There is therefore no one document which we can call our constitution, and an Act of Parliament can bring about a change such as the example given above. The system is flexible in that it can be readily adapted to changing political conditions and ideas.

The elements of Government

In Britain, like most other states, there are *three* basic elements or powers of government which have to be distinguished.

1. The *legislative* or law making power, which is the function of the Legislature.

    Laws are made in Britain by Parliament which consists of two Chambers, The House of Commons and the House of Lords, and the assent of the Queen is required before laws are put into operation, but this Royal Assent has not been refused since 1707.

    In certain instances, Ministers and local authorities and othe bodies can also make laws after such power has been delegated by Parliament.

2. The *executive* power is concerned with the administering or carrying out of the laws. Responsibility for this function rests with Her Majesty's Government which is in effect headed by the Prime Minister who appoints other Ministers, the most important of whom are members of the Cabinet. These Ministers are responsible for Government Departments which are staffed by career Civil Servants. Local goverment authorities, public corporations and other public bodies are also part of this Administration.

3. The *judicial* power is concerned with interpreting the laws and adjudicating in disputes. The Courts of law which perform this function range, from the House of Lords, which is the final Court of Appeal, to magistrates' courts. There is an important distinction between civil and criminal courts.

Note A more detailed description of the legal system can be found. It should be noted that these three ''powers'' of government are not completely separated. In particular, the legislative and executive powers are overlapping, as can be seen by the existence of a Cabinet which is made up of the leading members of the party which has the most seats in the House of Commons, the leader of which is the Prime Minister.

The House of Commons — An Elected House

The House of Commons consists of 635 members who represent county and borough constituencies. Certain people are disqualified from sitting in the Commons — including those under 21 years of age, clergymen, civil servants, members of the regular armed forces and Peers (who are entitled to sit in the House of Lords, although a peer can disclaim his title for life under the Peerage Act 1963 and seek election to the Commons).

The only people who are entitled to vote at Parliamentary elections are those whose names have been entered on the electorial register for the constituency in which they live, or who are service voters (including armed forces, Crown Servants employed abroad, and their wives). Certain people are disqualified from voting, including aliens, prisoners, and people who have been found guilty of corrupt and illegal practices at an election. No one can vote until he or she has reached eighteen years of age.

The British parliamentary electoral system is a simple and straightforward one, but is often criticised because it is unfair to the smaller political parties. In Britain a two party system operates, in that a Government will be formed by one of the two major parties, at present Conservative and Labour. The party with most seats after a General Election will become the Government party, and the leader of that party becomes Prime Minister and chooses the Cabinet. The electoral system tends to perpetuate this two party system, and there is no direct relationship between the percentage of votes cast for a party at an election and the percentage of Seats which it may gain.

The House of Lords — A non-elected House

The second Chamber survives to-day despite widespread criticism of its composition and functioning. But there is no way people can agree on any possible replacement.

The House of Lords consists of

(a) hereditary peers and peeresses, numbering approximately 900.

(b) Life peers and peeresses created under the Life Peerages Act 1958, numbering approximately 200.

(c) 2 Archbishops and 24 Bishops of the Church of England.

(d) Those Lords of Appeal in Ordinary (Law Lords) who have been appointed to carry out the judicial duties of the House of Lords.

The judicial function of the Lords is carried out only by those qualified to do so — the Law Lords. The Government of the day will have its representatives in the Lords, including the Lord Chancellor and a Leader of the House of Lords, now often the Lord Privy Seal, who helps to organise government business in the House. Besides its legislative function, the Lords also have an important function of deliberation — debating important political and social issues. Government policies can also be criticised and Government representatives in the Lords can be questioned.

Legislation

Parliament is the supreme law-making body in this country. It is thus described as "sovereign", which means that Parliament can make or unmake any law it wishes. Unlike the situation in some political systems, for example the United States, a statute passed by the United Kingdom Parliament cannot be challenged in the courts on the ground that Parliament had no authority to enact it. There is no legal limit to its powers except that one Parliament cannot bind its successors. This means that if Parliament made a law to-day, some succeeding Parliament can unmake it if its wishes. No matter how unpopular a statute may be, judges must enforce its provisions until such time as it is repealed. The repeal of a statute is the only way by which it ceases to be law. Although the social, political, or economic conditions under which it was passed may long since have ceased to exist, a statute does not become obsolete because of its age. For example, the Treason Act, 1351, was used in 1946 to prosecute William Joyce, a British subject, who broadcast German propaganda in World War II. Similarly, no doubt the person who began legal proceedings in the case of Ashford v Thornton, 1818, was horrified to discover that his opponent could validly claim to have their dispute resolved in trial by battle, a right given by a statute passed in the reign of Henry II (1154-1189). The courts do, however, exercise a great degree of control over the practical application of a statute because they have to interpret it so as to give true effect to the intention of Parliament when it was passed. This question of interpretation will be dealt with later.

An Act of Parliament is initially introduced as a Bill which is a draft version of the proposed Act. Bills are drafted by legal experts known as Parliamentary Counsel, usually under the supervision of a Minister of the Crown, and are divided into "clauses" which will later become "sections" in the Act itself.

The contents of the Bill will often be discussed with the particular interest group who can give their opinions on the Bill. e.g. The British Medical Association (BMA) representing doctors if a Bill relating to a health matter is proposed. It is an important part of the job of Civil Servants at the higher levels in Government Departments to maintain contact with such interest groups.

Types of Bills

The main distinction which should be realised is between public and private Bills. *Public Bills* are introduced in either House, predominately by the Government. The object of a Public Bill is to make an alteration or addition to the general law of the land. There are a few opportunities available for Members of Parliament who are not members of the Government to introduce Private Members' Bills which are also included in this category of Public Bills. Whilst as many as 50 or 60 Government Bills may eventually be passed in any one session of Parliament, only 6 or so Private Members' Bills will manage to gain Parliamentary approval.

Private Bills should not be confused with Private Members' Bills. Private Bills do not relate to the general law of the land, but are concerned with more particular matters, such as acquisition of land by a local authority or by a public corporation.

Stages in the passage of a Public Bill

There are five main stages through which a Bill has to pass in each House before it received the Royal Assent and can operate as an Act of Parliament.

First reading. No debate takes place. The Bill is announced to the House. Its title is read out.

Second reading. This is an important hurdle for the Bill to negotiate. The general merits or otherwise of the Bill are discussed, and a vote is taken. Non-controversial Bills may now be considered by a Special Committee to save time.

Committee stage. The Bill is studied in detail, clause by clause, and amendments may be made. A Standing Committee consisting of between 25 to 45 member will usually undertake this task. When a Bill is of major significance the committee stage will be undertaken by a committee of the whole House e.g. European Communities Bill 1972 (G.B. entry in E.E.C.).

Report Stage. The House now has an opportunity to consider the Bill and discuss it again, taking into account how it has fared during the previous stage. Further amendments may be made.

Third reading. The Bill is again considered in full, but only verbal amendments may be made to improve its wording.

Amendments in the other House. The above example has taken into account what happens to a Government Bill which starts out in the House of Commons. It should be remembered that certain Bills may start out in the House of Lords, but will be of a special nature, and certainly will be concerned with matters of which the House of Commons would not immediately require consideration. The House of Lords will consider Bills which have originated in the Commons and vice versa. Similar stages are undertaken in the appropriate House which can make any further amendments.

The Lords cannot amend finance Bills, however. All amendments must receive the final approval of the Commons, but if the Commons and the Lords cannot reach agreement, the Lords have the power to delay a Bill. e.g. 1976 — Lords delayed the Trade Union and Labour Relations Bill.

The Royal Assent. This is nowadays a formality, and the Monarch will not become directly involved with a particular Bill. No Monarch has refused the Royal Assent since Queen Anne in 1707.

It should be noted that the legislative process will inevitably be a lengthy one and several months may elapse before a Bill is eventually passed. Nevertheless, if full agreement of Commons and Lords is given, a Bill may go through very quickly, even in the space of a few hours. e.g. 1974 Anti Terrorism legislation.

Interpretation

A vital part of the Judicial function is the interpretation of statutes. It has already been mentioned that a statute, in the form of a Bill, is initially drafted by Parliamentary draftsmen, usually under the supervision of a Minister of the Crown. Where the wording of a statute is clear and unambiguous, there will be no need for interpretation of it. However, although great care is taken by draftsment to ensure that statutes are precise, points of doubt will inevitably arise, and so if the wording of a statute is ambiguous or uncertain, litigation will undoubtedly follow at some time. The statute will then have to be interpreted by the courts and a definite meaning given to the words of it. So in Customs and Excise Commissioners v Savoy Hotel, 1966, the court was called upon to decide whether an orange squeezed by hand was a "manufactured beverage", and if so, liable to taxation. Although such questions may seem petty, the interpretation of a word or phrase could be the dividing line between, for example, a person being found guilty or innocent of a criminal offence.

Thus in Fishers v Bell, 1961, a shopkeeper displayed a flick-knife in his shop window. It was described as an ejector knife and priced at 4/-. Under the Restriction of Offensive Weapons Act, 1959, it was an offence to "offer for sale" certain types of weapons including flick-knives. The court held that the shopkeeper was not guilty of an offence because the display of goods in a shop window does not, in contract law, constitute an offer to sell them. It is regarded merely as an invitation to treat; that is an invitation to potential customers to make an offer to the shopkeeper to buy them.

As Chief Justice Holt said in 1701: "An Act of Parliament can do no wrong though it may do several things that look pretty odd."

The essential purpose of a judge then, in interpreting a statute, is to discover what Parliament intended when the Act was passed. This is not always an easy task. Lord Justice Scrutton, for example, said: "If I am asked whether I have arrived at the meaning of the words which Parliament intended, I say frankly I have not the faintest idea." The general rule is that the judge can only refer to the words used in the assumption that the legislature has expressed its intention perfectly. However the courts themselves have developed several rules of interpretation and construction of statutes which must now be considered, although it is not possible to know in advance which of the rules the courts will favour.

The rules themselves

1. *The Literal Rule.* This states that the words used in a statute must be given their usual grammatical meaning. If a word appears more than once, it should be given the same meaning whenever it appears. So, provided the word is capable of only one meaning, the courts must assume that Parliament intended that meaning to be given to it. The fact that the interpretation may produce hardship is irrelevant, and in such a case the remedy is a new statute. Obviously, however, this rule cannot be used where the word in question is capable of more than one meaning.

2. *The Golden Rule.* This is an extension to the Literal Rule. In essence it provides that words should be interpreted according to their literal meaning *unless* this would make the meaning ridiculous or make it clash with the intention of Parliament when the Act is considered as a whole. In such circumstances, the ordinary meaning of the word can be modified so as to avoid the absurd result. The rule enables the court to deal with ambiguous words where, as we mentioned, the literal rule does not.

A classic example can be found in the interpretation given to s.57 of the Offences Against the Person Act, 1861, dealing with the criminal offence of bigamy. The section states that "Whoever, being married, shall MARRY any other person during the life of the former husband or wife" shall be guilty of the offence. At first glance this may appear to be a perfectly obvious statement. It seems clear that Parliament intended it to be an offence for a man to have more than one wife at the same time or a woman to have more than one husband. But one word in the statute, if given a purely literal meaning, would make it impossible for the offence to be committed. The offending word is the word "marry". This is because the legal definition of marriage says that both parties must be single. It would, therefore, be impossible for someone who is already married to "marry".

So we can see that the word "marry" is capable of two meanings in this context. It can be interpreted as "contracts a valid marriage" or alternatively "goes through a ceremony of marriage" since the first meaning would have made the statute ridiculous the courts applied the second meaning so as to remove the absurdity.

3. *The Mischief Rule.* The rule is also known as the Rule in Heydon's Case (1584) which was when it was first developed. Again it is usually used to resolve ambiguities in cases where the literal rule could not be applied.

It states that the courts can look at the Act to see what "mischief" (or defect) in the old law the Act was designed to prevent.

Heydon's Case itself established four things to be discussed and considered by the court. They are:

(a) What did the Common Law provide before the Act was passed;

(b) What was the defect in law for which the Common Law did not provide;

(c) What remedy had Parliament decided was necessary to remedy the defect;

(d) What is the true reason for the remedy.

After considering these questions, the court will then adopt the interpretation of the statute which will correct the defect.

The criminal case of Smith v Hughes, 1960, gives a good example of the operation of the rule. Here, the relevant statutory provision was s.1 of the Street Offences Act, 1959, a statute which was designed, amongst other things, to make the soliciting of customers by prostitutes illegal. The section provided that it should be an offence for a prostitute to loiter or solicit "in a street". In the case before the court, prostitutes had attracted the attention of people walking in the street from balconies and windows. The question before the court was whether the words "in the street" covered such conduct. In deciding that an offence had been committed, Lord Parker, one of the judges, said that the mischief at which the Act was aimed was to clean up the streets so that people could walk along them without being molested by prostitutes. Using that as a guideline, he then said that the precise place from which the prostitute approached someone walking in the street was irrelevant.

However, there are cases where a consideration of the mischief involved in the old law may lead to the statute being interpreted very narrowly. One such case was Rodgers v National Coal Board, 1966, involving s.31 of the Mines and Quarries Act, 1954. This provided that "the surface entrance to every mine shaft" should be provided with an efficient barrier designed and constructed in such a way so as to prevent any person from accidentally falling down the shaft. The case was brought by the widow of a man who fell to his death from a cage which was *inside* the shaft itself. The court decided that the mischief which the Act was designed to prevent was the possibility of someone accidentally falling down the shaft from the surface entrance. It therefore did not cover a case where a person fell from inside the shaft itself. As a result of this interpretation, the Coal Board were not responsible for the accident.

In addition to these three major rules, there are other minor rules of construction, some of which it is also essential to mention here.

(i) *Noscitur a sociis.* (the meaning of a word can be gathered from the context in which it is used.) Under this rule the precise meaning of any words which are doubtful can be gathered from considering perhaps the phrase or the sentence in which the words appear.

(ii) *The "Eiusdem Generis" Rule.* The term "E.G." means literally "of the same kind or type". It is quite common, where a statute is drafted to cover a wide range of things which are similar, that the Act will mention two or three specific things and then follow these with a general expression. The result is that the Act will apply to things which are "of the same kind" as the specific things mentioned.

An example will illustrate the way in which the rule operates.

The Betting Act 1853 prohibited the keeping of a "house, office, room or other place" for betting with people using it. The question which arose in Powell v Kempton Park Racecourse Co. in 1899, was whether Tattersall's Ring, which was an "other place" and so subject to the statutory prohibition. Applying the *eiusdem generis rule,* the court said that the words "other place" were not "of the same kind as" the specific things mentioned — that is to say, "house, office, room" which are all indoors and not outdoor places. Therefore the prohibition did not apply in this particular case.

(iii) *"Expressio unius est exclusio alterius".* This means that the expression of one thing implies the exclusion of another. That is, that where specific words in a statute are not followed by general words, then the Act applies only to the specific things mentioned. So, if a provision refers to "cars and motorcycles", then it would not apply to, for example, buses, lorries, or pedal cycles.

Statutory Assistance

In addition to the rules evolved by the judges themselves there are certain statutory aids which may help in the question of interpretation.

1. *The Interpretation Act, 1889.* This Act gives the definitions of words and phrases which are commonly used in statutes. So, for example, it provides that unless a particular Act provides otherwise, words of masculine gender include females; words in the singular include words in the plural and vice versa; the expression "person" includes a corporate body (such as a Limited Company), and the word "month" means a calendar month.

   Notice, however, that the Act to be interpreted might specifically provide that these general definitions do not apply.

2. *Interpretation Section.* Many statutes incorporate an interpretation section themselves. This will give the meanings of words *as they are to apply to that particular statute.* So, for example, s.62 of the Sale of Goods Act, 1893 defines the term "goods", although a different definition of the same term appears in s.34 of the Theft Act, 1968.

3. *Preamble and Long Title.* A preamble used to be common in Acts of Parliament. It is an introductory statement which appears before the provisions themselves, and sets out the reason for the statute being passed. It might, for instance, state the defect in the old law which the Act has been passed to remedy. Modern Public Acts, however, tend not to have a preamble, and so its importance as an aid to interpretation is declining.

   Now a statute tends to have a long title, which, although it is a part of the statute, is really a minor aid to interpretation. The Companies Act, 1948 (which is the short title, or the title by which the Act is commonly called) has as its long title: "An Act of Parliament to consolidate the Companies Act, 1929, the Companies Act, 1947 (other than the provisions thereof relating to the registration of business names, bankruptcy and the prevention of fraud in connection with unit trusts), and certain other enactments amending of the first-mentioned Act."

   One might have though that Parliament would have taken the opportunity, in using the long title, to state its reasons why the Act was passed, but in practice long titles tend not to explain the statute's purpose so much as to identify what it is about. This is why the long title is only a minor aid.

Presumptions in interpretation

A judge must also bear in mind several principles which are presumed in interpretation unless the Act itself expressly provides to the contrary. The main ones are:-

1. The Act applies to the whole of the United Kingdom but no further.

2. International law will not be infringed.

3. The statute is not retrospective, that is to say it does not apply to situations which existed *before* it was passed.

4. The Act does not alter the common law, that is to say it is presumed that Parliament did not intend the statute to alter the law unless the Act itself uses words showing this to be so.

5. The Act does not impose liability without fault. Generally if a person is to be found guilty of a criminal offence, it must be shown that he had a "guilty mind", or criminal intent. So, if a statute wishes to introduce an offence of strict liability (that is that a person will be guilty whether he had criminal intent or not), it must do so in clear and unambiguous language.

6. The Crown is not bound by the statute.

7. The jurisdiction of the Courts will not be ousted, that is to say, an individual will always be able to apply to the courts so that his rights in a particular situation can be determined.

8. The Act does not deprive a person of a right which he had before the Act was passed. Thus if a statute takes away someone's property, there is a presumption that he will be paid compensation for it.

9. The Act does not repeal any other Act.

In conclusion we can see that statute law forms an increasingly large part of the legal environment in which any organisation operates. If the organisation is subject to any statutory provisions then it is bound by them and it is for the courts to determine the nature of its rights and obligations through the interpretation of the Act where this proves necessary.

The role of the House of Commons

Besides carrying out this important legislative function, the House of Commons is the body which supports the government of the day i.e. the government remains in office so long as it retains the confidence of the House of Commons. In normal circumstances this can be expected, but the example provided by the Labour Government from October 1974 suggests that unless a government can call upon an overall majority at all times during its term of office, there will be times when its plans are reversed. At worst, as happened in April 1979, a government may be defeated on a vote of confidence, and unless it can get this reversed almost immediately, it must resign.

Other important functions of the Commons are:

Finance. The authorisation and control of the raising and spending of money. There are two important Select Committees of the Commons which support the House in this task, the Expenditure Committee and the Public Accounts Committee.

Scrutiny of government policy and administration — we do not expect the Commons to govern the country directly, but as the House which contains the elected representatives of the people, the Commons should be able to find out what Ministers and their Departments have been up to. During Question Time which is held every day except for Friday, Ministers can be questioned on policy issues and departmental matters. The Commons also spends a lot of time debating important issues, when the Opposition can highlight what it considers to be government failings. Select Committees are appointed and report back to the House. Besides the two Committees mentioned above, there are also Committees covering the nationalised industries. Science and technology, race relations and immigration and the work of the Parliamentary Commissioner for Administration (the Ombudsman).

Local Government

The local government system consists of a number of elected councils representing local areas. Each council, depending on its size, is responsible for a range of services. Whatever powers and duties a particular local authority has to carry out, must be sanctioned by an Act of Parliament or by particular measure made under the authority of an Act. Many services which are provided for people in this country are of a kind which demand a partnership of central and local government. For example, in the field of education, the Department of Education and Science has overall responsibility for education in the country, but the local education authorities administer the system of education and maintain the schools at the local level.

In England and Wales there are two types of authority which perform local government functions. There is the county authority which normally provides the large-scale local government functions, and the district authority which is responsible for the more local ones. The local government system was reformed with effect from April 1st 1974 as a result of the Local Government Act of 1972. Local government reform recognised the existence in England of heavily populated areas or conurbations and a special system of local government exists in six "metropolitan" areas in the country. London is the first metropolitan area, of course, and the local government system which operates in this area was reformed in the sixties. (London Government Act 1963 which took effect from April 1st 1965).

Local government expenditure in the late 1970's amounted to approximately some £20,000M per annum. A distinction is made between current and capital expenditure of local authorities. Current expenditure is financed by (i) Government Grants (about a half), (ii) Local rates paid by occupiers of land and buildings (almost a third), and (iii) Rents from council houses and other income from such things as leisure provisions, swimming baths and such. Current expenditure relates to one financial year, whilst capital expenditure which is usually financed by borrowing is more long term. Therefore, the wages bill which a local authority has to meet is part of current expenditure, whilst the costs of building a huge new Civic Centre will be part of the capital account.

Exhibit 3.1 shows how local government is structured, whilst Exhibit 3.2 gives examples of services available from local government.

Exhibit 3.1

Local Government Structure

Parliament

39 County Councils	6 Metropolitan County Councils	Greater London Council		8 Welsh Counties
296 District Councils	36 Metropolitan District Councils	32 London Boroughs	City of London Corporation	37 Welsh Districts
Local (Parish) Councils	Local (Parish) Councils			Local (Community) Councils

Metropolitan Counties

1. West Midlands
2. Greater Manchester
3. Merseyside

4. Tyne & Wear
5. South Yorkshire
6. West Yorkshire

Exhibit 3.2

Examples of Local Government Services

Services	Metropolitan County		Non-Metropolitan County	
	County Council	*District Council*	*County Council*	*District Council*
Strategic Planning Transportation Planning Highways Traffic Regulations Consumer Protection Refuse Disposal Police Fire Service	YES		YES	
Education Personal Social Services Libraries		YES	YES	
Environmental Health Housing Planning Applications Refuse Collection		YES		YES

Note: Other services such as off-street carparks, provision of museums, art galleries and parks are available at both levels, depending on local agreements.

Major departments

If we had to list the major activities of government, we would see that these are now many and varied. During the course of this century such activities have increased greatly. Of course, we can use certain categories into which particular activities can fit:
e.g.

(1) Maintenance of law and order.

(2) External affairs — Defence and Foreign policy.

(3) Economic and industrial affairs.

(4) Social services.

The major Government Departments are represented by a Minister in the Cabinet. There are other Ministers who are not in the Cabinet but who are responsible for a Department which has lesser importance. Some Departments or Ministries have been in existence for a long time, e.g. Treasury, Home Office, Foreign Office, although over the years they may have undergone a change of name. e.g. Defence Ministry established in 1964 although the actual function of "defence" has existed as long as any governmental system. Defence and law and order are the original functions of government.

There are also Departments which are clearly an invention of the 20th century — the Age of Technology e.g. Department of Energy.

The major Government Departments

Department	Main responsibilities	Examples of other Agencies associated with Department
Agriculture Fisheries and Food	Agriculture, horticulture, food and fishing industries. Control and erradication of animal and plant diseases. Safety and quality of food and food supply.	The Intervention Board for Agricultural Produce (implementation of market support arrangements and other aspects of EEC Common Agricultural Policy).
Ministry of Defence	Defence policy; control and admin of Armed Forces. Procurement of equipment for the forces.	Procurement Executive (Defence) — maintains liaison between the Service users and the machinery for procurement.
Education and Science	Promotion of all forms of education throughout England. Post-school education in Wales. Civil science. Library service.	Local Education Authorities (LEA's) i.e. Local Departments of the County Councils and in Metropolitan areas. District Councils. University Grants Committee (UGC). Research Councils. (e.g. Science).

Employment	Employment policy, industrial relations, pay policy. Payment of unemployment benefit.	The Manpower Services Commission (Employment and Training Services Agencies).
Energy	Energy Supply, usage and conservation. Coal, gas, electricity industries. Atomic energy. Off shore 'Natural' gas and oil resources.	National Coal Board. British Gas Corporation. CEGB (Central Electricity Generating Board). 12 area electricity boards. Atomic Energy Authority. British National Oil Corporation.
Environment	The physical environment – urban affairs, inner City renewal, new towns, local government and regional affairs. Housing and construction industries. Planning, development, control of land. Control of pollution. Sport and recreation. Water and sewerage. Maintenance of public and government buildings. Historic towns, buildings and sites.	Local authorities – Housing Departments. The Housing Corporation. (liaison role – encourages non-profit making housing associations and societies).
Foreign and Commonwealth	All aspects of external affairs, foreign policy, negotiations with other countries, protection of British interests, including citizens abroad.	In foreign countries – Embassies and consulates. Overseas Development (a Govt. Dept. subject to overall responsibility of Foreign Office).
Health and Social Security	Administration of NHS. Public health, hygiene, local authority Social Services. Collection of Social Security contributions. Payment of benefits.	Local authorities – Social Services Dept. Regional and Area Health Authorities (RHAs and AHAs).
Home (Office)	Internal affairs not assigned to other Depts. (England and Wales). Administration of Justice. Maintenance of law and order, treatment of offenders, probation, public safety, fire, Civil defence. Immigration, community relations. Control of firearms, dangerous drugs.	Metropolitan Police (directly under control of Home Office). Provincial Police Forces (Police Committees of local authorities). Probation offices. (local).

Industry	General industrial policy financial assistance to industry (regional policy). Nationalised industries – Iron and and Steel. Aircraft, shipbuilding. Post Office, Research and Development. Civil Aerospace Research. Technical services to industry.	The British Steel Corporation. British Shipbuilders. The Post Office. British Aerospace.
Prices and Consumer Protection	Policy and legislation on prices, consumer affairs, quality assurance and standards. Fair trading, monopolies, mergers and restrictive practices. Consumer and home safety.	The Price Commission. Monopolies and Mergers Commission. Consumer Councils (Nationalised Industries). Local authorities – Consumer Protection Officers.
Trade	Commercial policy – relations with overseas countries. Administration of British protective tariffs. Export services. Insurance, insolvency, patents, trademarks, copy rights. Civil aviation. Marine and shipping policy. Hotel and travel industries.	The British Overseas Trade Board. (directs official export promotion services). The Civil Aviation Authority. British Airways.
Transport	Inland transport industries, railways, buses, freight and ports. Planning and construction of motorways and trunk roads. Local transport. Road and vehicle safety, vehicle and driver licensing.	Transport and Road Research Laboratory (jointly sponsored by Trade and Environment). British Rail. British Waterways Board. The National Freight Corporation.
The Welsh Office	Child care, health, housing, local government, primary and secondary education. Town and Country planning. Agriculture (Wales), Roads, economic development, water and sewerage. Forestry. National parks. Tourism.	The Welsh Planning Board. The Welsh Council.

The Treasury

This important government department has a central role to play in the system of government. It takes primary responsibility for developing Britain's overall economic strategy.

There are 4 main Divisions or Sectors of the Treasury.

1. *Public Services Sector* – with responsibility for controlling public expenditure as a whole as well as individual programmes.

2. *Domestic Economy Sector* – with responsibility for fiscal, monetary and counter-inflation policies and also looks after the Treasury's contribution to industrial policies such as controlling the amount of public money spent on agriculture and industry.

3. *The Overseas Finance Sector* – with responsibility for balance of payments policies, foreign currency reserve, together with international monetary issues and financial relation with other countries.

4. *Chief Economic Adviser's* – with responsibility for the preparation of short-term and medium-term economic forecasts and for giving specialist advice on general economic policies.

The Treasury therefore heads the list of those government departments with economic responsibilities on a national scale. Others which can be cited are:

(1) Agriculture, Fisheries, Food.

(2) Employment.

(3) Environment.

(4) Energy.

(5) Industry.

(6) Prices and Consumer Protection.

(7) Transport.   (8) Trade.

Estimates

The financial year for the public sector begins on April 1st. and extends to the following March 31st. Each government department will submit its estimates of the amount of money which it requires to the Treasury. These estimates will be submitted in December i.e. some four months before the new financial year begins on April 1st.

Estimates require approval by the Treasury before being presented to Parliament in February or March. An appropriation Act is passed in July which sanctions the estimates. To cover the money spent for April to July, a Vote of Account is approved by Parliament in March.

In each session of Parliament 29 days (Supply or Opposition days) are allowed to cover discussion of broad issues of policy, with the Opposition choosing subjects for debate based generally on the estimates.

The Consolidated Fund

There are certain expenditures which do not require annual approval. They are covered by Acts of Parliament which allow payments to proceed from year to year.

Such payments will come direct from the Consolidated Fund, into which all tax revenues and other receipts are paid. The balance is held in the Exchequer Account at the Bank of England. Examples of Consolidated Fund payments include the Civil List which the Queen receives, and other provisions for members of the royal family; salaries and pensions for judges and the Parliamentary Commissioner for Administration (Ombudsman).

The National Loans Fund

This is another official account at the Bank of England which deals with much of the Government's domestic lending and borrowing.

The Exchange Equalisation Account

This covers official dealings in foreign exchange. The other two accounts mentioned above cover only sterling receipts and payments.

The Budget

The Chancellor of the Exchequer will make his Budget Speech usually in April. His main concern is to find means of raising money to finance government expenditure. Another aspect is the need to spell out the state of the economy and the Budget acts as an important instrument of economic management. Some changes in taxation are inevitable e.g. change in the basic rate of income tax or Value Added Tax (VAT). Whatever changes occur the Chancellor can affect the demand made on goods and services in the country. He may feel it is necessary to reduce the predicted level of demand on economic resources.

For the most part taxation proposals made in the Budget will bring about changes in the rates or coverage of existing taxes, and perhaps, new taxes will be introduced or existing ones abolished. There may also be changes in the administrative arrangements concerned with taxation.

The Finance Act

Whatever tax changes are announced in the Budget they will be incorporated in the annual Finance Act which is passed towards the end of July. This act also gives effect to provisions for non-Budgetary changes in the tax system and Government borrowing requirements.

Provisional Collection of Taxes Act

There is an obvious delay between April when the Budget is announced and July when the Finance Act is passed. The Government is allowed to collect certain taxes provisionally e.g. income tax under the above Act.

The Planning and Control of Public Expenditure

This is an issue of great importance as everyone who works in the public sector appreciates. Three main methods by which this is carried out should be noted:

1. *The Public expenditure survey* — produced annually, and cover the whole range of projected public expenditure, for the following five years.
2. *The Supply Estimates procedure* – which has been outlined previously.
3. *Cash limits* – operate for the financial year immediately ahead and cover roughly half of public expenditure. Whatever limit is laid down in terms of a fixed cash provision, this figure should not normally be exceeded.

Policy implementation and control

In Britain the decision making process whereby government policies are formed, is centralised with the Prime Minister and Cabinet playing the major part. The advice which is given by Civil Servants at the top level, based on many years of experience, should never be forgotten, however. The Central Government Departments are the major instruments through which government policy is implemented after Parliament has passed the necessary legislation. The experience gained by Civil Servants in implementing previous policies give them a sound basis for assessing the feasilibility and desirability of future policies. Government Departments will work with and through other bodies — local authorities and ad hoc bodies for example.

Rules, orders and regulations (delegated legislation) will be drawn up by such Departments and the other bodies when provision for further rule making has been authorised in previous Acts of Parliament. The Government Departments will obviously be the main bodies carrying out such provisions. We should bear in mind that Parliament has allowed delegated legislation to be drawn up in particular instances, and will endeavour to keep a check on any rules which are introduced. Ministers are also expected to exercise the necessary oversights of their Departments and those bodies which have some link with these Departments. The forms of control to which Government Departments are subject should be born in mind — internal controls are maintained by the Treasury, and the Civil Service Department. This Department was established in 1968 and is responsible for general management of the rest of the Civil Service, in terms of general organisation, pay, promotion and conditions of service.

External controls are maintained by Parliament and the Ombudsman, as well as the mass media generally. Adverse publicity directed against any Department or a particular decision may be taken up by the M.P.s and in some cases the decision may be reviewed or even withdrawn.

The Parliamentary Commissioner for Administration (OMBUDSMAN)

The Parliamentary Commissioner is an officer of Parliament and is therefore independent of the government and the Civil Service. The office was established in Britain in 1967. The Ombudsman investigates complaints of maladministration which are referred to him by M.P.s on behalf of members of the public. Such complaints against actions taken by central government departments must be related to the administrative functions of departments. Policy matters are outside the Ombudsman's jurisdiction, but M.P.s can question Ministers in the Commons on such matters, of course. The Ombudsman can check all relevant departmental papers and correspondence and will report back to the M.P. who referred the case to him.

Additionally, the Ombudsman presents a report to Parliament every year and may also present other reports on particular cases if he thinks it is necessary. A House of Commons Select Committee examines these reports.

Since the Office was established the main problem area consistently has been delay, in that a Department has not dealt with a particular matter promptly. The two Departments which have most contact with the public, Inland Revenue and DHSS, invariably find that they are complained about most. Considering the number of decisions which all Departments make every day, the 815 complaints referred to the Ombudsman in 1976 is not sufficiently high to cause concern, although some may disagree. Some people have argued that the Office should be given more publicity and members of the public should be allowed to refer complaints directly to the Ombudsman.

Health Service Commissioners

The present Ombudsman also has responsibility for investigating complaints about the Health Service. At present the three Health Service Commissioners For England, Scotland and Wales are combined with the duties of the Ombudsman. Complaints that a health authority has failed to carry out its statutory duties are investigated as well as maladministration and injustice or hardship as a result of some breakdown in a service. Whatever the nature of the complaint, previous notification must be given to the health authority to allow it time to investigate it and reply to the complaint. The Commissioner reports to ministers every year and such reports are then laid before Parliament.

Local Government

Since reorganisation of local government in April 1974 there are also independent statutory Commissions for Local Administration for England and Wales. Local Commissioners organised on a regional basis, each dealing with a given group of local authorities, investigate complaints of maladministration against local authorities.

Pressure Groups

Such groups can be referred to as organised associations of people which attempt to influence or modify government policy. Unlike political parties which aim to get candidates elected and control the machinery of government, pressure groups have more limited and specific aims. The pressure group will appeal to potential members on a narrower basis than the political party. Nevertheless, there are some groups which do seek widespread support for a cause — PROMOTIONAL groups, such as the R.S.P.C.A. and the N.S.P.C.C. There are other groups which can be called PROTECTIVE (or sectional) groups which exist to look after the special interest of their members. Under this heading further categories are often suggested — labour groups, professional groups and business groups can be cited. Examples — Labour groups, include the Trades Union Congress (T.U.C.), the individual unions, nearly all of which are affiliated to the T.U.C. together with the Co-operative Movement.

Professional groups include the British Medical Association (B.M.A.) and the Society of Civil Servants.

Business groups include the Institute of Directors and the Confederation of British Industries (C.B.I.) which is a body which represent more than 10,000 companies plus over 200 trade associations and employers' organisations.

Their methods

The most direct and significant method of operation is for the pressure group to approach the Executive — Ministers and the Civil Service. It is obvious that some groups will inherently have more success than others in this respect. There are those groups which in any case are called upon by Ministers and Government Departments to offer advice and information (advisory bodies). These groups are involved and are consulted and can contact the Department if they wish to press any further points.

Those groups which exist on the 'fringe' and are not a part of this network of involvement may try to contact Minister and Government Departments, but will have to rely on other methods also to publicise their own cases e.g. Lobbying M.P.s, use of the mass media, and perhaps more direct action, such as mass rallies and demonstrations.

Links with political parties

Of the groups previously mentioned, no prizes will be awarded for linking particular ones with certain political parties. The labour groups are obviously linked closely with the Labour party, whilst the business groups have close links with the Conservative Party. Both political parties, however, will often feel bound to widen the basis of their support in the country. Nonetheless, the financial backing for the two main parties from the groups with which they are associated is substantial. Whilst the trade union contribute approximately 75% of the Labour party funds, business firms contribute up to 70% of the Conservative party funds.

The main distinction between the two bases of support concerns the fact that the labour groups "affiliate" to, or actually join, the Labour Party, whilst the business groups have less direct links with the Conservative Party. The trade unions sponsor individual candidates, many of whom become M.P.s. No such sponsorship is undertaken by the C.B.I. and other business groups. It is not to say, however, that the informal links are any less significance than the formal ones. Nonetheless, the trade unions helped to establish the Labour party at the beginning of this century, and have an established position within the party at present. They can elect 12 of the 28 members of the National Executive Committee (N.E.C.) of the Labour Party. The N.E.C. is the management committee of the party.

Dominance of two parties

In Britain a two party system operates. This does not mean that there are only two parties since we can all name three or four, or even more? What it does mean is that, at present, only one of two major parties has the capacity to get enough M.P.s elected to be able to form a Government. Whichever party manages to achieve this feat will be the governing party, and the other one will form Her Majesty's Opposition. The other parties do not have such an "Official" status.

The political party has been seen as the main link between the "governors" and the "governed". In our political system an "Independent", that is someone who has no party links, has to take his chance against the organised political parties campaigning for our vote. Once again, we realise that the 2 major parties have distinct advantages — and finance is a very important factor. Money is required to launch publicity campaigns as well as to provide the necessary deposit of £150 which each candidate has to put up for a parliamentary election. This deposit is forfeited if the candidate fails to get at least one-eighth of the total votes cast in the election. There has been an increase in the support for the smaller parties during the last ten years of so, and therefore a decline in voting support for the Labour and Conservative parties. This may have the effect of making it difficult for either party to achieve and maintain an absolute majority in the Commons. If so, a government may have to accept that some agreement or "pact" with one or more of the minor parties is necessary to keep it in office e.g. the "Lib-Lab" pact 1978. In any case, there is now more likelihood of the smaller parties having some modifying influence on the government.

Public opinion

Pressure groups and political parties are both instruments through which particular opinions are expressed. Public opinion is a general term which accounts for the total beliefs or opinions of people on particular issues without necessarily showing unanimous opinion or majority opinion. In fact, there are occasions when minority views will be more influential if people can organise themselves effectively.

The mass media will invariably play a part in the process — people are informed by television and radio programmes and by reading newpapers. Public opinion will react in the face of governmental and other decisions e.g. a firm decides to close down a local factory, and particular opinions can be expressed by the political parties and the pressure groups. Public opinion can be gauged by means of opinion polls and we can discover which party leader is the most popular in the country at a given time, as well as the public's views on other issues e.g. capital punishment. The extent to which opinion polls can be relied on as completely accurate guides can be discussed with your statistics tutor. Probably the most direct way in which public opinion can be expressed on a given issue is means of a referendum. Such a measure was used in June 1974 when the people were asked whether Britain should remain a member of the European Community. The main problem with a referendum is whether people are able fully to understand the complex issues which will usually be involved. An important discussion point is involved here. Do we expect in our political system to be guided by the people we elect on such issues, or only on some particular issues? What issues can be suitably put to the people for a direct vote in a referendum?

Advisory bodies

An important aspect of Central government which is sometimes overlooked, is the existence of many advisory councils or committees which help Ministers and their Departments to take account of important issues when policies are being formulated. These advisory bodies have often collected information and undertaken research which can be vital in a highly technical world. There may even be a statutory obligation on a Minister to consult a Standing Committee before he reaches a decision. Nevertheless a Minister will often appoint advisory bodies simply to enable him to find out certain information and give him advice.

Membership This depends on the nature of the work involved but the members of advisory bodies come from a variety of backgrounds, e.g. Civil Servants, professional bodies, industrialists, trade unionists, academics.

Status Many advisory bodies are permanent standing committees or councils. From time to time the Government establishes AD HOC committees to investigate and report on a particular matter. A Royal Commission may even be established if a particularly important issue is to be considered. e.g. The Latey Commission which reported in 1968 on lowering the age of majority.

Whatever recommendations any advisory body, including a Royal Commission, may make, it is still up to the Government to decide what should be done.

Green Papers

When a government wishes to generate discussion of an issue, it may publish its own outline plans in an official document. The first such Green Paper was issued in 1967 concerning a regional employment premium. The idea is that all interested parties can contribute their ideas, and the Government can then decide whether any further steps need to be taken.

White Papers

These are used to state official government policy, which enables Parliament and the general public to gain vital information. The White Paper is therefore a more definite statement of the intentions of the government than the Green Paper. Legislation may follow publication of the White Paper in the course of time.

Law Reform Agencies

One of the more pleasing aspects of the law, and one of the more infuriating as well, is its constant change. But naturally as the needs and ideas of society change, so the law must change too. The number of statutes passed by Parliament in recent years, and statutory instruments issued under authority delegated by Parliament is indeed prolific. All of these are designed to add to, amend, or remove existing legal rules. Government policies affecting the operation of organisations may, once formulated, come out in the form of new Acts. The enactment of the Companies Acts

1967 and 1976 laying down regulations relating to publicity of information about a company's affairs are examples of this. Influence affecting government policy may come from Law Reform Agencies.

The idea behind the creation of such agencies is a simple one. For many years the law depended for its development upon the introduction of new legislation to meet some new change (but occasionally, for example with the Race Relations Acts 1965 and 1968, to lead public opinion) and upon the slow changes in the law brought about through case decisions. These traditional methods of law reform came to be recognised as inadequate, and the feeling developed that greater direction in the area of law reform was necessary.

The major break-through was achieved in 1965 with the establishment of a full-time Law Commission under the Law Commissions Act. Basically, the function of the Commission is to keep all aspects of the law under constant review. Its members are appointed by the Lord Chancellor and are responsible for making reports as to their findings to him and to Parliament. They have to approach the existing law from the point of view of its systematic development and reform, paying particular attention to possible codification (that is to say, combining all the law on one particular subject, for example The Theft Act 1968), simplifying and modernising the law, and repealing any statutes which are regarded as obsolete and unnecessary.

In addition to the Law Commission itself various other bodies, committees, and commissions may be appointed to examine some particular aspect of the law, and the comments which they make may influence government policy on particular matters. Several recommendations contained in the Jenkins Committee Report in 1962, for instance were included in the Companies Act, 1967.

Major Quasi-Judicial and Quasi-Governmental Bodies

Quasi-Judicial Bodies

Modern conditions, having required that there be increasing control by the State of the liberties of the individual, have also led to a growing number of disputes between people and the Administration. For example, the government pays pensions, unemployment benefit, and family allowances, but a dispute might arise between the individual who claims benefit and the State which maintains that he is not entitled to it. If all such disputes were to be dealt with by the courts, those courts would soon be overburdened with business. Additionally, the costs of judicial proceedings are high, the courts are slow and their procedure is very formal and elaborate, and in any event matters which involve public services are better dealt with by specialists. In modern legislation then, where it is anticipated that a dispute might arise, provision is often made for it to be heard by an Administrative Tribunal or by a Minister after holding an enquiry. Tribunals are quasi-judicial bodies. That is they are governed by procedural rules and apply legal principles but they are outside the actual courts system itself. They enjoy certain advantages over courts system:

1. Decisions can be given quickly, so delay in hearing disputes is avoided.
2. The hearing is less expensive than using the court's time.
3. The informal and straightforward procedure probably suits the parties better.
4. Detailed specialist knowledge in the field of the dispute is available.
5. Tribunals are essentially local by nature and so they have knowledge of local conditions.
6. They have wider discretionary powers than ordinary courts, and often develop their own policies.

The Tribunals and Inquiries Act, 1958, was passed to remedy criticisms that there was little publicity of a tribunal's findings, reasoned judgements were not always given, and decisions were unpredictable because of their wide discretionary powers. The Act established a Council on Tribunals to review the way in which they work. They must give reasons for their decisions, and so as to increase their independence and ensure that those appointed have appropriate qualifications for the job, the Chairmen of tribunals are appointed from a panel suggested by the Lord Chancellor. The law was consolidated in the Tribunals and Inquiries Act, 1971, which governs the present position as we enter the 1980's. Appeals can be made to the courts in some instances, and, in any event, tribunals are subject to control by prerogative orders issued by the High Court as shown in chapter 16.

For convenience, these quasi-judicial bodies may be divided into two major groups, and a selection of examples within each group can now be given.

Domestic Tribunals

These are disciplinary bodies formed to exercise controlling jurisdiction over professions, clubs, and other associations by settling disputes within the association itself. They may be established by statute of by agreement between their members. Thus doctors and nurses are controlled by the Disciplinary Committees of the General Medical Council and the General Nursing Council respectively; solicitors are subject to the control of the Disciplinary Committee of the Law Society. In cases of misconduct, members can be disbarred or may be suspended for a specified time. Various trading organisations producing and distributing particular products have also been used to control the sale, production, and pricing of their products, for example the Egg Marketing Board.

Other Tribunals

Industrial Tribunals can be included here. They hear most disputes which might arise as a result of recent statute law dealing with, for example, unfair dismissal, sex and race discrimination, equal pay, the payment of redundancy benefits, and disablement, injury or death arising in the course of employment.

Social security tribunals would deal with matters concerning family allowances and the Special Commissioners of Income Tax hear appeals against income tax assessments. The Lands Tribunal resolves disputes which might arise where land is to be acquired by local authorities or government departments under powers of compulsory purchase.

Finally, there are Rent Tribunals exercising powers given by the Rent Act 1977. An appeal to them can fix the rent to be paid for houses and flats and they can also give tenants security of tenure in rented accommodation.

It should be stressed once again that these are only a very few examples of the thousands of tribunals operating in the administrative field.

Quasi-governmental bodies

The important fact that the functions of the state have increased in the course of the 20th Century was emphasised in Chapter 2. The number of Central Government Departments and the range of their activities have likewise increased. The local government authorities have been entrusted with many more statutory responsibilities — powers which they have to carry out. Public administration should not be viewed merely in terms of the activities of Central Government Departments and local government authorities. There are also a vast number of quasi-governmental bodies, most of which have been established by statute to administer or manage what are considered to be special types of Public Services and activities.

Ad hoc bodies

These quasi-governmental bodies are also referred to as ad hoc bodies which means that they exist for a particular purpose. They are semi-independent bodies whose purposes are many and varied.

Whilst Central Government Departments have a Minister with direct responsibility for the particular activity, these ad hoc bodies are usually semi-independent boards or corporations which are responsible for the day to day administration of the activity.

Brief history

Such semi-independent bodies were not invented in the 20th Century, however, even though their numbers have increased greatly this Century. An early example can be seen with the Commissioners of Sewers, established in Tudor times to supervise the disposal of sewage.

In the 19th Century a number of ad hoc bodies existed at particular times, such as the Poor Law Commissions and the School Boards. An early 20th Century example is the Port of London Authority, established in 1908 to administer the London Docks.

Different types

It is a difficult exercise to place such bodies in particular categories, but so long as we recognise that most classifications are not rigid, the following classification of ad hoc bodies can be used;

(a) Those which are primarily *Managerial and Commercial* e.g. Public corporations. (nationalised industries).

(b) Those which have a *Promotional function* e.g. Industrial Training Boards, Research Councils (Social Research Council). etc.

(c) Those which are associated with *Social Service functions* e.g. The Supplementary Benefits Commission, The Criminal Injuries Board.

(d) Those which have a *Regulatory function* e.g. Licensing Board. (Transport); The Race Relations Board; Equal Opportunities Commission; The Charity Commission.

So whatever classification is used as a general guide we must realise that some ad hoc bodies may perform more than one function e.g. The Independent Broadcasting Authority (IBA) can be said to perform regulatory and commercial functions.

The Public Corporation

This particular type of ad hoc body is probably the most familiar of the quasi-governmental bodies which exist. Public corporations are associated with the gradual emergence of the state as the most important and influential organisation in our lives — with a direct intervening role in industry and commerce.

These corporations have been established as an alternative to Central Government departments and local government authorities as a means of managing certain public activities. Such activities are essentially specialised and a particular type of administrative structure can be established for each on a separate basis. When the Labour Government from 1945 onwards decided to nationalise certain industries, it was the public corporation which was chosen as the agency to manage the industry e.g. The National Coal Board (NCB) was established to manage the Coal industry in 1946. The idea is that the public corporation offers the "best of both worlds" i.e. there is a need for some control of the industry because it is a "public" industry — therefore ministerial, Parliamentary and consumer control should be exerted over the industry. Such control should, however, not limit the Board of the Public Corporation in its task of organising the day to day management of the industry on a commercial basis.

That was the original plan, anyway. Increasingly the achievement of "both worlds" has been seen as an impossibility. The nationalised industries are a part of the public sector, over which the Government has to exert controls and whose activities have to be co-ordinated. During the last ten years or so, governments have felt the need, in attempting to control inflation, to interfere with the running of industries e.g. Wage restraints. Public sector and private sector industries have been affected. Even so, there are still people who advocate more accountability for public industries, particularly more scope for the consumer councils which are attached to most corporations.

Assignments

1. Explain the terms Legislature, Executive and Judiciary.
2. What happens to a public bill during its passage through Parliament?
3. What are the main functions of the House of Commons?
4. Why is the Treasury one of the most important (if not the most important) of Government Departments?
5. "The most important pressure groups are inevitably those with economic interests which require protection." Discuss.
6. In what way does a White Paper serve a different purpose to that of a Green Paper?
7. "A vital part of the Judicial function is the interpretation of statutes." What are the rules that the courts themselves have developed to help them in their interpretation?
8. What advantages do Tribunals enjoy over the courts system?
9. "The traditional methods of law reform were found to be inadequate to keep the law up to date this century — new methods had to be found". What are these traditional methods, and how has the approach to law reform been altered to overcome their defects?

Chapter 4

Government Policy — Economic

Learning objectives:
At the end of your study of this chapter you should be able to:
1. describe the functions of the Bank of England.
2. summarise the various methods by which Government policies are implemented and controlled with particular reference to
   a) monetary policy
   b) fiscal policy
3. understand why 'national budgets' are introduced.

In the mixed economy of the United Kingdom it was stated that the Government tends to pursue certain major economic objectives.[1] In its attempt to achieve these objectives the Government puts into operation its economic policy which makes use of its economic organisations, such as the Treasury[2] and the Bank of England. Such organisations have a variety of instruments that help them to carry out the Government's policy. The instruments used are conveniently grouped together under major headings, namely: monetary, fiscal, direct and persuasive. The last two mentioned will not be discussed here. All are used to achieve Government economic policy, but the first two mentioned play more important roles.

In this chapter the intention is to provide information about the following:
1. Bank of England. A brief account of the Bank's functions will be noted.
2. Monetary policy. Stating in a concise form the various methods by which monetary policies are implemented and controlled.
3. Fiscal (or Budgetary) policy and its main instrument, the Budget.

At the top and in control of these three areas is the Government. They establish economic objectives to be achieved and determine economic policy. Government organisations gear their operations to the requirements of the Government.

Policy

Policy, simply stated, refers to the course of action adopted by the Government, but the term is difficult to define. One author stated that the word policy is like the elephant; difficult to define but once seen it is easily

1. Refer to Chapter 2.
2. Refer to Chapter 3.

recognised. It is difficult to give an exact meaning to monetary and fiscal policy because each has undergone many changes in emphasis and shifts of direction. The aims and instruments which give these policies effect are all conditioned by the changing economic situation and changing ideas from one period of time to the next.

It should also be noted that "The study of policies is the study of priorities — the distribution of limited resources, the choice between desirable but incompatible aims, and the decision to do one thing first and others later."[3] Policy, at national level, is very much conditioned by its environment, especially the political environment.

Bank of England

The Bank of England Act 1946 nationalised the Bank of England and since that time the Bank has become one of the public corporations. The Act gave the Bank the power to request information from and make recommendations to bankers, and with approval of H.M. Treasury to issue directions to bankers to obtain compliance with any such request or recommendation.

An up-to-date version of the Bank's role, and one which provides detailed information, was submitted, in July 1978, to the Committee to Review the Functions of Financial Institutions (the Wilson Committee) in connexion with the second state of its inquiry. Details of the submission have been made available to the public in the Bank's Quarterly Bulletin.[4]

The function[5] of the Bank of England can be conveniently listed under the following headings:

1. External or foreign duties, and
2. Internal or domestic duties.

External

The following functions relate to the transactions that take place between the U.K. and the rest of world.

1. *Managing the Exchange Equalisation Account.* This account was set up by the Finance Act of 1932. The main purpose was to provide a fund for buying and selling gold and foreign currencies in order to protect the value of Sterling on foreign exchange markets. The Account handles the country's reserves of gold, dollars and foreign currencies.

---

3. "Housing Policy Since the War" by D. V. Donnison, Occasional Papers No. 1 on Social Administration, 1960, p.7.

4. Refer to 'Papers submitted to the Wilson Committee' — a total of five papers in the Bank of England Quarterly Bulletin, Vol. 18, No. 3, September 1978 pages 379-400. Page 386 provides a useful listing of Acts relating to banks and banking but excludes Northern Ireland legislation.

5. The word 'function' refers to the kind of action or activity proper to the Bank of England — the Bank's duty in carrying out action to fulfil its purpose. The Bank's role.

2. *Administering foreign exchange control.* Policy is agreed between the Treasury and the Bank of England but the Bank administers the control. In this area the Exchange Control Act 1947 applies. Administration ensures that banks who are authorised to deal in foreign exchange keep to a series of conventions or agreements in practice, for example the type and size of transactions, according to the policy in force.

3. *Maintaining relations with other monetary authorities and central banks.* The Bank provides banking services for other central banks, and exchanges views and information.

4. *Participate in the work of certain international financial institutions.* The Bank acts as the Government's agent when it participates in such international financial institutions as the International Monetary Fund, the International Bank for Reconstruction and Development and the Bank for International Settlements. Participation enables regular and intimate discussions between the Bank and opposite numbers in an attempt to achieve close co-ordination with others in the interests of orderliness in international finance (including Balance of Payments problems).

Internal

1. *Acts as the central bank of the U.K.* As central bank of the U.K. the Bank is given the powers to control and supervise the money markets and the banking system, and, as noted, operate and participate in the international financial field. In order to carry out its duties in these areas the Bank monitors the economic and financial climate and takes whatever action is necessary in the regulation of the markets and systems. (Note: this function, the next and the last are typical functions of any central bank.)

2. *Acts as banker to the government.* The duties of the Bank, as banker to the government, are to keep the Consolidated and National Loans Fund (the central accounts of the Government). In performance of this duty it provides day-to-day services to the government just like any bank does to its customers with a current account. It receives moneys due and transfers payments out of the account. At times it gives temporary assistance when the government's account goes 'into the red'. The Bank is responsible for managing the government's borrowing from the market in financing the Exchequer.

3. *Controls token money.* The Bank authorizes the minting of coins by the Royal Mint. Notes are printed by the Bank and they are the sole issuer in England and Wales. Banks in Northern Ireland and Scotland have the right to issue notes but most of their issues are backed by Bank of England notes.

4. *Acts as banker to the commercial banks.* The government is the most important customer of the Bank of England, but next in importance are the commercial banks who deposit about one-third of their total cash

holdings with the Bank. In other words the commercial banks maintain a working balance with the Bank. They draw upon this account as required. They also settle debts among themselves after the day's 'cheque clearance' by transferring money from one bank's account at the Bank to another bank's account at the Bank.

5. *Manages the National Debt.* The term 'national debt' refers to the cumulative total of outstanding debt owed by the Government on behalf of the nation. When the Government has an overall surplus in the Budget the debt decreases, and an overall deficit will increase the debt. The Bank, as manager of the debt, sells Treasury Bills and bonds or buys them in the open market. Which operation takes place will depend upon the 'needs' of the Government and the health of its account at the Bank.

6. *'Lender of last resort' to the discount market and Government.* The Bank's lender of last resort facility is available only to the Discount Houses who operate in the discount market and the Government. Each Discount House has a discount account at the Bank. These organisations are prime lenders and borrowers of short term money and when they are unable to borrow from other sources (for example commercial banks) they are forced, as a last resort, to go to the Bank of England. When this happens the Bank is able to dictate the terms (rate of interest and time). The discount market is an important feature of the U.K.'s money market because the bulk of the Bank's open market operations go through this market.

The Bank, being banker to the Government, is obliged to see that the Government can always meet its financial obligations and, as such, acts as lender of last resort to the Government.

In addition to the above functions the Bank has the role[6] of:

1. *Supervising banks and other deposit-taking institutions.* In carrying out this function the Bank sets forth the current philosophy and practice in the conduct of that supervision.

2. *Supervises the sterling money markets.*

3. *Supervises the foreign exchange and currency deposit markets.*

4. *Supervises the gold market.*

5. *Supervises the non-statutory aspects of the securities markets.* The main institution being the Stock Exchange.

6. *Surveillance of the London commodity markets.* In this area the major markets are the London Metal Exchange and the London Commodity Exchange. The latter Exchange is concerned wtih deals in certain 'soft' commodities such as cocoa, coffee, oilseeds and fats, rubber, soyabean meal, sugar and wool.

---

6. These functions are based on details provided in the five papers submitted to the Wilson Committee which appeared in the Bank of England Quarterly Bulletin, September 1978 — pages 379 to 402.

The Bank of England acts as agent to the Government and it is primarily in this capacity that it carries out the above functions. In carrying out these functions the Bank is able to fulfil its overall and main function, that of: *Carrying out the many aspects of monetary policy.*

Monetary policy

The Bank of England, as the central bank of the U.K., acts on the behalf of the Government when it puts into operation monetary instruments in an attempt to achieve current central Government economic policy. The Bank is the link between the public and private sector in the monetary field.

Monetary policy simply stated is the course of action adopted by the Bank in the field of money and credit.

Monetary policy, although looked at in isolation here, must be considered, generally, in the context of economic policy. It, along with other economic policies such as exchange rate policy, to some extent incomes policy, and particularly fiscal policy, is implemented to achieve better economic management of the economy. There is wide agreement about the major objectives of economic policy and monetary policy: high employment, growth in the short and long term, and stable prices. There is less agreement about which should be first in priority.

The objective of monetary policy in the 1950s and 1960s was geared towards control of the structure of interest rates. In the latter 1960s emphasis changed, as inflation steadily increased, towards control of monetary aggregates. This change in emphasis in the U.K. took place in September 1971 with the publication of a document called "Competition and credit control". The first aim of competition and credit control was to move towards a system in which market forces could play a dominant role in controlling the rate of growth of monetary aggregates through the market instrument of interest rates. To do this it was necessary to move away from restrictive controls which were directed towards the banking system.

Monetary aggregates, known by abbreviations such as M_1, M_3 and PSBR (Public Sector Borrowing Requirements), will be covered in the chapter on 'Money'.

Monetary policy, therefore, has to do with monetary management which is aimed at managing monetary aggregates. Compared to fiscal policy, monetary policy is more flexible and change can be made at any time. This is important because the success of monetary policy depends upon it being adjusted to meet changes in economic and financial conditions. These changes, as well as changes in monetary conditions, do not move up and down according to a set of rules. Thus, according to the Governor of the Bank[7] "the conduct of monetary policy is an art rather than a science".

Before considering the various methods by which monetary policies are

---

7.   "Reflections on the conduct of monetary policy". A lecture (the first Mais lecture) given by the Governor at the City University, London on 9 February 1978 and published in The Bank of England Quarterly Bulletin, March 1978, p.31.

implemented and controlled, remembering that they are designed to influence monetary totals, it is important to note that implementation of instruments to achieve the aggregates will depend on knowledge that exists about the factors that influence the demand for money on the one hand and the components of money supply on the other.

The demand for money is related to the level of national income and temporary influences such as a temporary shift from demands that are slightly sensitive to interest rates (precautionary and transactions demand) to a type of demand that is more sensitive (speculative demand). The Bank works on the theory, according to the Governor of the Bank,[8] that interest rates are the main determinants of the demand for money given the level of national income and neglecting temporary influences. This is important to the Bank because it seeks "to manage the course of monetary aggregates by bringing about changes in interest rates. But it is, of course, difficult to predict the level and structure of interest rates at which the stock of money the public wants to hold will be brought into equality with the stock the authorities would like to see being held.". Not being certain how interest rates will be influenced by various factors the Bank concentrates on the supply side to find out something about demand. This can be done by considering the broader aspects of money — DCE (Domestic Credit Expansion) and PSBR[9]. These will show demand for money by noting the flow of money — demand for money to purchase government securities; demand for money shown by noting the amounts borrowed from the banking sector, etc. This enables the Bank to predict, but not accurately, what the "rate of monetary expansion" will be, assuming there is no change in interest rates. If equality exists (supply equals demand) the Bank will not intervene in the money market. If they get out of line, or diverge, the Bank may find it necessary to intervene by putting into operation different types of instruments used to control the money market.

Monetary instruments

The instruments that are used to intervene and control the market are normally classified as:

1. Open market operations.
2. Minimum Lending Rate (called Bank Rate prior to 1972).
3. Funding.
4. Special deposits.
5. Directives.

The oldest instruments used by the Bank are the first two mentioned. The last three were brought into existence during the 1950's. All of them have an impact on the 'money supply'.

---

8. "Reflections on the conduct of monetary policy" p.35.
9. Refer to chapter on 'Money' for details about DCE and PSBR.

Open market operations

Open market operations refer to operations carried out by the Bank of England when it sells or purchases government securities in the open market. The objective is to control the supply of money in the private sector. It does this by changing the reserve assets of the commercial banks, and in so doing it changes the 'reserve asset ratio'[10] of each bank. The ratio, presently 12½ per cent, is determined by the Bank of England and must be maintained by each bank.

Open market operations are implemented when the Bank of England broker, who takes his instructions from the Bank, buys or sells government securities on the Stock Exchange.

If the Bank has the desire to *reduce* the supply of money in the private sector the Bank's broker will sell government securities. Ultimately this will cause a fall in the balance that banks have with the Bank. Because this balance forms part of the reserve assets of each bank it will bring each bank's reserve asset ratio below the 12½ per cent. This will force each bank to take action to bring the ratio back to at least 12½ per cent.

How does the sale of government securities reduce each bank's balance at the Bank of England? The story goes something like this: Government securities sold on the Stock Exchange are purchased by the general public, banks and other financial institutions. Each purchaser will make out a cheque usually drawn on their banks in favour of the Bank of England. When these cheques are cleared it has the immediate effect of reducing money, held in accounts with the commercial banks, in the hands of the private sector. The banks meet payment of cheques drawn on them, as well as their own cheques if they purchase securities, by having money transferred from their account at the Bank to the account of the Bank. The banks will replace the lost money by recalling money from the Discount Houses, and results in the Discount Houses being short of money so they will have to go to the Bank of England to borrow money as last resort. The Bank will lend at the 'minimum lending rate'.

On the other hand the Bank's broker may be instructed to *purchase* government securities in the open market. The operation that takes place will be the reverse of what happens when the broker sells. Overall it tends to have the opposite effect:-

---

10. The reserve asset ratio was introduced on 16 September 1971. It is the relationship between the reserve assets of a bank to its eligible liabilities and is expressed as a percentage as follows:

$$\frac{\text{reserve assets of a bank}}{\text{eligible liabilities of a bank}} \times 100\%$$

Each bank is required to maintain reserve assets to at least 12½ per cent of its eligible liabilities.

For details of what comprises 'reserve assets' and 'eligible liabilities' refer to additional notes at the back of the Bank of England Quarterly Bulletin. For example, in the September 1978 issue of the Bulletin the information is provided under 'additional notes to table 3.

reducing the amount of government debt held in the private sector, and increasing the supply of money in the private sector.

There are limitations to the exercise of control if some of the activities are not carried out exactly in the manner prescribed, but if they are then the Bank of England is able to control the supply of money.

Minimum Lending Rate (Bank Rate)

Bank rate was first introduced in 1797.

It will be convenient to discuss Bank Rate and Minimum Lending Rate (MLR) in three stages.

1. Bank rate prior to 9 October 1972.

2. MLR from 9 October 1972 to 25 May 1978.

3. 25 May 1978 MLR.

The Bank rate is simply the rate at which the discount houses can borrow from the Bank of England. The most common method is that the Bank makes an advance to a discount house against Treasury bills.

The only time the bank rate was used was when the discount houses were forced to borrow from the Bank as lender of last resort. Its importance lies in the fact that it was used as a 'base' for determining other interest rates. The Bank used it to control the price and quantity of credit rather than the money supply. The method by which this was achieved was that the Discount Houses passed on the rate they had to pay the Bank when borrowing to the banks who borrowed from them. This automatic change of rates on bank advances and deposits would have an effect on domestic demand (and on the capital account of the balance of payments). An increase in the bank rate would curb domestic demand and a decrease would encourage an increase in domestic demand. In other words the higher the rate the general public had to pay banks when borrowing money would discourage them from borrowing in order to purchase goods and services, and vice versa.

In setting the bank rate the Bank would deliberately set it above (or below) the short term rate of interest in the money market. A small change would have little impact on the money market and domestic demand, but a sharp change (say, increased by 2½ per cent) would disturb these activiies and shake people into changing their course of action.

For full details of bank rate, implementation and effects, students are advised to read the relevant paragraphs in the Radcliffe Report.[11]

On 9 October, 1972 out went the old bank rate and in came a new one called the 'Minimum Lending Rate'. This put an end to the importance of the bank rate, because the intention was that the MLR should follow changes in the money market rate of interest rather than lead them. The commercial banks no longer had to tie the rates they charged for lending or paid on deposits to the MLR. They could set their own 'Base Rate' based on money market conditions they faced, and could do this independent of authorities.

11. Committee on the Working of the Monetary System — Cmnd 827, HMSO, Aug. 1959.

The arrangements for determining the MLR, the penal rate for assistance to the discount market, was to be calculated each week according to a simple formula which would link it automatically to the prevailing discount rate on treasury bills at the end of the previous week. The MLR (from 9 October 1972 to 25 May 1978) was calculated at ½ per cent above the average discount rate on treasury bills at the Friday morning tender rounded up to the nearest ¼ per cent and this new rate would then rule the following week. At the same time the Bank of England reserved the right to bring back the traditional bank rate if they wanted to secure the special effects associated with changes in that rate.

On 25th May 1978 the Bank announced that the MLR arrangements, noted above, should be terminated, and "For the future the level of MLR will be determined by administrative decision and any change will normally be announced to the market at 12.30 p.m. on a Thursday. It has been decided that MLR shall remain at its present level of 9% until further notice. No further announcement will be made until it is decided to change the rate. It is intended that MLR will continue to be adjusted flexibly, taking account of market developments.[12]

On 8 June 1978 the MLR was raised to 10% and on Thursday, 9 November 1978 it was raised 2½% to 12½%. Like the traditional bank rate the psychological effect was to create changes in the money markets. The Bank said that the new 12½% MLR "is intended to establish a new level of short-term interest rates appropriate for the continuing restraint of monetary expansion." One of the first institutions to respond were the building societies who raised their mortgage (borrowing) rate by 2%. Other interest rates in other money markets also changed.

How long will this new MLR operate?

Funding

Funding is the process, carried out by the Bank of England, of restructuring the 'national debt' in order to change the asset structure of commercial banks. This debt consists of different classes, based on different periods of time to maturity; the main types are:

Treasury bills — up to 3 months;

Short bonds — up to 5 years;

Medium bonds — over 5 years and up to 15 years; and

Long bonds — over 15 years and undated.

Restructuring takes place when the Bank causes a change in the distribution between the different classes, and it does this by selling one class of debt and buying another. If, for example, the Bank sells long bonds and buys Treasury Bills it will have the effect of changing the liquidity position of the commercial banks. This would have the effect of lengthening the debt and reducing the liquidity of the banks. As the banks have less liquid assets they will have to reduce the sum of money they lend to the private sector (credit),

12. Bank of England Quarterly Bulletin, Vol. 18, No. 2, June 1978, p.173.

and the private sector will find it more difficult to borrow money in the money market.

A restructuring of the debt in the opposite direction (buys long bonds and sells bills) will tend to have the opposite effect on the liquidity of the banks and the amount of borrowing by the private sector.

Special deposits

Special deposits, invented in 1958 but first introduced in 1960, gave the Bank of England the power to call for special deposits from the banks to be lodged with the Bank. In essence, deposits are 'forced loans'. When introduced they were intended to act as a signal to the banks and money market that the Bank was introducing a major change in the direction of monetary policy. Basically the Bank would call for special deposits if the Bank wanted to make the money market short of funds, and repayments would take place to achieve the opposite effect.

Another reason for introducing special deposits was that they were expected to achieve what open market operations were designed to achieve but did not do successfully. A weakness of open market operations was that they were voluntary and there was no guarantee that banks would react in the way they were supposed to. Special deposits on the other hand were compulsory and it was mandatory that banks act along desired lines. In other words special deposits were more effective than open market operations in achieving the same objectives. Not only were special deposits more effective, they were also a more flexible weapon.

The Bank may call upon the banks and finance houses for special deposits amounting to a certain proportion of their eligible liabilities at any time. All banks observing the 12½ per cent reserve assets ratio and all finance houses observing the common 10 per cent reserve ratio[13] must make special deposits with the Bank. Interest is paid on these deposits; paid at a rate adjusted weekly based on the average rate for Treasury bills issued at the latest weekly tender.

Supplementary special deposits

In addition to special deposits the Bank introduced a scheme referred to as 'supplementary special deposits'. The first deposits recorded were for July 17, 1974.

Supplementary special deposits was an additional weapon or instrument to ensure that certain institutions remained within a guideline (how much each bank was allowed to increase their interest bearing eligible liabilities) which was set by the Bank to keep the money supply under control. If a bank (other than Northern Ireland) or deposit taking finance houses exceed the guideline they are penalised and must make a 'non-interest-bearing special deposit' with the Bank. The rate of deposit is progressive depending on how

---

13. The 10 per cent reserve ratio was based on arrangements between the Bank of England and finance houses and came into operation on 16 September 1971.

much the growth of interest-bearing eligible liabilities exceed the guideline. It should be noted that the scheme operates directly on the liabilities (not the assets) of these institutions.

The operation of supplementary special deposits was suspended in August 1977 but was reactivated in June 1978.[14]

The press have dubbed the supplementary special deposit scheme as the 'corset'. It can be harmful to banks and the banking system if worn too tight for too long.

A major advantage of these deposits is that they do curb banks from taking on substantial lending commitments beyond the guideline. In doing this it helps to ensure that the 'domestic credit expansion' (DCE) and rate of growth of sterling money supply remains within the target limits set by the Bank of England.

Directives (recommendations and requests)

The Bank of England, as central bank of the U.K., was given powers in the Bank of England Act 1946 in controlling and supervising generally the banking system. The exercise of these powers are carried out by the Bank informally by means of recommendations and requests. The commercial banks treat these as though they were directives; they consider them as being mandatory because they know that obeying them are in their own best interests.

These official recommendations and requests are directed at the banking sector to restrict their lending, and have taken two forms:

1. *Quantitative.* Directives, when issued, tend to restrict bank lending to a certain percentage above or below the size of their lending at a specific time; month and year is stated. For example: banks may be allowed to increase their lending but it should not be more than two per cent of their lending based on a specified month and year.

2. *Qualitative.* Recommendations and requests in this area simply specify who the banks should give top priority to when providing loans. If economic policy is geared to rectifying a deficit on the current account of the balance of payments top priority for lending will be to exporters; if it is geared towards Development Areas then top priority will be towards firms setting up in these areas. On the other hand the Bank may specify who banks should not give loans to, for example: property speculators.

In the document 'Competition and Credit Control' of September 1971 the Bank declared that restrictions on bank lending have been removed and in the future control will be by special deposits and through interest rates. As such, the supplementary deposit schemes with their restrictions on exceeding guidelines can be visualised as combining quantitative directives with special deposit controls.

---

14. For details of the June 1978 reintroduced scheme refer to 'Credit control notices' in September 1978 issue of the Bank of England Quarterly Bulletin, pages 357-358.

Having developed the basics of monetary policy and monetary instruments it is now time to consider fiscal policy and its main instrument — the Budget.

Fiscal (or budgetary) policy

'Fiscal' refers to matters that relate to the public purse or public fund. So, when discussing 'fiscal policy' we can say that it refers to the course of action adopted by the Government in all matters relating to the public fund.

The fund is filled when the Government obtains money from taxation, and depleted when expenditures are made.

Public funds

The bulk of the financial transactions of the central Government comes from:
the Consolidated Fund, and
National Loan Fund.

The Consolidated Fund, the Government's main account with the Bank of England, is filled primarily from monies obtained from taxation. Money is taken from the Fund when Government departments, such as the Department of Education and Science, reequire money to make expenditures relating to their responsibilities. Estimates of these expenditures are submitted to and voted by Parliament annually. These revenue and expenditure transactions will, at the end of the accounting year, leave the Fund holding a surplus of money or be in deficit. It is at this time that the Consolidated Fund which is closely associated with the National Budget, becomes linked with the National Loan Fund.[15]

If there is a surplus the Consolidated Fund transfers it to the National Loans Fund. This Fund uses the money to reduce the sum borrowed by the Government so it can make loans to local authorities and public corporations. On the other hand, if there is a deficit then the National Loans Fund lends money to the Consolidated Fund — the money loaned is obtained by the Government selling securities to various sectors within the nation and from overseas, but primarily to the private sector at home.

A principal function of the National Loans Fund is that it services the National Debt.[16]

The total that can be loaned by the National Loans Fund is limited by law. It follows then that individual loans made by the fund do not specifically need the approval of Parliament.

These two central Government accounts are very important to the Chancellor of the Exchequer and the National Budget because they are at the centre of Budget decisions — decisions that relate to central Government activities.

15. National Loan Fund was set up under the National Loan Act 1968, section 5.

16. National Debt was defined earlier in this chapter. The debt arises when successive British governments raise funds over and above the amounts obtained by taxation in order to meet its expenditures.

National Budget

The National Budget, the major instrument of carrying out 'budgetary policy', can be referred to as the Government's balance sheet which shows the *estimated* revenue and *estimated* expenditure for the coming financial year.

This idea of laying the whole financial year's programme of estimated revenue and expenditure before Parliament is not new to the 20th century. It can be traced back to the 'younger Pitt' (William Pitt, 1759-1806).

Originally the purpose of the Budget was to enable the Government to raise sufficient money to meet expenditure needed to carry out essential central Government activities, such as expenditures on maintaining law and order and providing for defence against foreign aggressors, in the same financial year. This tended to be the practice right up to the commencement of World War II, but indications over time showed that there would have to be some change as the country moved farther away from a free enterprise economy.

Towards the end of the 19th century the Government increased its expenditures when it took over the responsibility for elementary education and, thus, needed more revenue. During the 20th century up to and including the second World War it took on further expenditures and found it necessary to raise taxes to obtain more revenue. As the scale of expenditure and taxation increased it was realised that the level of expenditure and the level of taxation had an important influence on the pattern of demand, the level of output and employment.

The traditional idea of 'balancing the Budget' (balancing expenditures with an equal amount of revenue) was discarded as the Government realised the Budget could be used as an instrument of economic management. Evidence of this change can be found in the 1944 White Paper on Employment which said that "there was no merit in a rigid policy of balancing the Budget each year, regardless of the state of trade". Since then Chancellors of the Exchequer have deliberately budgeted for an 'unbalanced Budget'; either having a surplus of revenue over expenditure or a deficit (expenditure greater than revenue).

Economic management begins when the Chancellor reviews the state of the economy and the Government's finances for the past year and then lays down new Budgetary measures for the year to come with the intention of steering the nation's activities along desired paths. These new measures are made known to the public when the Chancellor presents his Budget, usually during the month of April.[17]

For most of the post World War II period British policy makers have favoured the Budget in regulating the pattern and total of supply and demand of the nation's resources; monetary instruments being used in a

---

17. Details of the new Budgetary measures are set out in a Finance Bill which are discussed by Parliament and normally passed into law sometime in July.

supporting role.[18] However, devising Budgetary measures to regulate the economy entails considerable preparation.

As soon as one Budget is presented the Government's revenue departments (such as Customs and Excise and Inland Revenue) begin making forecasts of estimates of receipts for the next financial year. Naturally these are continuously being up-dated especially as Budget day draws near. On the expenditure side we find Government departments (such as Health and Education and Science) preparing their future expenditures; these are usually done between November and January and the sums are agreed with the Treasury. These expenditure are also up-dated in the light of changes taking place in the economy — as shown by economic indicators.[19] On this basis the Chancellor makes his major Budget decisions.

The Chancellor's decisions bring pressure on the production of and the demand for the nation's goods and services. The effect, however, will depend primarily on the overall balance of the Budget. It will depend on "whether the Government spends and puts back into the economy less than, as much as, or more than it takes out by taxation. Important secondary effects may also be secured by the selection of the Budget measures in that these may be designed to influence rapidly the decisions of business firms to spend on capital equipment, or the decisions of individuals on spending and saving."[20] We can also note that surpluses and deficits have an effect on the money supply — putting more money into the economy than it takes out by taxation or vice versa.

The information provided about the Budget, so far, has been simple and straight-forward. It is possible at this stage to discuss the various types of taxes and expenditures and their effects, but these will be developed later in the book. At this time, we return to the idea of 'Budgetary Policy'.

Budgetary (or Fiscal) Policy

The Budget, the main instrument of 'Budgetary' (or 'Fiscal') Policy, is introduced by the Chancellor of the Exchequer to lay down certain taxation and expenditure measures which indicates the action the Government intends to take to achieve its economic objectives. Action is geared to move

18. In the 1970's there has been considerable controversy about: –
    a) whether the Budget plays a more important role in managing the economy than monetary instruments, and
    b) the effectiveness of the Budget in stabilising employment and inflation.
19. Economic indicators would include details about the following:
    a) National suppy, which includes home output of goods and services and imports.
    b) National demand, which includes expenditures (or claims) made by various sectors of the economy, such as consumers, public authorities, business organisations and exports.
    c) Other indicators such as employment situation, change in purchasing power of the pound, and others.
20. Committee on the Working of the Monetary System, Cmd 827, Aug 1959, HMSO, para 516 (Radcliffe Report).

the country along a path of steady economic growth and, at the same time, maintain a high and stable level of employment without inflation. This is the prime aim of 'Budgetary' policy.

The *attempt* to achieve 'full employment without inflation' is often referred to as the Government's 'stabilisation policy'. To reach these two objectives the Government tries to manipulate the level of the country's economic activity by changing its expenditures and/or income.

Budgetary and monetary policies

Budgetary measures are not considered to be as flexible as monetary measures although over the last few years, with the introduction of more than one Budget a year, they have become more flexible. On the other hand fiscal measures are considered to have a more certain impact on the economy. It is, perhaps, because of this last fact that budgetary policy has, ever since the end of the second World War, been considered as the key in pursuing 'full employment without inflation'. At the present time, in the late 1970's, this is still accepted as being true but monetary measures are being given a more important role than in the past.

Both policies are important and necessary if the major economic objectives are to be achieved. Both are aimed at influencing the level of demand or expenditure. For this reason both policies are often discussed under the subject heading 'demand management'.

It is important to realise that the Government does not use 'budgetary' or 'monetary' measures in isolation. The measures associated with both are normally combined to achieve economic objectives. In fact, they are not only bound to each other but also combined with other Government economic policies, such as 'incomes policy' and 'exchange rate policy'. The mixing of one policy with others is called 'policy-mix'. Whatever the mix, the aim is always that of achieving the desirable economic objectives of:

steady economic growth, and
full employment without inflation.

Economic policies

It would appear, from what has been written, that the application of the above policies will achieve the above objectives. This is far from the truth, and the following provides some reasons why this is so.

Conflicting aims

Governments find that there are conflicts between objectives. For example, the closer the Government gets to reaching the fullness of full employment the more difficult it becomes to keep prices from rising. Knowing that such conflicts exist, the Government will have to make the choice between conflicting alternatives; gear the measures towards one objective first and then, at some later date when the first objective has been reached, to modify the measures that are more suitable to achieving the alternative objective.

Uncertain effects

Policy measures are implemented today to achieve certain targets in the future. When dealing with the future there is always the uncertainty of events that will take place. It is not easy to predict the future, and it is not easy to predict the effect that the implementation of one measure will have on some other factor. For example: how much additional money must be invested to obtain a certain amount of technical progress? This is impossible to predict.

Uncertainty increases when there are forces outside the control of the Government — its environment — which can destroy predictions made about the future. Can one predict a year in advance the type of winter the U.K. is going to have? Do you think the British Government could predict the severe winter of 1978 and early 1979? Casting one's net wider afield — is it possible to predict movements of exchange rates? Or, can one say what the actions of foreign Governments will be in their attempt to achieve their own objectives and the effect these will have on the U.K. economy through international trade, finance, and exchange rates?

Even if the U.K. Government had full control over all aspects of the economy (pure planned economy) it would still find it difficult to achieve economic objectives because they do not have full control over all forces operating in their environment.

Constraints

Policy measures may be put into operation with the intention of reaching targets but the targets aimed at may not be reached because their exists within the country certain conditions which can not be broken now or in the near future. These constraints, as they are called, can be classified under several headings such as Economic, International, Legal, Political, Pressure Groups, and Social. Some brief examples are given below:

Economic. The main constraint relates to the quantity and quality of the factors of production, such as labour and land.

International. U.K. is a member of many international organisations (European Economic Community, International Monetary Fund, North Atlantic Treaty Organisation, World Health Organisation, etc.) and is expected to abide by their rules and regulations.

Legal. Laws introduced in previous years can hinder Government action because they uphold old (rather than current) attitudes — and laws are made to be obeyed, even by Governments.

Political. The political party in power may not have a clear majority in the House of Commons, for example the Labour Government of the late 1970's.

Pressure Groups. The powers of various pressure groups, such as the Confederation of British Industry and the Trade Union Congress, restricts the power of Government.

Social. The attitudes of the population towards certain Government activities towards the community, family, home, job, etc. may constrain these activities.

The above are some of the forces that operate within a country which hinder Governments in implementing actions to achieve desirable objectives.

Government economic policy — community well being

The information given in this chapter is only a small part of a large and complex subject, but the end result is simply that the U.K. Government implements 'economic policy' in order to maximise the economic wellbeing of the community.

Assignments

1. What is understood by the terms 'monetary policy' and 'fiscal policy'? How does monetary policy achieve economic management of the economy?

2. State the major internal functions of the Bank of England and then write brief notes on at least *four* of these functions.

3. State and discuss the major 'economic weapons' that the Bank of England can use to achieve monetary objectives.

4. Take the most recent Budget presented by the Chancellor of the Exchequer to the nation and provide details concerning the following:

   a) balanced or unbalanced budget,

   b) economic objectives to be achieved, and

   c) measures to be implemented to regulate the supply and demand of the nation's resources.

5. Monetary and budgetary policies may find it difficult to achieve economic objectives. Why?

6. Originally the Budget was used to raise revenue to meet Government expenditure. Today it is the major instrument for regulating the economy. Explain and discuss.

Chapter 5

National Income

Learning objectives:
At the end of your study of this chapter you should be able to:
1. analyse the main components of the national income.
2. explain the practical importance of the national income concept.
3. explain, in simple terms, the factors that help a country to achieve economic growth.

In the spring of each year, the Chancellor of the Exchequer presents his annual budget to Parliament. Since 1941, he has also presented a White Paper containing the official estimate of national income and expenditure.

Later, each year, usually in August or September, the Central Statistical Office (CSO) produces a fuller publication than the White Paper, and this is known as the National Income and Expenditure 'Blue Book'. This has been published each year since 1952.

It must be remembered that the figures given in the 'Blue Book' are *estimates*. It would be virtually impossible to gain an exact appreciation of the national income in all its aspects.

National income defined

National income can be regarded as a flow of real goods and services made available to the community through economic activity over a specified period of time, usually one year, and is measured in money.

Income flow

Before we can gain a full understanding of how the national income is estimated, and what it represents, it will help us by considering a model of 'income flow theory' in a closed economy.

The simplest economic model is that which involves only households and firms, and as the economy is closed, no outflows or external inputs exist. This means that all economic activity takes places between households and firms. A diagram of this is shown in Exhibit 5.1.

Exhibit 5.1

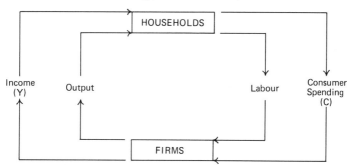

Income Flows in a Closed Economy
(excluding Government sector)

The exhibit shows the flows that occur in this simple economy. Firms produce output using the resources available (labour provided by the households) and this is sold to the households. The householders can purchase this output using the income they receive for providing their labour to the firms.

Assuming no saving exists and all income is consumed then Y (income) = C (consumption).

To make the situation more realistic, a government sector can be introduced. Still keeping the economy closed, the flows can only take place between the firms, the households, and the government.

The government revenue is in the form of taxes levied on both the firms (for example: corporation tax) and the households (for example: income tax). Government expenditure will be in the form of purchasing goods and services from the firms (for example: building materials for public works) and salaries to householders employed by the government (for example: teachers, builders of public works, etc.).

Exhibit 5.2 now shows the flows in this three-part economy.

Since, again, there is no leakage such as external inputs (called imports) and savings, then all those flows that enter the household sector must leave it. Likewise, all flows entering the firms sector and the government sector must also be utilised.

For households:	incoming flows	=	Y	plus	Gh
	outgoing flows	=	C	plus	Th
therefore:	Y plus Gh	=	C	plus	Th
For firms:	incoming flows	=	C	plus	Gf
	outgoing flows	=	Y	plus	Tf
therefore,	C plus Gf	=	Y	plus	Tf
For the government:	incoming flows	=	Tf	plus	Th
	outgoing flows	=	Gf	plus	Gh
therefore,	Tf plus Th	=	Gf	plus	Gh

74

Exhibit 5.2

Income Flows in a Closed Economy
(including Government sector)

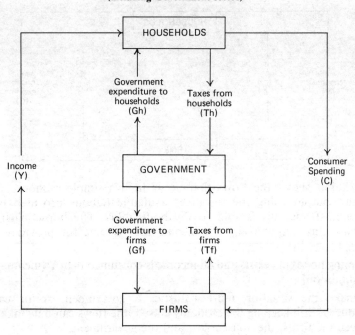

Now, it can be seen that there are three types of flow in an economy that are measureable. These are income, output and expenditure. In the model of the closed economy we have seen that each of these is equal to each other. This relationship is also true in an economy such as that of the United Kingdom today.

Logically, if a result is gained from measuring the total expenditure in the economy, then this is equal to the total income which, again, is equal to the total output. The relationship may be viewed as the three sides of an equilateral triangle as shown below.

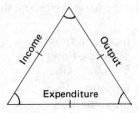

Income and output are more closely related, and can be regarded as 'positive' ways of measuring the national income. In fact, they tend to use the same set of figures, and Exhibit 5.3 is provided to give a rough idea of this relationship.

Exhibit 5.3

Hypothetical Table
to show
Relationship between Income and Output

(figures in £m)

Rewards to factors of production in producing goods and services	Output by Industry			Income Totals	
	Industry A	Industry B	Industry C		I N C O M E
Rent (Land)	12	20	30	62	
Wages (Labour)	60	20	75	155	
Interest (Capital)	12	50	30	92	
Profit (Enterprise)	16	10	15	41	
Output Totals	100	100	150		

———————————————— OUTPUT ——————————→ | 350 | ←

Exhibit 5.3 clearly shows the relationship between income and output. In fact, the exhibit tends to show more than this. It introduces the rewards (or incomes) paid to various factors of production for their efforts in producing goods and services. There are many industries operating in a country — we have shown three to illustrate the income-output relationship. One can note that each industry uses the factors of production in varying proportions. Industry A would be considered 'labour intensive', and industry B 'capital intensive'.

The third approach to measuring the national income is called 'the expenditure approach'; it can be regarded as a 'negative' or 'independent' method of gaining the same end result.

Some national income terms

Before showing the methods employed by the government (shown in exhibits 5.4 and 5.5) to measure the national income, it is probably wise to define some of the terms that will be used.

Firstly, the terms 'Domestic' and 'National' need differentiating. Where the word Domestic appears, such as Gross Domestic Product, this means the economic activity occurring within the country and making no allowance for economic activity undertaken by members of the community in foreign countries. National, on the other hand, means that this allowance has been made and 'net income from abroad' is included.

Secondly, we must understand the difference between 'factor cost' and 'market price'. When goods or services are sold, there is often a part of the price which is to cover taxation levied by the government. A good example being that of Value Added Tax (VAT). This means that the price is higher than the true total of returns to the factors (of production) that produced the goods or services.

This is made clearer by showing the make up of the price of a good by the returns to each 'factor of production; these generally being regarded as land, labour, capital and enterprise.

In the 'market', the price of good 'A' is 110 pence and this is made up as follows:

Rent	(return to land)	15p
Wages	(return to labour)	60p
Interest	(return to capital)	15p
Profit	(return to enterprise)................	10p
Total returns to factors of production		100p (factor cost)
Government tax at 10% of factor cost .... +		10p
Market price of good 'A'		110p

To gain the true cost of the good — the taxation part of the price must be deducted. Thus:

Market price   minus   taxation = Factor Cost.

Conversely, some goods and services, mainly those from the agricultural sector or from the nationalised industries are subsidised by the government. In this case, the government may wish the price, to the population, to be lower than its true cost. Milk is a good example. So, the market price of the good or service is lower than it should be if based upon the true value of returns to the factors engaged in its production.

Again, using good 'A' as an example — using the same figures for rent, wages, interest and profit — we have:

Total returns to factors of production	100p (factor cost)
(Less) Government subsidy .... −	20p
Market price of good 'A'	80p

So, in the case of subsidisation, we must add the amount by which the good or service is subsidised to gain the true factor cost. Thus:

Market price   plus   subsidy = Factor Cost.

Measuring the national income

The time has come to look at the measuring of the national income in reality. Exhibits 5.4 and 5.5 show the income/output and expenditure methods of measuring the National Income.

The diagrams show that both methods coincide at the point where the Gross National Product (GNP) at factor cost is gained. This term can be defined as the total income of residents of the U.K. before making provision for depreciation or capital consumption, and it is equal to the factor cost of all goods and services produced by the residents plus their income from economic activity abroad (this includes income from property held abroad). Finally, the corresponding income of non-residents of the U.K. has to be deducted.

Taking the income/output method step by step we see that the first step can be shown either by type of income or type of output.

Exhibit 5.4

Determination of National Income
by
Income/Output Method

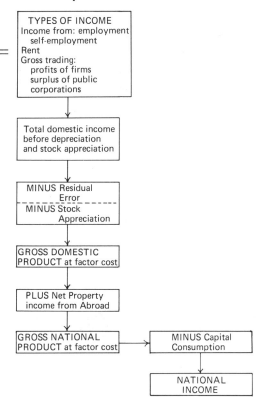

By type of income

Income from employment. In the National Income 'Blue Book', in the Income and Expenditure Account (table 4.1), income from employment is listed as the following:

Income before tax: Wages and salaries,
Pay in cash and kind of H.M. Forces,
Employers contributions,
National insurance, and
Others equals
Total income from employment.

Wages and salaries also includes an addition of any amounts deducted at source for payment of tax, as well as Directors' fees. A deduction is made for certain expenses of employment recognised for tax allowances (examples: for uniforms, special protective clothing, necessary tools, etc.).

Exhibit 5.5

Determination of National Income
by
Expenditure Method

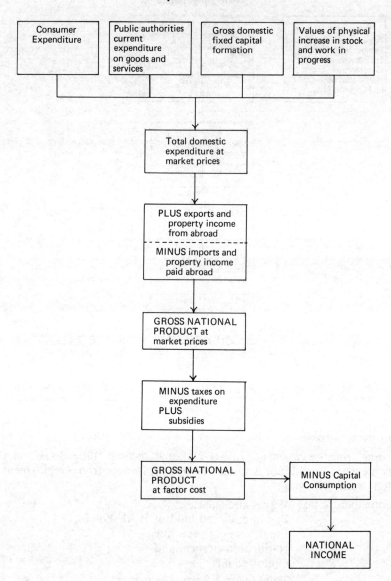

Employers contributions cover such elements as National Insurance (as listed) but also employers contributions to pension schemes and various compensation payments made to employees.

Income from self-employment. This section, found in the same table in the Blue Book lists:

> Professional persons,
> Farmers, and
> Other sole traders and partnerships.
> Total income from self employment.

The professional persons figure does not, of course, include salaried personnel who are already catered for under wages and salaries in the 'income from employment' section.

Interest in this section is the need to include profits in combination with labour income, and these two elements can not be regarded singly.

It must also be noted that no provision is made at this point for depreciation or stock appreciation and these incomes are measured after a deduction has been made for all business expenses.

Rent, dividends and interest. Rent represents total property income received by people by virtue of the fact that they own land and/or buildings.

Dividends and interest include the dividends and interest on securities of the public sector.

Gross trading. Listed under this heading are the profits of firms and surpluses from public corporations.[1]

As we have seen, this initial step can be taken in two different parts; by type of income (already dealt with) and by type of output.

By type of output

The measurement being made under this heading is that of the Gross Domestic Product (GDP) by industry.

In the 'Blue Book', table 3.1 lists each industry and shows the contribution of each to the GDP in 'millions of pounds'. This is the value of the product of each industry and is measured by taking the costs to the factors of production in each industry. Basically, what is happening here is that for each industry, wages and salaries, employers contributions, rent, profits, etc. are being measured as they were for the country as a whole.

Whether the measurement is made by output or by income, the total gained is that of Total Domestic Income but before depreciation and stock appreciation have been allowed for.

Points to ponder

Although the national income analysis is of great value to economists and others interested in the levels of economic activity of the economy there are several points that must be remembered.

---

1. As public corporations exist to serve the public interest, then very few are "profit" making concerns owing to the preference of lower prices for the consumer rather than profit for the state. Some public corporations do, however, end up with a surplus which is held for re-investment but needs to be included in the national income.

1. It must be pointed out that the estimates are given in monetary terms. This basically means that what may appear to be an increase in the level of economic activity of the community over a given period may not be so at all. In a period where the value of money itself has changed, then the national income estimates will change accordingly.

   In a period of inflation, it is likely that the monetary figures for the national income will be higher than those of the preceding period. To this end, the national income estimates are often shown in terms of a 'base year'. This means that the figures are shown in terms of the purchasing power of money in a previous year.

2. National income statistics only show economic activity relating to goods and services which have been sold for money, and to payments made through official channels. No account is taken of those services rendered by people who work without payment. Most housewives, for example, would come into this category.

3. No account is taken of the quality of goods produced. A change in the quality of a good is rarely shown as a change in the price of that good and yet it may well increase or decrease the wellbeing of the consumer. For example, if twenty years ago a light bulb gave an average one year service and today it only gives two months service, all other things being equal, this would be reflected as a six-fold increase in the purchasing of light bulbs simply because of a change in quality.

4. On similar lines, no account is taken of the service that durable goods give the consumer. Washing machines, refrigerators and televisions, for example, will probably give many years service to the consumer and yet will only be reflected in the national income statistics in the year that they are purchased.

Changes in the national income

We have now seen the basic components of the national income and some of the reasons why the totals may not show the whole 'picture' of the economy. It is reasonable at this stage to ask "why does the real value of the National Income change over any given time period?".

We will examine this question by looking at an *increase* in the *real* value of the national income over time. Since 'economic growth' is said to be the annual rate of increase of a country's *real* gross national product, then what is really being examined is why a country experiences economic growth, using national income figures as a measurement of the *rate* of growth.

If we take the figures for the Gross National Product of the hypothetical country 'Economica' for 1977 and 1978 we see that there has been a monetary increase of £100.

	1977	1978
G.N.P. (£)	1,000	1,100

This means that the *monetary* value has increased by 10 per cent. Only if the general price level has remained perfectly stable can we say that the country has experienced economic growth at a rate of 10 per cent. If the general price level had increased at a rate of 10 per cent then no growth would have occured, and the difference in the figures can be attributed totally to rising prices.

To combat this problem, and to allow the *real* growth to be analysed, national income figures for any one year are regarded in terms of a base year.

The National Income Blue Book (table 2.1) shows Expenditure and Output each year at the price level of a given year. For 1966 to 1976, 1970 prices were used and an index number for each year was calculated based on that year.

	1966	1967	1968	1969	1970	1971	1972	1973	1974	1975	1976
G.N.P. at Factor Cost	90.4	92.7	95.8	97.8	100.0	102.4	104.1	112.0	110.7	108.2	111.2

From the table it can be seen that a *real* increase of 2.4 took place between 1970 and 1971, or over a 6 year span of time, from 1970 to 1976, there was a real increase of 11.2.

To analyse what factors cause a change in the *real* level of the G.N.P. we will look in turn at each of the factors of production and note how changes in the quality and quantity of each will cause a change in the overall figures of the national income.

Labour

Any change in the size of the labour force will, if all other factors remain the same, result in a change in the size of the national income.

Let us look at an increase in the size of the labour force of the country. Such an increase may be the result of many factors[2]; an increase in total population, a lower school leaving age, a higher retirement age, more women going out to work, etc..

Increasing the size of the country's labour force is one method of stimulating growth if the hours worked and the number of days taken as holidays remain the same. It must be noted however, that the growth will not occur immediately (for reasons we will look at later).

An increase in the size of the general population stimulates growth by causing an increase in the level of demand in the economy. The increased population need food, clothing, housing, etc., and thus a greater amount of production is needed to meet this increased demand.

Taking our fictitious economy 'Economica' as an example:

The population of the very small country 'Economica' is exactly 100, all of whom work. They need only one pound of beans each, every day, to live. Thus the country's production level is 100 pounds of beans per day and the production of those beans needs all 100 people to work.

2.   Refer to chapter on 'population and employment' later in this volume.

If there is an influx of ten adults from the neighbouring country (who also eat beans), then obviously the demand in the economy has risen from 100 pounds to 110 pounds per day.

If we assume that the supply of beans is unlimited, and all that is needed to harvest or produce the beans is an extra 10 workers, we can see that the influx of 10 extra workers has caused the following:

1. an increase in the size of the population,

2. an increase in the size of the labour force,

3. an increase in general demand in the economy, and

4. an increase in the general level of production.

Now, if we assume that each pound of beans has a money value of £1, then we can see that the G.N.P. = 100 pounds of beans = £100, before the influx.

After the influx,

the G.N.P. = 110 pounds of beans = £110.

The price level has remained stable but the G.N.P. has increased by 10 per cent.

Obviously, this is a much simplified model. However, the basic relationships are the same in an economy such as in the U.K. today.

We said earlier that to increase the size of the population was a method of stimulating growth, but that this growth did not occur immediately. This is because of the relationship between labour, and capital.

If the economy is working at full capacity, then an increase in population will mean a greater demand level. However, if the level of capital does not increase too, then each worker will now be working with less capital than before and there will not be any growth in the first instance.

The growth occurs because the demand level has increased and thus producers see that the size of the market has increased. This prompts them to increase production and sell more. To do this they need to increase the working factors (more machines, more labour); thus the extra labour force is absorbed into the economy and the level of capital stock is increased.

It can be seen that the *general* level of demand is increased. This occurs because an increase in demand for one product will cause an increase in production of that good. To do this, perhaps more machinery is needed, thus there will be an increase in the demand for machine parts, oil to lubricate them, the service of maintenance personnel, etc..

Of course, there are other ways in which labour as a factor of production can increase production without a physical increase in the size of the labour force. One of these is by increasing the hours worked.

In 'Economica' the demand for beans increases from 100 to 110 pounds per day (because of a particularly cold spell, the 100 people all require a little extra to keep going). However, the size of the labour force remains the same — 100. How do they meet the increase in production that is needed?

If we assume that each person in 'Economica' normally works 10 hours per day to produce one pound of beans, then all other things being equal, if they all work 11 hours a day they will produce 1/10th of a pound more each. Tabulated, this will appear as follows:

	Before the increase in demand	*After* the increase in demand
Demand for *and* production of beans	100 lbs.	110 lbs.
Labour force	100	100
Hours worked per person per day	10	11
Total 'labour hours' per day	1,000	1,100
Production rate	100 lbs per 1,000 hours worked	110 lbs per 1,100 hours worked
Production per 'labour' hour (or 'per man hour')	1/10th pound	1/10th pound

We can see that *productivity* (defined as output per man per hour) has remained the same but that total production has increased by all the workers working for one extra hour every day.

Another way of increasing production with the same sized labour force would be to increase productivity. If all the workers in 'Economica', because they were becoming experienced bean producers, could produce 1 and 1/10th pounds of beans per day in 10 hours, then from the following:

Production.............110 pounds of beans.
Labour force............100
Hours worked..........10 per person
Total hours.............1,000

It follows that production is at a rate of 110 pounds per 1,000 hours worked, and this equals 11/100 pounds per man per hour; an increase in *productivity* of 1/100 pounds per man per hour.

Any method of increasing productivity will cause an increase in total output. Education of the labour force is an important factor leading towards increased productivity; better education will mean a more highly skilled labour force.

In our own society, skill training centres, management training, better schooling, and many other ways of improving the education of the labour force all point towards better methods of production carried out by more highly skilled personnel in a more efficient manner.

So, it can be seen that; by increasing the size of the labour force, increasing the hours worked, or increasing productivity will all increase total output. This, however, can only be true if there is scope for an increase in output. Without the extra demand, producers will lack the incentive to produce more, and without the extra capital, the work force will not have the means with which to increase production. This brings us to the second factor.

Capital

A change in the country's stock of capital will cause a change in the level of the national income, if it is used to produce more.

If a firm employs 10 machines to make 100 articles, then by employing 12 machines the level of production is raised to 120 articles. If over the whole economy more machines are employed then the country has increased its stock of capital. If all this machinery is then used to its full advantage, the level of production is increased.

In an economy such as that of Great Britain today, those people with some of their income remaining after they have bought all they need will tend to 'invest' it. It is investment over a period of time that allows the level of capital stock to be increased. When people invest in a firm (in return for a profit in their investment at a later date), the firm can utilise this money to increase its holding of capital with the aim of increasing production.

All investment undertaken in an economy over a given period is called 'gross investment'; when totalled up, however, some of this is lost in 'depreciation'. As capital goods are used they tend to wear out, needing new parts, servicing and eventually replacing (just like a motor vehicle). This is known as depreciation. For instance, if I bought a new car 3 years ago for £2,000 and today it is worth £1,400 then it would have 'depreciated' by £600. If it was now worth £2,600, it would have 'appreciated', but this normally only happens to very few goods such as collectors' items, vintage cars, old coins, paintings, etc..

If we take the total of all investment in an economy over a certain period (gross investment) and take away the total depreciation, we are left with 'net investment' and this is the rate at which the economy is *adding* to its capital stock.

Of course, manufacturers need the incentive to produce more — they must have a market for their product or they will not produce more. Basically, given that the demand for a product exists, there is an incentive to the producer to increase production and to the investor to invest.

So, given the demand for increased production, we can see that the GNP of an economy will increase if the capital stock is increased. Increasing the *quality* of capital goods is another way of increasing production. A new machine which can work more efficiently, produce more, and produce each unit at a lower cost are ways of increasing production. Obviously, a machine which can produce more than its forerunner is going to increase production but how about producing at a lower cost per unit? If a manufacturer finds he can utilise a machine to produce his goods at a lower cost, this releases more for investment in more capital or could result in a lower priced good and hence increase sales which means more profit and thus more investment.

So, investment goes not only into buying more capital of an existing type but also into improved methods of production and better machinery.

The major problem here is that to invest *now* in order to *grow later,* some present spending (known as current consumption) must be foregone in order to provide resources for investment. Once an economy is experiencing growth this problem lessens as the higher wages and salaries become in relation to the 'cost of living', the more there is to release for investment.

Land and natural resources

Very little can be done to increase the amount of land within a country. As a country grows however, it is necessary to release more and more land to build on, farm on and cultivate. The decision must be made as to whether land will be used to build factories and houses or to farm (or, indeed, be kept as parks and common land).

The natural resources available to a country vary greatly all over the world and this is a very important factor in world trade and thus to a country's national income.

A good example is that of the oil producing countries. The GNP of countries such as Kuwait or Saudi Arabia is high 'per person' (or 'per capita') in relation to industrialised countries such as Great Britain. This is so because of the exploitation of vast resources of oil that exist in these countries and that is sold to other countries.

A country having to import natural resources to produce has to pay other countries and this will affect the national income — (remember 'net income from abroad'?). If a country can uncover natural resources in its own borders then this will mean that less has to be imported and indeed may result in exporting. A good example of this is the North Sea oil fields off Great Britain. This will undoubtedly improve our own 'Balance of Payments'[3] over the years and increase the amount of 'net income from abroad' that results primarily from reducing imports of oil.

Better method of production with relation to natural resources also gives scope for increased efficiency in production. By-products from the coal industry are far reaching when coal is processed to make gas, as well as other products such as nylons and aspirins. By recycling natural resources, producers can use them again and again thus reducing the amount of natural resources that are needed. An example here is the re-pulping of paper.

Other factors affecting changes in national income

In addition to the factors of production we must look at other sources of growth, or increasing the GNP.

Firstly, we have mentioned *demand* several times. A high level of demand can lead to increased investment and production. As stated earlier, if the producer has the market for his product he will try to increase production to meet the demand, either by increasing capital stock or by increasing productivity.

3. Balance of Payments refers to the record of transactions kept between one country and the rest of world over a period of time, normally one year, and measured in money.

A more modern view, however, is that a high level of demand causes producers to sit back and relax as they know they have their market and do not have to compete to sell their products. This means that they do not feel they have to innovate or invest in increased production. This will eventually cause the economy to 'stagnate' and will not cause growth. This in turn will lead to a drop in the level of demand as incomes tend not to rise at the same rate as before.

Another factor that has to be considered is the amount of competition that exists between firms in the same market. A high degree of competition will tend to cause firms to try and improve efficiency and lower unit cost in order to have their good marketed at a competitive price. This means that improved methods of production are always being sought.

Of course, no one will work to try and improve methods of production to increase production unless there is 'something in it for them' — an incentive. These take various forms, such as profit to the investor or entrepreneur, bonus schemes to the workers, tax concessions to industry, higher salaries for management, a sense of achievement to the inventor combined with royalties for his invention.

Changes in the national income — summary

Basically we have seen that changes in national income figures are brought about by changing the balance of one or more of the factors of production. Remembering the definition of 'growth' in an economy, we talked about increasing the quantity and/or quality of the factors of production being the basis for increasing the GNP in real terms.

If the *incentive* exists for the labour force, the investor, and management, then *production* can be increased with appropriate rewards to the *factors of production* in terms of higher *wages* for the labour force, *profits* for the investor (on capital investment), higher *salaries* for management. This means that the *Gross National Product* is increased (on both sides of the equation — higher wages and salaries on the positive side AND expenditure coupled with increased investment on the negative side). If the increase of the GNP is measured in *real* terms, then by using a base year as an index we can see if *growth* has occurred over a given period of time.

Practical importance of national income statistics

Each government in power has various aims or objectives with relation to the economy. These objectives can be grouped under the following headings:

> Balance of payments equilibrium.
>
> Economic growth.
>
> Full employment.
>
> Stable prices.

Each heading incorporates a number of lesser objectives and covers a number of methods of how the government can manipulate the economy.

As usual in Economics, not all of these can be achieved at the same time using the same economic weapons and so the government of the time has to decide which objective is the most important or to what extent a certain objective can be sacrificed in order to achieve another objective. To enable them to make this decision, they have to know the state of the economy and how it is changing.

National income statistics provide the government with figures showing changes in the state of the economy. By comparing the latest national income figures with earlier years, the government can gain an idea of how the economy is changing, is being affected by current trends and current policies.

National income statistics help the government gain an idea of the growth of the economy by comparing the real increase (or decrease) of the Gross National Product over time. The figures reveal income distribution patterns — how the national income is distributed between the various sector of the economy — which is important when looking at investment and savings.

Expenditure patterns are revealed by the figures thus giving the government knowledge of where the nation's money goes, which types of goods are being demanded and in what amounts. This is important for taxation purposes and to gain an understanding of the standard of living.

Estimates on wages, salaries and profits also help to give an idea of the changing level of incomes which can be compared with expenditure tables, price movements and changes in investment.

Government and industry alike have a need to plan their future policies. Both need information upon which they can formulate such plans. National income statistics can give the government the information they need to prepare a basis upon which to 'plan' the future of the economy. They can compare present national income statistics with past figures and find the trends, or cycles that occur in the economy and use these to decide what *objectives* should take priority. An example is that of full employment — a situation, say, where no more than 3 per cent of the working population are not employed. If employment is falling below the limit set by the government as acceptable, then there are various courses they can take to try and remedy this. They may institute a large programme of public building — building hospitals, schools, public libraries, motorways, and so on. This will mean additional resources are needed, such as architects, builders, plumbers and surveyors; also building materials, electrical equipment and many others. This causes a flow of government money into the economy and an increase in the employment level. It may well mean that taxation may have to be increased to provide the money being expended and could cause more income to flow owing to the increased size of the labour force. As a result, certain prices may rise due to increased demand. On the other hand, less money will have to be paid in unemployment benefits.

It can be seen that such a step as instituting a large programme of building public works has a wide effect on many parts of the economy. To enable the government to make this decision they need statistics to show whether or not such a policy is viable, whether it has succeeded in the past, and whether or not it can be afforded.

Industry can learn much from national income statistics too. To achieve their aim of maximising profits, achieving low unit cost of production, etc. they need to know what investment levels are and what they are likely to be. They want to know what the economy's expenditure and income distribution is like and the possible future trends. By analysing present and past statistics they can gain an idea of the *trends* in each area they are interested in and act accordingly.

For example, a large firm that deals in a luxury good such as colour television but one that can also produce washing machines may decide to increase production of the latter whilst producing less colour televisions. Their decision to do this may be governed by the national income statistics showing an income distribution and expenditure pattern that means that the population in general cannot afford colour television but can find enough for a fairly essential washing machine.

It can be seen then that national income statistics are important in practice in today's economy to government and private enterprise to enable both to decide upon their *priority objectives*, then to decide what economic *weapons* they need to use to achieve these objectives. The statistics show past *trends* and the present state of the economy from which *estimates* for the future can be gained.

If you take a copy of the 'National Incomes Blue Book' mentioned at the beginning of the chapter, have a look at the various tables shown and note the large amount of information that is revealed by the statistics. Some of the details will be used in later chapters.

Assignments

1. Define national income. To what extent does the national income reflect the economic progress of a nation?
2. Explain precisely what is meant by:
   Gross National Product equals Gross National Income equals Gross National Expenditure.
3. Obtain up-to-date figures from a recent National Income and Expenditure Blue Book and place alongside each of the sections shown in Exhibits 5.4 and 5.5. Explain why type of output equals type of income.
4. Explain why the *real* value of the national income changes over any given period.
5. What is the practical importance of national income statistics?
6. What factors set limits to (or determines) the size of the national income?

Chapter 6

Money[1]

Learning objectives:
At the end of your study of this chapter you should be able to:
1. explain the nature of money.
2. explain the functions of money.
3. explain the methods of making payments.
4. explain the consequences of changes in the value of money.

In a primitive society, with its small population existing in virtual isolation, demand is mainly for biological goods (food, drink and clothing). The exchange system would be something like the following: one person (Mark) has more wool than he needs but is short of wheat; a second person (Luke) has excess wheat but requires meat; and a third person (John) has more meat than he needs but not enough wool. All would be satisfied by bartering. Mark would barter with Luke (wool for wheat), Luke with John (wheat for meat), and John with Mark (meat for wool). Their needs would be met by the system of bartering which is a slow and painful process. However, in a primitive society it proved to be a satisfactory method of arranging exchanges.

As we move towards the modern society, large population and virtually no isolation, demands for biological needs accelerates and there are new and accelerated demands for psychological and social goods and services (washing machines, deep freezers, swimming pools, boats, plumbing, electrical repairs, etc.). Bartering could not satisfy the vast number of transactions that are required to meet the needs of all persons. So, to make it easier for exchange to take place society invented two tools, namely, money and credit.

Money

Money is an important commodity in the study of any modern economy. The importance lies not in money itself but in the goods and services which can be purchased with it. Employees exchange their efforts and skills for 'money wages', but they do not want this money for its own sake but for the goods and services that can be purchased with it, that is to say 'real wages'. When calculating the income of the nation, national income, money is used to measure the flow (money income) but the importance to the community is the actual flow of goods and services produced and made available to the

---

1. Most of the first section of this chapter — from beginning to the sub-heading 'cheque clearance' — was taken from Vol II "Economics for Business Studies" Ed. N. L. Paulus.

community (real national income). It is important to realise the difference between 'money wage' and 'real wage', and between 'national income in money terms' and 'national income in real terms'.

What is Money?

Economist are always careful in defining money. Some go to great lengths in noting many details usually associated with money and then perhaps they will define it. However, this is usually followed up with a warning that it is not easy to decide a demarcating line that claims everything this side of the line is money and the other side is not, for example, arranging all assets alongside a liquidity line according to the length of time it takes to make them liquid.

Most writers on the subject would agree that coins and notes are money. Some would say that money in a current account is money whereas others may say it is not. Some include deposit accounts and others would not; banks may request you to wait for 7 days for withdrawals from deposit accounts. There is no general agreement on what money is.

Money can be defined as anything which is generally accepted in the payment for goods and services. In other words it can be notes and coins, or tobacco, or cattle, or beads, or diamonds, etc. which is widely accepted by the general public as a medium of exchange. Our employee above provides his labour to buy food, drink, tobacco and other goods. He is paid in notes and coins which he accepts because others accept these in payment for the goods mentioned. Notes and coins (money) become the medium between his skills and efforts in producing good A and his purchase of goods B, C, D, etc. produced by others.

If notes and coins are widely accepted they become money. On the other hand, if some other commodity becomes more widely accepted then that commodity becomes money.

For the time being, money can be defined as anything which is generally accepted as a medium of exchange.

Nature of Money

Nature, according to *The Concise Oxford Dictionary*, is a noun and it is defined as "thing's essential qualities". In *The New Century Dictionary* it is defined as "the particular combination of qualities belonging to a thing by birth or constitution". Thus, when considering the nature of money we should discuss the special qualities which make it acceptable.

Qualities of Money

A variety of commodities, such as gold, silver, diamonds, other precious gems, beads, cattle, etc., can act as money. However, to determine which material is best to serve as money we should consider each material against specific qualities associated with money. Each commodity should be graded from good to bad against each quality noted. That which has the best grading would normally be selected to act as money.

Acceptability. As already noted it is important that anything that is to act as money must be widely accepted as a medium of exchange.

Divisibility. Anything that is to be used as money must be easily divided into smaller units and at the same time the smaller units should be able to be brought together to form larger units.

Durability. If that which is to act as money is to last a long time it should not be a substance that will perish, nor as a result of frequent handling should it deteriorate through wear and tear.

Homogeneity. It is important that any commodity used as money should be similar, especially in quality. It should not be possible to distinguish one unit from another.

Malleability. Money normally requires identification and any material that is to be used as money should be able to withstand stamping, printing or moulding.

Portability. Money is usually transferred from one person to another. Any substance acting as money must not create difficulty nor inconvenience to anyone *carrying it about.*

Recognisability. If a material is to be used as money it must easily and instantly be recognised by the various senses such as sight, touch, and often by hearing.

Stability. This quality refers to the value associated with the commodity. The standard of value must be stable in order to value other commodities.

Transportability. It is important that the material acting as money can be transported over *long distances* without deteriorating. Also, it should not be expensive to transport from one place to another. The usual statement here is that it must have high value for its bulk.

The importance of these qualities can be judged when considering an economy as it changes over time. For example, Britain during the 14th century with its manors[2] and isolated pockets of population. Most of the needs of these isolated communities came from the land and the method of exchanging one good for another was by bartering. Money, as we know it today, had only a small role to play. However, as markets and fairs grew in importance, so did the need for some commodity to satisfy the qualities mentioned. Today, with national and international markets and isolated communities being a rarity and the tremendous increase in demand for many types of goods which the land cannot directly supply there was need for some commodity to act as a medium that was acceptable to buyers and sellers in the variety of transactions they were involved in. Bartering, acceptable in primitive societies, became impossible in our modern society. Notes and coins ultimately became the commodities that satisfied the requirements of today's modern exchange system.

---

2. Manors varied in size — about 100 to 200 inhabitants. These pockets of population, so it has been said, considered other pockets of population living, say, 18 miles away as foreigners.

Functions of Money

The commodity chosen to act as money must, if it is to fulfil its purpose, be capable of acting as:

1. a medium of exchange,
2. a measure of value,
3. a store of value, and
4. a standard of deferred payment.[3]

Medium of exhange. This is considered to be the primary or root function. It does away with bartering by facilitating exchange, but in order to do this it must be widely accepted in exchange for all other goods and services. Before it can be accepted as a medium it should fulfil certain conditions, as already noted, such as: divisibility, portability, recognisability, etc. Also it must be relatively scarce; not too plentiful, and yet not too scarce. The possessor of money must be satisfied that his wants can be obtained without difficulty. This becomes possible when money intervenes between one good and another in an exchange. By intervening (acting as a medium) it fixes the terms between the goods to be exchanged. Because it is accepted as a medium it facilitates the settlement of business transactions.

Measure of value. Quite often this is referred to as a 'unit of account'. In other words, the value of any good or service to be exchanged can be measured by reference to a standard unit or the commodity serving as money. Having such a standard it becomes easier to measure the value of all goods and thus facilitates exchange. It assists businessmen to calculate gains and losses and it enables society to establish a more accurate pricing system.

Store of value. A person who holds money often wishes to store it away in a safe place and bring it out for exchange at some future time. In the process of storing it this person would not want it to deteriorate; he should not suffer any loss. This can only be done if the commodity accepted is durable and at the same time its own value remains stable.

Standard of deferred payment. In the United Kingdom, a large proportion of business is conducted on the basis of credit, for example bank credit in the form of overdrafts and short term loans, and trade credit. Credit refers to an extension of time to pay for goods and services and for the use of money; briefly referred to as 'deferred payment'. Persons who arrange to receive payment at a future date must be assured that money received later will approximate the purchase of the same quantity of goods and services the money could have bought on the date the transaction was made. To ensure this the money in use must be sufficiently stable; it can change with small changes in supply and demand but not big changes. In other words the standard of value of today should have almost the same standard in the future.

---

3. These four functions might be remembered by the following rhyming mnemonic:
   Money's a matter of functions four,
   A measure, a medium, a standard, a store.

Credit

The fourth function of money 'standard of deferred payment' indicates the very close link between money and credit. Credit can be considered as simply an extension of money into time. As stated before, credit is defined as an extension of time to pay for goods and services and for the use of money. Thus, credit refers to a transfer of goods or money from one person or business to another person or business with a promise from the debtor (borrower) that the debt will be repaid at some future date. In both cases the creditor (lender) faces the risk of not being repaid, whereas the debtor has possession of the money or goods *now*.

There are different types of credit; those associated with money and those associated with goods. Exhibit 6.1 gives an idea of the type of transactions associated with money and goods.

Exhibit 6.1

Types of Credit

Associated with Money	Associated with Goods
Bank overdraft	Sales credit
Bank loan	Trade credit
Bank bill	Trade bill
Cheque	Hire purchase
Etc.	Etc.

Two basic elements in any credit transaction are:

1. the amount of credit to be provided, and
2. the length of time credit is given.

Qualities associated with credit

Confidence. This is perhaps the most important quality associated with credit. No creditor is willing to extend credit to anyone in whom they do not have confidence. Thus, the qualities associated with credit should be mainly considered from the point of view of the creditor. If the qualities do not exist then no credit will be given. It appears to follow that all other qualities are really principles associated with the giving of credit to determine the level of confidence the lender has in the borrower.

Safety. A loan must, above all, be safe. The creditor must make certain that the borrower is reliable and that he can repay the sum of money loaned within the period given. Further, because of the unforeseen events that might take place in the future that might prohibit repayment, the credit can be made safer by ensuring that the borrower offers some security as insurance.

Suitability. The giving of credit is often established on the suitability of the asset or the purpose for which the credit is extended. A banker would consider gambling and speculation as not being suitable. Hire purchase may not be given if the life of the asset is less than the period of time covered by the agreement. The less suitable the asset or purpose for which credit is to be used the less confidence the creditor will have.

There are other factors that are taken into consideration in the credit field but the above listed are the most important. All factors are considered to determine whether the creditor should or should not have confidence in extending credit.

Credit and the Banker

The following will be a simple exposition. Basically the banker will require knowledge about the borrower. If the credit to be given is small and for a very short period of time the knowledge required is little compared to the depth of knowledge for a large amount of credit for a long period of time. The knowledge required can be broken down into three time periods:

1. past,
2. present, and
3. future.

Past records are usually asked for to help the banker establish the suitability of the borrower. Has the borrower a meticulous record in paying off past debts? If the borrower is a business and the loan is large then the banker will, normally, ask for the accounts of the firm over the last few years.

Past records will assist the banker to assess the *present* creditworthiness of the borrower. Here the banker tries to establish the financial strength of the borrower. In other words, are the borrower's liabilities greater than his assets or vice versa? What are these liabilities? these assets? These are the type of questions that must be asked to establish the suitability of the borrower and provide the banker with confidence. If the borrower is not deemed to be creditworthy the banker will not, normally, give credit. If the borrower is considered to be creditworthy the banker may give credit but only if the risks associated with the future are not excessive.

The *future* involves the banker in establishing the risk that the bank will face in giving credit. The worst possible risk a company can face is liquidation; for an individual it would be bankruptcy. Thus, the banker would estimate the greatest possible risk associated with the repayment. If the risk is too great and there is no possibility of the bank recovering the money loaned after all prior commitments have been made, the banker would probably not give credit even though the borrower is at present creditworthy. On the other hand, if the risk is not too great the banker would probably give credit.

All these considerations are based upon confidence; confidence in the borrower from past records, present creditworthiness position and future. All periods of time must give the banker confidence in the borrower if he is to give credit.

Functions of Credit

When considering the functions of credit we are concerned with the action by which it fulfils its purpose. Sometimes it is easier to see these functions if we assume there is no such thing as credit. Considering it this way we would find:

1. There would be greater need for more notes and coins because all transactions would have to be in cash. Cheques, of course, reduce the need for notes and coins in circulation. Also, cheques are a form of credit because you pay by cheque today but it is not debited to your account until it has been cleared through the banks — a deferred payment for hours or days. Thus, one of the functions of credit is to reduce the use of notes and coins.

2. If all debts have to be settled in cash immediately, this may create considerable inconveniences. Thus, another function of credit is to make it convenient for borrowers to settle their debts.

3. Often it is not possible for certain trading activities to be carried out now in anticipation of demand later. For example, farmers wishing to purchase seeds for sowing in anticipation of demand for their crops at harvest time would face great difficulties if they had to pay for their seeds in cash. Thus, a function of credit is to enable purchasers to buy raw materials now and make payment to the lender later, after he has sold his finished goods.

4. If credit did not exist there would be difficulty in channelling savings into investment, and production would, probably, not be on as large a scale. Thus, a function of credit is establishing a link between savings and purchasing materials needed in the production process. Normally the big creditors (banks, finance houses, etc.) act as mediators in this channelling process, and through their credit policies they minimise the idleness of large sums of money. This last point, idleness of money, can also be considered as a function of credit.

5. If credit did not exist it would not be possible for financial firms, with excellent reputations, to transfer the use of their firm's names to another firm for trade.[4] Credit, functioning as it does, enables the reverse of this situation to take place.

Methods of Payment

There are a number of different methods by which one person in this country can make payment to another. Some of these are as follows:

Cash — coins and notes

Cheque.	Bank draft.
Credit card.	Credit transfer.
Promissory note.	Direct debit.
Postal order.	Bill of exchange.
Money order.	Travellers cheques.

Some of these will be discussed at length; the others will be noted.

---

4. Acceptance credits, a short term method of raising money, applies here. Refer to 'Bill of Exchange' on page 97.

Cash. A person can make a payment to someone else by paying in coins and notes. In making the payment there is a restriction on the amount that is handed over the counter; often referred to as 'legal tender'. This term simply states that there is a restriction on the currency a debtor can legally compel his creditor to accept. The figures for coins[5] are:

coins of bronze for payments not exceeding 20 pence,
coins of cupro nickel or silver of denominations not more than 10 pence for payment not exceeding £5, and
coins of cupro nickel or silver of denomination of more than 10 pence for payment of any amount not exceeding £10.

It should be noted that "coin" means coin which is current and legal tender in the United Kingdom, whereas any coin which is not current and legal tender is called 'bullion'.[6]

All bank notes, up to any amount, are legal tender.

All coins and notes are often referred to as 'token money' whereas legal tender money is sometimes called 'common money'. Nevertheless, cash is the normal method by which people pay for their purchases when shopping for everyday needs, especially when total outlay is reasonable.

Cheque. A cheque is not legal tender. It is the method that is most commonly used in paying debts. An increased proportion of the population use cheques as do businessmen when paying debts to other firms. Anyone who signs a cheque has a current account with a bank, and payments are actually made by altering amounts in the separate banks of payee and payer.

What is a cheque? It is an instrument used to transfer a sum of money from the banking account of one person to that of another. As such it is not money — it is a means of transferring money.

The procedure used in clearing cheques will be discussed later in the chapter.

Credit Card. Many retail establishments display signs showing that they accept credit cards as a method of paying for goods and services. Holders of these cards, two of which are 'Access' and 'Barclaycard', present their card to the retailer. He writes out a sales slip and imprints the details of the card on to the slip. The slip is presented to holder for checking details and signature. You receive the goods and a copy of the sales slip. The retailer obtains his money from the organisation that operates the credit card scheme. At a later date you pay the credit card organisation.[7]

Promissory note. This is simply a promise made by one person to another to pay a certain sum of money at some agreed date in the future. The debtor (person who borrows the money) draws the note — unlike a bill of exchange.

5. As stated in Section 1.1 of Decimal Currency Act, 1969.
6. Currency and Bank Notes Act, 1954, Section 3.
7. For full details obtain booklets from the banks that operate these schemes. Midland Bank for Access — Barclays Bank for Barclaycard.

Postal order. The Post Office provides this method of payment. These are most useful to persons who do not have bank accounts. Payments can be transmitted by post with relative safety; the amounts, however, are only for a few pounds.

Money order. The Post Office also provides this method of payment when payments are for much larger sums of money. Money order can be transmitted by post, or, if speed is essential in making the payment they can be transmitted by telegraph — known as 'telegraphic money order'.

Bank draft. This is nothing more than a cheque but the cheque is drawn on a bank. This ensures the cheque will be honoured and there is virtually no risk that the wrong person will be paid. It is quite useful in sending reasonable sums of money (say £10 or more) to persons in other countries.

Credit transfer.[8] Usually the gas, electricity and telephone bills have a section which can be detached which enables the debtor to pay a bill at any bank branch. Non bank customers can also complete a credit transfer slip in the same way. The bank then transfers the sum of money to the creditor's account at the bank where the creditor has his account.

Direct Debit. This method of payment requires a bank's customer to authorise his bank to pay his creditors on sight of an invoice which the creditor will send directly to the bank. The bank simply debits the customer's account. Many businesses find this useful because it tends to reduce the cost of administering debts and makes money available to the firm sooner.

Bill of exchange. This instrument is drawn by the creditor — unlike the cheque or promissory note. Businesses find this method of payment very useful in exporting and importing.

Bills of exchange are often discussed in finance as acceptance credits or bill finance. These 'bills' are nothing more than a special form of cheque which has been post dated; usually 90 days forward but could be for 30 days or even 180 days.

In law, a bill is "an unconditional order in writing, addressed by one person to another, signed by the person giving it, requiring the person to whom it is addressed to pay on demand or at a fixed or determinate future time, a sum certain in money to or to the order of a specified person or to the bearer".[9]

Bills can be classified under two main headings: trade bills and bank bills. The trade bill relates to a bill drawn by a seller or goods addressed to the buyer of goods who, when recovering it, either writes across the face 'accepted' and signs it, or, pays a commission to a financial institution to accept it on his behalf. As soon as it has been accepted the person accepting it substitutes his credit for that of the drawer — he accepts liability to pay the bill on the due date. The bank bill is originated before trade takes place

---

8.   The Midland Bank has published a folded two page pamphlet which provides useful information about credit transfers.

9.   Bills of Exchange Act, 1882, Section 3(1).

— the bill is drawn by a person seeking finance to purchase goods expecting to pay the bill on the due date. Normally a financial institutions, such as an Acceptance House, provides a business with a Letter of Credit which permits the firm to borrow money by drawing the bill on the financial institution, who, when accepting it assumes responsibility for payment of the bill on maturity.

Travellers cheques. These are a special form of cheque issued by banks or specialised organisations for the convenience of customers who purchase goods and services in foreign countries. Most overseas businesses are often unwilling to accept personal cheques but quite willing to accept travellers cheques.

Cheque Clearance

Banks are constantly receiving from their customers cheques to be paid into their accounts. Some of these may be from one customer of a branch bank to another customer at the same branch. These cheques are cleared by the branch bank itself. On the other hand a large number of cheques submitted to branch banks are drawn on other banking firms. They are cleared by a system, evolved by the banks called the *Clearing House system*.

The system involves the 'clearing banks, such as Barclays, Lloyds, Midland and National Westminster, along with the Bank of England. Each clearing bank has an account at the Bank of England.

Each day the branches of each bank send to their Head Offices all cheques that have to be cleared; those that cannot be cleared at local level. Each Head Office sorts the cheques drawn on each of the other banks and totals are calculated. For example, the cheques held by bank A which were drawn on bank B may, when totalled, be greater than the claim that bank B has on bank A. Thus, bank B owes A money. B pays A by having their account at the Bank of England debited and the sum is credited to A's account at the Bank of England. The cheques have been cleared. The same procedure is carried out by all other member banks of the 'clearing house system'.[10]

Now, each Head Office has its own cheques (drawn by its customers). These are sorted and delivered to their branch banks where each customer's account can be debited.

This completes the 'clearing system'.

Now that the basics of money and credit have been investigated we can turn our attention to other ways of looking at money.

Value of Money

One of the major internal economic objectives pursued by government is that of maintaining reasonable stability of the internal purchasing power of money. This is a formal way of saying that the government is concerned with the question: what can be purchased with a given sum of money? If the

10. Banks that are not members of the 'clearing house system' must clear their cheques through one of the clearing banks.

government can keep the value of the 'pound in our pocket' reasonably stable it will ensure the orderly life society. Failure will disrupt this ideal situation. The objective is — not to fail.

The value of money cannot be measured in terms of itself; it has to be measured in terms of the goods and services that can be purchased with it. Hence, the value of money is its purchasing power, as indicated by the general level of prices.

Stability of the general level of prices means stability in the value of money and enables the citizens of a community to go about their purchases in an orderly manner. There is no need to rush or panic in making purchases now because prices are expected to rise. Stable petrol prices, sugar prices, coffee prices, etc. means there is no need keep your stock of these goods at abnormally high levels; no needs to stand in long queues, and no need to upset your normal weekly budget. BUT, prices do not normally remain static. they change over time. It is not too bad if the changes are small; it does not disrupt the normal way of life. When changes in price are large and occur over a short period of time, it creates chaos to consumers, businesses and the government.

Changes in the value of money

Because prices of goods and services change over time, the purchasing power of money changes. The relationship established is that changes in the purchasing power of money are the opposite of changes in prices. Thus,

1. when prices in general rise the amount of goods and services that can be purchased with a given sum of money declines, and the value of money falls. And,

2. when the prices of goods and services fall then the amount of goods and services that can be purchased with the same quantity of money increases, and the value of money rises.

Inflation — A Note

Inflation generally means a persistent or sustained increase in the prices of goods and services. In other words, if we refer to point 1 above and insert a few extra words we will, probably, have a better understanding of inflation. It would read something like this:

3. inflation is created when prices in general persistently and steadily increase so that the amount of goods and services that can be purchased with a given sum of money persistently and steadily declines, and the values of money persistently and steadily falls.

Measuring changes in the value of money

Changes in the value of money, price change, and price inflation are expressed in pounds (£s) but measured by price indices.

Price indices are used to measures changes in the value of money over time; from one day to the next, from one year to the next. As the prices of goods and services change so does the value of money — an inverse relationship.

The United Kingdom has a number of price indices that can be used for measuring the purchasing power of money. Some of these are related, basically, to consumers purchasing power such as:

1. consumer price index based on national accounts,
2. index of retail prices for one pensioner households of limited means,
3. index of retail prices for two pensioner households of limited means, and
4. general price index of retail prices.

Other indices are important to businessmen and indicate their purchasing power, such as:

5. wholesale price index,
6. import price index, and
7. export price index.

The government, of course, is interested in all these indices.

Our basic concern will be the indices itemised as 1 and 4. However, before discussing these indices, a few points must be noted about index numbers.

Index Numbers

The pioneers[11] of index numbers were primarily concerned with measuring changes in the purchasing power of money.

Index numbers measure fluctuations of a large number of related variables[12] that can be averaged or expressed as a single number. The average at one point of time can be compared to the average at another point of time enabling us to express movements in single numbers.

It is important to realise that index numbers deal with things that do not remain constant, that is to say, not at one level. Because one level does not exist we should not use phrases such as price levels, production levels, temperature levels. For example, temperature changes are noted by the movement of mercury up and down a scale. This is exactly the way we consider changes in prices or production — moving up and down a scale, but in the case of prices the scale is provided by index numbers. The point of reference is taken at a specified point of time (1974, or January 1974) and is called the base or base year. The figure associated to this time is 100. Hence, the base is usually referred to as: 1974 = 100, or January 1974 = 100. The scale are figures below and above the figure 100. When prices have risen, relative to the base year, the scale moves beyond 100 and vice versa.

Prices relate to goods and services. There are hundreds of thousands of commodities entering into exchange and it would be impossible to compare *all* individual prices at one point of time with *all* prices at another date. For

11. For example: Jevons 1863 and Fisher 1911.
12. Variables refer to a thing, such as prices, wages, industrial production, temperatures, etc., that do not tend to remain constant; things that are able to assume different numerical values.

this reason a selection of commodities are chosen which are representative of the goods and services people purchase. This selection is normally referred to as 'a basket', or 'a basket of goods and services'.

To reflect the relative importance of the commodities in the basket logical weights must be employed; food being relatively more important than alcohol to the general consumer. It is extremely important to get the weights correct. If two different weights are used it could result in the final index numbers showing movements that are completely different in direction. To ensure weights are as accurate as they possibly can be for retail price indices, the government[13] carries out a 'Family Expenditure Survey'[14] to obtain the importance of consumer expenditure for one item relative to others. From this survey, carried out annually, weights are calculated. The pattern of expenditure gradually changes year by year and so new weights are established each January.

Once the weights have been determined the prices of commodities in the 'basket' are collected starting with the base date and at future dates. Changes are noted by referring them back to the base.

The overall index is a weighted average of all individual price changes of commodities in the basket. If the cost of the basket rises the value of money falls. If the increased cost of the basket is persistent or sustained we have, what is commonly called, inflation.

These indices are useful to businessmen, economists, market researchers, politicians, sociologists, etc. in an attempt to explain past trends and predict future trends.

Now, to look at two indices that throw light on:- consumer expenditures from given incomes, prices of commodities in the basket, and the internal purchasing power of the pound.

Consumer Price Index based on National Accounts (C.P.I.)

National accounts, for 1938 and continuously since 1946, includes estimates of consumers expenditure. It is this material that is used to calculate the C.P.I.

The index is calculated by taking the ratio of total consumer expenditure (TCE) in the United Kingdom at current prices to total consumer expenditure, in the United Kingdom, at constant prices and express it as an index number. In other words,

$$\frac{\text{TCE in the UK at current prices}}{\text{TCE in the UK at constant prices}} \times 100$$

---

13. In this case, the Department of Employment is responsible for the survey, its processing and publication of results. The Social Survey Division of the Office of Population Censuses and Surveys is responsible for the actual conduct of the survey.

14. Refer to Department of Employment Gazette, February 1978, "Family Expenditure — A plain man's guide to the Family Expenditure Survey" pages 137-147.

Two examples will be provided to clarify the above. The base year for the index is 1970, that is to say 1970 = 100.

Example 1. $\dfrac{\text{1970 TCE in the UK at current prices}}{\text{1970 TCE in the UK at constant prices}} \times 100 =$

$\dfrac{\text{£31,201 million}}{\text{£31,201 million}} \times 100 = 100$

Example 2. $\dfrac{\text{1976 TCE in the UK at 1976 prices}}{\text{1976 TCE in the UK at 1970 prices}} \times 100 =$

$\dfrac{\text{£72,380 million}}{\text{£34,904 million}} \times 100 = 207.4 \text{ (to one place of decimals)}$

Consumer expenditure here refers to *all* expenditures made by *all* consumers. It does not include expenditures made by central and local government, nor companies and financial institutions, nor expenditures made by tourists in the United Kingdom.

The TCE in the United Kingdom, as a percentage of total domestic expenditure in the United Kingdom, varies year by year, but appears to be around 60 per cent. In 1976 it was greater than this, and in 1970 it was less.

The C.P.I. is calculated by the Central Statistical Office and shown in the 'National Income and Expenditure' blue book. The figures[15] they give, using 1970 = 100, are as follows:

1963	73.3	1970	100.0 (base year)
1964	75.9	1971	108.3
1965	79.6	1972	115.6
1966	82.6	1973	125.3
1967	85.2	1974	145.9
1968	89.4	1975	180.3
1969	94.4	1976	208.0

This shows that prices for all consumers for all goods and services purchased in the United Kingdom rose from 100 in 1970 to 208 in 1976 — an increase in prices over the six year span of approximately 108 per cent.

From this table we can calculate the internal purchasing power of the pound for consumers as a whole. The method used to obtain this information is as follows:

$\dfrac{\text{base year C.P.I.}}{\text{year to be considered}} \times 100 \text{ pence}$

For example:

$\dfrac{\text{1970 base year C.P.I.}}{\text{1976 C.P.I.}} \times 100 \text{ pence} =$

$\dfrac{100}{208} \times 100 \text{ pence} = 48.1 \text{ pence (one place of decimal)}$

15. taken from table 2.5 of CSO's 'National Income and Expenditure 1966-1976' published by H.M.S.O., 1977.

This states the following about the purchasing power of the pound regarding its change in value. The pound in 1970 was worth £1 (100 pence) and it bought £1 worth of goods and services. In 1976 a consumer would require £2.08 to buy the same basket of goods and services. Therefore the £1 of 1970 was worth approximately 48 pence in 1976.

Another piece of useful information from the above figures is that prices rose by 108 per cent from 1970 to 1976. The rise, per year, on average, was approximately 18 per cent. This is inflation — a persistent and sustained rise in the general prices of goods and services (purchased by consumers).

The Central Statistical Office says that "the Consumer Price Index tends to increase rather more slowly than the General Index of Retail Prices."[16]

General Index of Retail Prices[17]

This index, one of several measuring retail prices, seeks to measure the weighted average change in retail prices of a representative sample of goods and services which are purchased by a particular section of the community. The commodities to be included, and the weights attached, must reflect the purchasing habits of the sector being analysed. It should be noted at the very beginning that it is a 'sample' and not a 'census' and therefore is subject to discrepencies even though they may be small.

This index is commonly, but erroneously, called the 'cost of living' index. There is no such thing as the 'cost of living' because, to mention a few points, what is reasonable for one person may not be the same for another. In fact, no one person's cost may be exactly the same as an index number. Also, over time the base subsistence required for living changes — a luxury before the second world war may no longer be a luxury today.

The reason for the error arises from an index carried out by the government called the 'Cost of Living Index' which was based on expenditure patterns of the working class for the period 1904-1914. The survey covered the consumption and cost of food in about 2,000 United Kingdom workmen's families living in urban districts. The 'Cost of Living' index was replaced in 1947 by an Interim Index of Retail Prices.

The most recent General Index of Retail Prices (RPI) uses a basket which is brought up to date in January each year from the latest Family Expenditure Survey results. The cost of the basket uses the reference base of January 15, 1974 = 100. This base is expected to remain in existence until at least 1980.

---

16. "The internal purchasing power of the pound" Note by C.S.O., in Statistical News, No. 13, May 1971 p13-14. Further information about the C.P.I. can be found in this article.

17. Information relating to retail price indices can be found in the following:
   i) "Measuring Price Changes" in Feb 1978 issue of Economic Progress Report, pages 6 and 7.
   ii) "Family Expenditure — A plain man's guide to the Family Expenditure Survey" in Employment Gazette, Feb. 1978, pages 137-147.
   iii) "An Unstatistical Readers' Guide to the RPI" in Employment Gazette Oct. 1975.

This was recommended by The Retail Prices Index Advisory Committee,[18] who felt that changing the base would create problems because the index is used in connection with inflation proofing for national savings schemes and pensions.

The weights for the index are changed each January for the broad sectors of expenditure covered by the index. Exhibit 6.2 shows the weight (or importance) of each of eleven major groups of goods or services in the basket and the index numbers associated with these groups towards the end of 1977.

Exhibit 6.2

General Index of Retail Prices

Expenditure Sectors	1977 Weight	Expenditure as % of Income	Index at Dec. 13, 1977 (Jan. 15, 1974 = 100)
Food	247	24.7	194.8
Alcoholic drink	83	8.3	188.3
Tobacco	46	4.6	218.2
Housing	112	11.2	163.8
Fuel and light	58	5.8	220.0
Durable household goods	63	6.3	174.7
Clothing and footwear	82	8.2	164.7
Transport and vehicles	139	13.9	196.4
Miscellaneous goods	71	7.1	197.5
Services	54	5.4	184.0
Meals outside the home	45	4.5	198.0
All Items	1,000	100.0	188.4

Source: Extracted (except for column 3) from Retail Price table located pages 262 and 263 in Department of Employment Gazette, February 1978.

The exhibit shows that the average householder which consist of practically all wage earners and most salary earners[19] have expenditures, based on market prices (includes expenditure taxes such as value added tax and excise duties), which approximate the weights. In other words, out of every £1,000, about £247 or 24.7 per cent of income is spent on food; about £112 or 11.2 per cent of income is spent on housing; etc.

The index figures for December 13, 1977 shows that the prices of all items in the basket have risen from 100 on January 15, 1974 to 188.4 on December 13, 1977, an increase of 88.4 per cent; fuel and light prices have been greater than this, from 100 to 220, an increase of 120 per cent; housing shows price changes of approximately 63.8 per cent (100 to 163.8) and so on.

Over a span of 4 years the prices of all items have risen by 88.4 per cent, an average rise per annum of 22.1 per cent; an indicator of high inflation. The

18. The Secretary of State for Employment, following the recommendation of the RPIAC, made the announcement in the House of Commons on Jan 11, 1978.

19. excludes one person and two person pensioners of limited means, people in institutions and households whose heads have the highest weekly incomes (in first half of 1977 this was £145 — figures are updated).

sectors that tended to inflate more than the average price figure of 188.4 were, from highest to lowest; fuel and light, tobacco, meals outside the home, miscellaneous goods, transport and food. Those below the all item index of 188.4, from lowest to highest, were: housing, clothing and footwear, durable household goods, services and alcohol. Over 60 per cent of income is spent on the most inflationary items. Each student can ask — does this represent the pattern of expenditure at our house?

The 'silver jubilee' of the Queen's reign took place in 1977. What was the pattern of expenditure for the average household in 1952? The first thing to note is that the number of sectors totalled 9 in 1952 compared to 11 in 1977. The sectors of expenditures and weights plus the expenditures as a percentage of income are shown in Exhibit 6.3.

Exhibit 6.3

Expenditure Pattern in 1952

Expenditure Sectors	Expenditure as % of Income	1952 Weights
Food	39.9	399
Alcohol	7.8	78
Tobacco	9.0	90
Rent and Rates	7.2	72
Fuel and light	6.6	66
Durable household goods	6.2	62
Clothing	9.8	98
Miscellaneous goods	4.4	44
Services	9.1	91
All Items	100.0	1,000

When comparing the details in exhibit 6.3 with those in 6.2 some striking features take shape .... remembering two sectors (transport and vehicles, and meals outside the home) are not represented in the 1952 expenditure pattern. The expenditure pattern has changed considerably. Food in 1952 took, on average, 39.9 per cent of expenditure compared to 24.7 per cent in 1977. We tend, on average, to spend less on food and tobacco but more on alcohol and rent and rates (housing), out of every £100 of income.

Weights, as stated before, must be treated with great care. They must be as accurate as possible if the index is to be meaningful. Weights are based upon the 'family expenditure surveys' carried out each year, but there are problems in obtaining accurate details. For example, to mention a few problems, the basket can never be absolutely up to date. Also, expenditures are obtained from only 7,000 households although over 10,000 households are sampled, and these may not be truly representative of all households. The survey is a sample (not a census) and there is bound to be a sampling error. Often, false information is given, for example there is a tendency to understate tobacco expenditure. However, this item can be cross checked by comparing them with government revenue raised from tobacco, and the error removed.

Index numbers give interested parties a good idea of price changes and changes in the value of money, but the changes should not be treated as being perfect. An index number of 103 may be anywhere between, say, 102 and 104. When politicians (government or opponents) use the RPI to make statements about retail prices, inflation or purchasing power remember that they give a reasonably accurate idea of these movements, but not a perfect one.

The monthly figures for the 'General Index of Retail Prices' from January 1962 is provided in Exhibit 6.4.

Exhibit 6.4

General Index of Retail Prices (all items) (January 1974 = 100)

	Annual average	Jan	Feb	Mar	Apr	May	Jun	Jly	Aug	Set	Oct	Nov	Dec
1962	53.0	52.1	52.2	52.4	53.1	53.3	53.6	53.4	53.0	52.9	52.9	53.1	53.3
1963	54.0	53.5	54.0	54.1	54.2	54.2	54.2	53.9	53.7	53.9	54.1	54.2	54.3
1964	55.8	54.6	54.6	54.8	55.3	55.8	56.0	56.0	56.2	56.2	56.3	56.7	56.9
1965	58.4	57.1	57.1	57.3	58.4	58.6	58.8	58.8	58.9	58.9	59.0	59.2	59.5
1966	60.7	59.6	59.6	59.7	60.5	60.9	61.1	60.8	61.2	61.1	61.2	61.6	61.7
1967	62.3	61.8	61.8	61.8	62.3	62.3	62.5	62.1	62.0	61.9	62.4	62.8	63.2
1968	65.2	63.4	63.7	63.9	65.1	65.1	65.4	65.4	65.5	65.6	65.9	66.1	66.9
1969	68.7	67.3	67.7	67.9	68.7	68.6	68.9	68.9	68.7	68.9	69.4	69.6	70.1
1970	73.1	70.6	71.0	71.4	72.5	72.7	72.9	73.5	73.4	73.8	74.6	75.1	75.6
1971	80.0	76.6	77.1	77.7	79.4	79.9	80.4	80.9	81.0	81.1	81.5	82.0	82.4
1972	85.7	82.9	83.3	83.6	84.4	84.8	85.3	85.6	86.3	86.8	88.0	88.3	88.7
1973	93.5	89.3	89.9	90.4	92.1	92.8	93.3	93.7	94.0	94.8	96.7	97.4	98.1
1974	108.5	100.0	101.7	102.6	106.1	107.6	108.7	109.7	109.8	111.0	113.2	115.2	116.9
1975	134.8	119.9	121.9	124.3	129.1	134.5	137.1	138.5	139.3	140.5	142.5	144.2	146.0
1976	157.1	147.9	149.8	150.6	153.5	155.2	156.0	156.3	158.5	160.6	163.5	165.8	168.0
1977	182.0	172.4	174.1	175.8	180.3	181.7	183.6	183.8	184.7	185.7	186.5	187.4	188.4
1978		189.5	190.6										
1979													

Source: "The Internal Purchasing Power of the Pound", October 1977, table 1 page 3, by Central Statistical Office, from a 10 page article made available by the Press and Information Service of the C.S.O.

From this exhibit it is possible to give estimates of changes in prices or in purchasing power between any two months.

To find the percentage change in prices between June 1977 and February 1978 the calculation is:

$$\frac{\text{RPI February 1978 } - \text{minus} - \text{ RPI June 1977}}{\text{RPI June 1977}} \times 100\%$$

$$\frac{190.6 \text{ minus } 183.6}{183.6} \times 100\% = + 3.8 \text{ per cent}$$

The change in purchasing power, for the same two periods of time, is calculated as follows:

$$\frac{\text{RPI June 1977}}{\text{RPI February 1978}} \times 100\text{p}$$

$$\frac{183.6}{190.6} \times 100p = 96.3 \text{ pence}$$

The purchasing power of money has fallen by 3.7 pence, or the pound of June 1977 could purchase £1 worth of goods and services but 8 months later it has command over 96.3 pence worth of goods and services.

This tells us something about the change in the value of money. Now, to find out more about 'money'.

Types of Money

There are three types of money and they must all be restricted in supply if they are to obtain their value. They are:

1. commodity money,
2. token money, and
3. banking money.

Commodity money. This type of money must contain in itself its worth. As such it has a value outside its exchange function; it has value for its own sake. Gold coins, such as gold sovereigns, and silver coins, such as the United States silver dollar, are good examples of commodity money; coins of intrinsic value.

Commodity money was normally kept relatively scarce and enjoyed qualities of being fairly durable, easily divisible, reasonably portable, and above all else, widely acceptable. They had, when minted, uniform quality in content and weight, but later were prone to being debased for as they passed from one person to the next there was a tendency to shave the edges,before passing them on in exchange. Debasement *also means* producing coins of similar value but contains less gold or silver.

Supply of this money could be increased only by a physical increase in the quantity of coins in circulation. This was made possible by an increase in the amount minted, through a surplus arising from international trade, or by debasing the coinage (more coins from a given quantity of gold or silver).

The seal or stamp of the issuing authority on coins became important in the commercial field because it established authenticity to 'uniform quality'. It followed from this, quite naturally and eventually, that the State should become the sole issuer of coins.

Token money. This type of money does not, normally, have value outside its exchange function. Bronze coins, cupro-nickel coins and bank notes are examples of token money. In the United Kingdom, the issue of this type of money is entrusted and controlled by the Bank of England subject in general to the State.

Coins, in the United Kingdom, are minted by the Royal Mint who then sell them to the Bank of England. The Royal Mint's account at the Bank of England is credited with the amount sold. There is no limitation on the minting of coins, but the Bank of England does control the issue of coins to the public; normally, as the public demands.

Bank notes, on the other hand, in terms of printing and issuing are controlled and regulated by law. *Notes issued* means the notes that the Bank of England is authorised to issue. *Notes in circulation* refers to the note issue that is circulating in the community.

The control of the note issue goes back to a Bank Act of 1844. This stated that the Bank of England could issue notes to the value of the gold reserves plus, £30,000,000. This £30,000,000 was called the 'fiduciary issue'; it was not backed by gold. An Act of 1928 raised the fiduciary issue to £280,000,000 and, an Act of 1939 increased it to £300,000,000. The latest Act, operating in 1978, is the Currency and Bank Notes Act, 1954. It states that the Bank of England may only issue notes of denominations approved by the Treasury. The Act raised the fiduciary note issue to £1,575,000,000 and made provisions whereby this amount could be varied by the direction of the Treasury. The directive would be effective for six months but could be renewed but had to be terminated at the end of two years except by virtue of an order made by statutory instrument subject to negative parliamentary procedure.

Today, a proportion of bank notes are backed by gold coin and gold bullion held at the Bank of England; the remainder is made up from the fiduciary note issue.

Token money, coins and bank notes, is not as important as the type of money called 'banking money'.

Banking money. This type of money is, by far, the most important of the three types mentioned and, therefore, there is greater need to control it.

The most usual way of paying debt today is by the signing of a cheque, and a cheque can be converted into token money. Hence, the Bank of England can control bank money by restricting the amount of token money held by banks (clearing banks and merchant banks).

Cheques require a person having an account with a bank. So, by banking money we do not mean Bank of England notes, but accounts that people and businesses have with banks. Some accounts originate when cash is deposited with the banks, but others originate when the banks loan money to individuals, businesses, and other organisations. This latter type of account is the base of 'bank money'; money that is not backed by token money. In other words, all the accounts of the banking sector, when totalled, are much greater than the token money held by the banks.

Our modern 'money system', consisting of token money and banking money, had its begining over 250 years ago. A brief look at the scene then will help to explain the link and development of the three types of money.

Goldsmiths and three types of money

The London goldsmiths, who were really the first bankers in this country back in the 17th century, provide the link between the three types of money noted.

The strong rooms of the goldsmiths were ideal for persons to deposit their cash (commodity money) for safe keeping. In return, they were given a receipt. The receipt could be used by the holder to make payment for his debts by endorsing the receipt in favour of his creditor. The ultimate holder of the receipt could claim the cash held by the goldsmith. Later, the goldsmiths found it beneficial to issue several receipts, in small denominations, for cash deposited with them stating that the issuer promised to pay the bearer an equivalent amount of commodity money on demand. This was the beginning of paper money — bank notes.

The goldsmiths noted that their promissory notes would, normally, be used many times for paying debts before demands were made upon them to honour their promise to convert the note into gold and silver. This is the idea of convertibility. This delay led to the next development.

Idle money could be put to good use by lending it to others; and it was profitable. But greater profits would be made if the goldsmith could encourage more people to deposit their cash with them. So, the idea was formed of paying interest to those who did this. The intention being that the goldsmith would then lend the cash to other persons, keeping a record of the account (banking account), but always keeping some cash in reserve to meet demands on the original notes. This meant that the receipts were in circulation as well as the cash. This is the background to what economists call 'banks creating money'. Bankers argue that this is not true because they need cash deposited with them before they can loan the cash to someone else; money is, therefore, not created. Despite arguments, this is how 'bank money' was developed.

It is often claimed that the goldsmiths originated the idea of cheques; where the depositor of cash signs receipts which lay claim on the cash deposited. This is not strictly true. The Bank of England, in its earlier years, introduced the version of the modern cheque. "Drawn notes were written on special forms prepared by the Bank having a 'check' pattern running across the paper."[20]

It follows, from the above, that Bank of England notes ultimately developed from the notes issued by the goldsmiths; issued and signed by bankers. Banking money developed from the goldsmiths but cheques, signed by the depositor, originated with the Bank of England. Convertibility refers to the situation whereby bank notes can be converted into gold and silver. Today, in fact since 1931, notes in the United Kingdom cannot be converted into gold and silver; they are inconvertible. On present day bank notes the statement 'I promise to pay the bearer on demand the sum of ———' means you can obtain coins and/or notes totalling that sum but not gold and silver.

The previous details given explains something about money, types of money, development of money, but what constitutes the money supply?

---

20. "The Bank of England note: a short history" in Bank of England Quarterly Bulletin, Vol. 9, No. 2, June 1969, p212.

Money Supply

Money is used to pay debts. However, as a modern society progresses the number of exchange transactions increase and often, one type of money in existence is inadequate in supply to meet the needs of society. When transactions increased and commodity money was short in relation to the increased transactions a gap was created. This gap required a new type of money. Later a new gap appears and a new type of money emerges. Gradually, one definition of the stock of money becomes unsatisfactory; there is need for 2 or 3 or 4 definitions. Such is the case in the United Kingdom.

The authorities (Government, Treasury, Bank of England) whose job it is to control the money supply have created several definitions. The problem is that they are subject to change from time to time — "the stock of money can be defined in various ways according to the selection of bank deposits chosen".[21]

At the present time (1978) there are three major definitions of money supply used in official statistics. They are called M_1, sterling M_3, and M_3. The original definitions were agreed in 1970 but these have been changed or modified. Sterling M_3 was introduced in May 1975.

What is the make up of the definitions?

M_1. This is a narrow definition of money supply and consists of:

1. Notes and coins in circulation with the public, plus

2. United Kingdom private sector sterling sight deposits.[22]

Sight deposits are classified under two headings.

    a) non interest bearing sight deposits — obtained after deducting 60 per cent of transit items[23], and

    b) interest bearing sight deposits.

This definition, as well as the others, can not be measured direct; they are estimates. Estimated figures mean that one should not treat them as being 100 per cent accurate.

M_1 represents money (coins and notes) and very near money (funds that are available on demand). Very near money refers to bank accounts that can be turned into coins and notes in a matter of minutes or hours.

Sterling M_3. This, relative to M_1, is a broader definition of the money supply. Since early 1975 it is officially "presented as an alternative

---

21. "Summary of Articles Vol. 1-10, 1960-1970" in Bank of England Quarterly Bulletin, p532.

22. Sight deposits refer to funds that are available on demand. It also includes money at call and money placed overnight.

23. Transit items refer to money in transit between banks. The deducting figure follows a rule of thumb measure and allows for delays in clearing cheques through the banking system. These figures are estimates.

definition of the money stock".[24] This new definition makes it possible to discuss the broader definition of money supply of the *domestic* stock because it excludes foreign currency deposits.

Sterling M_3 consists of:
the components of M_1, plus

3. United Kingdom private sector sterling time deposits (which take time to be turned into coins and notes, such as deposits accounts), plus

4. United Kingdom public sector sterling deposits.

M_3. This definition is broader than 'sterling M_3'. It consists of: the components of M_1 (items 1 and 2) and sterling M_3 (items 3 and 4), plus

5. United Kingdom residents deposits in other currencies.[25]

Sterling M_3 and M_3 take into consideration 'near money' items; those that can be turned into coins and notes after a delay of days.

All definition indicate that there are many kinds oi money. Money that is immediately money (coins and notes) and various bank deposits which are not really money, but can be turned into money over time. The shorter the time the nearer it is to money, and the farther in time it takes to convert into money the farther away it is from being money. All, however, fulfil the functions of money.

All definitions are based on *estimated* figures, and are calculated from the liability side of the consolidated balance sheet of the banking sector.

Money Supply in Figures

The following exhibits (6.5, 6.6) puts figures to the above definitions.

Exhibit 6.5 provides some useful information. It shows the size of each item making up the various definitions. However, to be more useful secondary statistics would be required. Below are only a few of these secondary considerations.

The broad definition of money supply, M_3, in the course of one year changed by £4,097mill, or by approximately 10.7 per cent. Sterling M_3 rose by £2,891mill, or roughly 8.1 per cent. M_1 increased by £2,388mill or about 15 per cent. This is an indication that people, during this period, wanted to remain fairly liquid; hold token money and very near money.

Previously it was stated that coins and bank notes were not as important as banking money. Exhibit 6.5 proves this statement. Let us look at the second quarter of 1975; coins and notes represent approximately £14.066 out of every £100 of money supply (M_3) and the remainder (£85.934) is made up of deposits in the banking sector.

---

24. "DCE and the money supply — a statistical note" in Bank of England Quarterly Bulletin, Vol. 17, No. 1, March 1977, p39.

25. U.K. residents may have foreign currency deposits only for purposes approved by the exchange control authorities. Examples: oil and insurance companies who require other currencies for their international operations.

Exhibit 6.5

**Money Supply Definitions
in Figures**

(figures are unadjusted)   (figures are in £m)

Items	Second quarter figures 1975	1976
Notes and coins in circulation with public	5,371	6,188
Sterling sight deposits (UK private sector)		
non-interest bearing	8,819	9,947
interest bearing	1,712	2,155
M_1 money supply	15,902	18,290

M_1 money supply	15,902	18,290
Sterling time deposits (UK private sector)	19,043	19,332
Sterling deposits (UK public sector)	879	1,093
Sterling M_3 money supply	35,824	38,715

Sterling M_3 money supply	35,824	38,715
Foreign currency deposits (UK residents)	2,359	3,565
M_3 money supply	38,183	42,280

Note: 2nd quarter of each year chosen because the new statistical returns began in 2nd quarter of 1975.

Source: based on figures from table 11 in Bank of England Quarterly Bulletin, June 1977.

The exhibit does not show the amount of coins and notes separately. Estimates show that the value of coins in circulation, during this period, was approximately £425mill and notes £4,946mill. From these figures we can show that coins represent about £1.113 out of every £100 of money supply (M_3) and notes £12.953.

This information supports the idea that control over money supply must be geared towards the activities of the banking sector, and to do this it is necessary to control the quantity of bank notes in circulation. In support of this statement it can be noted that the banking sector deposits account for approximately 84 to 85 per cent of the domestic money supply (sterling M_3).

Other relationships can be calculated. The student might like to find out the overall breakdown of each item as a percentage of M_3, or out of each £100 or M_3. What was the size of increase in each of the items from the second quarter of 1975 to the second quarter of 1976 relative to M_3. What do these figures tell us about the way the various sectors of the economy hold their money?

What has been the trend of money supply? To establish the trend it is necessary to look at each of the money supplies over a longer period of time. Exhibit 6.6 provides this information for the period from the first quarter of 1970 to the first quarter of 1977.

Exhibit 6.6

Growth of Money Supply
1970-1978

(figures are unadjusted)   (figures are in £m)

Money			1st quarters of each year					
Supply	1970	1971	1972	1973	1974	1975	1976	1977
M_1	8,507	9,691	11,225	12,333	12,772	14,735	17,801	19,566
Sterling M_3			20,882	26,047	32,165	34,903	37,321	40,155
M_3	16,161	18,192	21,411	27,146	33,938	37,422	40,471	44,434

Sources: for 1970 and 1971 figures was Bank of England Quarterly Bulletin, Vol. 14 No. 4, Dec. 1974, taken from table 12.
for 1972 onwards figures came from table 11 of Bank of England Quarterly, June 1977.
Note: There have been a few changes in calculating the 'money stock'. For details refer to 'additional notes' that follow the tables at the back of the Bank of England Quarterly Bulletins. In mid May 1975 there was a slight break in the series as new statistical returns were introduced.

Exhibit 6.6 shows that over the period of 7 years from the first quarter of 1970 M_1 and M_3 have increased substantially; M_1 has more than doubled and M_3 has increased 2 and 3/4 times. Sterling M_3, over a five year span (from 1st quarter of 1972) has almost doubled. All three definitions show a continuous rise; a pronounced upward trend.

As stated before, we do not want money for its own sake, we want it for the goods and services it can purchase. To this end, it would be interesting to compare money supply changes (M_1 and M_3) with changes in the 'consumer price index', 'retail price index', and with the 'gross national product in real terms'.[26]

The gross national product at 1970 market prices was as follows for 1970 and 1976: for 1970 it was £51,463mill and for 1976 it was £57,871mill. The index numbers for 1970 = 100 and for 1976 = approximately 112½; an increase of 12½ per cent. By holding prices constant we remove changes in prices and note increases in goods and services made available to the community.

To carry out the relationships, it is necessary to make an index for M_1 and M_3. These indices have been calculated and are shown in Exhibits 6.7 and 6.8.

26. To obtain the GNP in real terms: take one year (1970) and use the prices in that year as being constant throughout the range of years. Multiply the prices by the quantities in each year that follows. For example: prices in 1970 times quantities in 1970; prices in 1970 times quantities in 1971, etc.. Take the money values obtained and form an index. 1970 = 100.

114

Exhibit 6.7

Indexing M₁ Money Supply

Year[1]	M₁ (£m)	Index Numbers							
1970	8,507	100	—	—	—	—	—	—	—
1971	9,691	114	100	—	—	—	—	—	—
1972	11,225	132	116	100	—	—	—	—	—
1973	12,333	145	127	110	100	—	—	—	—
1974	12,772	150	132	114	104	100	—	—	—
1975	14,735	173	152	131	119	115	100	—	—
1976	17,801	209	184	159	144	139	121	100	—
1977	19,566	230	202	174	159	153	133	110	

Note: 1 ..... time refers to first quarter of each year.

.... use 1st column of index numbers to compare with GNP and CPI. Their base year is 1970.

.... use 5th column of index numbers to compare with RPI (base year is 1974).

Indexing M₃ Money Supply

Year[1]	M₃ (£m)	Index Numbers							
1970	16,161	100	—	—	—	—	—	—	—
1971	18,192	113	100	—	—	—	—	—	—
1972	21,411	132	118	100	—	—	—	—	—
1973	27,146	168	149	127	100	—	—	—	—
1974	33,938	210	187	159	125	100	—	—	—
1975	37,422	232	206	175	138	110	100	—	—
1976	40,471	250	222	189	149	119	108	100	—
1977	44,434	275	244	208	164	131	119	110	

Note: (same notes as given in exhibit 6.7 applies)

These indices, when compared with the CPI, RPI, GNP or Gross Domestic Product, must match the base dates and ending dates as near as possible to having meaning. When this is done the more reliable the comparisons become. But, the relationship should be treated with care because the various indicators used have been over simplified.[27] There have been several empirical investigations showing the relationship of money supply to prices and national income statistics. Virtually all have been criticised that their investigations have been too simple; that complex econometric models should have been used.

However, what we can note is this — there is a positive relationship between money supply and prices, money supply and the real gross national product. Changes in money supply appear to influence movements of the indicators noted above, but how strong the influence and how certain the movements is debatable. Money supply does matter but there are other factors that matter too.

27. More detailed knowledge is required to establish firm relationships. There is need for monthly or quarterly changes over many years; need to remove seasonal variations; need to establish leads and lags between the indicators, need to consider central government revenue, taxes and borrowing requirements, interest rates, etc..

Domestic Credit Expansion

In 1969 the government introduced a new concept called 'domestic credit expansion' (DCE) to measure the total credit extended to the domestic economy from the banking sector in the United Kingdom and from overseas.

On 15 December, 1976 the Government stated, in its letter of intent to the International Monetary Fund (IMF), that its primary monetary objective would be expressed in terms of the rate of DCE rather than the growth of M_3. To this end it was necessary to redefine DCE to get it in line with the IMF's definition.[28] The aim was to bring the definition of DCE closer to the concept of 'money' generated domestically'.

Domestic credit, measuring credit or money, must be calculated from the assets side of the consolidated balance sheet of the banking sector. The banking sector's assets show who they lend to.

DCE can be defined as:

1. the change in domestic non-banking holdings of notes and coins, *plus*
2. all lending by U.K. banks to the overseas, private and public sectors, *plus*
3. bank lending to the public sector in foreign currencies, *and* overseas lending to the public sector.

There is an alternative presentation of the DCE. It includes:

1. the public sector borrowing requirement (PSBR), *minus*
2. purchases by the non-banking private sector of public sector debt, *plus*
3. the increase in bank lending in sterling to the private sector and overseas sector.

The new definition excludes all foreign currency lending, but includes all sterling bank lending to the private sector.

Exhibit 6.9 shows the alternative statistical presentation of DCE, and shows the importance of the PSBR in calculating DCE.

Public Sector Borrowing Requirement

The public sector includes central government and its agencies, local government and the nationalised industries. When the government's revenue is less than its expenditure, it has to borrow to make the additional expenditures. It is this borrowing that is calculated.

Who finances this borrowing? Basically, three sectors, namely:

1. the general public,   (sterling)
2. the banking sector, and   (sterling)
3. the banking sector and overseas. (foreign currency)

Borrowing sterling from the general public takes place in two ways. First, the general public needs more cash to finance daily transactions. The government meets these increases by issuing notes and coins, and this adds

---

28. Sterling M_3 was to be given greater official emphasis at the same time.

Exhibit 6.9

PSBR and DCE
(Changes in period for year ending April 20, 1977)

(figures in £m)

PSBR. Central government (surplus −)	plus	5,706
PSBR. Other public sector, and Purchases (−) of public sector debt by private sector (other than banks). Other public sector debt.	plus	1,519
Purchases (−) of public sector debt by private sector (other than banks). Central government debt.	minus	6,068
Sterling lending to private sector.	plus	3,026
Bank lending overseas, in sterling.	plus	38
D.C.E.	plus	4,221

Source: based on table 11/3, Bank of England Quarterly Bulletin, Vol. 17, No. 2, June 1977.

directly to DCE and money supply. The government sees this as a form of interest free borrowing. It represents 1/10th or less of total PSBR. Notes and coins are deposited with banks; banks are able to increase their loans (create money) which adds to the money supply and increases bank credit to the community. This does expand domestic monetary conditions. Secondly, the government borrows from the general public by selling national savings certificates and gilt edged securities (long term commitments). This does not expand credit, and so the government obtains about ½ of PSBR by using these methods. The general public, in purchasing these securities, parts with cash normally by drawing on their deposit accounts with the banks. This flow of money back to the government tends to offset its excess of expenditure over its revenue.

Borrowing sterling from the banking sector is kept to a minimum because it expands the money supply (liability side of bank sector's balance sheet) and also expands domestic credit (assets side). When the government finds it difficult to finance its borrowing from the general public it must turn to the banks, but by doing this, it increases money supply and DCE beyond, what it might consider to be, a reasonable level. It is borrowing of this type by the public sector that is considered to be the main way to affect the money supply and DCE.

Borrowing foreign currency is difficult to explain in simple terms.[29] Basically, this method of finance has helped the government "to offset the effect of the PSBR on the money stock". In fact, this method of financing has little or no effect on the money supply (sterling M_3). Borrowing from overseas is associated with the current account of the balance of payments.

29. For an explanation, including diagrams, refer to page 5 and 6 of Economic Progress Report, No. 58, January 1975.

Money Supply

The previous information points very clearly to the fact that the most important factors affecting money supply are:

1. actions exercised by the government, and

2. the machine-like operations of the banking system.

The causes that change the money supply, already discussed, can be briefly stated as variations in:

1. PSBR,

2. bank lending,

3. government securities in the hands of the general public, and

4. the balance of payments.

Money Demand

The demand for money can be related to the functions of money and, these functions are necessary for the price mechanism to operate. Basically, there are two main factors that determine the demand for money. They are:

1. the volume of transactions carried out by the community to satisfy their needs, within a given time, which requires the use of money, and

2. the needs of the community to satisfy foreseen and unforseen events of the future ('precautionary' plus 'speculative' motive).

Quantity Theory of Money

We have noted that as the sterling value of the gross national product has grown, so has the money supply. It appears that there is a connection between 'goods' and 'money'. The Quantity Theory states that there is a strong connection between the level of gross national product and the level of money supply measured in money terms, and shows this in the form of an identity: $MV = PT$.[30]

The Quantative Theory of Money (QTM) sought to establish an arithmetical relation between the volume of money and the level of prices; stating that the value of money depends on the quantity of it in circulation. In the 1930s attention was paid to it to show the connection between money trends and national income trends. Recently, the QTM has been brought back into prominence by suggesting that the control of the money supply is the best way to manage the economy.[31]

$MV = PT$ is simply M times $V = P$ times T, where:

M.. is the 'stock of money', or quantity of money available in the community;

---

30. This theory was known by 18th century economists but not under this name. It was Irving Fisher, an American political-economist-mathematician, who put the theory into a 'quantity equation' in the early part of the 20th century. The equation has many different forms, with meanings very similar. American economist tend to prefer $MV = PQ$.

31. by Milton Friedman, an American economist and the Chicago School.

V.. is the 'flow of money', or the velocity of money circulating in the community; often discussed as the 'turnover' of money;

P.. is the average price level of goods and services, measured by some price index, for example, the Consumer Price Index; and

T.. is the number of transactions of goods and services which are exchanged for money, normally taken to be one year.

What the theory says, goes something like this. Assume that the velocity of circulation (V) remains stable. Then, the government, by controlling the stock of money (M) the volume of transactions in goods and services (T) will be controlled, or the price (P) will be controlled, or both. For example: V is stable at 5; each £1 note circulates 5 times in the year. M, the independent variable, is controlled by the government (assume this is in the first instance to be £1,000). Thus: M times V = P times T,

$$£1,000 \times 5 = £5,000$$

PT can not be larger than £5,000. M, therefore determines PT. Now, if the government wanted to lower prices but keep the number of transactions stable (keep standard of living stable; assuming, of course, no population change) it could to this by lowering the supply of money. Thus, if M was changed to £800 the following would result:

$$£800 \times 5 = £4,000$$

The argument is that P can increase only with the increase in M. Thus, if prices are to be kept stable, especially in the long run, then P must not be allowed to grow faster than the growth of the gross national product in real terms (economic growth). The control is through M. Any inflationary movement or any increase in demand (in relation to goods and services made available to the community being stable) can be corrected by the government simply by controlling the stock of money available to the economy.

So, it can be seen that if the government did fix the stock of money it would affect spending; spending is limited by the size of money stock. However, spending is not limited to the amount of money existing in the community because V is not stable. As the Radcliffe Committee said[32], "The fact that spending is not limited by the amount of money in existence is sometimes argued by reference to the velocity of circulation of money." They then went on to say "We have not made more use of this concept because we cannot find any reason for supposing, or any experience in monetary history indicating, that there is any limit to the velocity of circulation; it is a statistical concept that tells us nothing directly of the motivation that influences the level of total demand." On the other hand an article in the Midland Bank Review[33] stated that since more attention is being given to the supply of money again, "it is perhaps timely to reconsider the relevance of the velocity of circulation, more especially as, in the ten years since the Radcliffe Committee reported, it has ceased to rise as quickly as it had in the previous ten years".

32. Committee on the Working of the Monetary System, Cmnd 827, August 1959, published by H.M.S.O., para 391 page 133.

33. "Money Supply and the Banks" in M.B.R., Feb. 1969, p.6.

The following exhibit (6.10) is a simple example to show the change in the velocity of circulation from 1970 to 1976. Because MV = PT then

$$V = \frac{PT}{M}$$

where PT equals the gross national product at current market prices, and M equals the value of money supply, M_1 and M_3.

Exhibit 6.10

**Velocity of Circulation
1970-1976**

(figures in £m)

Col 1	Col 2	Col 3	Col 4[a]	Col 5	Col 6[b]
	P × T	M	V	M	V
	GNP	M_1	Velocity	M_3	Velocity
	at current	Money	of	Money	of
Year	market prices	Supply	M_1	Supply	M_3
1970	43,924	8,507	5.16	16,161	2.72
1971	49,656	9,691	5.12	18,192	2.73
1972	55,492	11,225	4.94	21,411	2.59
1973	64,815	12,333	5.26	27,146	2.39
1974	74,958	12,772	5.87	33,938	2.21
1975	93,978	14,735	6.38	37,422	2.51
1976	110,259	17,801	6.19	40,471	2.72

Notes: a ... Col 4 = Col 2 divided by Col 3. Figures correct to 2 places of decimal

b ... Col 6 = Col 2 divided by Col 5. Figures correct to 2 places of decimal

Source: Col 2: Table 1.1 page 3 of "National Income and Expenditure 1966-76" Blue Book, published by HMSO, 1977.

Col 3 and 5: refer to exhibit 6.6

In the period from 1970 to 1976 the following changes took place.

1. The GNP has increased by approximately 151 per cent.

2. M_3 has increased by approximately 150 per cent.

3. M_1 has increased by approximately 109 per cent.

It is a fact that the GNP has climbed faster than M1, but the rise in GNP has been matched by the rise in M_3. This is a simple fact based on a simple example.

The velocity of circulation of M_3 has remained fairly constant over these years, varying between 2.21 and 2.73. On the other hand the velocity of M_1 has varied quite considerably, ranging from 4.94 to 6.38. It can also be seen that the velocities of M_1 and M_3 do not seem to have strong relationship with each other. Looking at the velocity changes from one year to the next, only twice did they move in the same direction; twice when the velocity of M_1 moved down the velocity of M_3 moved upwards; and twice the reverse of this occurred.[34]

34. In all years, M_3 has been greater than M_1; ranging from 1.9 to 2.7 the size of M_1. This might be explained by noting the year to year percentage changes of M_1 and M_3 (in exhibits 11.7 and 11.8). When M_1 percentage change is greater than M_3 the velocity of M_3 rises, and when the percentage change of M_1 from one year to the next is less than that of M_3 the velocity of M_3 falls. So the answer may be found if we knew why the percentage change relationships of M_1 and M_3 change the way they have over recent years.

We know, today, a lot more about M, but not so much about V. What causes V to vary? Is the answer related to P? Is it related to the rapid rise in prices (inflation)?

The favourite question asked in recent years is: should economic policy be based on the QTM? This is a highly debatable question. There are many who say 'No', that money does not matter because it does little to achieve the major economic objectives of employment and economic growth. On the other hand, there are many who say 'Yes', that money does matter because it can control money incomes and inflation. The cause of the debate, it would appear, depends on the stability of V.

Inflation

Inflation, as noted before, generally means a persistent or sustained increase in the prices of goods and services; rising prices for the factors of production (land, labour, capital, enterprise), rising prices for bread, cars, cigarettes, petrol, bus rides, haircuts, etc.. On the other hand, the general public recognise inflation not only by persistent prices rises, but also by a persistent and steady fall in the value of money.

Degrees of Inflation

Inflation is by no means a stranger to the people in the United Kingdom, nor for that matter to people, generally, anywhere in the world. Over time, however, the degree of inflation differs, and has been very noticeable in the U.K..

Economists have put names to various degrees of inflation. The following it is hoped, will clarify these terms.

Creeping inflation. In 1962, using the RPI as the price indicator, the rate of inflation for the year was less than 2.5 per cent. In 1963 prices rose by 1.5 per cent. From January 1962 to December 1963 the increase was approximately 4.2 per cent; showing a steady and continual rise. However, the annual rate of inflation was less than 3 per cent. When the degree of inflation is 3 per cent or less it is called creeping inflation.

Moderate inflation. In 1965 inflation increased by about 4.2 per cent, and in 1966 by a further 3.5 per cent. In these years the United Kingdom had what is called moderate inflation; where the degree of change is greater than 3 per cent but less than 6 per cent.

Accelerated or galloping inflation. In 1970 the rate of inflation was around 7 per cent, and in 1971 it was near 7.5 per cent. This degree of inflation is normally given the term accelerated or galloping inflation. Once it gets up to this speed it is very difficult to stop. This degree of inflation, it is claimed, sets in around 6 per cent and ends around 15 per cent.

Hyper inflation. In 1974 inflation in the U.K. was approximately 17 per cent, and in 1975 about 21.5 per cent. This level of inflation was a stranger to the people in the U.K.. When degrees of inflation go beyond 15 per cent per annum we normally call it hyper inflation.[35]

Student should not be dismayed by the above. The degree of inflation in the U.K. is winding its way downwards; from a hyper inflation situation to an accelerated position. From almost 14 per cent in 1976 to just over 9 per cent in 1977. Perhaps we can term a downward movement of this type 'decelerated inflation'.

The greater the degree of inflation the greater the degree of intensity required to stop it. The usual saying is that inflation can not be cured, but it can be halted. The degree of intensity relates to the pressures applied in society; the need is to apply just the right amount of pressure in the right places.

Creeping inflation is considered to be beneficial to a country with great growth potential, for example, India at the start of the 1960s. In a country such as the U.K. in the 1960s, with full employment and low potential growth rates, it does little harm to our orderly economic and social life. We can easily learn to 'live with it'. However, as inflation accelerates the economic and social consequences become more and more unsatisfactory. These will be discussed later in this chapter. In the meantime, it should be remembered that consequences become more and more unsatisfactory the higher the degree of inflation.

Causes of Inflation

The typical question asked is: What causes inflation?

In chapter 2 it was established that there is a relationship between demand, supply and price; as noted by the price mechanism. Changes in prices, and therefore inflationary prices, can be considered by looking at changes that affect demand *and* changes that affect the cost in supplying goods and services. A third element arises in the mixed economy; the tendency by the government to interfere with the price mechanism and therefore price movements. In other words, it is widely accepted that there are three causes of inflation, namely:

1. excess demand pressures,

2. increase in the costs of production, and

3. certain government activities.

Before discussing these, it must be noted that once an inflationary situation develops it becomes difficult to isolate the cause with any precision. For example, an expansion of demand *pulls* up prices. The response to this change, after a time, is for production costs to rise (example: wage

35. Hyper means 'excessive'. The U.K. problem of 1975 was not as great as Germany in 1923. In a period of just 4 months in 1923, the German wholesale price index showed price rises by about 1,000,000,000 or one thousand million per cent. What special name should we call this? super-hyper-inflation?

increases) which *pushes* prices upwards. Increased incomes generate increased demand which is responded to by increased cost, and so on. Inflation, as noted here, is self-generating which develops into an inflationary spiral; known as 'wage-price spiral' or 'price-wage spiral'. With every new demand *pull* situation price increases, and with every new cost *push* situation another twist is given to the inflationary spiral.

Demand-pull inflation. This inflationary situation arises from excess demand in relation to the present price situation. Consumers are willing to purchase more than the quantities being produced. To put it another way, at the current price, demand exceeds supply; there is disequilibrium in the market.

An increase in demand, in relation to a given supply situation, comes about mainly through increased expenditures by the various sectors of the community, such as the general public and government.

From the general public's point of view, this may arise in a variety of different ways, but mainly because more money is available for spending. More money may come from increases in income, or because people are saving less and spending more out of a given income, or because credit facilities have been widened making expenditures possible on goods not previously included, or new credit facilities are introduced.

The government, on the other hand, may wish to increase its expenditures on social service facilities. Increased expenditures may be backed by revenue from taxation, or borrowing from other sectors in the U.K. economy or from overseas.

Whatever the situation, demand exceeds supply and prices are pulled upwards. Some situations may arise generally, affecting the supply of all goods and services; creating shortages in supply in relation to demand. For example, this tends to occur during wars, immediately after wars, or may arise from a 'general strike'. In war time resources are shifted from consumer to war commodities. Consumer demands will exceed supply and pull prices upwards; unless the government is successful in its rationing programme. After the war, pent-up demands will be released but because it takes time to change production from war to consumer goods, supply is short; demand exceeds supply and we have demand pull inflation. General strikes stop the production and supply of many commodities and thereby create a shortage of supply in relation to demand. The result: prices pulled upwards.

Specific situations tend to affect the supply of certain goods and services, although demand may not have changed. These are often referred to as 'bottleneck inflation' situations. It can be caused by many factors such as strikes at one plant. This reduces supply at the strike plant and perhaps at other plants. The longer the strike the greater the problem of supply. Another situation may arise when suppliers dump or burn or hold back supply from the public, for example coffee or oil. This does not, immediately alter the level of demand; so demand will exceed supply and prices for these goods will rise. If such goods are very important to purchasers (high weight in RPI) it will tend to raise the RPI to a figure higher than a commodity that has low weight. In either situation prices will rise but one is more inflationary than the other.

Regardless of whether expenditures remain the same or increase it must be related to the supply situation to determine changes in prices. As long as demand exceeds available supply we have increases in prices and price pull inflation.

Cost-push inflation. This is an inflationary situation that is viewed primarily from the supply side of the price mechanism; the increase in cost in the production of goods and services. It makes no difference whether the increased cost arise from within the community (wage increases) or outside (raw material price increases), as long as it adds to the cost of production it can be viewed as 'cost-push inflation'. This assumes, of course, that there is no change in productivity (output per man does not change). Cost, as a result, will push up the price (unless producers absorb the cost by reducing their profits).

In the United Kingdom, at the present time and over the past few years, the general concensus of opinion, other than that of the Trade Union Congress, is that the inflationary problem has been cost inflation.

The claim is that an accelerated rise in import prices set off the general rise in prices in recent years. Following this there was a substantial rise in internal costs. When these internal costs were superimposed upon the import prices the RPI was bound to move into accelerated and hyper inflation.

Income from employment (wages and salaries), especially wages, are usually singled out for demonstrating 'cost-push' inflation. The reason for this is that income from employment represents a high proportion of the 'gross national product'. In 1966 it was over 68 per cent, and in 1976 over 71 per cent of the GNP. As income from employment took a greater share of the GNP, the gross trading profits of companies fell (from 13.7 per cent in 1966 to 11.3 per cent in 1976). Lower profits, generally speaking, discourage businesses in carrying out investment programmes.

Pure cost inflation situations tend to arise when employment, real output[36] and profits are falling, but wages and prices are rising fast.[37] The United Kingdom has recently experienced the above situation. Wage earners have pushed up supply costs because they are reluctant to accept reductions in wages or changes in real income (what they can purchase with their wages). Wage earners, through their trade unions which have grown considerably in strength at the bargaining tables, have sought wage increases by comparing their situations to past, present and future situations. They compare their wages based on experiences they faced in the past; compare their wages with other people's earnings at the present time; and compare their wage needs to compensate for price changes expected in the future.

36. Real output fell (using gross domestic product at factor cost at 1970 prices) in 1974 compared to 1973, and 1975 compared to 1974.

37. These conditions are often referred to as 'stagflation'.

Most cost inflation situations normally arise from demand inflation situations.

Demand and Cost Inflation

We have seen that demand and cost inflation can be distinguished. Usually they exist at the same time, one tending to feed the other (the inflationary spiral).

Government and Inflation

The government may cause inflation by carrying out certain actions or policies. Increases in taxes on expenditure, such as the value added tax, will push up prices and this can result in a demand for increased wages so wage earners can offset the price increases of the 'basket' they purchase. On the other hand, an increase in taxes on income may make it difficult for wage earners to purchase the same 'basket' as they did before. This would bring pressure from them for increased wages and, thus, add to the cost of supply.

The government controls the money supply. It may simply print more notes in order to finance expenditures that are not covered by revenue, rather than use the tax system, and inflate the economy.

On the other hand the growth of real general government expenditures (GGE) on goods and services has grown faster than the gross national product.[38] This growth of general government claims on resources leaves less for the private sector, and this tends to lead to counter-pressures for increased wages and increased profits which produces accelerating inflation.

These are a few of the examples that could be quoted.

Consequences or effects of inflation

Any change in inflation, up or down, must create gainers or losers. Changes in price movements upwards must have its own special effects. In this section we shall attempt to highlight some of the major consequences.

Inflation and the functions of money. The word 'standard' was used frequently when discussing the functions of money. Standards must be maintained, or, if changed must not be allowed to change by big amounts. Perhaps the one force that tends to erode standards is the considerable change that takes place when purchasing power of money falls (price inflation).

Briefly, a high level of inflation may lead towards the rejection of one form of money (notes) and acceptance of another form which is considered to be the better medium (Germany in 1923). Also, inflation would create chaos to those who use it as a unit of account because it makes it difficult to calculate gains and losses (inflationary accounting problem). Who wants to store

---

38. Both GGE and GNP are at 1970 prices. From 1966 to 1976 total GGE expenditure on goods and services rose by 26 per cent, and the GNP at market prices rose by 24 per cent.

money today knowing it will not have the same value one, two or three years in the future? The same picture can be painted for those who were once willing to wait for payment; inflation would make them less willing to act in the 'deferred payments' field because future money would not have the same purchasing power as it does at the present time.

High rates of inflation tends to erode standards and thus erodes these functions.

Inflation and credit. Rapid inflation also tends to disturb the area of credit. Creditors tend to lose in an inflation because the payments made to them in the future are reduced in value in terms of goods and service they can buy. During an accelerated or hyper inflation, creditors are reluctant to give more credit, and on the other hand, they urge debtors to pay their debts sooner. Debtors gain from inflation. The real value of their debts is reduced; they make payments in depreciated pounds. On the other hand, if they are businessmen they stand to gain because they buy raw materials now (when credit is given) at lower cost and sell at a future date when prices are higher. In an inflationary period debtors are reluctant to pay sooner, in fact they tend to take a longer period of time before repaying their debts.

Inflation and incomes. Some individuals, many old age pensioners, many wage earners who are not in highly organised trade unions, and others, whose money incomes fall behind the rate of inflation will experience a fall in the amount of goods and services they can purchase (real income declines). Others, whose earnings rise faster than the inflationary rate will benefit because they can buy the same basket of goods and services as before and have money left over to increase their standard of living, that is they can purchase more goods and services than they could before.

Persons whose money incomes rise faster than the rate of inflation can purchase real assets, such as land and houses, whereas those who have money incomes that can not keep pace with the inflation may have to sell their real assets, such as land and houses, simply to maintain their standard of living. One sector of the community increases its wealth, and the wealth of others falls.

Inflation then creates a redistribution of wealth and incomes because inflation does not have a social conscience.

Inflation and consumption-savings. Inflation is likely to increase the level of consumer purchasing in the economy. People who expect inflation to continue into the future may rush to purchase now when prices are low rather than later when prices are high. This, naturally, creates production problems for businessmen.

People who hold their spare money in savings accounts (deposit accounts, building society accounts) are likely to receive interest that is far below the inflation rate. They may no longer find the down payment on a house they had hoped to purchase is the same as before; the price paid to savers for savings falls in relation to the rise in price of houses for sale. Leaving their money in these accounts will result in a loss of purchasing power in the future. As a result, many will withdraw their money and purchase other goods which they expect will hold their own value during the inflationary movement. They might buy antiques, diamonds, gold or rare stamps.

Inflation tends to lower the amount being saved and increase consumption.

Inflation and business activity. Creeping inflation tends to stimulate aggregate demand and economic growth of the economy. Businessmen, in the attempt to supply the increased demand will increase output with existing plant in the hopes of making higher profits, and where necessary invest in new plant (assuming resources of the factors are available). As long as the inflation rate at home does not exceed the inflation rate of foreign competitors the businesses should prosper.

However, when a country is faced with accelerated or hyper inflation, such as the U.K. has recently faced, then businesses and the community tend to suffer. The prices of home produced goods and services tend to rise at a rate faster than foreign economies. Although aggregate demand may increase, it will be directed towards lower priced foreign goods. U.K. export prices rise relative to prices in countries that normally purchase U.K. goods and services; demand for U.K. production declines. In both cases, home producers face a fall in aggregate demand. Firms cut back on production, making less use of existing plant and other factors of production. Factors will gradually become unemployed. Lower production increases the cost per unit of output and pushes up prices. Inflation is fed with inflation. Profits are less than before and there is no need to invest in new plant and machinery because firms have unused capacity. Not a happy situation for U.K. businessmen, nor for any business organisation in any country that is faced with hyper inflation.

Inflation and the balance of payments. The effect of inflation will depend on the level of inflation in the home country and inflation in countries that normally trade with the home country. However, inflation of all types, and especially hyper inflation, tend to push up home prices more than overseas prices. As a result: imports become cheaper than home produced goods and consumers and producers tend to purchase from overseas rather than at home. The volume and value of imports rise. On the other hand the prices of goods and services of the home country when sold abroad tend to be higher than the prices of similar commodities in the overseas trading country. The volume of exports will fall, and even though prices have increased the value will also tend to fall. The relationships between total receipts from exports and total payments for imports is that payments exceed receipts. In other words, the home country, such as the U.K., is bound to suffer a deficit on her trade balance (current account of the balance of payments). If the home country already has a deficit — the deficit will grow larger.

Inflation and the government. As stated before, one of the major internal economic objectives is that of maintaining reasonable stability of the internal purchasing power of money; maintaining a high and stable level of employment; and achieving a steady growth of the economy and improving the standard of living for members of its society. Creeping inflation does not normally require the government to take drastic actions to keep this type of inflation in check. But, accelerated and hyper inflation creates abnormal problems.

All one has to do is to look at the action of the government in the last few years to see the enormous problem faced by the government seeking to achieve those objectives: especially controls to check and lower the rate of inflation.[39] For example, it was reported in an article of the Economic Progress Report that: "A tough new policy for attacking inflation was outlined in Parliament by the Prime Minister on 11 July (1975)." Also, that "A sharp reduction in the rate of inflation is now an over-riding priority for the nation and a pre-condition for a reduction of unemployment and an increase in investment. This will not be possible without greater restraint on the rate of increase in wages and salaries."[40] Its intentions then were set out.

Creeping inflation we can live with; it does not disrupt, to any great degree, our orderly way of life. But, hyper inflation creates chaos; it does nothing but disrupt the orderly way of life.

Money

As we have seen, there are many aspects of money; some are relatively easy and others difficult to explain and comprehend. However, there is much more to this subject than that given here, as students will find out as they progress through this and other business books. It is a complex subject but it is one businessmen should understand better. Their business life revolves around money.

Yet, important as money is in business life, and to life in general, it should be remembered that it is something we do not want for itself — we want it for the goods and services that can be purchased with it.

---

39. Students should search out information in Economic Progress Reports which are prepared by the Treasury's Information Division and issued monthly. Look at calendar of events in the above mentioned reports and in other publications, such as National Institute Economic Review, The Journal of the Economics Association publication 'Economics', etc..

40. "The attack on inflation" in E.P.R. No. 65, August 1975, page 1.

Assignments

1. What functions are performed by money? Briefly examine the effects that inflation has on the performance of these functions.

2. What does inflation mean and how does it arise? What do you suggest might be done to cure it?

3. You are asked by the Financial Director of your organisation to prepare an essay on 'The decline in the value of the pound sterling during the period 1970 to 1979'. You are requested to submit the essay within seven days.

4. "Any change in inflation must create gainers and losers". Develop this idea by relating it to:

   a) credit,

   b) incomes, and

   c) wealth.

5. The Quantity Theory of Money is expressed as an identity $MV = PT$. What is the meaning of each of these letters? What does it say?

6. M_1, sterling M_3 and M_3 are different definitions of money supply. Explain these definitions in words. Explain why you would not be happy to accept the figures associated with each of these as being absolutely accurate.

Chapter 7

Population

Learning objectives:
At the end of your study of this chapter you should be able to:
1. explain the relationship between the world population and land.
2. explain the relationship between the population and the land in the United Kingdom.
3. explain the present structure of United Kingdom population.
4. identify the major changes that have taken place in the U.K. population structure.
5. identify the major changes that have taken place in the composition of the U.K. population structure since World War II.

Population is a large and complex subject but, as Sir William Beveridge said, "The problem of population, for a variety of reasons, is one of the most interesting as well as one of the most important in the whole range of social science. It has as many aspects (economics, political, sociological, biological, psychological) as there are branches of social science. It takes a different shape from one generation to another".[1]

The changing shape probably affects all social institutions, but in different ways and to different degrees. Institutions are affected because it is not possible to isolate the people that make up the population from (a) their activities (births, deaths, divorce, marriage, work, etc.) and (b) their close associations with organisations (business, social, political, etc.). There are many inter-relationships of population and institutions at a point in time and over time.

These inter-relationships, to understand them properly, require a vast amount of knowledge covering the many disciplines mentioned above. In fact, the material in this and the few chapters that follow on population must be seen as simply "skimming the surface" of the topic.

Population Defined

The term population, as used by statisticians, consists of all objects and things from which one obtains information relevant to an inquiry. For example, if obtaining information on family expenditure then the family is the population; if seeking information on forests then trees are the population. Our task, in this chapter, is to seek information about the total

1. "The Population Problem" in the Political Quarterly, April-June 1946 p133.

number of persons inhabiting the United Kingdom[2]; its present structure and composition since world war II.

Population — 3 pieces of information

1. Population studies relate to the flow of persons over time and, therefore, must be seen as a dynamic rather than a static subject.

2. Vital statistics refers to statistics concerning life, or the conditions affecting life and the maintenance of population. They are *strictly figures* that relate to the population as a whole, and probably, the most vital of statistics is that of how many people a country has. Other statistics that are vital to the whole population are births, deaths, marriages and migration.

3. Demography is a science that makes use of vital statistics. It is concerned with *facts about changes* that take place within the population (births, deaths, disease, divorce, marriage, migration, etc.). The demographer tries to measure population change and predict its future behaviour.

Collecting Population Statistics

Vital statistics are obtained, in the United Kingdom, by taking a census of population and by registration of certain events, such as births, deaths and marriages.

A census (Latin word meaning 'count') of population provides us with a snapshot of the population. It provides the chance of getting in touch with every single person in the community, at a point in time (a certain time on a specified date in the year). It is carried out periodically — in the United Kingdom a census of population has been carried out every ten years since 1801, except for 1941. In 1966 a sample of ten per cent of the population was taken.

In order to note the number and condition of the people, a series of questions are asked, and answers required, about:

age, sex, occupation, nationality, etc.,

whether single, divorced, married,

number of children born of marriage,

education, occupation, and

details of the household and relationship to the head of the household. Sometimes other information is required, for example, in the 1951 census questions were asked about household arrangements: fixed bath? kitchen sink? etc..

---

2. British Isles is an embracing term covering England, Wales, Scotland, Northern Ireland, Eire, and the off shore islands immediately surrounding these countries.
    United Kingdom is a shortened version of 'United Kingdom of Great Britain and Northern Ireland'. It consists of England, Wales, Scotland and Northern Ireland.
    Great Britian refers to England, Wales and Scotland.

Because the census is taken every ten years it leaves too big a gap to record the progress in the size of the population; the Registrar General wants to know year to year details. To this end he makes estimates from information gathered together under 'registration data'. Registration data mainly consists of:

Births.   This usually gives data such as date of birth of new child, its sex, age of mother, length of marriage, number of previous children.

Deaths.   Data collected usually consists of sex of deceased, age at death, occupation, cause of death, place of death, whether single, widowed or divorced at time of death.

Marriages.   These are registered at the time of marriage. Data collected from marriage certificates contain such items as age of man and woman, condition of each, that is to say, single, widowed, divorced, occupation of persons concerned.

These statistics, census every ten years and registration data every year, enable comparisons to be made. They throw light on important changes but they do not explain the changes.

World's Land and Population

Before discussing the population of the United Kingdom or of the world it is important to consider the area of land that supports the population.

The land mass of the earth, represents approximately 29 per cent of the globe's surface. This surface is not entirely habitable: it includes forests, mountains, ice covered land, deserts. These prohibit, to a significant extent, their being used by the human race.

The land mass in the world totals approximately 36,232,230,000 acres (or 56,613,000 square miles or roughly 14,662,685 hectares). When we remove deserts, ice covered land, etc., to arrive at an area of land suitable for cultivation and grazing for feeding the world's inhabitants, it would total, roughly, 4,800,000,000 acres.

This is land which feeds the world's population. In 1950 the population of the world was approximately 2,400,000,000. If we relate this population to the world's area of land we would find that each person would have, if land were equally shared, about 15 acres, However, only 2 acres of this would be cultivated and grazing land.

World population does not remain constant; the tendency is for it to increase. In 1974 it was estimated that the population had risen to approximately 4,000,000,000. This is an increase, over a span of 24 years, of almost 57 per cent. Thus, in 1974 each person would have about 9 acres of land but only 1.2 acres of cultivated and grazing land. Population may increase but the land area does not, or if it does it does not increase by very much. This creates a problem of feeding the world's population.

When looking into the future, say to the year 2000, all forecasts indicate the world's population will be more than 6,000,000,000. Some simple arithmetic will immediately show that the acres per person becomes much less than in 1974. In fact, each person would have about 6 acres of land but less than 1 acre of cultivated and grazing land; 0.8 acres to be more exact.

The big question is: can the world support an ever increasing population? What does this mean in terms of feeding the world's population? While there is no answer to how much food is needed for a full healthy and active life, the conclusion reached by the Food and Agricultural Organisation,[3] in 1952, indicated that there are probably few communities whose daily minimum requirements are less than 2,200 calories. In the early 1950's it was calculated that over 2/3rds of the world's population did not have enough to eat, and this was considerably higher than the period before world war II when it was calculated to be about 1/2.[4]

There is definitely an indication that there is a tendency for the food supply of the world to be less than that required. Although man has been able to increase the yield per acre of foodstuffs it, apparently, is not sufficient to feed the increasing population of the world. Practically all the best land is being cultivated. It is true that land under cultivations can be increased by reclaiming land (Holland) or by irrigating desert land (Egypt) but there is the opposing force of soil erosion which is more noticeable in less soil-educated countries of the world.

Neither land, nor people, are spread evenly throughout the world. Some regions in the world have a larger number of persons per square mile than others. The following shows the density of population in 1950.

Region	Area in square miles	1950 population	Density per square mile
Africa	11,053,000	199,000,000	18.00
America	16,663,000	328,000,000	19.68
Asia	17,008,000	1,272,000,000	74.79
Europe	3,700,000	594,000,000	160.54
Oceania	3,299,000	13,000,000	3.94
	51,723,000	2,406,000,000	46.52
Artic and Antarctic	4,890,000		
	56,613,000		

(Note: Population figures from "Population Bulletin No. 1" United Nations, published in December 1951. European figures include Asiatic U.S.S.R.)

The table clearly brings out the unequal distribution of land and population. It does not tell us what the situation is today or what it will be be in the future. Nor, does it tell us about the nations in the regions, that is to say those that are developed, such as the U.S.A., U.K., West Germany, etc., and those that are developing, such as Bangladesh, India, Mexico, etc..

Most of the developing nations of the world are located in Asia (excluding U.S.S.R.), Africa, and the Americas south of the U.S. border. The developed countries are located mainly in North America and Europe.

3.   FAO's "Second World Food Survey"

4.   From "World Population and Resources", P.E.P. Report, Sept. 1955, p24.

In 1950, over 65 per cent of the world population lived in the developing nations; in 1970 the figure was over 70 per cent. Looking into the future, in the year 2000, it is expected to be over 78 per cent. These figures must be considered against the background of poverty which has already been mentioned. World poverty is centred mainly in the developing nations, and yet it is in these nations that the 'population explosion' occurs. It can only lead to increased world poverty, and fear that increasing world population can only lead to more and more misery.

'Population explosion' is best explained by noting the words of Robert S. McNamara, President of the International Bank for Reconstruction and Development. He stated that: It took mankind more than a million years to reach a population of 1,000,000,000. But the second billion required only 120 years; the third billion 32 years; and the fourth billion 15 years.[5] Mr. McNamara notes that rapid acceleration in the rate of growth of the world's population has finally reached its peak or is about to in the 1980's yet he claims, there is need for 'far more attention' to be given to world population growth.

The above was related mainly to feeding the world population. Not only must humans be fed they must be sheltered, clothed and provided with other material necessities. This requires the use of a variety of raw materials supplied by the earth and unlike agricultural products, are not annually renewable, such as oil, coal, lead, zinc, etc.. These materials, at the present time, are not spread evenly over the globe, nor are they everlasting. Energy materials will not last forever. In fact, it has been calculated that the world should run out of oil reserves around the year 2005, followed 20 years later by natural gas, and uranium by 2070. Coal, the energy source of the first revolution, should be available until the year 2220. Of course, all these figures are based on present day consumption levels. If the increasing population of the world increases their level of consumption, then increased production will tend to lower reserves so they will be depleted earlier than the year stated.

Why the increase in population? Basically, the answer is very simple; more children are being born and people are living longer. Behind the simple answer lies a large number of occurrences; the factors of which are linked to the economic and social environment. For example, in the past there was improvement in nutrition and this tended to reduce mortality among infants and young children. Families were not only having larger families (less died at child birth and early years) but the health of the children was better than before. Later, improvements in medicine and medical care increased fertility. Behind these forces was the increased use of children to improve the circumstances of the family (more income, more food, etc.); in other words to improve the standard of living and quality of life of the family. At

5.   A speech given at the Massachusetts Institute of Technology, Cambridge, Massachusetts, U.S.A., on April 28, 1977 and reported in 'Finance and Development' quarterly publication of the IMF and IBRD, June 1977, p8.

the upper end of the age structure, people were living longer. Before world war II, on average, a person living in the developing nations could expect to live to his early thirties. Improvements in nutrition and medicine/medical standards raised the age expectancy of life to about 50 in the latter 1960's. During this time the place of the woman was in the home and to raise children.

The slowing down of population growth has been attributed to many factors, such as: improvement in education; planning the family and use of contraceptives; changed status of women; further improvements in health and thus need for smaller family size, etc..

Nevertheless the growth of population is still increasing although at a slower rate; in the early 1970's the rate per annum was between 2 and 2.2 per cent. The world, and the developing nations especially, is faced with the age-old problem formed by the Reverend T. R. Malthus that population is outstripping the food supply. This idea will be discussed in the next chapter.

This is the world in which we, in the United Kingdom, live.

United Kingdom's Land and Population

The British Isles began to take shape about 10 million years ago but the land features changed considerably since that time to the shape and size that it is today.

Today, the United Kingdom has a land area, excluding inland waterways, of approximately 59,562,240 acres,[6] which is less than one-fifth of one per cent of the land area of the world. The approximate area, in acres, of each of the countries making up the U.K. are:

England	32,060,800
Scotland	19,069,440
Wales	5,100,160
Northern Ireland	3,331,840

A large proportion of the U.K. land area, like the world, is not satisfactory for cultivation and grazing. In fact, agricultural land under crops and grass, in June 1975 was approximately 29,729,000 acres and rough grazing totalled about 16,198,000 acres,[7] a total of 45,927,000 acres.

This is the land that supports the home population of the U.K.. Home population refers to persons who are actually present in the area of the countries making up the U.K.. These figures are less than 'total

---

6. Acres and square miles are imperial measurements of area. To convert acres into square miles divide total U.K. acres by 640 acres. Square kilometres is a metric measurement. To obtain square kilometres divide total U.K. acres by 247.105 acres. To convert to hectares, another metric measurement, divide total U.K. acres by 2.47105 acres.

7. Non cultivation and grazing land was about 13,635,240 acres, of which forest area was 5,048,355 acres. Information obtained from Annual Abstract of Statistics 1976, HMSO, Table 1, 247 and 254.

population'.[8] The home population of the U.K., for various years, was as follows:

mid-year 1951	50,290,000
mid-year 1961	52,807,000
mid-year 1971	55,610,000
mid-year 1975	55,962,000[9]

Mid-1951. The population of the U.K. in mid-1951 was over 4,000,000 greater than that taken in the 1931 census; an increase of approximately 9.2 per cent. The annual average increase in population, over the 20 year span, was slightly less than ½ per cent. When relating the home population in mid-1951 to the land area of the U.K. it shows that the number of acres per person was about 1.18.

To make these 1951 figures more meaningful we can relate home population to 'density per square mile' so we can compare it with the densities of the world and its regions; shown a few pages before. On average, there were approximately 540 person for each square mile.[10] This was more than 3⅓ times greater than Europe, and more than 11½ times that for the world as a whole. In other words, the U.K. was, in mid-1951, one of the most densely populated areas in the world.

Mid-1951 to mid-1971. The population of the U.K., over these 20 years, increased by 5,320,000; more than in the previous 20 years. The increase in percentage terms was slightly less than 10.6; an average annual increase of just over ½ per cent. The size of the U.K. population was increasing at an increasing rate.

Mid-1971 to mid-1975. This 4 year span showed a population increase of 452,000 or just over 4/5ths of one per cent; an annual average increase of 1/10th of 1 per cent. Although the population is increasing in absolute terms the rate of increase is at a decreasing rate. The population of the U.K. is increasing but at a much slower rate.

Mid-1975. At this time the home population of the U.K. was estimated to be 55,962,000. The number of acres per person has fallen from the 1951 situation to 1.06 (1951 it was 1.18), and the density or number of persons per square mile increased (from 540 in 1951) to 601.

Future. What will be the size of the U.K. home population in 2000 or 2001? Will it be 66,500,000 or 60,000,000 or about the same as it was in mid-1975? It is not possible to predict the size of population 25 or even 20 years into the future with certainty. It is not possible to predict the way people will act — marriage, having children, etc..

8.   According to the Central Statistical Office on p.6 in the Annual Abstract of Statistics — total population consists of the home population *plus* members of H.M. forces domiciled within the area but serving overseas or in another part of the U.K. *minus* members of H.M. forces, Commonwealth forces and foreign armed forces present in the area but not domiciled in it.

9.   Taken from table 6 of the Annual Abstract of Statistics 1976, by C.S.O., published by HMSO, 1976.

10. Divide the mid-1951 home population of U.K. by 93,066 square miles.

136

A document written in 1970 stated "The total population of Great Britain is approximately 56 million; by 2001 that is in thirty years time, it is projected that the population will have risen to 66½ million".[11] On the other hand, the total population projection for the U.K. made by the Office of Population Censuses and Surveys was 58,300,000.[12] In estimating the size of population in 2000 or 2001 one must consider the base population and variations of certain elements (births, deaths, migration) taken year by year into the future.[13] A chart in Social Trends (chart 1.6, page 65, Social Trends No. 7) shows the population of Great Britian ranging from approximately 54,500,000 to about 59,350,000. Naturally, U.K. figures would be higher than this by about 2 million. Between these ranges it would appear that the U.K. in the year 2000 would have a population approximating 57,000,000; higher than mid-1975.

Changes in the U.K. population there will be!

At this time it might be worthwhile to note the changes in home population from one year to the next in terms of percentages; starting with the change from 1951 to 1952 and ending with 1974 to 1975. This is best represented diagramatically and is shown in Exhibit 7.1.

Exhibit 7.1

U.K. Home Population Annual Rate of Change
Mid-1951 to mid-1975

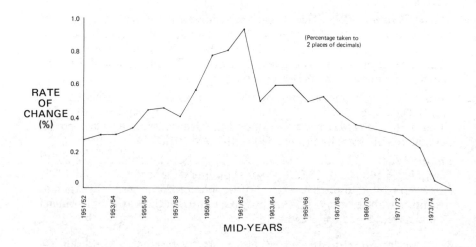

(Percentage taken to 2 places of decimals)

RATE OF CHANGE (%)

MID-YEARS

11. "Population" A document prepared by the Research Department of the Labour party for presentation to the 48th National Conference of Labour Women, 1971. page 2.

12. Taken from table 1.1 page 62 in Social Trends, C.S.O., published by H.M.S.O. Table source was 'Census of Population Reports, "Population Projections 1975-2015"'

13. For further details about population — refer to page 235 Social Trends, No. 7, by C.S.O., published by H.M.S.O., 1976.

1951-1975 — Yearly Rates of Change

From mid-1951 to mid-1975 the home population of the United Kingdom increased by 5,672,000. From one year to the next, over this period of time, population steadily increased until mid-1974. From 1974 to 1975 it decreased by 3,000. Overall the population was increasing but the rate of increase did not always increase.

From mid-1951 to mid-1962 U.K. population was increasing and Exhibit 7.1 shows the rate of increase was also moving upward. From mid-1962 to mid-1974 the population was still increasing but the rate of increase was falling. In other words, U.K. population was increasing, but at a decreasing rate. From mid-1974 to mid-1975 population decreased and the rate of population change was still on the decrease.

Why did these changes take place? What forces in our society were operating to create this situation? What problems do such changes create? What effect will it have on the future population of the U.K.? There are many questions that can be raised. As stated previously, these statistics throw light on important changes but they do not explain the changes. The inter-relationships are many, individual knowledge small, and it is impossible to attempt answering all these questions or others that may arise.

Countries of the U.K.

Previously we noted the land area, in acres, of England, Scotland, Wales and Northern Ireland, but we did not associate the population of each country to the land. Briefly, the relationship between the population and the land are as follows:

Country	Mid-1975 Population	Acres per Person	Persons per square mile
England	46,454,000	0.69	927.32
Scotland	5,206,000	3.66	174.72
Wales	2,765,000	1.84	346.97
Northern Ireland	1,537,000	2.17	295.24

The land area relates to all land, not only to cultivated and grazing land. Thus, the figures in the last two columns exaggerate the true relationship between population and land. If we only considered the supporting land the acres per person would be less, and persons per square mile more.

England is the most densely populated of the four countries. The change from 1951 has been considerable; rising from 823 to 927 persons per square mile, and this makes England one of the most densely populated countries in the world. In fact, the average density per square mile for the world in 1975 was approximately 78 which means England's density is almost 12 times higher. It is understandable why people often state that this is beyond the 'optimum population'[14] — an ideal position between the land and its people.

14. This subject will be discussed in the next chapter.

Smaller Areas

Where are the greatest population densities in the U.K.? How can one compare social and economic conditions in one area of the country to another? Because one section of the country is not like others in all respects it is important to collect statistics for smaller areas. The Government has found it useful to create boundaries between one region and another; one county and another, etc..

The areal unit (for example: regions, counties, wards, etc.), once chosen, establishes a standard classification of area, and the statistics collected for these areas makes it possible to compare one area with another for different variables (employment, unemployment, mortality rates, birth rates, migration, housing, health, etc.). This information is vital for planning an policies.

New counties were created by local government reorganisation in England and Wales in 1974,[15] and Scotland in 1975. As a result, some counties disappeared off the political map. The areal unit had to be reconsidered. As a result standard regions in England were revised in 1974 to bring them into line with the new counties. There are now 11 standard regions in the U.K.: 8 regions in England, and one each for Scotland, Wales and Northern Ireland.

Standard Regions and Counties — England

The standard regions for England, defined in terms of new counties, are as follows:

EAST ANGLIA	—Cambridgeshire, Norfolk, Suffolk.
EAST MIDLANDS	—Derbyshire, Leicesterhire, Lincolnshire, Northamptonshire, Nottinghamshire.
NORTHERN	—Cleveland, Cumbria, Durham, Northumberland, Tyne and Wear.
NORTH WEST	—Cheshire, Greater Manchester, Lancashire, Merseyside.
SOUTH EAST	—Bedfordshire, Berkshire, Buckinghamshire, East Sussex, Essex, Greater London, Hampshire, Hertfordshire, Isle of Wight, Kent, Oxfordshire, Surrey, West Sussex.
SOUTH WEST	—Avon, Cornwall, Devon, Dorset, Gloucestershire, Somerset, Wiltshire.
WEST MIDLANDS	—Hereford and Worcester, Salop, Staffordshire, Warwickshire, West Midlands.
YORKSHIRE AND HUMBERSIDE	—Humberside, North Yorkshire, South Yorkshire, West Yorkshire.

15. Local Government Act, 1972. Came into effect on 1 April 1974.

Geographical Distribution of U.K. Population

Chapter one noted that the U.K. is a mixed economy and that many decisions are made by central and local government. This, of course, requires a break down of national population (and resources) details into smaller areas. When decisions are planned forward, it becomes more important to have these regional statistics.

The National Plan, when formulated in the early 1960s, set targets for growth in terms of total output five years forward. This necessitated more detailed information about the regions, especially manpower, to ensure these targets could be met. Thus the need to obtain more details about the regions; past, present and future. To plan for the future "the General Register Office, now the Office of Population Censuses and Surveys (OPCS), became more and more involved in providing data — in particular up-to-date population projections — for the policy studies carried out both by central government departments and the Regional Planning Councils."[16]

The geographical distribution of the home population for the standard regions, existing at 1 April 1975, was as follows:

South East......................16,936,000
North West......................6,577,000
West Midlands...................5,178,000
Yorkshire and Humberside........4,894,000
South West......................4,233,000
East Midlands...................3,728,000
North...........................3,126,000
East Anglia.....................1,780,000
Scotland 5,206,000
Wales...........................2,765,000
Northern Ireland 1,537,000

All regions have increased in size from 1911 to 1971, but as the population of the U.K. has slowed down in its growth it is not surprising to note that some regions are declining in size.[17] Of the 8 English standard regions, 5 have moved downwards. The most surprising of these is the South East which has traditionally been one of the fastest growing areas in the country. As Richard Campbell said "the 'drift to the South East' appears now to have ended." His projections of this region up to mid 1991 (based on mid 1974 data) shows a continuing decrease. This decrease for the South East is noticeable from 1972, as well as the North region. The North West shows the start of a decline since 1973 and since 1974 so do the West Midlands and Yorkshire and Humberside. The three remaining area (East Anglia, East Midlands and the South West) have continuously shown increases and projections to mid 1991 shows that the trend is likely to continue.

16. "Local population projections" by Richard Campbell, in Population Trends 5, Autumn 1976, p9.
17. 1975 figures (table) based on Table 17 and changing situation noted from Tables 16 and 17 in Annual Abstract of Statistics 1976, HMSO.

Another way of looking at the geographical pattern is to note the urban/rural split. Taking a look at the U.K. the trend showed a movement towards urban areas from 1911 to 1951 and somewhere between 1951-61 the movement has been back towards rural districts. The following figures, percentages, based on census details,[18] are as follows:

U.K. Urban/Rural Split
1911 to 1971

	1911	1931	1951	1961	1971
Urban areas	75.8	78.1	78.9	78.3	76.9
Rural districts	24.2	21.9	21.1	21.7	23.1

Prior to local government reorganisation in 1974 there were, in England and Wales, 1,366 local authorities, and it was reasonably easy to separate urban and rural populations. However, in 1974 the number of local authorities was reduced to 403 and a principle behind the reorganisation was that towns and country could be combined in a single administrative unit. This creates problems for separating population into the urban/rural split.

Geographical patterns can also be established by breaking down national population into 'metropolitan counties'[19] and other counties. Three of the metropolitan counties, in mid-1975, had populations over two million (in order of size: West Midlands, Greater Manchester, West Yorkshire), and the other three had populations between 1,193,000 and 1,588,000.

Cities, too, are important in establishing population patterns. The largest city in the United Kingdom is London. Inner London, in 1971, had a population of 2,772,000; Outer London 4,680,000; these two together form Greater London. The second largest city was Birmingham (1,015,000), followed by Glasgow (897,000), Liverpool (610,000) and Manchester (544,000).[20]

Shape of Total Population

Knowledge about population in various areas within a country is important to planners and policy makers, but so too is information about the make-up of total population. Is population growth in the U.K. normal? What shape does it take?

Normal Population Structure
The age distribution of the population of Great Britain, in 1891 and 1901, took the shape of a pyramid, shown below, and was considered to be a 'normal distribution of population'.

18. Percentages are based on figures in Table 16 of Annual Abstract of Statistics, 1976, HMSO.

19. Metropolitan counties being: Greater Manchester, Merseyside, South Yorkshire, Tyne and Wear, West Midlands, West Yorkshire.

20. Students can find information about their towns, cities by looking at Census of Population publications.

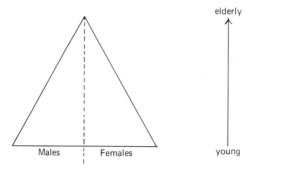

It can be seen that every age group at the base of the pyramid was larger than the next older group, and this group was larger than the next, and so on.

The reason for this shape:

births in 1891 were larger than any preceding year; the year before that larger than the previous year, and so on, and

each group, as they progressed through life, became smaller and smaller as deaths took their toll year by year.

In other words, the elderly came from a much smaller number of births compared to the younger generation, and as they became older many of their age group died each year and the size of this group became smaller and smaller year by year.

Abnormal Population Structure — 1947

Any shape that differs from the above is considered to be abnormal; often referred to, today, as a bulging population.

In 1947, the population structure for Great Britain looked roughly as follows:

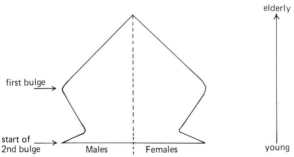

The above shapes are like snapshots of the British population taken in 1891 and 56 years later. Noticeably, there has been considerable change. To understand what has happened in the intervening years we would need many snapshots at different points of time, or better yet, a moving picture. Basically, the change took place because of changes in the number of births, deaths and migration. These would have to be studied to have a better understanding of population movements.

In 1947, the picture shows two bulges in the population structure. The first bulge occurred in the age group 35 to 44, and the second in the 0 to 4 age group. The last bulge came into existence in the period immediately after the end of world war II.

The 35 to 44 age group were those born between the years 1903 and 1912. In 1947, this age group formed a part of the population that makes up the work force of the country. In 1975 the survivors of this group formed the 63 to 72 age group (much smaller in size than in 1947). Many had already retired and other were soon to join their ranks. These 'senior citizens', in their life time, have witnessed two world wars and the big depression in the early 1930's.

The 0 to 4 age group in 1947, now, in 1975 formed the 28 to 32 age group. They have gone through the educational system and many make up the work force whilst others are unemployed. This age group have lived in a period of rising standards of living. They have never witnessed a major war, nor a deep-seated depression.

The contrast between these age groups, at the present time, and over time, invites attention.

An interesting feature of a bulging population is the impact it has or will have on various social and economic activities. For example, a larger number of births at one time compared to a smaller number of births in previous years would require more midwives and health visitors, or, if this was not possible then it would require an increased work load from the existing number of midwives and health visitors. Eventually, these children would start school. Forming a much larger group than previous entrants there would be need for more teachers and teacher training. Additional schools would have to be built and more educational materials made available. If none of these educational improvements took place it would mean, very simply, that these children would have to study in larger groups, and in overcrowded classrooms.

Already we can see the problems that would arise as they go into the next age group replacing a group that was smaller in number. Conversely, when smaller numbers follow larger numbers then the opposite situations occur, that is to say, less need for training teachers, smaller classes and under utilised schools.

A considerable amount of forward planning must be carried out if the members of a bulging age group are to have similar opportunities and advantages to the age groups just in front of them.

Now, we begin to understand why we cannot consider a bulging population as a normal population.

Students should follow their age group through the years; through their educational years at further and higher educational institutes; through their work life and eventually into retirement. Note the problems that arise if the group is larger than or smaller than the previous group or the age group just behind. Note the number of organisations that directly and indirectly affect your lives. What are the likely problems and what are the likely effects of population bulge on economic, legal, political and social institutions? Later in the book certain areas will be investigated in greater depth, for example education and employment. Here, we are simply setting the scene for future consideration.

The main factor between 1891 and 1947 has been the trend of annual births — upwards to 1903 and declining (except for odd years) to 1941. From 1947 the trend was once again upwards. We have already noted changes in the home population and rates of change year by year (exhibit 7.1), but it would be interesting to look at the age group structure in the 1970's.

Abnormal Population Structure — 1975

In mid-1975 the snapshot of the United Kingdom (not Great Britain as previously shown) shows another shape; different from the 1891 and 1947 age group structure. An idea of this shape is shown below:

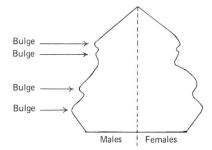

This shape shows four bulges. An interesting situation is that the 0 to 4 age group is smaller than the 5 to 19 age groups. This is not noticeable from the above shape, so a more accurate picture is provided in Exhibit 7.2.

Exhibit 7.2 shows the age structure of the mid-1975 population; the population being separated into male and female sectors. We previously noted that the home population for this point of time was estimated to be 55,962,000. Of this, the male sector totalled 27,232,000 and females the remaining 28,730,000. Females outnumbered males by almost 1½ million. A closer look at the exhibit will show that there are more males than females in age groups up to 40-44 and from 45 years of age onwards females outnumber males. This has not always been the case.

In the British population of 1947 males outnumbered females from birth to age group 20-24 and then the reverse situation occurred. In 1891 females outnumbered males from age group 5-9 onwards. Thus, males are not dying in their early years in recent years at the rate they were at the end of the 19th century.

In each of the years noted, 1891, 1947 and 1975, there have been more males than females in the early years of life. The reason for this is that there is a natural tendency for more boy babies to be born than girls; an event noticeable throughout the world. Rough estimates indicate that out of every

Exhibit 7.2

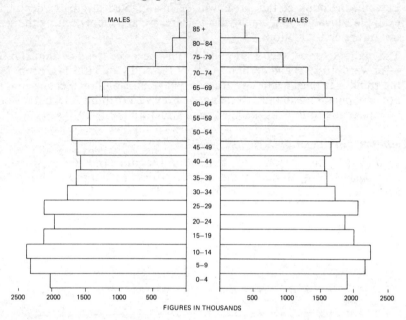

Mid 1975
Bulging Population of U.K.

FIGURES IN THOUSANDS

100 births, 51 will be boys. This information may not immediately seem worthwhile, but it would be to firms producing clothing for children (blue for boys, pink for girls).

What is the male-female relationship in the countries of the U.K.? The following provides this information, (population figures are in thousands).

| | | Males | | Females | |
| | Home | | As %
Home | | As %
Home |
Country	Population	Total	Pop.	Total	Pop.
England and Wales	49,219	23,968	48.7	25,251	51.3
Scotland	5,206	2,504	48.1	2,702	51.9
Northern Ireland	1,537	760	49.4	777	50.6
United Kingdom	55,962	27,232	48.7	28,730	51.3

Females outnumber males in all U.K. countries; the ratio is approximately out of every 100 persons, 49 males to 51 females. The ratio differs, however, at the low and high end of the age structure:

Under 2 years: 51.5 males to 48.5 females

Aged 80 plus: 28   males to 72   females.

Where is the equality between the sexes here? Do you think you could use this material to argue the case that males should retire from work at 60 and females at 65?

When comparing the male-female relationship from 1951 to 1975 there is a noticeable closing-up of the ratio. In other words the ratio of 49 males to 51 females in 1975 is closer to a 1 to 1 ratio than it was in previous years. For example:

mid 1951	48.0 males to 52.0 females
mid 1961	48.3 males to 51.7 females
mid 1971	48.6 males to 51.4 females
mid 1975	48.7 males to 51.3 females

Will the trend continue?

Another feature of the population structure is that of dividing the population into convenient age groups to separate the dependent population from the working population. This can be done in a variety of ways but it has been decided to use the following break down:

1. the under 5's — the pre-school population,

2. the school population — 5's and under 16's,

3. the potential labour force; younger working population — 16's and under 45.

4. the potential labour force; older working population. This is divided into 2 sections: 45 and under 65 for males; 45 and under 60 for females.

5. the elderly population — 60 and over for females, and 65 plus for males.

The following exhibit shows the break down of the mid-1975 home population.

Exhibit 7.3

Age Distribution by Major Groups of Mid-1975 U.K. Population

Age Groups	Total Population ('000)	Male Population ('000)	Female Population ('000)
Pre school	3,953.6	2,034.8	1,918.8
School	9,978.2	5,121.9	4,856.3
Potential labour force (younger)	21,172.6	10,732.4	10,440.2
Potential labour force (older)	11,340.0	6,309.4	5,030.6
Elderly	9,517.6	3,033.9	6,483.7
Totals	55,962.0	27,232.4	28,729.6

	% of Total	% of Total	% of Total
Pre school	7.1	7.5	6.7
School	17.8	18.8	16.9
Potential labour force (younger)	37.8	39.4	36.4
Potential labour force (older)	20.3	23.2	17.5
Elderly	17.0	11.1	22.5
Totals	100.0	100.0	100.0

Note: Population figures based on table 11, page 15, Annual Abstract of Statistics 1976, C.S.O., H.M.S.O.

Before discussing the contents of exhibit 7.3, it might be convenient to digress for a moment. The economic implication of population begins from the premise that there are 55,962,000 consumers in our society and this involves us in studying consumption problems. On the other hand there are less than this number of producers and this requires an understanding of production problems. Over 100 years ago J. S. Mill pointed out that the economic problem was providentially solved for 'with every mouth, God sends a pair of hands'. Being that there are more hands than mouths, there should be no problem of producing the needs of consumers. The above table helps us to look at the 'mouth and hands' situation more realistically, and to look at other situations (voting population, education population, ageing population, etc.) later in the book.

Basically, the exhibit gives us a rough idea of the relationship of the potential producers in the community to the total home population. In the form of a percentage this becomes:

$$\frac{\text{potential producers}}{\text{home population}} \times 100\%$$

$$= \frac{32,512,600}{55,962,000} \times 100\%$$

$$= 58.1 \text{ per cent.}$$

So, out of every 100 persons in the home population approximately 58.1 are potential producers and the remainder (41.9) are not. There are many more hands than there are mouths — but are there?

There may be more than 32½ million potential producers but a large number of these do not form part of the employed labour force.[21] In fact, in mid 1975, the employed labour force totalled 24,413,000 (15,055,000 males and 9,369,000 females). This means that only 75 per cent of the potential labour force were at work, and changes the relationship of producers to consumers:

$$\frac{\text{employed labour force}}{\text{home population}} \quad \frac{\text{(or producers)}}{\text{(or consumers)}} \times 100\%$$

$$= \frac{24,413,000}{55,962,000} \times 100\%$$

$$= 43.6 \text{ per cent.}$$

Now, the true relationship between 'hands and mouths' is that out of every 100 persons in the home population 43.6 are producers and 56.4 non producers. Or, 43.6 workers must support 100 people; one worker must support himself, another person and slightly more than ¼ of an additional person.

21. When the minimum school leaving age was raised to 16 on 1 September 1972 this reduced the size of the potential producer population and the size of the work force. Many students beyond the age of 16 remained at school and studied full time in further education establishments. For example, around 650,000 students aged 16, 17 and 18 remained at public sector schools. Added to these were about 828,000 unemployed plus those in ill health and others who, for one reason or another, found it unnecessary to work.

A more detailed look at the employed labour force, employment, etc. will be carried out in a later chapter.

Electoral Population

A rough but quick way to estimate the number of electors in the U.K. is to subtract the 'under 18s' from the total population. For example, in mid 1975:

	total population	55,962,000
less	under 18s	15,610,000
	electoral population	40,352,000

The Home Office provides more accurate figures. In fact, the figures for the U.K. Parliamentary elections 1964 to 1974 were:

	15 Oct. 1964	31 March 1966	18 June 1970	28 Feb. 1974	10 Oct. 1974
Number of electors (millions)	35.89	35.96	39.62	39.80	40.26
Number of votes recorded*	27.66	27.26	28.34	31.33	29.19
Number of votes recorded as percentage of electorate	77.1	75.8	71.5	78.7	72.5

Note: *number of votes cast relates only to voting for contested seats.
Source: top section of table 12.1, Social Trends No. 7, 1976, HMSO.

A glance at the figures for 1966 and 1970 shows a considerable increase in the number of electors. The reason for this is that the voting age was lowered to 18 from 16 February 1970. This had the effect of adding more than 2,300,000 young persons to the register.

The new group of electors made up almost 6 per cent of all electors in mid 1975. The elderly, as shown in exhibit 7.3, formed a much larger 'bloc of voters'; slightly more than 16 per cent.

By adding the younger generation to the electoral register it had the effect of diluting the voting importance of the previous electors.

Naturally, these electors are scattered over the country. If students wanted to find out the number of electors in their constituency it would be advisable to make contact with a local government official. On the other hand, electoral registers are normally available in libraries; showing a street by street break down of electors for districts within a constituency.

So far, our attention has been drawn to the fact that the population structure of the U.K. has undergone considerable change, and that we are about to witness further changes. Further, we have noted that a change in the population structure from a pyramid to a bulging shape brings increased economic, legal, political and social problems.

Associated with the changed structure we have noted some important features, such as:

geographical distribution of population,

rise and decline in annual rates of increase,

switch towards preponderance of males in earlier age groups, continued preponderance of females at upper end of age scale, and others. On occasion we have considered some likely events that arise from the changed features.

Basically, it is the age and sex composition of the population, as noted, which are responsible for the main processes of change. It is to these main processes of change that we must now discuss.

Factors determining population change

The main processes of change are:

1. number of births,
2. number of deaths,
3. number of emigrants, and
4. number of immigrants.

It is these that determine whether the population grows or declines. In other words:

rate of population growth = excess of births over deaths PLUS excess of immigrants over emigrants.

rate of population decline = excess of deaths over births PLUS excess of emigrants over immigrants.

Birth Rate

The birth rate is a factor which statisticians find they are not capable of predicting accurately. This rate, very simple and crudely, refers to the number of live children born each year in proportion to the size of the total population. To put it another way it is the number of children born per 1,000 of the population in a year. Because it relates births to the total population it is called 'crude birth rate'. As such it is inadequate and misleading. A truer way of measuring the birth rate would be that of relating births to the number of women of child-bearing age; approximately ages 15 to 44. Women in these age groups are considered fertile and capable of producing children, and when used it is called a 'fertility rate'.

One further measure of birth rates, used since the 1930's, is the 'reproduction rate'. This rate shows to what extent the women in the fertility age groups are replacing themselves from one generation to the next. In this measurement boys are removed from the calculation. When the rate is calculated it tells us whether the population is replacing itself.

The crude birth rate for the U.K. has been steadily declining; in 1964 it was 18.8 and the provisional figure for 1975 was 12.5. In the period before this, from 1951 to 1964, the trend was upwards; it was 15.8 in 1951.[22] It should be noted that the birth rates refer to live births.[23]

22. Crude birth rate =
    $$\frac{\text{number of live births in U.K.}}{\text{U.K. home population}} \times 1,000$$

23. total births equals live births and still births. Still births are not included in birth rates. The trend of still births has been on the decline since 1961 — from 19,000 to 8,000 in 1974.

Fertility rates also show a decline. In the census year 1961 the rate was 90.6 and in 1971 it was 84.8. The highest fertility rates, in both these years, were for women in the age group 20 to 29, and the lowest for women aged 40 to 44. This appears to be quite natural from one year to the next.

Sometimes it is more interesting to look at long term trends; say from the beginning of the 20th century. For example, the fertility rate in the U.K. has been declining over the past three-quarters of a century: 1900 it was approximately 115, in 1975 it was 64 — a fall of more than 44 per cent. When looking at the countries making up the U.K. we can note that the rates for England and Wales were nearly the same as the U.K. rate, Scotland was higher (122 to 66) and Northern Ireland lower (100 to 88).

Of course, over this time, there have been movements upwards and downwards around the trend. It was low just after World War I, especially low in the early 1930's (similar to the rates of the early 1970's). In the period of the 'great depression' the birth rate was a little above 'replacement levels'. Immediately after World War II there was the 'baby boom' and this was followed by a fall, a rise and the present decline.

Most of this information can be assembled in the form of an exhibit.

Exhibit 7.4

Facts associated with Births
in United Kingdom
1901 and 1975

	1901	1975
U.K. Home Population	38,237,000	55,962,000
of which:		
Males	18,492,000	27,232,000
Females	19,745,000	28,730,000
age group 15-44		
Males	8,788,000	11,173,200
Females	9,513,000	10,856,300
Sex ratio*	924	1,029
Live births**	1,095,000	697,000
of which:		
Males	558,000	359,000
Females	537,000	338,000
Crude birth rate	28.6	12.5
Fertility rate	115.1	64.3

Source: Figures obtained from Annual Abstract of Statistics, 1976, No. 113, HMSO — Tables 6, 8, 11 and 25.
Notes: * sex ratio .... males per 1,000 females
       ** average figures 1900-1902

The majority of births are to married women. Statistics substantiate this statement, but the trend shows an increase in illegitimate births; for example, in 1951 the number of illegitimate births constituted about 4.8 per cent of all live births, and in 1974 the figure was up to 8.7 per cent.

The social events associated with births are 'marriages and the size of families'. It is to these we will now look.

Marriage and Family Size

In 1974 the total live births, in the U.K., numbered 737,000; of this 672,881 babies were born legitimately. Thus, it is obvious that births will depend first upon whether people marry or remain single, and second at what ages they marry. If the greater proportion of marriages take place early (late teens) then the chances are that it will be possible for more babies to be born; if later (late twenties) the less likely the size of families will be large.

There were more married persons in Great Britain in 1974 (27½ million) than in 1901 (12½ million); more than doubled. Also, there were more marriages in 1974 (426,000) than in 1901 (291,000).

The average age of first marriages was lowered for males and females. 27.2 was the average age at which males married, in Great Britain, in 1901, and 24.8 in 1974. The respective average age for females was 25.6 and 22.7. It was noticeable in the 1960's that more teen-age marriages were taking place. This trend was more pronounced in the 1970's.[24]

It would appear from the foregoing that the number of children per family should rise, but this was not true. In the early 1860's the average number of children was slightly more than 6. The average for the early 1970's is slightly more than 2.

The population of the U.K. has stopped growing, and the main reason for this has been the decline in the number of births.

Why the decline in births?

The decline in the number of births can be viewed alongside many social developments; some important factors are:

1. Birth rates tend to fall during a recession or slump in economic activities; noticeable as unemployment figures rise beyond the million mark.

2. Children, since the beginning of the 20th century have stayed at school longer and thus became a liability rather than an economic asset to parents. Children at school put a strain on the family purse. Parents react by restricting births so they can concentrate their finances on a smaller number of children.

3. The status of women has changed. Today people believe that a wife's role is no longer that of being a mother and housekeeper. More mothers go out to work and this has had considerable impact on the number of children born.

4. Contraceptives, known and accepted by the middle class in the latter part of the 19th century, have recently been widely accepted by other classes. This enables parents to 'space' the birth of children.

5. Family planning services have been provided to help parents to plan the size of their families.

24. The trend towards more marriages in the teens was strongly affected by the Family Law Reform Act 1970 which lowered the age at which people could get married without the consent of their parents. Age was lowered to 18.

6. Women have found it easier to have abortions. The number of abortions under the 1967 Act increased to a peak in 1973 and since then has shown a slight decline.[25]

7. Social attitudes have changed as to what constitutes the ideal family size.

Births have been registered in England and Wales since 1837; the year the Registrar General[26] set up the register. Deaths, since that time, also have to be registered.

Death Rates

Another factor, other than births and net migration, that affects the size of the population is the number of deaths.

The crude death rate, one measure of mortality, measures the number of deaths to the entire population; like the crude birth rate. However, care must be taken when comparing the crude death rate of the U.K. with any other country because the number of deaths depend very much upon the age composition (shape) of the population.

In the U.K., annual total deaths since the beginning of the 20th century has been fairly constant ranging mainly between 310,000 and 340,000 for males and 290,000 and 330,000 for females.

At the turn of the century (1900 to 1902) the average number of deaths per year were 662,732; males 340,664 and females 322,068. In 1974 the figures were 667,359; males 337,263 and 330,096 for females. The crude death rates for each of these periods were:

1900-1902   —   17.3

1974   —   11.9

In other words, although the total number of deaths for the two different periods were nearly the same, the number of deaths per 1,000 of the population were substantially different, a fall of 31 per cent.

These crude figures do not show the specific ages at which death occurred. An investigation into deaths at specific age groups overtime would show dramatic changes. Exhibit 7.5 brings out these changes.

The death rate of young children has fallen considerably over the 74 years; from approximately 35 out of every 100 deaths to just over 2. The decline was primarily attributed to the advance in medical knowledge, such as vaccinations and better maternal facilities.

Over the same span of time expectation of life has increased greatly. This has been due to several factors such as a higher standard of living, improved medical knowledge, better working conditions and improved standards of hygiene. It, therefore, seems natural to expect a higher rate of deaths in the over 65 age group; from 24½ to 73½ out of every 100.

25. "Fertility and abortion inside and outside marriage" by Jean Thompson, in Population Trends 5, Autumn 1976, p3.

26. On 11 May 1970 the Government Social Survey Department and the General Register Office were merged into a new organisation called the 'Office of Population Censuses and Surveys'.

Exhibit 7.5

Deaths of the young and old
in United Kingdom
1900-1902 and 1974

	All Ages		Young 0 — 4		Old 65 plus	
		as % of		as % of		as % of
	Number	total	Number	total	Number	total
1900-1902						
Totals	662,732	100	230,000	34.7	162,110	24.5
of which:						
Males	340,664	51.4	125,076	18.9	74,648	11.3
Females	322,068	48.6	104,934	15.8	87,462	13.2
1974						
Totals	667,359	100	14,640	2.2	490,341	73.4
of which:						
Males	337,263	50.5	8,487	1.3	226,445	33.9
Females	330,096	49.5	6,153	0.9	263,896	39.5
	U.K. Crude Death Rate*		**0 — 4 Age Specific Death Rate****		**65 plus Age Specific Death Rate****	
1900-1902	17.3		6.0		4.2	
1974	11.9		0.3		8.8	

NOTES:

* UK Crude death rate = $\dfrac{\text{total UK deaths}}{\text{UK population}} \times 1{,}000$

**Age Specific death rate = $\dfrac{\text{deaths in age group}}{\text{UK population}} \times 1{,}000$

UK population in 1900-1902 was approximately 38,237,000
UK population in 1974 was approximately 55,965,000

SOURCE: Numbers of deaths obtained from table 30 of Annual Abstract of Statistics 1976, No. 113, H.M.S.O.
Percentages and death rates calculated by author.

Age specific death rates tells us the extent to which differences in the U.K. crude death rates, for 1900-02 and 1974, are the result of differences in the age composition. In other words, in 1974 the age specific death rate for the 65 and over age group was 8.8, whereas the U.K. crude death rate was 11.9. Thus this elderly age group's deaths was 8.8 of the 11.9 (74 per cent of all deaths); all other age groups made up the difference of 3.1 (26 per cent).

An investigation of the causes of death in the 65 and over age group shows they resulted mainly from cancer, heart diseases, and pneumonia.

The shape of deaths over the various ages takes on a 'J' pattern. High during infancy, diminishing to a low level in early adolescence, rising slowly to the 40s and 50s and then an upsurge from those ages upwards.

Associated with mortality are life expectancy details. In fact, life expectancy tables are simply a measure of mortality. For example, according to life tables for 1974-75[27], 811 out of every 1,000 baby boys, in England and Wales, can expect to reach the age of 60, and 586 the age of 70. Comparable figures for female babies, on the other hand, are 882 to age 60, and 752 to age 70. These figures vary according to regions (regional health authority regions). More babies, boys and girls, can expect to reach ages 60 and 70 if they live in East Anglia and Oxford, and less than the figures quoted above if they live in the north and northwest regions.

Natural Change — Births minus Deaths

The natural increase of the U.K. population is the result of births being greater than the number of deaths. For example:

mid years 1974 to 1975 births exceeded deaths by 49,600, and

mid years 1975 to 1976 births exceeded deaths by 7,400.

Of the countries that make up the U.K. it can be noted that England and Wales, in the 1975-76 period, showed a natural decrease whereas Scotland and Northern Ireland had a natural increase.

Births, deaths and migration are factors that affect the size of the population. It is changes in these interacting factors that bring about changes in the trend of population.

International Migration

International migration is the third factor or component affecting changes in the overall size of the population. The figure relating to changes is the 'net' difference between the number of persons permanently leaving the U.K. (emigrants) and those taking up residence here (immigrants). Persons who are temporarily residing in the U.K. from foreign countries are termed 'aliens'.

Emigration, over recent years, has caused considerable controversy. For example, in the early 1960's emigration aroused considerable public interest. So much so that a special working party was set-up, in November 1966, to study the 'brain drain'. This was the title of the report submitted by the Committee.[28] The first point in their summary stated that "There is a serious brain drain of young engineers, technologists and scientists from the United Kingdom".

Immigration, even more recently, has had its impact on society, and on the attitudes of the indigenous population. In terms of population, the first impact is on the size of the population, whether it increases or decreases the size. The secondary impact is the extent to which migration causes the number of births and deaths to differ from that which would be expected had migration not taken place. It is normally argued that immigrants do not replace the people who are leaving the country; immigrants typically, are manual or clerical workers.

To understand migration, it is necessary to understand the 'push' and 'pull'

27. "Life Expectancy: Variations Among Regional Health Authorities" by Dr. Martin Gardner, in Population Trends 10, Winter 1977, HMSO, Tables 3(a) and 3(b) on page 11.
28. "The Brain Drain", Report of the Working Group on Migration, Cmnd 3417.

factors. What forces operate within a nation that 'pushes' people from their homelands, and what attracts or 'pulls' migrants to other countries. There are many factors, such as religious persecution, social dissatisfaction, dislike of political regime, penalising tax system. If these are push factors then the reverse, freedom of religion, low tax systems, etc. might constitute pull factors.

In the U.K. the most reliable information on migration comes from the Census of Population. Registration data up to 1969 was not very helpful. However, since 1969, birth and death registration requires details that help us to view the impact that migration has on the size of population. Birth registration now requires information about the place of origin of parents of new babies. Death registration requires the origin of birth of the person who died.

'Net' Migration

The U.K., from one census to another, from 1871 to 1931 has had a net loss by migration. Rough calculations put the loss as approximately 4 million. From 1931 to 1961 the U.K. had a net gain of almost ½ million.

From mid-1964 to mid-1974 over 2,800,000 people left the U.K. to live abroad and 2,300,000 came from abroad to live in this country.[29] On balance this represented a net loss of ½ million. There was a further net loss in 1975 and in 1976.

Overall, over the last 100 years, the U.K. has had a much larger flow of persons outward than inward. There does not seem to be much of a problem in terms of the effect migration has on the size of the population.

Where do immigrants come from?[30]

In the period 1931-41 "The immigrants of this period consisted to a rather small extent of political refugees from Germany and other European countries, to a rather greater extent of immigrants from Eire, but as to the great majority they were Britons returning from abroad ....."[31]

In the period from 1964 to 1973 they came from:

New Commonwealth · 36%
of which
African Commonwealth (11%)
Indian Sub-Continent (14%)
West Indies (5%)
Other Commonwealth (6%)

29. "Migrants entering and leaving the UK 1964-74" by Norman Davis and Christopher Walker, in Population Trends 1, Autumn 1975, HMSO, p2.

30. Material for this section and the next is taken or based, mainly, on 'Migrants entering and leaving the UK 1964-74' by Norman Davis and Christopher Walker, pages 2 and 5 in Population Trends 1, Autumn 1975, H.M.S.O.

31. Royal Commission on Population Report, June 1949, Cmd 7695, HMSO, para 45.

Old Commonwealth	·	21%
of which		
New Zealand	(3%)	
Canada	(5%)	
Australia	(13%)	
Foreign	·	43%
of which		
South Africa	(3%)	
U.S.A.	(10%)	
Europe	(23%)	
Other Foreign	(7%)	

Many of the immigrants to Britain are British. Davis and Walker stated that in the five year period 1969-73 "over half of the immigrants from Commonwealth countries and nearly a third of those from foreign countries were UK citizens.". To make the percentage figures given above realistic, they refer to 2,300,000 immigrants.[32]

Where do emigrants go to?

Emigrants, up to the Second World War, went, mainly, to Commonwealth countries, particularly to the older Commonwealth nations, and the U.S.A..

In the period from 1964 to 1973 they went to:

New Commonwealth	·	15%
of which		
African Commonwealth	(6%)	
Indian Sub-Continent	(3%)	
West Indies	(3%)	
Other Commonwealth	(3%)	
Old Commonwealth	·	47%
of which		
New Zealand	(5%)	
Canada	(13%)	
Australia	(29%)	
Foreign	·	38%
of which		
South Africa	(6%)	
U.S.A.	(10%)	
Europe	(17%)	
Other Foreign	(5%)	

These percentages relate to 2,800,000 emigrants.

32. It should be noted that the International Passenger Survey, used by Davis and Walker for their survey defined an immigrant as someone who, having lived abroad for at least 12 months intends to reside in this country for at least 12 months, and vice versa for emigrants. A statistical definition; one "unrelated to the laws defining those whose entry into the country is subject to immigration control".

Many of the emigrants from Britain are non-British. For the period 1969 to 1973, Davis and Walker noted that "over a quarter of all people leaving the UK .... were either foreigners or citizens of Commonwealth countries; that over a third of emigrants to foreign countries were aliens and nearly a fifth of emigrants to Commonwealth countries were already citizens of Commonwealth countries".

Measuring International Migration

The Brain Drain Report (para 22) states that there is a large flow of people into and out of the United Kingdom each year. People come to the United Kingdom to visit, to study, to work, perhaps for a short while, perhaps permanently. They are part of the growing international flow of people.

The Brain Drain Committee, although concerned primarily with qualified people, stated that it was important to have available regular and comprehensive statistics on the emigration and immigration (however defined) of qualified people. Better migration statistics are becoming available. The author found considerable information on migration but found it difficult to isolate material relevant to his needs in this section.

For up-dated international migration figures, based on International Passenger Survey data, it is advisable to consult the most recent publication of 'Population Trends'. These tables provide 'in' 'out' 'net' and 'age group' details.

Components of Population Change

The basics of the components that affect the size of the U.K. population has now been considered, and it is possible to produce a table to show population changes as they are affected by these components. These are shown in Exhibit 7.6.

This exhibit shows, as noted previously, that the size of the U.K. population has increased continuously from 1961 to 1975, and then decreased from 1975 to 1977. In all years shown, natural increase was always 'plus' and net migration always 'negative' except for 1961-62.

Some Relationships

Before taking up other areas of population study it might be worthwhile to briefly look at some relationships relevant to previous material.

Birth rate. It is not certain what determines the birth rate of a country apart from fertility. We have considered some changing factors (social status of women, etc.) that do change. Fertility (ages 15 to 44) does not tend to change.

On the other hand, birth rates do influence the 'number of hands and mouths' in the nation and the potential structure of the population.

Sex structure. This is determined by the proportion of boys to girls at birth, and in later years by the proportion of deaths, in each age group, of boys and girls and later men and women.

Exhibit 7.6

Components of population change
United Kingdom

thousands

Mid-year to mid-year	Population at start of period	Births	Deaths	Natural increase	Net migration	Other changes*
				Components of change (mid-year to mid-year)		
1961-2	52,807	965	636	329	+ 112	+ 26
1962-3	53,274	981	657	324	− 31	− 14
1963-4	53,553	1,000	606	393	− 32	− 28
1964-5	53,885	1,006	616	390	− 33	− 24
1965-6	54,218	987	648	339	− 58	+ 2
1966-7	54,500	982	609	373	− 88	+ 15
1967-8	54,800	948	658	289	− 37	− 4
1968-9	55,049	943	646	296	− 54	− 28
1969-70	55,263	899	667	232	− 60	− 14
1970-1	55,421	915	639	276	− 39	− 48
1971-2**	55,609.6	862.3	660.8	201.5	− 44.2	+ 13.8
1972-3**	55,780.7	807.6	671.9	135.8	− 4.6	+ 0.7
1973-4**	55,912.6	751.7	664.0	87.7	− 76.7	− 1.3
1974-5**	55,922.3	720.7	671.1	49.6	− 71.9	+ 0.5
1975-6**	55,900.5	688.6	681.2	7.4	− 28.7	+ 6.4
1976-7**	55,885.6					

* Changes in numbers of armed forces plus, for England and Wales, adjustments to reconcile population change between 1961 and 1974 Censuses with estimates of natural change and net civilian migration.

**Recalculated estimates from new series — See 'In brief', page 5 of 'Population Trends 10'. Reproduced from Social Trends, No. 10 by permission of H.M.S.O.

This structure helps to determine the size of the working population and the ages at which people marry. For example, if there are more males than females in the 'teens and early twenties then more marriages will tend to take place earlier in life.

Age structure. This is influenced by the sex structure and deaths from one age group to the next, as well as past and present birth rates. The influence, of the age structure, on society is considerable. It influences: the number of households and therefore the number of houses, the size of families and therefore the type of houses (2 bedrooms, 3 bedrooms, etc.). Also the size of the working population and the mobility of labour. It influences education and educational facilities, health and health facilities. The type of goods and services to be produced and imported, and many other areas.

All that we have said here, and are about to say later, is about people, and it is people who form the basic resource of any community.

Areas of Population Study

This chapter on population involved us in looking at the collection and measurement of population data for the U.K., whenever possible, at different points of time. Information was provided on births, deaths, migration, and other characteristics of the inhabitants of the country, such as size of family and marriage. A deeper penetration into this field of study would have taken us to scenes behind the components of population: illegitimacy, abortions, marital conditions, diseases that cause death, and others. All these areas are of interest to actuaries (for example, experts in insurance companies who compute risks according to probabilities indicated by the recorded facts) and demographers. This is one area of population study.

A second area of population study is that of studying the relationship of population change with changes in economic, social, political and other institutions.[33] As population changes from one time to another there is a tendency for institutions to change. Small population changes, of course, will probably have little effect on some institutions and virtually none on others. Large population changes are likely to effect all institutions.

What are the economic, social and political implications of a change in the shape of the population structure? What are the implications of a four-bulge population (U.K. in mid 1975)? How do these population changes affect education? employment? national production? markets? government expenditure? others?

The next few chapters provide some of the material that is needed to get to grips with these questions.

---

33. Institution can be defined as:
  a) an established law, custom, usage, practice, organisation, foundation.
  b) an establishment or organisation set up for the promotion of a particular object.
      Examples:

schools, colleges, universities	—to educate members of society
charitable foundations	—to provide charity
manufacturing organisation	—to produce goods
trade union	—to unify labour
church	—to provide spiritual guidance
parliament	—to make and unmake the law
courts of law	—to administer the law
market	—to provide contact between buyers and sellers.

Assignments

1. Argue the case that agrees *or* disagrees with the following statement. In the year 2000 it is estimated that the world population will be approximately 6,000,000,000, and the surface of the earth can support 6,000,000,000 mouths.

2. The population of the United Kingdom, from 1962 to 1974, increased at a decreasing rate. Explain this statement.

3. Explain, using simple diagrams where necessary, the following terms:
   a) population explosion,
   b) normal population, and
   c) abnormal population.

4. In mid-1975 the United Kingdom had several bulges in its population. What problems do you foresee arising from these bulges?

5. In the 1860's the average number of children per family was more than six. The average for the early 1970's was slightly more than two. What reasons can you give for this decline?

6. Do you or do you not agree with the fact that there are too many immigrants coming into the United Kingdom? State why.

Chapter 8

Population — General Information

Learning objectives:
At the end of your study of this chapter you should be able to:
1. define the concept of the "optimum population".
2. evaluate the concept of the "optimum population".
3. explain, in simple terms, the theory postulated by Malthus.

World population has been increasing ever since Adam and Eve. At first it increased slowly and then from the early 1800s to the present time it increased at an 'exploding' rate. This explosion can best be seen by using a graph, as in Exhibit 8.1.

Today, many people are aware of the population explosion, but more than 180 years ago the Reverend Thomas R. Malthus published a depressing essay called "An Essay on the Principle of Population as its Affects the Future Improvement of Society". This essay, published in 1798, we might say was the beginning of investigations into population growth, economic growth and their associated problems. Malthus' essay may have been written many years ago but it is still brought back into prominence every now and then; even in the mid 1970s. For example, an article published in 1975 stated: "At the present annual rate of about 2 per cent, world population will rise to about 5.3 billion by the year 1990. Meanwhile, without a massive investment in the agricultural sector, world food grain production will be about 1.6 billion tons in 1990 while expected demand at that time will be about 1.9 billion tons. The world, and the developing countries particularly, could be said to be facing the Malthusian specter once again".[1] At the beginning of this 1975 article it stated that "Food and population are two of the major problems facing mankind". This is exactly the way Malthus saw the situation.

Malthusian pessimism

Malthus postulated his theory in the 1790s when the population of the world was estimated to be around 750,000,000 and that of the U.K. slightly more than 10,000,000. At this time — more than 80 per cent of the U.K. population was engaged in agriculture, and the so called 'industrial revolution' was beginning to take-off.

---

1. "Population: Exploring the food-fertility link" by Shahid Javed Burki and Shahid Yusuf in Finance Development, December 1975, p.29.

Exhibit 8.1

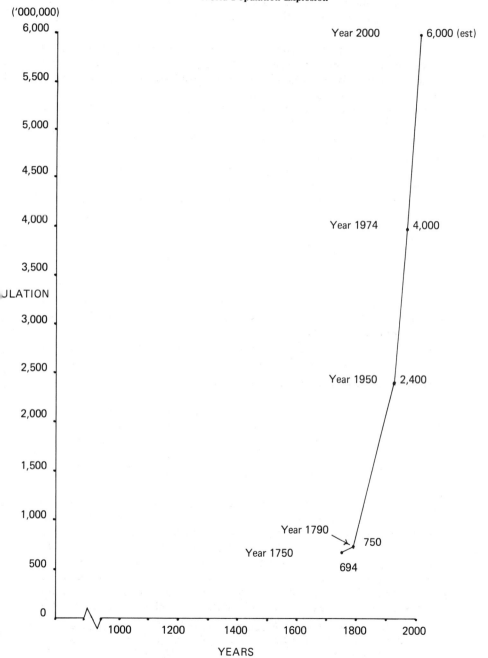

World Population Explosion

Malthus noted that an increase in the standard of living encouraged the growth of population, and this, in turn, led to increased demand for agricultural goods. However, the amount of food that can be produced from the land, which was fixed, would eventually reach its limit and this would check the growth of population.

In other words, Malthus claimed that if the rate of fertility (of giving birth to children) remained constant at the rate prevailing, then for succeeding generations population would increase in a geometrical ratio (1 plus 2 plus 4 plus 8 plus 16 plus 32, etc.) whereas food production or the means of subsistence would increase only in an arithmetical ratio (1 plus 2 plus 3 plus 4 plus 5 plus 6, etc.). It follows that humans were destined to a life of poverty and misery unless the rate of population growth was checked.

Very simply, there had to be a balance between population growth and production from the land. If an imbalance was created, in that population increased faster than the food supply, it would lead to certain evils such as: high death rate, disease, famine and war. Thus, imbalances were brought back into balance by positive checks such as: disease, famine and war.

Malthus concluded that positive checks would not be sufficient to keep the population in check so human controls had to be introduced. He suggested that:

(1) apprentices should be forbidden to marry during their apprenticeship,

(2) the Speenhamland system[2] of poor relief which favoured large families, and provided foodstuff for legitimate as well as illegitimate children, should be abolished,

(3) marriages should be postponed until income and money saved was enough to cater for a family, and

(4) restraint should be taken during marriage.

Today, human controls are also advocated, for example, people should be educated on how to establish a smaller family norm (family planning and use of contraceptives), and the status of women should be raised to make them more equal with men economically, politically and socially. Some people even suggest euthenasia, but this is not so acceptable to the general public.

From the time of Malthus to the present day the population of the world increased by more than five times; the population of the U.K. also increased by more than 5 times. However, the fears of Malthus have been offset by a variety of improvements. Science has enabled larger yields of crops to be produced, and certain foods to be produced synthetically. Communications and transport have been improved and enables one country to make up its needs from other nations in the world. World food production has, more or less, kept up with the increase in population — and we have not even begun

2. Speenhamland was the name of a district in Berkshire where the Berkshire justices held their meeting in 1795. The decision of the justices of the peace was to supplement the wages of the local agricultural labourers out of the rates, according to size of family and the price of bread.

yet to farm the sea. But, as we have previously noted, more and more people are faced with poverty today than ever before.

Today there is still the fear that population growth is outstripping available food supplies.

As far as the population in the U.K. are concerned the Malthusian theory would operate if it were not for international trade. As one author said: "One of the most tragic instances of a wide disparsity between numbers of people and the carrying capacity of the land on which they live is twentieth-century Great Britain". Later, this author claimed that "despite superb agricultural techniques, she cannot possibly produce enough food at home to support what we consider a decent standard of living. She is perilously close to her condition in 1600."[3] Students can consider: what foods would we have to do without if we did not trade internationally?

We might ask ourselves the typical question: what is the optimum population of the U.K.?, and, what is the optimum population of the world?

Optimum population

Before considering the 'optimum population' concept, a few words must be said about the word 'optimum'. This word refers to an ideal position and is usually shown under static conditions. However, the world in which we live is dynamic, conditions are always changing and this means that the optimum is constantly shifting. As conditions relating to the optimum change, so the optimum must change.[4]

According to the economist, optimum population refers to that number of persons which, when combined with the factors of production, such as existing land and existing capital, will produce the greatest output per head of the population. Naturally there are many relevant factors, other than those mentioned, which relate to the community: their habits and customs, the level of education and training, and the nature of the environment. When any of these vary, the optimum changes.

The above statement can be considered visually in the following simple diagram.

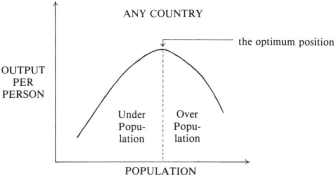

3. "Road to Survival" by William Vogt, William Sloane Associates, 1948, p 70 and 71.

4. There are many types of optimum: population, output, plant size, etc.

This diagram states than any country that has a population below (to the left of) the optimum position simply has too few people to use effectively the available resources of the community. In other words, the community is under-populated. An increase in population, with its given amount of cultivated and grazing land and capital, would lead to an increase in output per head — and a movement towards the optimum. Considering this idea of 'available resources' we might ask: Are countries with vast stretches of desert, such as those in the Sahara, under-populated or over-populated? Is Greenland with its ice covered land under or over populated? The answer, of course, depends on whether the population is less than or greater than the ideal position.

The population to the right of the optimum position indicates over-population. This means that there are too many people to use effectively the given resources of the community. A reduction in population will lead towards an increase in output per head; a movement towards the optimum. A country with a large land area may be poor in natural resources and lacking capital and yet may have a small population and economically would be over-populated. Greenland? Is India over-populated? or China? or the U.K.?

Over a period of time conditions are liable to change and what was formerly the optimum may cease to be so, and a new optimum position occurs. This can change our ideas of under-population and over-population; depending, of course, on which way the optimum moves. To the right of the previous optimum? to the left? Let us assume certain conditions change (new capital is injected into the economy, or a river has been controlled to irrigate large tracts of desert land) that would push the optimum to the right. Diagrammatically, it would be as follows:

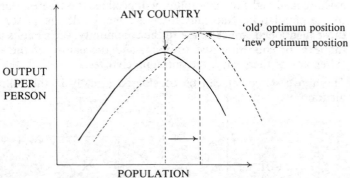

This changes the under and over-population situation. A country that was over-populated may now be at or near the new optimum, but a country that was under-populated would be farther away; much more under-populated.

Of course, the optimum could change again.

The foregoing states a theoretical situation; it lays down a number of assumed conditions. In reality there are many factors operating at a given time, and they are extremely complex and difficult to measure. Further, one factor influences other factors, these influences other factors, etc. and makes it all the more complex and difficult to measure.[5] Who can really say what the optimum population is?

The above is not a piece of useless information. It does help us to understand the forces that operate within the concept, and helps us to seek improvements that move us towards the ideal position.

Are there other concepts of optimum population? The simple answer is 'yes', but it depends upon the criteria people wish to use. Which criteria should one use? welfare? religion? military? electoral?

Military powers evidently feel that the optimum population is that which not only provides maximum output per person in foods, houses, roads, guns, ships, etc., but also sufficient numbers to man guns and ships which is necessary to maintain their independence or expand their empires. In other words their optimum is a population that is greater than the economic optimum.

Often one states a population to be at an optimum when considering availability of food supplies; the population can be fed at a predetermined standard of nutrition by its own agriculture and what it imports. Is the U.K. beyond the optimum in this sense? It has been claimed that using the best possible techniques in agriculture it is possible to feed perhaps 40,000,000. The surplus of U.K. population, about 16,000,000, survive from what we import. Is the U.K.'s balance of payments problems basically a problem of over population?

Is there an optimum population for the world? By what standard should we consider it? For example, let us *assume* that all countries in the world are equal to the U.K. in terms of resources and capital; which, of course, they are not. Also, let us *assume* that the mid-1975 population of the U.K. was at an optimum. We could then state what the optimum population of the world should be.

Now each person in the U.K. has 1.06 acres, and the number of persons per square mile was 601. Some simple arithmetic would indicate that the world population optimum would be approximately 31,000,000,000. This appears to be a lot of nonsense because we know that shortly after World War II something like 2 out of every 3 persons in the world were living in a state of poverty; the world population then was about 2,400,000,000.

Anyways, not all countries are alike. The U.K. is a developed nation and many countries in the world are still developing. Also, we do not know if the mid-1975 U.K. population is at an optimum.

When action is to be taken about the size of population (population policy) the idea of the 'optimum' is not satisfactory as a practical guide to action. A

5. Students can compare the above to a simple situation, using a 'still pond' as a static situation. Then introduce new factors into the pond (large stones, small stones, sticks, leaves, etc.) and note the small and large actions and inter-actions that take place. These dynamic changes make it more difficult to describe what is happening and doing it accurately. This can be likened to the static theoretical and dynamic real situations applied to the optimum.

more useful measurement is to consider rates of increase and/or decrease — on trends.[6] An example of using rates of change is provided by this Fabian statement: "The continuance of a net reproduction rate below unity will probably involve a falling standard of life, a hardening of our political arteries, a reduction in military power, a diminished influence in world affairs, a less adventurous and less vital social life." And, that it follows from this that it is "essential in the national interest that the present decline in the birth rate[7] should be arrested......".

Thus, the 'optimum' is a useful theoretical tool, but is not very useful from a practical point of view in establishing population policy and action. It is much better to concentrate on trends, and it is the trends that should indicate whether the government should encourage or discourage certain activities (family planning, contraception, equality of sexes, etc.).

Governments are concerned about population size — looking at its inhabitants as 'numbers'. But, concern normally extends beyond this; these are 'people' and they have certain needs.

6. This was the attitude of the Fabian Society when giving evidence to the Royal Commission on Population (Cmd 7695, June 1949). A Fabian Society booklet "Population and the People. A National Policy" contains the 'Memorandum of Evidence' they gave to the Royal Commission. Sir William Beveridge's "Population Problem" article in The Political Quarterly, April-June 1946, page 134 agreed with the Fabian Society saying that the Society rightly rejected the economic concept of an optimum population as a practical guide to action.

7. Present decline referred to the situation before 1948. It can be noted that the U.K. experienced a similar situation in the mid 1970s.

Assignments

1. The optimum size of a country's population, for example the United Kingdom, can be determined. Critically examine this statement.

2. "The world, and the developing countries particularly, could be said to be facing the Malthusian specter once again." Explain, in simple terms, the theory postulated by Malthus.

Chapter 9

Needs

Learning objectives:
At the end of your study of this chapter you should be able to:
1. identify the major social needs of the population.
2. identify the major material needs of the population.
3. appreciate the relationship that exists between these two needs.
4. understand the problem of 'poverty' in the world.
5. understand the basic causes of poverty in the U.K.

Dictionaries[1] are useful books giving meaning to words. The word *need* refers to necessity arising from the circumstances of a case; a case or instance in which some necessity or want exists, such as one's daily needs; commonly, a condition of want or destitution, lack of necessaries or poverty whence the word *needy*.

Often the word need is prefixed with another word to qualify its meaning — such as 'material needs' and 'social needs'.

Material, as used here, is concerned with bodily comfort or well-being of members of the community. Should a person (or family) fall below a certain level of material well-being[2] we can claim they are in *need of materials* to bring them back to that standard or level which society considers satisfactory. To ensure that no member of a society perishes from hunger it is essential to meet his needs and provide him with 'food materials'; when a person is in need of clothing supply him with 'clothing materials' to keep him warm and decently dressed. The situations that create these and other similar material needs must, in our type of society, be recognised and measures taken to secure minimum standards for all individuals and families at all times.

Social has many meanings but when used in an area dealing with population it means we are concerned with the mutual relations of human beings in the community. The effort in most countries in the world, including the U.K., is to improve the 'conditions of life' of the people; to improve the 'quality of life'; to make people happy or give them happiness. When the quality of life or happiness of an individual, family or community has deteriorated below a specified set of conditions there is a *social need* to rectify and restore the situation to standard conditions.

1. In this case: The New Century Dictionary and The Concise Oxford.
2. Material well-being is normally referred to by economists as 'economic welfare'. The level of material well-being is usually called 'standard of living'.

Social needs refer to situations not directly associated with material needs. It is true that social needs may arise from material needs such as the conditions that arise out of poverty. Poverty directly makes a person liable to material degradation and this can lead to social degradation; people going around dirty, ragged and in ill-health. But, normally social needs are non-material; they are concerned with conditions associated with ill health and distress, concerned with conditions creating affecting the well-being of the aged, the disabled and the young; concerned with the conditions creating break-down in personal and family life.

Bringing these two types of need together means we are dealing with one big subject called 'welfare' or 'well-being' of the community. On the one hand material needs are normally discussed as 'economic welfare' and social needs as 'social welfare'. The word 'need' simply states a situation in both areas of welfare which society feels must be rectified because below a certain level people no longer have well-being.

Changing definition of need

In moving from historical times to the present day we find that definitions of words change, for example the word 'need'[3] would be different in the 1600's (giving poor relief and treatment of paupers) from that of early 1900's and again different at the present time.

Need in the early 1900's was conceived as an individual matter instead of a family problem. For example the National Health Insurance Act 1911 provided cash payments for a married man equivalent to a single man and gave no concern to wives and children of such workers. Two years later another Act provided medical care for insured workers but wives and children were excluded. Classes of persons in need were treated but not families and social groups in distress. It was not until the latter 1940's that wives and children were included (cash payments and medical care).

Social obligations had to be widened before 'need' covered more than insured persons. The Beveridge Report[4] which was published in 1942 laid down the recommendations to the government for widening these social obligations.

Beveridge report

The Beveridge Report which was regarded as a unique contribution to economic and social reform investigated the social area of want (want is the state of being without something needed, for example, to be in want of money). The Committee looked at the past and then made 23 principal changes which should be provided in the future. They noted various causes that put a strain on the finance of the individual and family.[5] In brief, lacking money invariably means that the 'head of the house' is not able to

3. Another word that has changed its meaning over time is 'charity'.

4. Report on Social Insurance and Allied Services, HMSO.

5. These causes and the post-war legislation introduced to remove most of them are discussed in the chapter on 'Population and Social Implications'.

buy those goods and services that are necessary to maintain an acceptable standard of living. In other words such persons would probably find themselves and their families living in a state of poverty.

Poverty can indirectly create other social problems which disturb the quality of life for the individual and family — such as disease and squalor. The Beveridge Report made note that there was a social need for society to remove these other conditions at the same time as they were to remove want. Solving these social evils did not simply mean giving money — they required a separate sort of social assistance.

Two other social needs (social evils) were also recognised by the Report, namely idleness and ignorance. Again there was the social need to better the life of the people who were faced with these socially undesirable conditions.[6]

The terms of reference of the Beveridge Report did not ask them to report on these last four social evils nor the many other social needs of society that did not come into the category of want. Thus they did not investigate the social need of the blind, deaf, dumb, backward children, mentally disturbed persons, loneliness of the elderly or other forms of distress. All these required separate investigation and separate legislation. Some social needs not covered by statutory organisations are helped by voluntary organisations. On the other hand there are still (in the latter 1970's) special social needs not covered by any organisation.

Need changes with time. It changes as the shape of the population, and as economic and social conditions change. These points should be kept in mind when studying 'poverty'.

Material need — poverty (world)

'The poor always ye have with you'.[7] The known world centuries ago was smaller than the present time. Poverty existed then and it exists today. In 1973 it was claimed by Robert S. McNamara[8] that 'absolute poverty' was the lot of 40 per cent of the peoples of the developing countries — something like 900,000,000 (roughly 16 times the population of the U.K.) were in this situation. He considered absolute poverty as a condition of life so degraded by disease, illiteracy, malnutrition and squalor as to deny its victims basic human necessities. In later speeches on poverty Mr. McNamara referred to a type called 'relative poverty' and this referred to those whose average income was less than one-third of the national average.

It can be seen from the above that one can qualify different levels of poverty but they are still, nevertheless, poverty.

Poverty is a major social problem of the world.

6. These 4 social evils — disease, squalor, idleness and ignorance — are discussed in the chapter 'Population and Social Implications'.

7. John, XII, 8.

8. President of the World Bank (IBRD) made the statement in his address to the Annual Meeting of the World Bank and International Monetary Fund in Nairobi. Refer to 'Finance and Development' June 1978 for the definition given.

Poverty — definitions

How many people in the U.K. or in the world are living in a state of poverty? To obtain an estimate it is first necessary to define the word poverty.

Definition can be either subjective or objective. Recently there have been movements towards subjective measurements of poverty and other social indicators. These simply try to find out the degree of satisfaction or dissatisfaction felt by people with various aspects of their life; trying to find out something about their 'quality of life'. In the field of poverty this would mean asking individuals for their own views of whether they feel poverty stricken or not. Their response would tend to be guesswork and probably unrealistic because answers would be based on their attitudes, circumstances, expectations and experiences and what they feel the attitudes of society are through their reading of newspapers, watching television, etc..

In the past poverty definitions have been concerned wtih objective conditions; measurements being based on objective standards. Naturally we can have different objective standards and therefore different definitions. Traditionally definitions were centred on physical health; that which is just sufficient for physical efficiency. Other definitions are based on social or economic standards. Social standards would include more than the minimum physical materials; it would include other material goods which society would expect a person to have, perhaps for the elderly this might mean extra coal or certain types of toys for children. Economic standards are concerned with the materials that are needed to make a person economically efficient; a teacher needs books, a worker dealing with blast furnaces needs extra liquids, a person doing extra heavy work needs extra foods, etc..

Poverty surveys

Poverty studies in the U.K. began with surveys of Booth and Rowntree. They provided information on the extent of poverty and advanced our understanding of the causes of this social problem.

Charles Booth produced 17 volumes on "The Life and Labour of the People in London". The first volume was published in 1889.

B. Seebohm Rowntree studied the social conditions in York and his findings were published in 1901 under the title "Poverty, A Study in Town Life".

Both used specific sums of income to determine whether people were or were not living in poverty — an objective approach. Rowntree used a *minimum* income which was considered necessary for expenditures on materials required for physical efficiency; in other words the minimum income required by families of different sizes (Victorian families tended to have larger families than they do in the 1970's) to provide the *minimum* of food, clothing and shelter needed 'for the maintenance of merely physical health'. Families who were below this minimum income level (often called the 'poverty line') were considered to be living in 'primary poverty'. His calculations showed that 9.9 per cent of the people of York were below the poverty line.

Rowntree went on to explain what this idea of 'merely physical efficiency' meant in terms of materials that could not be purchased. They could be purchased but if they did they must do with less food; they must sacrifice physical efficiency. What could they not buy? They could not buy:
tickets to ride on railways or buses,
postage stamps to post letters to absent children,
dolls, marbles or sweets for their children,
beer or tobacco for themselves, nor
coffins to bury their dear ones.
Also, they could not afford to:
pay subscriptions to friendly societies,
pay the doctor, and
more than anything else they could not afford to be absent from work even for one day.

The above gave an idea of primary poverty. Rowntree also described a situation known as 'secondary poverty', where families had total earnings sufficient to keep them out of primary poverty but because money was misspent they appeared to be in primary poverty. This objective definition is more difficult to measure and less accurate relative to primary proverty.

Rowntree carried out a second survey of York in 1936. He used the same kind of primary poverty measurement but added additional material needs which their income had to buy, for example:
subscriptions to trade union,
contributions for compulsory insurance,
purchasing a daily newspaper,
paying travel fares to and from work, and
other odds and ends.

A similar list of material needs were used in the third survey of York, by Rowntree and G. R. Lavers, in 1951 "Poverty and the Welfate State".

In the ten years before World War II a considerable number of surveys on poverty in particular areas were carried out. Some of these are listed because some students may find them interesting because their home town has been studied.

Bolton — 1915 — A. L. Bowley and A. R. Burnett-Hurst, A Survey of Five Towns: "Livelihood and Poverty".
    1925 — A. L. Bowley and M. H. Hogg, "Has Poverty Diminished?".
Bristol — 1938 — H. Tout, "The Standard of Living in Bristol".
Kingstanding (Birmingham) — 1942 — S. Soutar, E. H. Wilkins, P. Sargant Florence, "Nutrition and Size of Family".
London — 1889-1902 — C. Booth
    1930-1935 — many contributors, "New Survey of London Life and Labour".
Merseyside — 1934 — D. Caradog-Jones, "Social Survey of Merseyside".
Miles Platting (Manchester) — 1934 — J. Inman, "Poverty and Housing Conditions in a Manchester Ward".
Northampton — 1915 and 1925 (see Bolton).
Plymouth — 1935 — "A Social Survey of Plymouth".

Reading — 1915 and 1925 (see Bolton).
Sheffield — 1934 — A. D. K. Owen "A Survey of the Standard of Living in Sheffield".
Southampton — 1934 — P. Ford "Work and Wealth in a Modern Port".
Stanley — 1915 and 1925 (see Bolton).
Warrington — 1915 and 1925 (see Bolton).
York — 1901 and 1941 — B. S. Rowntree.
     1951 — B. S. Rowntree and G. R. Lavers.

A recent article[9] stated that "Although government policies affect poor people and attempt to combat poverty, there is no overall assessment of how they are succeeding". Mr. Field presents a considerable amount of useful up-dated material in his articles and students would benefit if they read it in its entirety.

He pointed out that "The most commonly accepted definition of poverty is that laid down by the government in the supplementary benefit scale rates.", and then noted that mean-tested supplementary benefits do not accurately portray poverty for two likely reasons. The first being that many people do not take-up these benefits, and secondly that there was need to consider supplementary benefit scale rates as a proportion of average earnings; a relative situation.

It was shown that there were in Great Britain, in 1974, approximately 2,681,000 persons receiving supplementary benefits but this excluded the unemployed who received no payments during the week of inquiry. Thus, this figure under estimates the true situation, and it further under estimates the figure because some persons could but do not take-up the benefits.

This is one way of looking at poverty in this country. In terms of a relative situation we might use the definition of 'relative poverty' provided by Mr. Robert S. McNamara[10] which states that the "relative poor were those whose average income was less than one-third of the national average." Applying this definition to U.K. data for the period 1974-75 we would arrive at a figure of almost 4,000,000 being in relative poverty before income tax has been deducted, and approximately 2,500,000 after income tax is paid.[11]

No matter how you look at it (supplementary benefits or relative) the number of persons at or near the poverty line in the U.K. can be counted in the millions. When we take into consideration that this income has to be

9. "The Poor" by Frank Field in Society Today, Dec. 1977, p8.
10. Mr. McNamara is President of the World Bank (IBRD) and his definition of relative poverty was noted in "Changing Emphasis of the Bank's Lending Policies" by Mahub ul Haq in the Fund and Bank's publication "Finance and Development", June 1978, p.13.
11. The figures are based on Exhibit 5 in the section 'Population and National Income'.
    Pre-tax figures showed the mean income being £2,287. One-third of this is £762. When looking at incomes near this level we find that this would include all incomes in the bottom 10 per cent and almost half of those in the next higher 10 per cent of incomes. Post-tax figures: mean income £1,868. One-third of this is £623. The great majority of bottom 10 per cent incomes are below this figure. The number of income units noted, in both cases, was 28,300,000.

spread among members of the household then the number of persons rises to possibly twice the number stated (8 million before tax; 5 million after tax) in relative terms.

Poverty — causes

In the twenty years before the beginning of the 20th century the surveys of Booth and Rowntree showed that the major causes of poverty were:
low wages,
unemployment, and irregular employment.
Of these low wages were by far the most important single cause.
The next most important group were calculated to be:
large families,
death of chief wage earner,
illness, and old age.
Other causes noted were:
drink,
unwise spending, and
loafing, but
these last causes were associated mainly with secondary poverty.

In the inter-war period (1919-1939) surveys listed virtually the same causes but the order of importance had changed. For example, low wages were removed as the primary cause as the wages of unskilled labour increased and the introduction of Trade Boards set up minimum wage schemes for certain occupations.

The principal cause of poverty throughout the 1920's and 1930's was unemployment.

After World War II unemployment was removed from being first in the list as the U.K. economy advanced into a 'full employment' situation. At the top of the list we now insert 'old age'. In 1974 in Great Britain slightly more than 2 out of every 3 persons receiving supplementary benefits were over retirement age. Even with unemployment as high as 1½ million it is doubtful that it will take over first place, but it will make unemployment the second most important cause of poverty in the latter 1970's.

Poverty — cure

In seeking to cure poverty it is necessary to define the material needs a person or family should have to maintain a certain standard of living. Then a survey would have to be carried out to determine the causes that create poverty. Once the causes have been recognised the community must provide special treatment to remove each cause.

We have already noted that 'low wages' becomes less of a problem by instituting minimum wage levels and that these had to be above the amount of money needed to purchase the materials needed to keep above the poverty line. Of course it would be possible to remove 'low wage poverty' by providing these materials at subsidised prices but this method is not asacceptable as the first.

When people fall into poverty because their earnings have been interrupted (illness, industrial injury) then it might be cured by establishing some form of state assisted insurance against these uncertainties.

When the bread winner dies the wife can be guarded against poverty by providing her with a pension which will be sufficient to purchase the basic material needs required to meet the standard. Also, giving money to pay for funeral expenses will remove an immediate problem.

An income that keeps husband and wife above the poverty line may not be sufficient when a child is born. The remedy may be that of providing a lump sum of money at the time of birth to meet the immediate additional expenses and later provide allowances for children. These should keep the family above the poverty line at birth and over the period of time the child grows to adulthood. As the child grows the community can help by providing free milk and if necessary free school dinners.

Unemployment can be removed as a cause by creating employment. Simply said but not always easy to achieve.

Of course someone has to provide the extra sums of money to remove many of these poverty situations. The state may be the provider of monies but initially the money is mainly provided by those who are above the poverty line. The state takes money away from these in the form of taxes and redistributes the money to those below, at or near the poverty line.

Old age is a special problem. Normally the payment of insurance money during working life will help to meet the money needs of the elderly after retirement. However, inflation pushes up the price of material needs and therefore there is need for the state to make further money provisions to help them remain above the poverty line (in the U.K. this additional help is called 'supplementary benefits') or lowering the prices they have to pay for their basic material needs.

What the solutions are for the causes of secondary poverty (drinking, betting, gambling, ignorant or careless home keeping, etc.) is anybody's guess. Putting taxes on beer or betting may simply drive a person further down the wrong side of the poverty line. On the other hand subsidising drinkers may encourage more drinking. Maybe the answer, at least for some, is to treat their problems as a social need and set-up special services to help them remove the habit.

It is not always possible to find the right cure for everyone. To this end a net must be slung under all special treatments to catch anyone who finds themselves still in poverty. In the U.K. the net is called 'supplementary benefits' and usually people have to take a test showing they do not have sufficient means to keep them at or above the poverty line.

At the present time (latter 1978's) there are over 40 means tests. 14 means tests are related to national benefits; for example one means test is necessary to obtain supplementary benefits, and another to obtain free welfare milk and foods. Local authorities also provide benefits which require means tests, such as rent rebates and grants for students taking their first degree.

The essence of a means test is that a person must justify his need by proving lack of means.

Means test benefits depend on people applying for help on their own initiative. Many people may be ignorant of the benefits available. Others may know about the benefits but refuse to seek them because they are associated with their idea of charity and consider living in poverty is less degrading than taking charity.

The only thing certain about this whole area is that needs change and means change and therefore it is necessary to maintain a continuous examination and analysis of poverty to ensure less people are trapped below the poverty line. To do this there is need to find a standard that is adequate and not misleading; perhaps the best indicator is the 'relative deprivation' or 'relative poverty' method.

Poverty — an advantage

One thing that is normally not associated with poverty is that there is an advantage. Perhaps there is one. As one writer put it those that are poverty stricken do not have to fill out tax forms or worry about tax inspectors.

Poverty — important areas

In discussing material needs we have often made note of three areas but have not developed them, namely, employment and unemployment, incomes, and distribution of incomes. These will be discussed more fully in other chapters of this book.

Social needs

Having laid the basics relating to material needs, it is now time to take a look at social needs; the mutual relations of human beings and social conditions in the community.

The Beveridge Report made recommendation to implement various social security measures, designed to bring happiness materially within the reach of every person in the community. It took other investigations and legislation to cover other needs of special groups such as the elderly, the handicapped, problem families and many other social groups.

The course of action and the extent of assistance provided by the government to help these groups and their social problems is determined by its social policy.[12]

Government action normally takes place by providing services — social services. Now the government provides many services so we must be clear how to distinguish a social service from other services. We might classify a social service as one where the people associated with providing the service are more concerned with the effect the service has on the people making use

12. Social policies are formed by precedent or by information made available to the government as to the extent of social need. Social policy refers to the course of action the government adopts to remove these needs.

of it and not so much concerned with the object being provided. For example, hospitals are institutions which are mainly National Health Service administered but the aim of these hospitals is to achieve a better quality of life for those who are afflicted with diseases, injuries, mental disturbances, etc. who have need of the services provided. We are not concerned, in this area, with public utility services where the object (gas, electricity, water, etc.) is the concern of the people associated with the service and not so much the people who use them.

Social services are applied to the collective provision for certain social needs, and they all have the same aim — helping each user to obtain a better quality of life. On the other hand each service fulfils the overall aim by having different aims. One service may have the aim of 'prevention', another 'curing', another 'protection' and yet another 'rehabilitation'. Each service can be geared to one or more social needs and different aims. There are different types of hospitals in the health service (general hospital, maternity hospital, geriatric hospital, mental hospital) each providing a different service. In each hospital there are different specialist personnel whose services cater for different social needs. The same can be said for other major service areas; different services geared for different social needs.

How much assistance is provided by the social services will depend upon the concept of need and the concept of social responsibility. These can change over time depending upon the social conscience of the community. Since the end of World War II the categories of need and the specialities of services have widened. As gaps appear the social services are widened to take in the newly found social need.

Some gaps may not be covered by the state. These may be noted by an individual or group who feel some form of service should be provided and carry out the service on a voluntary base. At some later stage the community may become aware of the need and pressurise the state to either take over the servicing of this need or help the voluntary organisation with financial assistance.

Social needs cover a wide range of activities, and they are not all covered by social services, for example anti-social activities such as crime and delinquency.

One problem that arises with needs is defining the need and setting the standard. Some areas are easy to define and set standards. This is true for material needs but more difficult for social needs.

It is very difficult to define needs and set standards in education. We normally are made aware of the difficulty when we read about controversies relating to comprehensive versus grammar schools, or the taking of examinations at certain ages (the old eleven plus), or the size of classes, etc. What the needs are and what standards should be set may be acceptable to one sector of the community but not another.

Needs associated with the health service are fairly easily defined but it is more difficult to set the standards of treatment. Recently debate has taken place on how long or whether people should be kept alive by machines after they have been found to be clinically dead. Another debate centres around the priority of money associated with kidney patients relative to other patients.

Housing is another area where defining needs is difficult. What constitutes a slum? What is the standard we should use here? We might also ask: when does a house become unfit for human habitation? What basic amenities (hot and cold water system, inside lavatories, fixed baths, etc.) should be provided? What is overcrowding?

There are many social needs related to housing. High rise flats provide shelter but they have been considered to be nothing more than 'boxes on stilts' built without due consideration of the people who had to live in them. If high rise flats are not the answer to solving the problem of housing what type of house should be built for the married mother with young children or the elderly who have disabilities? Lord Beveridge said the first need of all people, old and young is housing — a place to live in comfortably. What standard do we set for 'comfort'?

Education, health and housing are broad social need areas. There are many social problems associated with individuals which must also be considered under the term 'social need'. Consider the broken home problem. In such a situation is there a greater social need to protect children under five relative to children who have reached adolescence? On the other hand we might consider the social need that arises from mothers going out to work. Surely there is greater need to assist mothers who go out to work to maintain self and children relative to a mother who goes out to work because she prefers work and not compelled by a need to do so.

These last 2 examples show there are various categories of need.

The elderly not only require material needs. They are prone to physical defects and are greatly in need of care and attention to help them lead a comfortable and normal life. Services are provided for them in their own homes, such as meal on wheels, home help and visits by the district nurse. On the other hand some may become more settled in their way of life if they were catered for in special institutions.

Social need situations are vast in terms of numbers and it follows that there is need for a large number of specialist services. It is impossible to make note of all social needs and specialist services and to discuss them in depth. Consider some of the following:

1. The ill, injured and disabled (mental or physical impairment such as the blind and deaf) need special rehabilitation services to help and train them to become active in economic life once again.

2. Certain social problem groups such as delinquents and unmarried mothers are provided with specialist services which offer moral guidance.

3. The young have to be protected, and specialist services exist to protect them from being battered, neglected or exploited in the labour market.

These are some of the areas of social need. They are determined by society who then takes responsibility for rectifying the situations. Both needs and responsibilities find expression in the form and scope of what we liberally call the social services.

It is impossible to give as much help as society would like to all areas of social need because providing assistance requires resources — it is expensive to provide the services. To this end, society normally sets minimum standards for all but aims to provide more than the standard for certain areas. In other words social priorities are determined; decisions must be made as to which is more urgent. Should more resources be made available for health and less for housing? Should education be given priority over health? Is the education of children more important that caring for their teeth? Should primary education be given priority over secondary education?

Not only must priorities be determined for each broad sector of need but also within each broad sector. Within each area of priority other priorities must be determined. The Government determines these priorities on behalf of the community.

Much has been left unsaid; it is impossible to give a comprehensive view of all areas of social need. On the other hand students should, through special case studies and reports, have a wider acquaintanceship with these matters. Some help is given in a later chapter 'Population and Social Implications'.

Material and social needs

The overall object of providing for material and social needs is to give respect to the individual and family — to give them happiness and to give them a better quality of life.

Is not this what society owes each member of the population?

Assignments

1. The word 'need' states a situation which society feels must be rectified. Carefully distinguish between 'material needs' and 'social needs' and explain why society feels these situations must be rectified.

2. Write brief notes on each of the following social evils:
   a) want,
   b) ill-health, and
   c) squalor.

3. Carefully distinguish between 'absolute poverty' and 'relative poverty'. Which definition do you prefer and why?

4. It has been claimed that the number of persons at or near the poverty line in the U.K. can be counted in the millions. Argue the case that this is so.

5. What, normally, are the major causes of poverty and what suggestions can you make to remove this social evil?

Chapter 10

Population and Economics Implications: General

Learning objectives:
At the end of your study of this chapter you should be able to:
1. **identify and explain the main economic implications of major demographic characteristics in contemporary Britain.**

The previous chapters on population provided details which showed that the population of the U.K. is in a continuous state of change. The implications of change in broad general terms were then noted but now, in the next two chapters, we must consider the general implications of population changes relating to the economic and social environmental areas.

General economic implications

The population of the U.K. has been steadily increasing and is expected to increase in the future, although at a slower rate.

An increase in population can result from any of the following:
1. an increase in the birth rate,
2. a decrease in the death rate, and
3. immigration.

A decrease in population results from the reverse of these.

In March, 1944 a Royal Commission was set up to "examine the facts relating to the present population trends in Great Britain; to investigate the causes of these trends and to consider their probable consequences; to consider what measures, if any, should be taken in the national interest to influence the future trend of population and to make recommendations".

The Report was published in June 1949.[1] They noted that the population of Great Britain would keep on growing and, as such, they considered some of the consequences of increasing numbers.

During the early 1970s further attention was paid to population growth, and a population panel was set up to assess the available evidence about the significance of population growth in Great Britain now and in the future, and to make recommendations about further work required. They submitted their Report (Cmnd 5258) in March 1973. One of their conclusions was that the U.K. would, in the long run, do better with a stationary rather than an increasing population.

1.   Royal Commission on Population Report, Cmd 7695, June 1949, HMSO. Chairman was Hubert D. Henderson.

Thus, the first consideration should be that of looking at the consequences of an increasing population. It should be noted that the Royal Commission stated that the consequences may be of various kinds; economic, social, psychological, political and strategic. They said (para 255) that "The industrial progress, the standard of living and the security of the British people, ... the influence of British ideas, traditions and institutions throughout the world may all be affected subtly but powerfully by demographic changes." They further noted that the above reactions can not be precisely assessed, and that some consequences, namely those belonging to the economic category, had greater weight than others.

Economic advantages and disadvantages of increasing population

Briefly stated (para 261) the economic advantages and disadvantages are as follows:

The disadvantages:

"(1) the amount of land available per head of the population diminishes as numbers in any country increase;

(2) the growing numbers have to be supplied with capital equipment of every sort (house room, public utilities, industrial plant, etc.) and productive resources have to be devoted to this purpose which might otherwise be used to raise standards."

As to the advantages:

"(1) facilitate an increase in the scale of production and supply a stimulus to technical improvement;

(2) if due to a high birth rate, are associated with a low average age of the population;

(3) make the economic system more flexible and may thus make it easier to avoid a waste of productive resources through obstinate mass unemployment;

(4) tend to increase the nation's internal influence and so in various ways to strengthen its economic position."

The above statements do not put weights to the advantages and disadvantages, nor do they mention whether the increase takes the population beyond the optimum.

If we were to consider the consequences of an increasing population to the optimum we might say that the advantages will tend to outweigh the disadvantages as long as the population increase continues to make more effective use of the available resources. Conversely, the disadvantages will tend to outweigh the advantages when population increase goes beyond the optimum size for this means there are too many people to utilise effectively the available resources.

It is a necessary condition of economic well-being that population should approximate to the optimum.

Economics implications — birth rates

With changes in the size of population go changes in its composition such as increasing or decreasing birth rates. An increase in the birth rate increases the total population, and a fall in birth rate lowers it.

Increasing birth rate

The immediate consequence of an increase in the birth rate is that it brings about an increase in the number of consumers. These young children must be supplied with goods (milk, nappies, powder, pins, cribs, etc.) and services (midwives, health visitors, doctors, etc.). These new demands must be met by the existing labour force and capital. If the existing labour force does not increase their production then there will be a lowering, on average, of everybody's material well-being. In other words, providing these new members of society with goods and services means that others will have less. They become a burden upon the adult population; resources and time must be devoted to their upbringing. Alternatively, had the increase not taken place, the existing population could have used these resources and time for raising their own standard of living.

The first impact is on the family. They must provide for their child from their income which, prior to World War II in the U.K., did not increase simply because they had a child. At the present time 'Family Allowances' are given by the state.

An increase in the size of the family would, normally, require bigger houses; a further outlay out of a given income.

These additional family outlays tend to create a standard of living gap between families and single persons.

Years ago children brought income (cash or kind) to the household and this tended to offset the cost of their upkeep. Today, as the school leaving age increases and restrictions are placed on employing school children, these children place a strain on family income.

The community as a whole is faced with more person living on the land; land available per person diminishes. More maternity hospitals, schools, etc. will be needed and these encroach upon available land.

As dependant children progress through their pre-working life they will need more goods and services; food, clothes, toys, cycles, schools, health visitors, teachers. As long as they are consumers and not producers it means a continued reduction, on average, in the standard of living of the community — especially the family.

Finally, they become producers and society should benefit from the goods and services they produce. This is true as long as they work. If they remain unemployed or emigrate to another country then the country of their birth loses their output.

When these persons marry they will have children. One would expect them to have more children that their parents and many more than their grandparents generation.[2] The economic consequences of more children are the same as before but the impact is greater.

Overall, when considering the economic consequences, remember the idea of the optimum.

Decreasing birth rate

When the birth rate decreases the size of the population falls, and the base of the 'population shape' is smaller than the previous year.

The immediate result is the opposite of what was said previously about the increase in birth rates. There will be:

fewer children, fewer consumers,
fewer 'dependant' population,
standard of living, on average, will not fall,
less need for producing baby foods, nappies, and later nurseries, schools, etc., and less need for services of doctors, health visitors, teachers, etc...

Economic implications — death rates

A decline in death rates tends to increase the size of the population and an increase the reverse of this.

Declining death rate

The immediate result of a declining death rate is that there will be an increase in the number of consumers. The overall result will depend upon which age groups are affected most by the decline in deaths.

If the decline is associated with infants then we have a situation similar to an increase in birth rates. If the decline is noticeable in the working population age group then we should expect a larger potential labour force. Assuming there were jobs for everyone we would expect an increase in goods and services, and a rise, on average, in the material well-being of the population.

If the age expectancy of life is between 30 and 35 (such as it was in the U.K. in the early 1800s, and India just after World War II) a decline in the death rate would simply raise the age of expectancy. This will probably increase the number of births and size of families (the age of fertility has been increased). Again, we could anticipate economic consequences similar to those associated with increasing birth rates.

Perhaps the age of expectancy is 60. A decline in the death rate at this age level will tend to increase the dependancy population (assuming the age of retirement is 60). This would result in the country having economic consequences associated with an 'ageing population':

more retired persons and need for pensions, national assistance and possibly the need for higher taxes from the work force,

an increase in the number of consumers relative to producers and therefore, on average, a lowering of the material well-being of the community,

2.   A generation is considered to be one-third of a century.

an increasing need for the existing labour force to produce more goods and services for the dependant population; not necessarily the type usedby the rest of the community,

the elderly find it difficult to accept technical change,

the number of persons staying in jobs to 60 and beyond will hold up promotion for the younger generation, and

numerous other consequences.

Increasing death rate

The impact of this event will depend upon deaths specific to certain age groups. The opposite to that noted above occurs. Briefly:

specific to young children: there will be less dependants — less 'mouths' to feed and shelter — later, a loss of potential workers — but, an increase in the standard of living for others.

specific to working age group: less workers — less output — a decline in standard of living.

specific to elderly population: less dependants — less mouths to feed — less goods and services especially needed by the elderly — an increase in the standard of living.

overall: there will be more land per person.

Migration

An increase in immigrants will increase the size of population, and an increase in emigration will cause a decrease in population.

Economic implications — immigration

An influx of people from abroad will increase the size of population and immediately increase the number of consumers. If they are of working age, and work is available, they will contribute to total output. On the other hand, if they are dependants (too young and too old to work) they will place a strain on the existing working population and lower the average standard of living.

Immigrants, quite naturally, are accustomed to a different way of life. They may have need for foods not grown in the new country and, as a result, will tend to purchase these from abroad. This will add to the import bill.

The dependant young will have to be educated, and if their language is not the same as the host country this will require special resources (books, teachers, etc.). This reduces the resources available to the non-immigrant population.

Most countries place restrictions on immigrants to ensure the existing population are not made to suffer a fall in their material well-being. Normally, host countries accept immigrants who can make a positive contribution; to enhance the material well being and quality of life of the indigenous population.

Economic implications — emigration

The size of population declines as people leave the country and the immediate effect is that the country loses consumers. However, like immigrants, much will depend upon the age of those leaving.

If emigrants form part of the work population the country loses their output. Great expense may have gone into their education and training (doctors, engineers, etc.) and their loss can not be easily nor quickly replaced. The host country gains all the advantages of their capabilities at the expense of the country they leave.

The 'Brain Drain Report' gives a better insight of the migration situation as it affects the United Kingdom.

Emigration and immigration

Why do people migrate? To answer this question it would be necessary to find out the forces that 'push' people out of one country, and 'pulls' them to a new country. There are many factors; social, political, economic, etc.. The economic forces vary from one time to another. Some recent 'push' forces are:

taxation .... too high at home compared to new country
salaries .... too low at home compared to new country
promotion .... better opportunities in new country
material well-being ..... better conditions in new country

Optimum population

In considering the general economic implications of these demographic factors it is useful to be guided by the concept of the optimum population. When considering the relationship between population and other economic areas is it important to remember the size of the population in relation to available resources.

Population and balance of payments

An economic problem that has faced the U.K., off and on, since the end of World War II in 1945 has been that of having a deficit in the balance of external payments. Quite simply, this may be the result of having too large a population.

We have already noted that agriculture in the U.K., even using modern techniques and equipment, is probably not capable of supporting the present U.K. population of approximately 56,000,000. If increased agricultural goods cannot be met by home agriculture then to ensure a high standard of living for all, the U.K. must import foods. Of course, there are certain foods which the U.K. can not economically produce (coffee, tea, cocoa, grapefruits, lemons, etc.), and, in order to supply the inhabitants with these desirable goods they must be imported from other countries. As population grows the greater the volume of imported foods are needed if the material well-being of each inhabitant is to be maintained.

Similarly, there are many basic raw materials which this country does not have in sufficient quantities (timber, copper) or not at all (cotton, jute, tobacco). To provide increasing numbers with these it is necessary to increase imports.

All these will add to our import bill. The larger the increase in population, the larger the import bill. To pay for these it is vital to export goods (manufacturing) and services (shipping, insurance). The larger the import bill the greater the efforts to export more (assuming the price relationship has not changed).

This may be the typical situation facing the U.K. today, but it may not have been the case had there been no world wars.

When this country was considered to be the 'workshop of the world' in the 19th century British money was invested in the business activities of foreign countries. The returns on these (dividends, interest and profits) were large and enabled the U.K. to pay for increases in the imports of goods and services. Unfortunately, the two world wars required the sale of a large part of these investments. The result being that these are no longer sufficient to pay for our present day import requirements. We, more or less, must meet our present import bill with what we can presently export.

The U.K. balance of payments prior to world war I were normally on the 'credit' side. This was possible even with an increasing population. Today, the story is different.

The U.K. relies heavily on trade with foreign countries, and so do many other countries. In total this reliance simply increases the world demand for certain goods which are kept in, more or less, fixed supply. The result is an increase in the prices we have to pay. This pushes our import bills higher and makes the previous problem a much bigger problem. It does not necessarily follow that the goods we export will rise to the same extent. As more and more countries become industrialised the U.K. exporters will meet stiffer competition, as evidenced, in recent years, by the motor vehicle industry. This means that more manufactured goods will have to be exported. Thus, the U.K. has had balance of payments problems.

A decrease in population, overall, would tend to reduce the problem.

The Royal Commission on Population in 1949 said (para 269) that "an increase in the population of 10 per cent would raise our import requirements by about 15 per cent". This suggests that the U.K. balance of payments difficulties might be materially eased by smaller numbers.

There is a strong relationship between the size and make-up of the U.K. population and its trade with other countries.

Population and government revenue and expenditure

In a 'welfare state', such as the U.K., the State, directly and indirectly, makes an impact on the life of the individual from the time of his/her entry into the world until his/her burial.

Those on the receiving end receive money, such as family allowances and pensions. Indirectly the State provides money for the services provided, such as midwife services and hospital services. These government expenditures increase as the size of the population increases.

Expenditures are normally met by the government raising money from the general public. The revenue is obtained from taxation, national insurance contributions and from borrowing. The size of the revenue will depend upon the expenditures which depend upon the size of population.

Population and demand

A change in the size and composition of the population will cause a change in demand. An increase in the size of population will tend to increase demand and a decrease in the size of population will tend to decrease demand. The more young children in a population the greater the need for goods and services to meet their requirements. The less elderly there are, the less the need for goods and services associated with them.

At the turn of the century approximately 5 out of every 100 persons in the country were elderly. In mid-1975 it was roughly 17 out of every 100. An ageing population will want goods and services quite different from the young; walking sticks instead of cricket bats; tea instead of milk; special chairs instead of high-chairs. Production will have to be switched to meet the increased demands of the elderly. We could multiply these examples indefinitely.

Population and markets

The term market means different things to different people. In economics a market is said to exist in any area where dealings between buyers and sellers take place for any good or service. There are many types of goods and services and many ways of bringing buyers and sellers together. At this time we are primarily concerned with buyers.

An increasing population provides, normally, an increase in the demand for goods and services. As population continues to increase *new* demands will be transmitted by buyers for the production of more goods and services. An increase in the demand for goods will tend to create new demands for the factor of production markets, for example, labour market, capital market. In other words, the size of the various markets tend to increase with an increase in the size of population.

Of course, the extent of the market for any product is limited by the facilities for transport. Prior to the industrial revolution most markets were small and local and the population were, generally, self-supporting. Over time transport facilities have improved and markets grew from local to national and international; more people depend on others for their needs. Gradually the movement is from self-supporting locally to self-supporting nationally. When population grows beyond a certain size international markets grow in importance. The history of the U.K. from the early 1800s bears this out.

Basically, increasing populations means more buyers in the market. More buyers require an increase in the output of goods and services.

Population and economies from large scale production

When local markets tend increasingly to become less restricted and therefore become mass markets (national and international markets) firms are able to achieve greater economies of scale. The size of the market is a major factor contributing to the growth of firms, and economies of scale.

Economies of scale, simply stated, refers to a general fall of costs in producing goods (or services) as the firm grows in size. Falling costs are the result of producing on a larger scale. They refer to economies in finance (easier and cheaper to raise financial capital), in buying (obtain bigger discounts), in applying division of labour (an employee does one small part of the production process), and others.

The above becomes possible because an increase in population tends to increase the number of buyers and the increased demand enables firms to grow in size by producing on a larger scale.

The larger the population the greater the opportunity for economies of scale to be achieved. For example, the U.S. has a population that is more than four times that of the U.K. This makes it possible for the motor vehicle manufacturers in the U.S. to achieve greater economies of scale than their counterparts in the U.K.

Economic implications of population

Most of the above provide an insight into the relationships between population and economics. Most situations, and there are many economic situations not considered, have been treated generally and briefly. Now, it is time to look at two specific areas in economics in greater depth; employment and national income.

Assignments

Age Composition of the U.K.

(figures in thousands)

Ages	Mid-1975	Mid-2011
under 5	3,954	3,986
5 and under 20	13,268	11,878
20 but less than 65	30,996	34,926
65 and over	7,825	8,235
Totals	56,043	59,025

Source: Abstracted from table 15 page 21 of Annual Abstract of Statistics, 1976, H.M.S.O.

1. What effect will the changed composition of the U.K., as shown in the above table, have on consumption?
2. What effect will the changed composition of the U.K., as shown in the above table, have on production?
3. The growth of population in the U.K., as shown in the above table, can only lead to a deficit in the balance of external payments. Explain why this is likely to be true.

Chapter 11

Population and economic implications: Employment[1]

Learning objectives:
At the end of your study of this chapter you should be able to:

1. identify and explain the main economic implication of major demographic characteristics with reference to employment.

2. contribute to a discussion on sex equality in terms of employment.

3. define and identify occupations.

Population not only provides a country with consumers but also producers. However, as noted earlier, not all consumers are producers, nor are all potential producers actually producing. Some who are capable and willing to work are unemployed or idle.

The Beveridge Report[2], in 1942, stated that society owed its members those resources that would remove the five giant evils of disease, ignorance, squalor, want and idleness, and that the way to remove idleness was to provide employment.

The Government, in a White Paper in May 1944[3], stated that they "accept as one of their primary aims and responsibilities the maintenance of a high and stable level of employment after the war". They also stated (para 39) that if fairly regular cycles of unemployment, which is evidence of instability in the economic system, is to be banished three essential conditions must be satisfied:-

"(a) Total expenditure on goods and services must be prevented from falling to a level where general unemployment appears.

(b) The level of prices and wages must be kept reasonably stable.

(c) There must be a sufficient mobility of workers between occupations and localities."

To this date, evidenced by the Budget of April 1978, the maintenance of a high and stable level of employment is still a major economic (and social) objective. It was stated that "the Budget measures are ...... designed with a number of closely related objectives. First, to give a stimulus to the economy which will get unemployment moving significantly down".[4]

1. The greater part of this section comes from "Economics for Business Studies" Vol. II Chapter 7, Ed. N. L. Paulus, Publishers: Polytech.

2. Report on Social Insurance and Allied Services, Cmd 6406, HMSO.

3. "Employment Policy", Cmd 6527, HMSO, p.3

4. "The Budget" in Economic Progress Report Supplement, April 1978, A Treasury Broadsheet, p.1.

Now to look at the link between population and employment.

Some terms clarified

Labour means all kinds of human effort undertaken for a reward. The efforts may be physical or mental, skilled or unskilled. It would include, to mention a few, the efforts of managing directors, foremen and operators on production lines or in offices, also central and local government officers and clerks, and health visitors, social workers and teachers.

The size of the labour force will depend, in the first place, on the number of people that are, by law (for example, employment of school children) or nature (severely handicapped) able to work. Our concern is with that part of the population who actively participate in economic activity in producing goods and services.

Economically active persons, according to the Census of Population 1971,[5] are those who are in employment plus those temporarily out of a job. Excluded are retired persons, students in educational establishments, persons doing unpaid domestic duties, and au pair girls. In other words it tends to exclude those never in employment, those not seeking work, and those not seeking work for a monetary reward.

Statistical material is used to indicate the size of the labour force and their occupations. Information comes from a number of sources, but for this chapter the basic source (at least for 1971) is the Census of Population.

Size of labour force

What is the size of the labour force in relation to the population of Great Britain? Exhibit 11.1 shows this relationship for two census years, 1961 and 1971.

Exhibit 11.1   Relationship of
Economically Active Population (EAP)
to
Total British Population

	1961[1]			*1971*[2]			*1961-1971*	
							Changes	
	Totals	*%*	*%*	*Totals*	*%*	*%*	*Totals*	*%*
Total Population	51,284,000	100·0	—	53,802,700	100·0	—	2,518,700	4·91
EAP[3]	23,816,000	46·44	100·0	25,002,600	46·47	100·0	1,186,600	4·98
of which								
Males	16,076,000	—	67·5	15,866,500	—	63·5	− 209,500	− 1·30
Females								
Married	3,886,000	—	16·3	5,781,100	—	23·1	1,895,100	48·77
Other	3,854,000	—	16·2	3,355,000	—	13·4	− 499,000	-12·9

Source:
1—Extracted from Table A1 of Census of Population 1961 entitled 'Occupation and Industry', National Summary Tables, HMSO, 1965.
2—Based on Tables 1 and 13 of Census 1971 Great Britain, Summary Tables (1% Sample), HMSO, 1973.
Note: Figures for both years are based on population aged 15 and over.

5.   Census of Population 1971 Great Britain-Summary Tables (1% Sample), HMSO, page 189.

The 'economically active population' is not the same as the 'working population'. The difference, using 1961 as an example:

Economically active population 23,816,000
    plus total of armed forces abroad
    plus 'net' figure of seamen at sea
    less foreign armed forces in Britain

Working population 24,026,000

The figures given in Exhibit 11.1 refers to all persons economically active *within* Great Britain (including foreign armed forces) at the time of the Census and excludes those *outside* the country.

Exhibit 11.1 provides some interesting facts. For example:

1. population grew, between 1961 and 1971, by nearly 5 per cent,

2. the EAP rose by approximately the same percentage,

3. the change in the EAP (1,186,600) was approximately 47 per cent of the change in total population (2,518,700).

4. the increase in the EAP was the result of many more married women taking jobs.

5. over the ten year span, there was a fall in the number of single females (including widows and divorced) at work; also the number of males. The two, together, represents a fall of approximately 708,500.

6. the EAP, in each census year, remained virtually the same proportion of total population; 46.44 per cent in 1961 and 46.47 per cent in 1971.

The exhibit does not tell us what part of total population are males, and what part are females. Nor, does it provide information about the future. A look into the future of the EAP was carried out by the Department of Employment.[6] It showed that the EAP will increase in absolute terms but the rate of increase will be less than the 1961-71 change. They also forecasted that the number of females, especially married, will constitute a larger part of the increased EAP. This is shown by the following example:

For every 100 economically active persons the breakdown of males to females approximates the following:

	Males	Females
1961	67.5	32.5
1971	63.5	36.5
1981	61.9	38.1
1991	61.2	38.8

This is an indication that personnel managers will need to look more and more to the female sector to fill job vacancies, and Trade Unions must accept more female members. Of course this assumes that the U.K. does not have a large unemployed male force.

What will the situation be in 1981? This we will know when the Census of Population 1981 is published. A point to be noted when comparing 1971

6.   "Labour force projections: 1973-1991" Department of Employment Gazette, April 1974, pages 304 to 310.

EAP figures with those of 1981 is that the 1971 EAP figures include the 15 year olds whereas the 1981 figures will exclude them. This does affect the size of the labour force and it results from a government decision raising the statutory leaving age by one year to 16 on 1 September 1972. The first effect of this was that in January 1974 pupils whose 16th birthday fell on or after 1st September 1973 were required to remain in school at least to Easter 1974.

Coming back to the Census of Population 1971 it is time to note more about the EAP and the 'economically inactive population' (EIP). Exhibit 11.2 attempts to widen our knowledge of these areas.

The first fact appearing from Exhibit 11.2 is as noted before, that there were, in 1971, more women than men making up the population; out of every 100 persons something like:

51½ were women, and
48½ men.

However, the relationship is not the same when looking at the age groups '15 and under' for males form a larger part of the total. On the other hand, females exceed males in the '15 and over' group.

Some other facts emerging from the exhibit are as follows:

1. the potential working male force totalled 19,474,000 but only 15,866,500 were economically active; 81½ per cent of the total.

2. the female potential working force was 21,353,100 but only 42.8 per cent (9,136,000) were economically active.

The above points can be expressed more simply as follows:

out of every 100 males 15 and over . . . . . 81 were economically active, and
out of every 100 females 15 and over . . . 43 were economically active.

The above is a clear indication that any growth in the labour force, in a period of full employment, would have to come, mainly, from the female sector.

Exhibit 11.2 makes known that not all economically active persons are in employment. Invariably there will always be some who are temporarily sick and others who are temporarily unemployed. However, of those who are employed we can note that they are employed under four major 'status' categories. Out of every 100 in employment:

approximately 7.5 are self-employed,
approximately 7.0 are managers,
approximately 4.1 are foremen and supervisors, and
approximately 81.3 other employees.

The economically inactive group (15 and over) provides some interesting information. For example, the retired and permanently sick are not available for employment and they constitute, almost, 37 per cent of the economically inactive total.

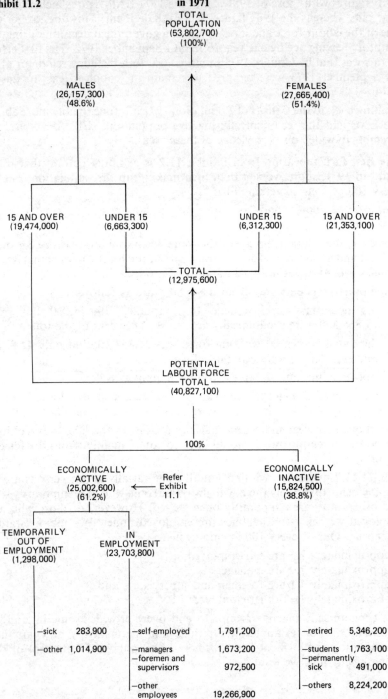

Source: Extracted from Tables 1 and 13 of Census 1971 Great Britain, Summary Tables (1%
Sample), 1973, HMSO.

The student population are potential employees, as are many of those noted under 'others' — a considerable proportion of these being females. One can suppose from these figures that the potential economically active group, at the time of the census in 1971, would total just under 35,000,000. However, the use of all these would create problems: no students and virtually all housewives working.

The exhibit and all that has been noted does seem to bring out the point that in 1971 there was a scarcity of labour.

This is very interesting information but it does not recognise that labour is a 'heterogeneous factor'. It says nothing about how these people are employed. What are their occupations? How many miners and quarrymen are there? How many woodworkers or textile workers?

Occupations

According to the general explanatory notes issued at the beginning of the 1% Sample of the Census 1971 it stated that "The OCCUPATION of a person is the kind of work which he or she performs, regard being paid to the conditions under which it is performed. This alone determines the occupational group to which the person is assigned. The nature of the factory, business, or service in which the person is employed has no bearing upon the classification of his occupation, except to the extent that it enables the nature of his duties to be more clearly defined. Thus, a crane driver may be employed in a shipyard, an engineering works or in building and construction, but this has no bearing upon his occupation and all crane drivers are classified to the same occupational group."[7]

Occupations — changing structure

Occupations are subject to change. Some occupations that exist today may have existed for hundreds of years (thatchers) whereas others (electronic engineers) may have recently arrived on the scene. Some occupations, over time, have been declining in importance, (thatchers, agricultural occupations) and others increasing (service occupations).

At the beginning of the 19th century the greater part of the British population lived off the land; most workers were occupied on the land. In the 1970s, the occupational structure of the British labour force is quite different. Small number of workers are required for agricultural occupations, many are demanded by manufacturing, and many more are required for occupations in the service sector of industry. The change has been from 'toilers' to 'blue collar' to 'white collar' occupations.

Occupations change in relation to changes in the demand for goods and services. They reflect the use society has for the efforts of labour. Thus, there is need for occupation mobility — it has been claimed that during the life time of a worker it can be expected that he will change his occupation three times.

7.   Census 1971 Great Britain — Summary Tables (1% Sample), HMSO, 1973, p. xii.

An understanding of occupations and occupation changes is needed for manpower planning by businesses and the government. An example of this is found in the National Plan.[8] The forecast for labour indicated that there would be a shortage of skilled and qualified manpower, and there was a need to accelerate training and retraining, and provide for those becoming redundant. Economic growth requires forward planning of labour as well as other factors of production.

1971 occupations

The Census of Population 1971, carried out by the Office of Population Censuses and Surveys, classified occupations into 27 occupation unit groups (OUGs). Each of these were subdivided into various occupations which fitted into each OUG; all in all 223 occupations were listed. Some OUGs had only 2 and others 3 or 4 or more. Group XXV (Professional, technical workers, artists) had 40 sub groups. It would take too long to make note of all these groups and sub groups, but it is worthwhile indicating the 27 groupings and the male and female make-up of each group. This has been done in Exhibit 11.3.

Exhibit 11.3 shows that the two largest OUGs are in the service sector of industry. OUG XXI (clerical workers) represented 14.8 per cent of the economically active in employment, and OUG XXIII (service, sport and recreation workers) was 12.1 per cent. These two OUGs constitute more than one-fourth the people in employment in 1971. In both these groups females outnumber males; the ratios are as follows:

Clerical workers . . . . 1 male to 2.359 females, and
Services, etc. . . . . 1 male to 2.382 females.

Further, the number of females in these two groups total nearly 51½ per cent of all economically active females; more than 1 in every 2 females have occupations in these broad areas.

The third largest group (OUG XXV) is also in the service section of industry and is male dominated; ratio of 1.6 males to every 1 female.

The fourth largest group (OUG VII) is in the 'secondary production' area and is male dominated; ratio of 6.4 males to every 1 female.

These four largest OUGs, in terms of employment, absorbed approximately:
49½ per cent of the total economically active population,
66½ per cent of all economically active females, and
39½ per cent of all economically active males.

From Exhibit 11.3 can be extracted the proportions of employment in primary, secondary and tertiary areas of production.[9] Primary production refers to the production of goods which are made available in a natural form, for example agricultural goods. Secondary production refers to the production of goods derived from the primary product, usually taken to be manufactured goods. Tertiary production is the production of services such as banking, retailing, transporting, wholesaling.

8. "The National Plan" Cmnd 2764, HMSO, September 1965 pages 39 to 43.
9. Actual demarcation of the OUGs into these areas of production is open to debate.

Exhibit 11.3   Importance of Occupation Groups

Numbers Employed

OUG No.	Occupation Unit Groups	Totals			
		Actual	as %	Males	Females
	All Occupations	23,703,800	100·0	14,998,600	8,705,200
	of which				
I	Farmers, foresters, fishermen	729,700	3·1	629,400	100,300
II	Miners and quarrymen	235,400	1·0	235,300	100
III	Gas, coke and chemicals makers	127,400	0·5	114,000	13,400
IV	Glass and ceramic makers	93,000	0·4	63,600	29,400
V	Furnace, forge, foundry, rolling mill workers	157,400	0·7	150,300	7,100
VI	Electrical and electronic workers	599,900	2·5	522,300	77,600
VII	Engineering and allied trades workers	2,654,800	11·2	2,373,100	281,700
VIII	Woodworkers	407,000	1·7	395,000	12,000
IX	Leather workers	110,400	0·5	55,000	55,400
X	Textile workers	292,200	1·2	134,800	156,400
XI	Clothing workers	394,600	1·7	73,600	321,000
XII	Food, drink and tobacco workers	359,400	1·5	254,100	105,300
XIII	Paper and printing workers	306,700	1·3	212,600	94,100
XIV	Makers of other products	298,200	1·3	194,200	104,000
XV	Construction workers	539,400	2·3	538,100	1,300
XVI	Painters and decorators	270,600	1·1	263,800	6,800
XVII	Drivers of stationary engines, cranes, etc.	296,800	1·3	293,500	3,300
XVIII	Labourers not elsewhere classified	1,090,100	4·6	948,100	142,000
XIX	Transport and communications workers	1,350,500	5·7	1,202,700	147,800
XX	Warehousemen, storekeepers, packers, bottlers	773,500	3·3	482,200	291,300
XXI	Clerical workers	3,498,100	14·8	1,047,600	2,450,500
XXII	Sales workers	2,194,300	9·3	1,153,400	1,040,900
XXIII	Service, sport and recreation workers	2,877,400	12·1	850,700	2,026,700
XXIV	Administrators and managers	928,100	3·9	849,100	79,000
XXV	Professional, technical workers, artists	2,686,900	11·3	1,653,300	1,033,600
XXVI	Armed forces (British and foreign)	247,200	1·0	236,400	10,800
XXVII	Inadequately described occupations	185,800	0·8	72,400	113,400

Note: Percentage figures do not add up to 100 per cent due to rounding.
Source: Extracted from Table 22 pages 118-119 of 1% Sample Summary Tables publication of 1971 Census of Population.
Percentage figures calculated by author.

Out of each 100 actively employed persons the relationship would be, approximately as follows:

4 in primary production	(OUGs 1 and 2)
34 in secondary production	(OUGs 3 to 18)
62 in tertiary production	(OUGs 19 to 27)

In terms of production Great Britain, in fact the United Kingdom, is definitely a 'service' type economy; often, but not always, the sign of an 'advanced economy'.

Of the 27 OUGs listed there are only 6 where female workers outnumber the males. When considering the 223 occupations that make up the OUGs we would find that female workers dominated 40 occupations; the remainder (183) were male dominated.

Exhibit 11.4 shows 18 occupations dominated by males, and Exhibit 11.5 shows the main occupations dominated by females.

Exhibit 11.4

**Male Dominated Occupations
in 1971**

OUG Number	Occupation Number	Occupation	Males	Females*
II	007	Coal mine—workers underground	200,700	0
XV	095	Plasterers, cement finishers, terrazzo workers	45,700	0
XIX	133	Stevedores, dock labourers	43,300	0
XIX	118	Drivers, motormen, second men, railway engines	36,400	0
XVII	102	Boiler firemen	34,800	0
XVIII	106	Railway lengthmen	25,700	0
VI	026	Linesmen, cable jointers	23,700	0
XIX	115	Deck, engineering officers and pilots, ship	18,900	0
II	010	Surface workers not elsewhere classified— mines and quarries	17,900	0
III	011	Furnacemen, coal gas and coke ovens	17,900	0
XV	094	Masons, stone cutters, slate workers	15,800	0
XIX	119	Railway guards	14,500	0
VIII	058	Pattern makers	13,000	0
XIX	124	Shunters, pointsmen	10,400	0
XIX	117	Aircraft pilots, navigators and flight engineers	8,800	0
XXV	202	Metallurgists	8,000	0
XVI	101	Coach painters (so described)	7,000	0
VII	034	Steel erectors, riggers	4,100	0

Note: *figure "0" in this column signifies "nil or negligible".
Source: Extracted from Table 14 of 1% Sample, Census of Population 1971.

Exhibit 11.4 shows 18 occupations where males almost completely dominate these jobs, and it is unlikely that there will be a large influx of female labour. The Sex Discrimination Act 1975 provided a comprehensive piece of legislation outlawing sex discrimination in employment, training and other matters, and makes it possible for females to work underground in coal mines or become stevedores on the docks. However, a close look at the occupations shown in Exhibit 11.4 shows they are the type that normally:

    require heavy lifting, or
    are very dirty, or
    are very dangerous, or
    are very hot.

Not jobs that the typical female is likely to choose. These occupations will be penetrated by a few females, for example there are two women who qualified as 'dock slingers' at the Royal Naval Dockyard, Chatham.[10] Rates of pay normally take these adverse conditions into consideration, but a female who carries out similar activities as men under the same conditions can legally be expected to receive equal pay. The Equal Pay Act 1970 became fully operational, after a five year transitional period, in December 1975 (the same period of time that the Sex Discrimination Act 1975 came into force).

On the other hand, none of the 223 occupations listed showed females dominating any occupation where there were nil or negligible males employed. This can be seen in the 18 occupations listed in Exhibit 11.5.

Exhibit 11.5   **Female Dominated Occupations**
                              in 1971

OUG Number	Occupation Number	Occupation	Males	Females	Ratio*
XI	076	Hand and machine sewers and embroiderers, textile and light leather products	800	230,100	1—288
XXIII	158	Domestic housekeepers	400	34,800	1—87
XXI	141	Typists, shorthand writers, secretaries	10,700	758,900	1—71
XXV	189	Occupation therapists	200	6,000	1—30
XXIII	164	Maids, valets and related service workers not elsewhere classified	15,200	427,600	1—28
XXIII	161	Canteen assistants, counter hands	10,800	293,400	1—27
XXV	183	Nurse	37,300	394,400	1—11
XXV	188	Physiotherapists	900	7,500	1—8
XXIII	166	Charwomen, office cleaners, window cleaners, chimney sweeps	65,800	456,400	1—7
XXI	140	Office machine operators	23,900	152,700	1—6
XXIII	157	Housekeepers, stewards, matrons and housemothers	5,000	31,900	1—6
X	066	Winders, reelers	4,500	26,900	1—6
XIX	127	Telephone operators	18,600	88,700	1—5
XXIII	163	Kitchen hands	21,200	100,400	1—5
XXII	144	Shop salesmen and assistants	182,300	786,100	1—4
IV	016	Ceramics' decorators and finishers	2,200	7,800	1—4
XXIII	167	Hairdressers, manicurists, beauticians	34,600	124,200	1—4
VI	029	Electrical and electronic fitters	13,000	37,900	1—3

Note: *Ratios are taken to nearest whole number.
Source: Extracted from Table 14 of 1% Sample, Census of Population 1971.

Exhibit 11.5 lists the top 18 occupations that are female dominated, starting with the greatest dominated occupation moving towards the lesser ones. The first listed is, by far, the exceptional female dominated occupation when compared to the rest. A glance at these occupations seem to indicate the lack of conditions noted for male dominated occupations. On the other hand, female occupations are the type that normally:

require neatness of handling.

10. Evidence of females entering occupations normally preserved for males and vice versa can be found in the April 1978 issue of "Employment News", The Department of Employment Newspaper.

This covers many aspects, such as softness of touch,
                        nimbleness of fingers, and
                        feeling towards helping others.

People differ in sex but these differences are not so important as they were once thought to be. The big differences in one sex performing jobs in these occupations better than others is the result of training given throughout their educational life. For example boys are trained in woodwork and metalwork whereas girls are trained in domestic and office work. Just recently (1978) two males completed their training course as midwives.

The last two exhibits clearly bring out the point that labour is not a homogeneous factor. Of course, it is possible to break down the occupations listed into more narrowly defined groups; more homogeneous groups. For example, in Exhibit 11.5 the 7th occupation shown 'Nurse' could be divided into 'hospital nurse', 'district nurse', 'midwife', 'health visitor'.

1972 — New list of occupations

While the Census of population classifies occupations under one system, the Department of Employment developed, in 1972, a new and comprehensive 'Classification of Occupations and Directory of Occupational Titles' (CODOT), and provided a list of key occupations.[11]

The Department stated that "These are occupations for which it has been agreed that figures are needed and can be collected at national level. It is not possible to collect and publish statistics on a national scale about every occupation; for practical reasons it is necessary to concentrate on a fairly limited number." They also stated that "To ensure compatibility between CODOT and the key list, all key occupations are identified and defined in CODOT and grouped in the same broad structure of 18 major groups." The following Exhibit (11.6) gives these groupings and the number of occupations listed under each.

This appears to be a much better system of classifying occupations. Nurses are classified in the list of key occupations under several occupations, for example:

Nursing administrators and nursing executives.
State registered and state enrolled nurses and state-certified midwives.
Nursing auxiliaries and assistants.

Midwives and Health Visitors are still not separately classified. Perhaps CODOT, with about 3,500 coded occupations, will break larger groups (like Nurses) into more homogeneous occupations.

What is the purpose of providing 402 key occupations? According to the Department of Employment, it is to identify those occupations for which national statistics are most needed with the aim of helping government and industry in the light of current needs.

It is imperative that labour is directed into the right occupations, and that businessmen and the government establish training systems relevant to the changing occupation structure — to prepare for present and future needs.

Exhibit 11.6

CODOT Grouping and
Number of Key Occupations in each group

Group	Group Listing	Number of Key Occupations
I	Managerial (General Management)	2
II	Professional and related supporting management and administration	21
III	Professional and related in education, welfare and health	24
IV	Literary, artistic and sports	9
V	Professional and related in science, engineering, technology and similar fields	31
VI	Managerial (excluding general management)	26
VII	Clerical and related	15
VIII	Selling	7
IX	Security and protective services	9
X	Catering, cleaning, hairdressing and other personal service	26
XI	Farming, fishing and related	13
XII	Materials processing (excluding metal)	29
XIII	Making and repairing (excluding metal and electrical)	53
XIV	Processing, making repairing and related (metal and electrical)	69
XV	Painting, repetitive assembling, product inspecting, packaging and related	14
XVI	Construction, mining and related not identified elsewhere	22
XVII	Transport operating, materials moving and storing and related	28
XVIII	Miscellaneous	6
	TOTAL	402

Economic growth depends upon us making the most efficient use of our labour force and this can be achieved, partially, by ensuring specific occupational shortages do not occur. Equilibrium between the demand for and the supply of specific occupations (for all occupations) is the goal to be achieved to satisfy economic growth.

Assignments

1. Any growth in the U.K. labour force in the last two decades of the 20th century will have to come, mainly, from the females sector. Use statistical material to support your explanation why this is true.

2. Occupations are subject to change. Give examples of four occupations that existed in the early 19th century but are considered to be a declining occupation today and then explain why the decline has taken place.

3. To have true equality of the sexes we must have females working underground at the coal face and as stevedores working on the docks. Do you agree? State reasons for making the decision you did.

Chapter 12

Population and Economic Implications: National Income

Learning objectives:
At the end of your study of this chapter you should be able to:
1. relate the effects of changes in population to the size and distribution of the national income.
2. appreciate the recent position of wealth distribution in the U.K.
3. discuss with confidence the distribution of income in the U.K.

In relating the effects of population change to the size and distribution of the national income it is important to have a clear understanding of the terms 'population' and 'national income'. To this end it will be beneficial to reproduce the definitions already given in previous chapters.

Population refers to the total number of persons inhabiting the U.K. This is the population that will be used when discussing the distribution of the national income. However, when discussing the size of the national income the term population will refer, mainly, to that part of the population that are economically active.

National income can be regarded as a flow of real goods and services made available to the community through economic activity over a specified period of time, usually one year, and is measured in money. Other terms associated with national income will often be used, for example: gross domestic product (GDP), gross national product (GNP), etc..

Population change
Briefly, changes that occur in the population are:
change in size of population, and
change in shape of population.

Allied to these are changes in birth rates, death rates, economically active population, dependant population, and many other aspects of population change noted in previous chapters.

The linking of population change to national income is a complex subject — it must be treated with great care. The following information does not cover all aspects of the situations, but is does provide an insight into the relationship of population change to national income.

Population — size of national income (economic growth)

The size of the national income, or to put it another way the total of goods and services produced, depends upon many factors. Perhaps the most important of these are:

1. the rate of increase or decrease in the quantity of a country's resources in capital, labour and land,

2. the rate of increase or decrease in the quality of the above resources,

3. the stability or instability of the government,

4. the state of technical knowledge, and

5. the level of aggregate demand.

There are other forces, important but considered to be minor, such as hours of work, religion, weather, work attitudes, and others.

The way to increase the size of the national income (making use of the five factors itemised) is to increase the quantity and quality of the country's resources, have a high state of technical knowledge and level of aggregate demand, and at the same time have a stable political atmosphere. The opposite of these will tend to lower the size of the national income.

A term that is normally used to describe an increase in real goods and services made available to the community through economic activity is "economic growth". More precisely the term is usually phrased as follows: "... to describe an increase in GDP or GNP at constant prices.". Achieving economic growth is important "because it provides the increased resources needed for industrial modernisation and development, for the improvement in the public services required for a growing population, and for a continuing increase in living standards."[1]

Having laid down some preliminaries about the size of the national income and economic growth in general we can now return to the specific forces (the five noted above) associated with population that help to determine a country's volume of production. At least we now know that population factors alone are not the only forces that determine the size of the national income.

Of the five factors listed we can isolate only that part of item 1 relating to the factor of production 'labour' and item 5 as being areas that can be discussed under the heading of population. First, to consider the fifth item.

It is claimed that population growth will increase the level of aggregate demand, and that the increase in internal and external markets leads towards economic development.

In the first instance the increase in demand will not be immediately met by an increase in supply, and this will result in a lower standard of living; the same amount of goods and services must be divided among more people. Later, because it facilitates an increase in the scale of production and supplies a stimulus to technical improvement more goods and services will be made available, on average to each person in the population. In the

1. "The National Income" Treasury Broadsheets on Britain No. 1, Dec. 1970, p4.

U.K., growing population can be beneficial if certain industries, such as those that cater for a mass market (electricity, gas, motor vehicle, water, etc.), can produce on a large scale. The cost per unit of these industries tends to fall as they more fully utilise their facilities.

An increase in the size of markets will normally create an additional amount of investment in factories, houses, etc. and this favours an increase in capital equipment. We might say that population growth initially stimulates aggregate demand and economic development but the more important factor is the level of investment in capital goods.

Thus, population growth will, in the long term, encourage businessmen to produce goods in sufficient quantities to satisfy steadily expanding demand; it is favourable, generally speaking to increasing the size of the national income.

Population growth not only creates larger markets but also, after education has ended, provides the nation with a larger labour force to produce goods and services to meet the demands of additional numbers.

In considering item 1 we should note that the 'quantity of labour' is one among many factors that determine the size of the national income. What does the 'quantity of labour' depend upon? It depends upon:

1. the size of the working population — taking into consideration the age when people leave the educational scene and join the work force, and the age of retirement.

2. the nature of the working population — taking into consideration the ratio of younger workers to older workers, females to males, and married females to total females.

3. the time given to work — taking into consideration the number and duration of holidays, the number of hours worked, and retirement.

Eventually we will discuss these situations in general terms. First a warning must be given to treat comments with care because the relationship between quantity of labour and national income is complex and many factors operate in the economy that affect the size of the national income and the utilisation of the labour force.

Very simply, we would expect that adding a new unit of labour to the work force would tend to raise output and so raise the size of the national income. On the other hand we would expect the reverse to be true, but this may not be so. It is possible to increase the size of the national income with a smaller labour force if each unit of labour exerted greater effort in producing more goods and services.

Sometimes we will meet a situation, as in the U.K. from the end of World War II to the early 1970s, where we have a fully employed economy.[2] In this

---

2. Roughly speaking, full employment means that the percentage of unemployed remains below 3 per cent; a situation where all who are available for work are at work. The unemployed are made up, mainly, of those whose job has come to an end, those who are looking for a better job, and those who are between jobs. Anyone who wants a job can get a job fairly quickly.

situation additional units of labour will be absorbed into the work situation — output will increase and the national income will rise to a higher level (in terms of real goods and services).

On the other hand the U.K. has had more than 3 per cent unemployment since 1975. It was estimated to be more than 1,600,000 (more than 6 per cent) in July 1978. People who were capable of work and looking for a job were not able to find one. In this case we would expect that additions to the work population would not be employed — it is unlikely that the national income would increase.

Utilizing additional labour will depend upon the level of aggregate demand, degree of competition from foreign competitors, amount of labour saving equipment in operation, and the state of the economy in general. The size of the working population is only one factor in determining the level of national output. Other factors must be favourable if they are to work.

What is the make-up of the labour force? What occupations are they in? What is the ratio of males to females? These, and other questions, have already been noted in the previous section.

In this section we had to establish a simple link between that part of the population which form the 'work population' (quantity of labour) and the size of the national income.

Population — distribution of national income

In the chapter on the 'mixed economy' we saw that the U.K. Government, during the 20th century, increasingly interfered with the operation of the market system. This was necessary, it was claimed, because the market created imperfections in many aspects of economic activity. Interference was speeded-up during and after World War II and has continued right on into the 1970s. One area in particular received a great deal of attention — the area associated with income; poverty, distribution of income and redistribution of income. The most recent information on this subject comes from the Diamond Commission.

In August 1974 the Government set up the Diamond Commission[3] which "should issue to inquire into, and report on, such matters concerning the distribution of personal income, both earned and unearned, and wealth, as may be referred to it by the Government.". The standing reference on the Distribution of Income and Wealth include the following: "To help to secure a fairer distribution of income and wealth in the community there is a need for a thorough and comprehensive enquiry into the existing distribution of income and wealth. There is also a need for a study of past

3. Royal Commission under the chairmanship of Lord Diamond. Up to the end of 1977 the Commission submitted 5 reports, 3 of which have been reports on the standing reference, and 4 'background papers'. There are two publications that are of interest to this section:

Report No. 5 which is the 3rd report on the standing reference— Distribution of income and wealth, Cmnd 6999, HMSO, November 1977.

Background paper No. 3 which was a background paper to Report No. 5 on The effects of certain social and demographic changes on income distribution, HMSO, 1977.

trends in that distribution and for regular assessments of the subsequent changes.''. The Labour Government, in office in 1974, set the scene in its pursuit of 'equality' for the population of the U.K..

It is impossible to cover all aspects of income (and wealth) of the U.K. population in this section but a fair attempt will be made to record some essential points. Income will be treated in greater depth than wealth.

Basic information starts with definitions.

1. Income (para 13). Income is a *flow* and is composed of various components which add to the command over resources accruing to an individual or household over a stated period of time. There are three main issues associated with this definition: the coverage of income, the nature of the income-receiving unit and the time period of measurement.

   However, in reviewing definitions the Commission felt that there was a need for a number of alternative definitions because income may be received in a variety of forms which are not always directly comparable.

2. Wealth (para 26). Wealth is a *stock,* representing the capitalised value of resource claims at a given point in time. As with income, the Commission said there was a need for a number of alternative definitions because wealth can be held in a variety of forms which are not always directly comparable.

When considering the nation's output of goods and services (national income) it should be remembered that all forms of income and wealth may be seen as representing claims or conveying command over resources; claims may take different forms and arise in different ways.

First, a brief treatment of wealth.

Wealth

Wealth, according to the Commission, can be divided into marketable (liquid) and non-marketable (illiquid) assets. This definition does not agree with the economist definition of real wealth — financial assets, for example, would not be included. However, they included the following under the various headings:

1. Marketable assets. Includes cash, bank accounts, government securities, company shares, land and dwelling. People have the right to dispose of these assets.

2. Non-marketable assets. Includes more border-line items: occupational pension rights, state pension rights, net worth of companies, and wealth held by the public sector. These assets are such that the holders have the right to income but not the right of disposal.

When considering wealth and the command it has over resources there are two approaches: wealth that can be converted into cash and command resources at a given point in time (marketable or liquid assets), and those stock of assets which provide a flow of income and has a command over resources over time (non-marketable or illiquid assets).

How has personal wealth been distributed in Great Britain and United Kingdom? Exhibit 12.1 provides this information.

Exhibit 12.1

The Distribution of Personal Wealth
1962, 1968 and 1974
of the Total Population aged 18 and over

(Figures are percentages)

| Quartile Group | Great Britain | | | United Kingdom |
	1962	1968	1974	1974
Top 1 per cent	27.2	24.2	18.4	18.3
Top 5 per cent	48.8	45.2	36.7	36.7
Top 10 per cent	60.7	57.1	49.0	49.1
Top 20 per cent	73.9	71.2	64.9	65.0
Bottom 80 per cent	26.1	28.8	35.1	35.0
Gini coefficient	72	68	63	63

Source: Part of Table 33, page 76, of Royal Commission on the Distribution of Income and Wealth. Original source is Inland Revenue.

Note: The Gini coefficient is a convenient summary measure of the overall degree of inequality in the distribution of income (or wealth). It may be defined as one half of the average of the differences between the income (or wealth) of each individual and that of every other individual in the population divided by average income (or wealth). It is estimated here from grouped data and expressed as a percentage: the larger (closer to 100 per cent) the coefficient the greater the degree of inequality.

Exhibit 12.1 uses Inland Revenue estimates and for 1974 covered less than half the total adult population; 19,300,000 wealth owners. The most important fact is that there has been a trend towards greater equality, as shown by the gini coefficient. The introduction of Northern Ireland into the figures had virtually no impact on the equality/inequality situation. The table clearly brings out the fact that the top 20 per cent of wealth owners were gradually losing their share of wealth, and the bottom 80 per cent gaining. This was due to the effect of 'estate duty' which operated over a long period of time. Evidently the very top wealth owners found it beneficial, because of the progressive nature of the tax on higher wealth figures, to distribute their wealth to less wealthy members of their families. The effect of estate duty has been that of distributing wealth and creating a movement towards equality. It is expected that the 'capital transfer tax' (tax imposed on deaths after 12 March 1975) will have a stronger effect than estate duties in bringing about equality of wealth.

The Diamond Commission also provided information on personal wealth in the U.K. for 1975. The total wealth was valued at £190,290,000,000 and was divided among an estimated 21,000,000 wealth owners. There were 15,533,000 wealth owners who had less than £10,000 of net wealth — total amount was £55,400 million (just over 29 per cent of total net wealth). Those holding more than £10,000 totalled 5,488,000 and holding total net wealth of £134,800 million (almost 71 per cent of total net wealth). Of this total, net wealth dwellings (43 per cent) and life policies (15.3 per cent) formed more than two-thirds of the total.

Evidence shows that there is still great inequalities of wealth distribution in the U.K. but over time the movement has been towards greater equality.

Income

The income of the U.K. population is derived mainly from home or domestic production (GDP). As such the 'net income from abroad' part of the national income is excluded. In other words:

Gross National Product		Net income		
or	minus	from	equals	GDP
National Income		abroad		

In the first instance the GDP will be considered at 'factor cost' because this enables us to consider incomes without being involved with taxation or subsidies. It provides us with the original money incomes people earn.

An attempt to show the development of income distribution, using 1965 and 1975 as two points of observation, according to official statistics is made in Exhibit 12.2.

Exhibit 12.2

**Distribution of Domestic Product
by Source of Income Before Tax**

Source of Income	1965 £m	1965 as % GDP	1975 £m	1975 as % GDP
Wages and salaries	19,111	60.6	59,292	60.9
Forces pay	467	1.5	1,296	1.3
Employers national insurance, etc.				
contributions........................	831	2.6	4,043	4.2
Employers other contributions	883	2.8	3,550	3.6
Total Income from Employment	21,292	67.5	68,181	70.0
Professional persons earnings	423	1.3	1,322	1.3
Farming income........................	592	1.9	1,767	1.8
Other sole traders and partnership income...	1,495	4.8	5,616	5.8
Total Income from Self Employment	2,510	8.0	8.705	8.9
Company profits.......................	4,741	15.0	10,387	10.7
Public corporations and other public				
enterprises surplus....................	1,100	3.5	3,012	3.1
Rent	1,896	6.0	7,144	7.3
*GDP at Factor Cost** *	31,539	100.0	97,429	100.0

Source: Income figures taken from table 1.1 on page 3 and table 4.1 on page 26 of 'National Income and Expenditure 1965-75', HMSO, 1976.

Percentage figures calculated by author.

Note: **GDP at Factor Cost does not include depreciation, stock appreciation and residual error.

Exhibit 12.2 implies that the share of 'wages and salaries' as a percentage of the GDP has increased slightly, probably less than many people would think with the large increases achieved by trade unions for wage earners. On the other hand the 'total income from employment' shows a fairly substantial percentage increase. This arises from the larger contributions made by employers to employees. Whereas the change in wages and salaries shows hardly any change in the equality of distribution of income the latter consideration does indicate a more pronounced movement towards equality. Coupled to employers' contributions is the much smaller share of domestic income attributed to 'company profits'; this implies a further move towards greater equality of incomes. Another noticeable change is 'rent'; a larger share of domestic product indicates a move towards inequality in the distribution of incomes.

Overall, the period 1965 to 1975 shows income distribution moving towards 'greater equality'. When incomes have been redistributed, after tax and subsidies have been applied we would expect to find a further movement towards equality of incomes.

In terms of the working population each member of the employed labour force had, on average, a 'money income' of £924; there were 25,747,000 employed persons. In 1975 the figure had risen to £3079; there being 24,968,000 employed persons. A decline in employed persons but an increase in 'money income' on average; approximately a 233 per cent increase. However, we want money for the goods and services it can purchase. The purchasing power of these money incomes show an increase of approximately 45 per cent. In 'real income' terms each member of the employed labour force are better off but not to the extent that the 'money income' figures show.[4]

Readers should note that more recent Blue Books (National Income and Expenditure) will, in the light of later information, revise previous figures so that the percentage shares of sources of income will not always remain the same, but usually the difference is not great and the figures used are fairly representative of the true situation. As the Diamond Commission said (para 56) "For 1975 the effect of the various changes has been to increase total personal income from the estimate of £95,700 million ..... to £97,051 million ...". This last sum is more or less in agreement with the figure shown in Exhibit 12.2.

The Diamond Commission also used the Blue Book as a major source for its investigation into income distribution because it included, unlike other material from other sources such as the Inland Revenue, non taxable incomes and incomes below the effective tax exemption limit.

---

4. Using the CPI as shown in the chapter on 'Money' using 1970 = 100 pence: each one pound in 1965 had a value of £1.26 — that of 1975 only 55 pence. These figures are used to revalue 'money income' in each year. Thus, the £924 in 1965 could buy goods and services based on 1970 prices to the sum of about £1,164, and the money income per employed person of £3,079 in 1975 could purchase £1,693.

The previous exhibit does provide us with some but not all details of personal income. According to the Diamond Report, personal incomes are *estimates* taken from three sources, namely:

earned income,
investment income, and
transfer income.

The make up of these, and their share of the domestic product is shown in Exhibit 12.3.

Exhibit 12.3

U.K. Personal Income
1975

Major components	Percentage share of major components before tax	Relative change 1971 = 100
Earned income	80.0	
Income from employment	70.8	204
Income from self-employment	9.2	203
Investment income	9.4	
Imputed rent of owner-occupiers	3.6	235
Rent, dividends and interest received	9.1	187
Less mortgages and other interest paid	− 3.3	275
Transfer income	10.5	213
National insurance other othe cash benefits from general government		
Total personal income (£97,051m)	100.0**	202

Source: Percentage shares based on Table 2, p.17 of Diamond Report, and relative change taken from table provided as part of para 58.
Note: **Items do not add to total.

It can be seen immediately that earned income forms the biggest percentage share of personal income, and that more than £1 out of each £10 comes from transfer incomes.

Transfer incomes do not alter the total income available to the community, but it does alter the ultimate distribution of income within the community.

It is important to make clear the difference between 'earned income' and 'transfer income'. Earned incomes are types of income derived from the use of the factors of production in the process of producing goods and services. They are earned in making a contribution to production. On the other hand, transfer incomes (such as state pensions, sickness benefits) represent a redistribution of income. People who receive these do not make any contribution to the production of goods and services; they receive cash from general government, a term used to cover both local and central government, based on some non-production criterion.

The index part of the exhibit shows us which of these major components of income are increasing faster or slower than total personal income over the five-year period from 1971 to 1975. The relative rate of change of 'mortgages and other interest paid' showed the greatest increase, probably a reflection of many movements in housing (increase in number of dwellings, increase in owner-occupiers, increase in house prices, and increase in mortgage interest rates). Rent, dividends and interest received, on the other hand, has not increased as fast as imputed rent of owner-occupiers or any other of the major components of personal income.

Personal income is not all at the free disposal of earners. Some of this income is taken by the government in taxation on income and national insurance contributions, and some of this the government uses to make transfer payments and finance social services which they hope wiH increase the welfare of the whole community. Other deductions are made. That which remains can then be freely disposed of by persons to buy the goods and services they consider most desirable; we call this 'disposable income' or 'personal disposable income'.

According to the Blue Book[5] personable disposable income is equal to total personal income   less   U.K. taxes on income, plus National insurance
contributions, plus
Other contributions, plus
Transfers abroad (net), plus
Taxes paid abroad.
Relating this equation to 1965 and 1975 we have the following:

		1965	1975
(a)	total personal income	30,083m	95,700m
(b)	deductions as indicated....................	5,009m	21,973m
(c)	personal disposable income	25,074m	73,727m
	(c) as a percentage of (a)....................	83.55%	77.04%

This is strong evidence that the trend is evidently to take more away from personal incomes, or to put it another way less is being left in the hands of income earners to freely dispose of as they wish in achieving their economic welfare.

How income earners dispose of their 'personal disposable income' is another story. Very briefly, the disposal of personal disposable income is as follows:
expenditure on current goods and services at factor cost, plus indirect taxes (such as purchase tax from 1940 to 1973 and since 1973 value-added tax).

Whatever remains is saved. Savings in 1965 constituted 8.9 per cent of personal disposable income, and in 1975 it was calculated to be 14 per cent.

When considering income distribution we must note two major types of taxes. Direct taxes are placed directly on income receivers. Indirect taxes are placed upon goods and are not payable until goods that have tax imposed upon them are purchased.

The Diamond Report (table 2) shows taxes on income and expenditure as a percentage of total personal income from 1967 to 1976. This information is shown in Exhibit 12.4.

5.   At bottom of table 4.1, page 26, 1965-1975.

Exhibit 12.4   Taxes on Income and Expenditure
as percentages of Total Personal Income

Year	Total Personal Income	UK Taxes on Income plus NI Contribution*	Taxes on Expenditure**	Total Taxes plus NI Contribution
1967	100	17.9	14.1	32.0
1968	100	18.7	14.6	33.3
1969	100	19.2	15.2	34.4
1970	100	19.8	14.7	34.5
1971	100	19.5	14.1	33.6
1972	100	18.9	13.2	32.1
1973	100	19.6	12.9	32.5
1974	100	21.0	11.6	32.6
1975	100	23.1	11.4	34.5
1976	100	23.6	11.5	35.1

Source: Diamond Report, Table 2 page 17

Notes: * Includes additions to tax reserves. Omits capital gains tax and death duties.
      **Includes customs and excise duties, motor vehicle licence duties, selective employment tax, local rates.
      Total taxes on expenditure are expressed as a percentage of total personal income.

Exhibit 12.4 shows clearly the relationship of taxes and national insurance contributions to total personal income. Direct taxes remained fairly steady from 1967 to 1973 but then rose rapidly from then to 1976. "Two factors identified as contributing to the increase experienced up to 1975" according to the Diamond Report (para 59) "were the combination of unchanged tax allowances and rapidly rising monetary earnings and the increase in 1974-75 of the basic rate of income tax. Increases in national insurance contributions were also reflected in the rise of these percentages." The reversal of these, mainly through Budget measures in 1977 and 1978, should curb further increases.

Taxes on expenditure, after an initial rise, have tended to decline from 1967 to 1969.

The overall tax situation was clearly stated in an 'Economic Progress Report' (September 1977) which said: "Total tax paid by the British taxpayer, measured as a proportion of national income, has averaged around 40 per cent over the past decade, in line with other industrial countries. Within the total however the emphasis has shifted noticeably from indirect taxes, which fall on final expenditure or enter the cost of production, to direct taxes on income, mainly personal income tax".

The Diamond Report in its chapter on 'The Distribution of Personal Income' produced 26 tables because "It is not possible to explain the complexity of the income distribution by reference to a single set of data". Exhibit 12.5 which uses Blue Book data because it provides the most suitable set of data available for measuring the overall distribution of income, is an attempt to select certain material from Tables 4 and 5 of the Diamond Report to show how personal income was distributed in 1964, 1969-70 and 1974-75.

Exhibit 12.5

U.K. Distribution
of Personal Income
1964, 1969-70 and 1974-75

Quartile Group	1964 % Shares of Income Before Income Tax	1964 % Shares of Income After Income Tax**	1969-70* % Shares of Income Before Income Tax	1969-70* % Shares of Income After Income Tax**	1974-75 % Shares of Income Before Income Tax	1974-75 % Shares of Income After Income Tax**	1974-75 £ per annum Income Range (Lower Limits) Before Income Tax	1974-75 £ per annum Income Range (Lower Limits) After Income Tax**
Top 1 per cent	8.2	5.3	7.0	4.7	6.2	4.0	8,585	5,856
2—5 per cent	11.3	10.7	10.8	9.7	10.6	9.7	4,983	3,846
6—10 per cent	9.6	9.9	9.4	9.2	9.8	9.5	4,097	3,260
Top 10 per cent	29.1	25.9	27.2	23.6	26.6	23.2	4,097	3,260
11—20 per cent	15.5	16.1	15.5	15.6	15.8	15.8	3,238	2,670
21—30 per cent	12.6	12.9	13.0	13.3	13.1	13.2	2,732	2,250
31—40 per cent	10.9	11.1	11.0	11.4	11.0	11.4	2,296	1,926
41—50 per cent	9.2	8.8	9.4	9.7	9.3	9.4	1,913	1,604
51—60 per cent	7.4	8.0	7.6	8.1	7.6	7.8	1,509	1,315
61—70 per cent	5.8	5.6	6.1	6.7	5.8	6.4	1,168	1,080
71—80 per cent	4.3	5.1	4.7	5.2	4.6	5.3	909	870
81—90 per cent	} 5.2	6.5	{ 3.3	} 6.4	{ 3.6	4.4	680	676
91—100 per cent			{ 2.2		{ 2.6	3.1	—	—
Number of tax units covered	27,500,000		28,200,000		28,300,000			
Gini coefficient (per cent)	39.9	36.6	38.0	33.5	37.1	32.4		
Mean income (£)			1,170	988	2,287	1,868		
Mean income at 1976 prices (£)			2,641	2,230	3,160	2,581		

Source: Diamond Report, part of information shown in Table 4 and 5.

Note: *The estimate for the earliest years in the financial year series are rather uncertain because of the difficulty of analysing the available data retrospectively. See para 60 of Diamond Report.

**Post tax distribution involves some re-ranking of the population from that implied in the pre tax distribution caused by variations in the amounts of tax paid at the same income level.

The first thing to be noted is the size of the population covered by the table — 28,300,000 for 1974-75; slightly more than 50 per cent of the 1975 population of the U.K.

A second point to be observed is that over the period shown there has been a reduction in inequality; illustrated by the Gini coefficient. The trend over time has shown a movement towards equality of incomes before income tax has been deducted and after. Naturally the biggest movement towards greater equality of income takes place because the income tax system taxes incomes at the higher levels at much higher rates than the lower income levels. This reduction in inequality can also be seen by looking at the 'income range' shown in the last two columns. At the lower limits of income the top 1 per cent had pre tax incomes of £8,585, and after tax had only £5,856; £2,729 less than before.[6] As we move down the columns it can be seen that the difference between pre-tax and post-tax personal incomes becomes narrower.

Over the whole of the period the share of the top 1 per cent has declined continuously; the share of the next 2-5 per cent has declined but not continuously. On the other hand the bottom 20 per cent increased their post-tax share of total income for each period considered, and in each year considered their share of total income was higher after income tax was deducted than before. All information shown shows a definite movement towards a reduction in equality of income distribution.[7]

Now, we can make an attempt to link income distribution with demographic and social change; to link national income with population change. It must be made clear at the outset that the resources that are made available to the community (national income or gross national product) is determined by many factors. It is exceedingly difficult to say with certainty the effect that one social or population factor has on the size of the national income or the way it is distributed. The claim that individuals (or households) make on the resources of the community will be determined, to a great extent by the final income they have to dispose of.

To reach 'final income', the third main stage of the distribution process, the following steps must be taken.

Start with the first main stage of distribution: *original income* which consists mainly of earned income.[8]

The second main stage of distribution is reached by adding direct cash benefits and then take away direct taxes. This leaves a sum called *net income* or disposable income.

Final income is arrived at by deducting from net income indirect taxes and adding direct benefits and indirect benefits in kind.

Carrying out the calculations over the three stages of distribution we consider two sets of flows. The first flow is the movement of money away from original income and net income holders to the government in the form

6. This information relates to the lower limit of the top 1 per cent. When considering the average income of this group the figures are more astounding. The average pre-tax incomes of the top 1 per cent was calculated to be £14,091, and the post-tax figures was £7,461 — a fall of £6,630.

7. Students would find it useful to use a statistical measure called the Lorenz curve to see the changes of income distribution at one point in time or over time: a square box with each axis measured from 0% to 100%, vertical axis is labelled for cumulative percentages of total income and horizontal axis cumulative percentage of total income recipients. A diagonal line would show perfect equality — each successive 10 per cent of earners would have earned 10 per cent of total income. A movement away from the diagonal would show inequality — the farther the curve from the diagonal the greater the inequality.

8. Investment income normally forms the original income of the top income earners.

of taxes. The State then redistributes this income to members of the population by giving direct cash benefits and direct and indirect benefits in kind. These last three items make up the 'transfer incomes' that we previously noted.

When these flows have been finalised recipients have incomes which are termed 'final incomes' and these incomes represent the claims on goods and services that were produced by factors whose rewards were 'original incomes'.

Transfer incomes, as noted, take the form of:

1. Direct cash benefits. These include old age and retirement benefits, unemployment benefits, supplementary benefits, family allowances.

2. Direct benefits in kind. These include benefits associated with the National Health Service and State education plus scholarships, school meals, milk, welfare foods.

3. Indirect benefits in kind. These include all forms of subsidies, such as housing subsidies (rent rebates) and food subsidies.

Individuals (or households) have different final incomes — depending on the sum of transfers made by the State to each of them.

The Diamond Report (para 138) said that the ratio of final income to original income is a convenient summary of the net effects of redistribution. Overall, the four major factors mentioned in getting from original to final income have a substantial effect which tends to reduce inequalities of income. Individually, the factors have the following effect:

1. Direct tax. Works towards equality of income distribution.

2. Benefits in cash. Same effect as direct tax.

3. Benefits in kind. Tends to make income distribution more equal.

4. Indirect tax. Works *against* a movement towards equality of income.

If the political party in power is geared to reducing the inequality of income it would favour the first three mentioned factors. If the opposite were the aim it would switch its policies in favour of indirect taxes.

From the foregoing it can be seen that the ultimate situation of final incomes depends upon social factors (health, education, welfare, etc.) and population factors (shape of population, size of families, etc.). Because social and population factors change, so do final incomes. It would be difficult to isolate a single force and say that that force has that specific effect on producing the national income (often called the 'national cake') and consuming it. In 1975 almost 25,000,000 persons were making the cake but nearly 56,000,000 were consuming it. Further, changes in income distribution must be viewed in the context of more general changes in the economy (inflation, incomes policies, etc.). Thus, any conclusion reached when isolating one or several factors must be treated with care — statistical information involves a certain amount of estimation and definitions adopted are not necessarily ideal, and other factors are operating in the economy at the same time.

"Of the purely demographic changes during the 1950's and 1960's" according to the Diamond Report (para 229) "the only change likely to have a significant impact on the overall distribution of income was in the age structure of the population; this can be summarised as an increase in the proportions of young and old in the population, at the expense of the intermediate age ranges. The strongest link between age and income is economic activity (i.e. participation in the labour force). Both the young and the old have low rates of economic activity relative to the intermediate age groups, so these demographic changes would be expected to lower the overall level of economic activity of the labour force. In the case of young people two factors were at work. As well as an increase in their numbers there was also an increased tendency to remain in full-time education after the minimum school leaving age had been reached."

The above statement has already been substantiated in the chapter on population and will be further discussed in the section on education. By taking the shape of the population structure and the number of births each year it would be possible to make simple calculations on the changing scene of the economically active to the inactive.

Above it stated that the age structure of the population has an impact on the distribution of incomes. This is true at all age levels because redistribution takes place at some time or other over the life span of nearly everyone. Professor Richard M. Titmuss stated this very clearly when he said "children put nothing in and take out in the form of education, subsidised milk, family allowances, income tax reliefs (if their parents are better off), medical care by doctors largely trained at the community's expense and so forth. As adults, people are constantly moving in or out of the territory of socially provided or subsidised services according to varying need and circumstances. In old age, as in childhood, most people take out more than they put in."[9]

Thus to see how much a person puts in to the economy (produces goods and services) or takes out (lays claim on goods and services produced) would require a continuous assessment over the life span of each member of the population.

The initial impact on putting in and taking out depends upon the shape of the population at a given time and the relationship between those who are economically active and those that are inactive.

At this point it might be best to itemise, rather than elaborate, some of the *likely effects* of certain social and demographic factors as they effect income distribution. The following are based upon information provided by the Diamond Report; measuring changes from Census of Population 1951 to 1971.

9.   "Crisis in the Social Services" in The Listener, Feb. 14, 1952.

Factor being considered	Likely effect on income distribution
1. changes in occupational and industrial structure of employment changes in the significance of the divorced, widowed and single and one parent families changes in the forms of income and in the sharing of income within families	none of these changes was found to be suitable for examination in quantitative terms
2. increased proportion of population which are elderly	increases the number of people in low income conditions depresses the income share of the bottom 20 per cent of income range therefore widening inequality at the lower end of income distribution likely to increase Gini coefficient — increasing inequality of incomes
3. increase in the number of married women likely to be working	raises the average level of incomes and tends to depress the share of personal incomes going to those at the bottom accounts for some of the decline in the income share of the top 1 per cent likely to lower Gini coefficient
4. increase in proportion of young people in further education (direct effect on economic activity)	decreases the number in labour market and is likely to lead to an increase in the latter's per capita income may result in some increase in the rate of pay going to young people at work likely to increase Gini coefficient
5. more people married	likely to lower Gini coefficient
6. more people married and the age structure combined (greater impact coming from age structure)	tends to increase Gini coefficient
7. factors listed under items numbers, 2, 3, 4 and 5	joint effect accounts for a significant amount of the alteration in the distribution of income in all but the top 10 per cent of incomes. The increase in the number of women in economic activity was the only factor that accounted for some of the decline in the top level of income earners. joint impact was to slightly raise the Gini coefficient and thus creating increased inequality of incomes.

It can be seen that trying to establish the relationship between population and national income is a difficult task, and it is made more difficult when trying to isolate factors from many others that are operating or are in a state of change at given points of time.

In the period from the end of World War II to the mid 1970's the people in the U.K. have seen many important social and demographic changes, as noted in the book, which were likely to have affected the distribution of income. Of the purely demographic factors the only change likely to have had a significant impact on the overall distribution of income was in the age structure — the shape of the U.K. population.

What will be the implications of population change on national income in the future? The future is never easy to predict but perhaps the continued fall in the birth rate in the 1970's will have the greatest potential long term significance. Added to this must be the increased interference by the state in many social and economic areas including policies for incomes; the increased proportion of the GDP represented by public expenditure, and that part of this that is accounted for by the increase in transfer payments. All these, plus others, must have an impact on the size and distribution of the national income now and in the future.

Assignments

1. Population factors, such as a change in the size of the labour force and level of demand, do determine the size of the national income. How true is this statement?

2. Explain the difference between 'national wealth' and 'national income', and the difference between 'earned income' and 'transfer income'.

3. Evidence provided by the Diamond Commission has shown that there has been a movement towards equality of income distribution after-tax compared to pre-tax. What, exactly, do we mean by 'equality of income distribution'? Explain how inequalities are reduced.

Chapter 13

Population and Social Implications: General

Learning objectives:
At the end of your study of this chapter you should be able to:
1. identify and explain the main social implications of major demographic characteristics in contemporary Britain.
2. identify the social evils in society and their social implications.
3. relate the importance of legislation to changes in the major social service areas relating to the removal of the social evils want, idleness, disease and squalor.

Queen Victoria died in 1901, a year of prosperity in the United Kingdom that was not shared by the country's 38,000,000 inhabitants. It has been calculated, by Peter Laslett,[1] that "something like a quarter of the whole population, perhaps even more than that, was living in poverty. And poverty ..... was strictly defined. Families were in poverty whose total earnings were insufficient to obtain the minimum necessaries for the maintenance of mere physical efficiency". Further, "one person in every five could expect a solitary burial from the workhouse, the poor law hospital, the lunatic asylum".

Break up of poor law
The Poor Law, which had its origin in 1601, dominated the lives of a great proportion of the population at the turn of the 20th century. The only public social service on a nation wide basis outside the poor law was education.

The break up of the old Poor Law, and the development of the present day social services took place slowly from around the 1890s to the close of the second World War. Changes were taking place, albeit slowly, due to many forces. Some of these, briefly noted, were:
1. Individuals. Researchers (Booth and Rowntree on poverty) and reformers (the Webbs) encouraged reform of the existing social scene.
2. Political parties. There was a rise of political parties that favoured social change.
3. Trade unions. Their increase in strength had a large impact on the political and social scene.

1. "Social Change in England 1901-1951" in The Listener, Dec 28, 1961 p1095

4. Unemployment. The great depression of the 1930s made the social evils more prominent.

5. Voluntary organisations. Those provided aid in fields which were not State aided.

6. Votes. A large number of voters demanded social change.

7. Wars. The Boer War and World War I created a desire for the next generation to be healthier.

Social change took place slowly. For example, in 1936 it was estimated that more than 30 per cent of the working class were in poverty.

The Second World War speeded up the evolution of the present day social services. It has been claimed that a country at war plans for peace, and this statement is substantiated by the publication of the Beveridge Report; Report on Social Insurance and Allied Services, appointed in June 1941, chaired by Sir William Beveridge, and reported in 1942. It was this Report which spearheaded the movement towards a Welfare State.

Social evils in our society

As noted previously, the Beveridge Report stated that there were five giant evils in our society: disease, idleness, squalor, want and ignorance. That it was necessary to solve the five evils simultaneously, it was not possible to treat one without the others, and that the removal of these was the responsibility of society if it was to provide its members with the basics of good living. This meant that the State, on behalf of society, should:

1. provide members of the community with facilities that would make them healthy; to remove disease and idleness,

2. create employment to remove idleness,

3. properly house its inhabitants to remove squalid conditions,

4. give the minimum support, mainly through social insurance, to its members so they could acquire the necessities of life and thereby remove want (extreme and distressing poverty), and

5. to educate the masses to remove ignorance.

The big 'positive push' to do something about redressing these evils took place in the period 1944-48 when the State, through a variety of Acts, took on the responsibility to provide services that were to be universal in scope and comprehensive.

It is important to realise that the value of the social services and housing cannot be measured in financial terms. We can put money figures to the services, but this can only be used to give us an idea of society's attack on these evils. Exhibit 13.1 attempts to show how much public expenditure has been provided in 1975 and in the census years of 1961 and 1971.

Exhibit 13.1   Public Expenditure on Solving Social Evils
in the U.K.
at Various Years

	1961		1971		1975	
	Money Spent (£m)	How Each £ of Public Expenditure Was Spent (pence)	Money Spent (£m)	How Each £ of Public Expenditure Was Spent (pence)	Money Spent (£m)	How Each £ of Public Expenditure Was Spent (pence)
Social Services:						
Social Security	1,628	15.8	4,309	17.7	8,918	16.4
Health and Personal social services	1,088	10.5	2,784	11.4	6,707	12.3
Education	1,012	9.8	3,023	12.4	6,840	12.6
Housing	555	5.4	1,240	5.1	4,291	7.9
Social Services and Housing Expenditure	4,283	41.5	11,356	46.6	26,756	49.2
Other Public Expenditure	6,036	58.5	12,971	53.4	27,709	50.8
Total Public Expenditure	10,319	100.0	24,327	100.0	54,465	100.0

	1961	1971	1975
Social Services and Housing Expenditure per head of population	£81.11	£204.20	£478.11

Source: Based on data from Social Trends No. 7, 1976 and Annual Abstract of Statistics 1976.

The above exhibit clearly shows that the State has increased the proportion of total public expenditure going to the social services and housing; from 41½ pence out of every one pound of total public expenditure in 1961 to just over 49 pence in 1975 — an increase of approximately 15.7 per cent. Removing 'want' has received the most attention, and housing the least.

When considering government expenditure per head of population the amounts have soared from just over £81 in 1961 to more than £478 in 1975; a six-fold increase. Of course, inflation has been continuous over this period of time.[2] A person, in 1975, would have needed about £2.60 to purchase what a pound could buy in 1961. In other words £210.60, in 1975, would buy what £81 would have bought in 1961. So, figuratively speaking, if each person in the 1975 population received £478 they would be able to purchase twice as many goods and services as they could have in 1961. It would seem that the State has increased its attack on the social evils.

Another way to view the attack on the social evils is to consider the expenditure by the state on social services and housing as a percentage of the 'gross national product'. This method also indicates an increase in attention to the evils as shown below:

1971 — 22.9% of the GNP was spent on social services and housing, and 1975 — 28.4%

2.   Refer to the chapter on 'Money'.

To maintain a positive check on the social evils it is essential that the country remain prosperous. Resources (goods and services) needed to remove the evils can only be given if the resources are available. This depends on many factors, but to a large extent it depends on the relationship between the active and inactive members of the population.

Now to look at each of the services noted.

Social security (want)

Social security normally refers to services needed to maintain incomes at specific levels should a person's income, for one reason or another, be less than is needed.

Beveridge noted many things that happened during the lifetime of an individual that put a strain on the finances of the individual and family. These events comprised:

1. maternity,
2. sickness or disability (example: blindness),
3. unemployment including loss of earning by a married woman in gainful occupation for some time before and after confinement, also loss of livelihood by a person not dependent on paid employment,
4. child rearing,
5. orphanhood and widowhood,
6. marriage,
7. incapacity of a wife for household duties,
8. loss by a wife of her husband's support through separation or desertion,
9. old age,
10. death from industrial accident or disease, and
11. death.

Of all these, item 6 is about the only one left out of present day social security benefits. Overall, the basic idea was to consolidate the entire nation into a community of insured persons as a step leading to social equality; to assist in removing financial stress from the cradle to the grave.

Social security payments

To be effective, social security benefits must be geared to the changing needs of the population.

In the period 1974/75 over £6,500,000,000 was paid out in social security payments of different kinds. If one were to add administrative and miscellaneous expenses the figure would reach £6,863,000,000. This was more than 50 per cent of that spent in 1961/62.[3] National insurance payments constituted, by far, the greater part of this total. Both, in 1961/62

3. For a list of benefits given under social security refer to table 13.16 page 204 in Social Trends No. 6, 1975.

and 1974/75, more than 70 per cent of social security payments were in the form of national insurance payments, and in both periods the greatest number of recipients were those receiving retirement pensions: over 8,000,000 in 1974/75 compared to approximately 5,800,000 in 1961/62.

An idea of the estimated number of recipients receiving social security benefits, under different headings, is given below for the period 1974/75.

4,585,000 families received a total of £360,000,000 in family allowances,

1,073,000 persons (based on monthly averages) received sickness benefits,

538,000 received death grants,

309,000 persons received unemployment benefits totalling £225,000,000, and

2,790,000 persons received supplementary benefits[4]; £875,000,000.

Supplementary benefits refers to assistance given to persons who are without resources to meet their requirements. When other benefits are insufficient to maintain a specified standard of living a second line of benefits is made available to keep such persons out of poverty. In other words supplementary benefits form a net under national insurance benefits to catch those whose national insurance benefits are not high enough to provide them with a specified standard of living.

The basic acts

The above provides us with some details of recent years. The background to the present scene started, mainly, with the recommendations made by the Beveridge Report. The Acts Implementing the recommendations were:

1946 — National Insurance Act

1946 — Industrial Injuries Act, and

1948 — National Assistance Act.

The three Acts completed the State provision that put an end to the former Poor Law system which dated from 1601, and positively attacked the social evil of 'want'.

Pensions to elderly

Before moving to the next social evil, it is important to make note about 'pensions' to the retired population (the elderly). The size of this population has increased and so has the size of the money being paid to them. Their size will continue to increase as a proportion of total U.K. population as long as the following influential factors exist:

1. Continued advances in medicine in preventing, detecting and curing certain diseases associated with the elderly.

2. A lowering of the number of children per family and a lowering of the birth rate. These indicate a decrease in the young as a proportion of the population, and therefore an increase in the elderly proportion.

4. Supplementary benefits replaced the term 'national assistance' from November 1966 onwards.

3. Emigration being greater than immigration where emigration consists mainly of members of the work population (plus their young children). Again this tends to boost the proportion of elderly in the U.K.

In the U.K. of today, we are more prosperous than our grandparents. Will our grand-children be more prosperous than us in 50 years time? The make-up of our population will help provide the answer.

Social security (idleness)

Idleness refers to someone who is not kept busy or is unoccupied; idle hands. We shall call it 'unemployment'.[5]

When a person becomes unemployed it invariably puts that person (and his family) into a demoralising situation, and sooner or later, puts him in need of assistance to remove him from the social evil called 'want'.

Unemployment — pre 1942

The Beveridge Committee, sitting in 1941-42, used pre World War II unemployment figures when they considered the problem of unemployment. In the words of W. H. B. Court[6] "During the 1920's the number of people officially registered as unemployed had never fallen below a million — about 8 per cent of the insured working population. The slump of 1929-32 drove the number up to over two millions for four years, 23 per cent of all insured workers being out of work when things were at their worst, in August 1932." These figures relate to those that were insured against unemployment which means the actual number of unemployed was much higher. For example, in Great Britain, out of a total population, in 1931, of 44,831,000 something like 21,055,000 formed the working population. Of these 21 million approximately 12,000,000 were insured against unemployment. This high level of unemployment is the type of situation that the Beveridge Report recommended should be removed; full employment should be a primary objective of government.

Unemployment — post World War II

Full employment, considered to be a situation where less than 3 per cent of the working population are unemployed, is of prime importance for a population that still remembered the long and bitter experience of large-scale unemployment between 1919 and 1939. This social evil was not eradicated after the war but it was kept below 2 per cent up to 1967. It was in 1969 that it rose above the 3 per cent level (3.2 per cent) and this happened again in 1975 (3.4 per cent). In 1976 unemployment figures rose above the 1,000,000 mark. In the period between October 1977 and 1978 the unemployed figures remained between 1,420,000 and 1,485,000 (more than 5 per cent of the working population). Of course, these figures were swelled by school-leavers. Finally, in March 1978 the number unemployed fell to

---

5. The term 'unemployment' did not appear in the dictionary until 1880.
6. "A Concise Economic History of Britain From 1750 to Recent Times" Cambridge University Press, 1954, p.294

1,399,000.[7] Unemployment in the 1970's is once again a big social and economic problem in the United Kingdom.

Unemployment, no matter how it arises, whether it comes from the pressure of international competition, or improvements in technology which increases the output of a worker, or other movements, is a social evil and must be removed.

Unemployment benefits

We mentioned previously that in the period 1974/75 benefits totalling £225,000,000 were paid to 309,000 persons; slightly more than £728 per person. If there had been 1,400,000 unemployed (1977/78 figures) and they were paid £728 it would have increased government outlays to more than £1,000,000,000. At the same time there would have been, in economic terms, a loss of output of goods and services made available to the community. A very rough estimate in money terms of lost production for 1,400,000 unemployed would come close to £5,250,000,000 for 1975. Increased government expenditure and loss of real goods and services are two results of unemployment. But the most harmful result of this evil is the effect it has on the person who is unemployed (and his family).

Some people want to remain unemployed, especially those who receive more in unemployment benefit than they would do from work, but the vast majority of unemployed want to work.

Unemployment, however it comes about, creates social and economic inequality.

Health and personal social services (diseases — ill health)

Disease refers to the morbid (or unwholesome) condition of the body or part of the body. Very simply, it means sickness of illness. The health and personal social services expenditures by the State are aimed at preventing illness and curing those that do become ill. In other words the object is to secure good health for everyone; to raise the level of well-being of the individual and the nation. Good health would enable individuals to do the things they would like to do.

Hospital development goes back to medieval times.

Public health measures in the 19th century grew up mainly to prevent disease and thus remove poverty. It was realised that there was a close connection between the two.

Personal health services are largely a development since the beginning of the 20th century.

Basic health act

The National Health Services Act, 1946, (Section 1) stated that the duty of the Minister of Health was "to promote the establishment in England and Wales of a comprehensive health service designed to secure improvement in the physical and mental health of the people of England and Wales and the

7.   1977/78 figures were taken from 'Economic Indicators' p.4 of Employment News No. 54, April 1978 — provided by The Department of Employment.

prevention, diagnosis and treatment of illness....''. The service was available to everyone, and one group of people who started to benefit immediately were the old. It was around this time that a new word 'geriatrics' was introduced into our vocabulary.

Recent legislation

Since that time there have been many changes that have affected the health services. Some recent legislation in this field are as follows:

Children and Young Persons Act 1969 which made the child care services in England and Wales the responsibility of the Department of Health and Social Security.

Chronically Sick and Disabled Persons Act 1970 which required local authorities to find out how many such persons lived in their areas and make provision for them.

National Health Service (Scotland) Act 1972 unified the Health Service in Scotland, setting up 15 Health Boards and the Common Services Agency.

Health and Personal Social Services (NI) Order 1972 provides a new administrative structure to the health and personal social services in Northern Ireland.

National Health Reorganisation Act, 1973.

April 1, 1974 local authority health (other than public health) services transferred to National Health Service.

17 December 1976. Publication of Report which reviewed the existing health services for children (under chairmanship of Professor S. D. M. Court).

Overall, the period 1970-76 has seen great change in the National Health Service which, in 1976, brought together the hospital services, the local authority health services, school health, ambulance services and family practitioner services under one single structure. On the other hand, the personal social services remained the responsibility of local authority social services departments and are directed towards many different groups of people in need.

Life expectancy

Great strides have taken place in making the people of the U.K. healthier. A look at age specific death rates provide us with a useful indicator of the health of the population. For example, 3/4ths of all deaths are men and women aged 65 and over, and the expectation of life at birth has gradually increased. In 1974 the figure for males was calculated to be 68.3 years and 75.5 years for females.

Helping the young

The Court Report noted that approximately 24 per cent of the total population are children but only 9 per cent of health service expenditure is allocated to them. Although they use these figures to substantiate a case for more resources for the child health services, it can be seen as an indicator of the success of 'health and personal services'.

In the child population, between 1 and 15 years, the principal cause of death is not illness but accidents.

Children, of course, are one of the most important group of people given personal social services. In March 1975 approximately 490,000 under 5's were provided for by nurseries, play groups and registered child minders.

Helping the disabled

At the same period of time the number of registered disabled totalled 811,000. This was double the figure resgistered at the end of December 1969 under the National Assistance Act 1948. The increase arose, mainly, because local authorities were required to find how many of these disabled persons existed in their areas (Chronically Sick and Disabled Persons Act 1970).

Helping the elderly

The elderly form the biggest proportion of the health and personal social services population. This is only natural because there has been a considerable increase in the number of elderly in the population. The older the person the greater the demand placed upon the health and personal social services. The over 85's require more meals served and more home help. In fact, the number of meals served to this group increased by more than 50 per cent between 1970 and 1975. The 65 and over, in 1975 required more home helps than in 1970; more than 8 per cent of this group, in England and Wales, received this benefit. In Scotland the home help service increased by 15 per cent between 1970 and 1974.

The 65 and over, in Great Britain, constitute almost half of all persons reporting long-standing illness, with females forming the larger group.

The above points out very strongly that the elderly proportion of the population require and need the health and personal social services more than any other group in the population.

Prevention — vaccination

In the vaccination area of preventive medicine in Great Britain, in 1975 relative to 1968, some interesting facts can be noted. For example:

1. There was a noticeable decline, in percentage terms, of children vaccinated against diptheria, poliomyletis and tetanus; from approximately 75 per cent (1968) to 57 per cent (1975).

2. The percentage of children vaccinated against whooping cough declined; from 76 per cent in 1968 to 32 per cent in 1975. This disease is dangerous to life mainly in the first year of life. The reason for the decline was attributed to an investigation, although not proven, that there was a connection between this vaccination and brain damage.

3. In 1968 the percentage of young children vaccinated against smallpox was 37 per cent. No figures are recorded since 1971 because the World Health Organisation has been successful in eliminating this disease from the world scene (barring the Birmingham incident in 1978).

4. In 1975 the number of people under age 16 who were vaccinated against measles totalled 350,000 and 298,100 were vaccinated against rubella.

5. Tuberculosis vaccinations, available to all persons, has shown a steady increase from 1968 (over 590,000) to 1975 (more than 684,000).

Prevention is better than cure; the success against smallpox proves this.

Cure — hospitals

In the hospitals there is a constant stream of patients, and each year the waiting list seems to get bigger, but not necessarily all that bigger. In 1951 it was estimated that 500,000 patients were waiting to be admitted, and in 1975 it was 704,000 (657,000 being surgical). The size of U.K. population, it should be noted was greater in 1975 relative to 1971 — by approximately 5,672,000.

How busy were the hospitals in 1975 in the United Kingdom? The following will give some indication:

1. The number of in-patients who were discharged or died was over 6 million.

2. The number of new patients seen in out-patients departments was nearly 9¾ million, and the average attendances per new patient was 4.2.

3. Almost 10,000,000 new patients were accident and emergency patients.

Add all these together. Now decide how busy hospitals were.

Ill health — expensive

All the above plus other details not included in this section (family planning, health visiting, maternity services, etc.) were serviced, in the mid 1970s, by slightly more than 1,000,000 health and local authority social services personnel; about 4 per cent of the employed labour force.

When it comes to expenditure on these services we can expect it to be expensive; a total of approximately £7,000,000,000 in the period 1975/76. Of this, slightly more than £6,500,000,000 was on current expenditures (services in hospitals, local authority personal social services, general medical, dental and other family practitioners, school milk, etc.).

£7,000,000,000 is almost 7½ per cent of the gross national product in 1975. In terms of money it is expensive, but it is necessary if the health of the population is to be improved.

Housing (squalor)

Squalor refers to the state of being squalid (dirty; filthy; hence, wretched, miserable, or degraded). These squalid conditions are normally associated with low standards of housing, and when located in a thickly populated squalid part of a city they are referred to as 'slum'. 'Bad housing' is linked to apathy and disease.

The social importance of 'good housing' to the community can not be over-emphasised. It has a direct and important bearing on the family and individual because it promotes better health and creates pride and self-respect.

Housing problem (and legislation)

Legislation on housing is not new to the 20th century; in the 19th century we had the Labouring Classes Lodging Houses Act, 1851, and the first housing Act — Housing of the Working Classes Act 1890. However, the period after the 1914-18 war witnessed more Housing Acts. The Housing and Town Planning Act, 1919, acknowledged housing as a problem calling for national planning and the introduction of improved standards of housing. The Housing Act 1936 remained the operative act after the Second World War although amended in some respects by The Housing Act 1949. The 1936 Act followed the basic pattern as the earlier Acts;

1. building of new houses,

2. demolishing houses unfit for human habitation,

3. relief of over crowding, and

4. slum clearance.

How serious was the housing situation after World War II? The Census of Population 1951 provided some details, for example:

1. 7,000,000 households had no fixed baths (either public or tin baths),

2. 3,000,000 households were entirely without a water closet or must share the W.C.,

3. 2,000,000 must share or do not possess a kitchen sink, and

4. 1,000,000 households share or were without a cooking stove.

The Second World War did not help the problem of housing families. It was estimated that more than 200,000 houses were blown up or burnt down, another ¼ million were so badly damaged that people could not live in them, and a further ¼ million were severely damaged. A lot of work had to be done to achieve 'good housing' for all.

Legislation took place continuously since the 1949 Act. Some recent legislation, so far, in the 1970s has been:

1. The Housing Executive Act (Northern Ireland) 1971 which set up the province wide organisation, the 'Northern Ireland Housing Executive' to cover the function of former housing authorities to cover the entire field of housing.

2. Housing Act 1971 which increased improvement grants, in Great Britain, for the development and intermediate areas.

3. Housing Finance Act 1972 provided for rent rebate and rent allowance schemes. A new system of housing subsidies was introduced for housing authorities including increased rents for many council tenants.

4. The Housing (Scotland) Act 1974 which gave local authorities the power to give substantial grants, with financial support of The Exchequer in special areas and smaller grants to other areas.

5. Circular on Homelessness (DHSS 4/74) on 7 February 1974 recommended that housing authorities should increasingly undertake the prime responsibility for homeless people and their accommodation.

6. Rent Act 1974 extended protection to unfurnished tenants of absentee landlords. This protection was given to furnished tenants under previous legislation.

7. Homeless Persons Act 1977 came into force in December 1977. An Act, according to the Daily Express[8] which "invited families from outside the U.K. to obtain a place to live at the expense of British people who have been on a waiting list for months".

Much legislation and activity has gone into housing since the end of World War II but — with what success?

According to the Daily Express, in a five part investigation into housing,[9] housing is a disaster story. In the lead into these investigations it was claimed that "After 33 years of post-war development, housing is still the great British disaster story. Incredibly we now have more homes than families — but the homes aren't where people want to live, and the statistics of human distress are grimmer than ever."

Although 1978 statistics are not readily available, it would appear from the census of 1971, at least in Great Britain, that a lot would have to be done to raise the number of basic amenities to remove human distress. There were approximately 18,300,000 households in 1971, and of these a substantial number were without certain basic amenities. For example, there were:

1. over 1,600,000 without a fixed bath,
2. over 200,000 without an internal or external water closet,
3. over 2,100,000 without an internal water closet, and
4. over 1,180,000 without a hot water tap.

Improvement was taking place as the government stepped-up the number of improvement grants to local authorities and private owners for improvement and conversion, and the continued clearance of unfit properties. As stated in Social Trends "Reflecting this improvement activity and the continued clearance of unfit properties, the proportion of households living in accommodation lacking basic amenties continued to decline".[10]

8. The Daily Express, 25 July 1978, p.10

9. First part of investigation appeared in The Daily Express on Mondy, July 24, 1978, page 10.

10. "Social change in Britain: 1970-1975" by Central Statistical Office, in Social Trends No. 7, 1976, p.28.

Number of households

The supply of houses should reflect the demand. Basically, an important factor relating to the demand for houses is the rate of formation of new households, and this depends on the trend in the changing structure of the population.

The number of households depend on the number of adults (not the total number of persons) in the population. Older persons are more likely to be heads of households rather than young single people. The latter group tend to share dwellings. Thus, it is very possible that the population of the country may increase but not the number of households. What is important in determining the number of households, so it seems, is the composition of the population — with various peculiarities brought about by bulges in the birth rate at various times.

Household size

Household size will depend upon the number of children that are still dependent upon the family. Those that have become independent (moved to another area, married, etc.) must be considered as members of other households. We would expect the household size to be less in the 1970's, when the average number of children per family was a shade over two, compared to the early 1860's when the Victorian family had an average of six children.

What is the realistic situation between size of population in recent times and the number of households?

The data that is used here is for Great Britain, for the census years 1961 and 1971.[11]

In 1961 the population was 51,284,000 and 53,979,000 for 1971. The total number of households, respectively, were 16,189,000 and 18,317,000. This can be looked at as follows: for example in 1961 there was 1 household for every 3.2 members of the population, and 1 for every 2.9 inhabitants in 1971. This movement appears to reflect the point that the fertility rates of women was lower in 1971 than in 1961; that couples are planning smaller families.[12] In fact when comparing 1961 with 1971 we find that there was an increase in the number of married couples with no children (from 25.6 to 26.7 per cent of all households).

Tenure of dwellings

Since the end of World War II the size of families has decreased as the average person in the U.K. has become more affluent. In support of this affluency we might make use of the noticeable change that has taken place in the tenure of dwellings. At the end of 1950, in the U.K., there were approximately 14 million dwellings and by the end of 1975 this had increased to nearly 20⅓ million (The South-east, which includes Greater London, had the greatest concentration (6,190,000) — in the whole of Northern Ireland there were 480,000). The change in tenure, measured as a percentage of the total for each is, roughly, as follows:

11.   Information obtained from table 2.1 in Social Trends No. 7, 1976.

| | % of Total Dwellings | |
| | End of | End of |
Type of Tenure	1950	1975
Owner occupier	30	53
Rented from local authorities and new town corporations	18	31
Other rented dwellings	52	16

Owner occupiers and local authorities have increased their share of total dwellings, from 48 per cent, at the expense of private owned rented accommodations.

Building of dwellings

Considering a 11 year span of time, 1965 to 1975, owner occupiers were completing more new houses and flats (over 19,500,000) than local authorities (14,000,000). However, owner occupiers appear to prefer houses (91.4 per cent of total) rather than flats, whereas local authorities produced slightly more flats (50.1 per cent of total). It would seem from this that the 'high rise' and 'multi flats' that local authorities seemed to favour is not the type of dwelling people would choose is they had a free choice. Recent experiences at Birkenhead, Manchester and other large populated centres seem to bear this out. As stated by Janice Morley "In the seventies it seems, for the sake of expediency and inconvenience, they built homes which displayed all disregard for the essential element — the people who had to live in them."[13]

Dwellings should relate to the desires of householders. Families with children and the elderly, in general, do not prefer living in high rise or multi-flats for a variety of reasons, for example, individual physical problems and hooliganism. Mothers with young children living in flats (and there were 20 per cent of all children under the age of 2 living in flats in 1973) must feel depressed at the prospects that face them each day.

On the other hand there are many people who are homeless and others who are living with their parents who would appreciate a dwelling; even a flat.

Housing is one problem that political parties have not been able to solve, at least up to the present time. Perhaps some success has been achieved to remove squalid conditions but many families still live in miserable conditions.

The market system, supply and demand, still operates in housing even though there is government interference. The State does not have a monopoly. However, their share of supply (and their determination of demand) has increased from the end of World War II.

It is probably true to say that the demand for houses and flats will never be completely satisfied. As old dwellings are pulled down new ones must take their place. Additional houses and flats must be completed to cater for the increase in the number of marriages. Newly weds do not want to share a home with others, they want a separate home. The elderly, growing in

13. "They are the architects of disaster", Janice Morley, Daily Express, July 24, 1978 p.11.

numbers, require special homes preferably near their relations; this would result, immediately, in their making less demands on the health and personal social services. Lord Beveridge said "the problem of happiness in old age is not essentially one of money but of care and companionship, and of housing conditions to make these natural and easy."[14]

As standards of living rise in the U.K., and the work population work shorter hours, there will be a demand for better homes with gardens and extra rooms.

Demand for 'good' homes and flats will never be satisfied, but every effort should be made to achieve this object because the health and general quality of the population are enhanced by 'good housing'.

There are other social problems associated with changes in population other than the four social evils already discussed and that of ignorance, discussed in chapter 14. A brief look shall be made into at least two of these areas.

Population and environment

Environment, as noted before, refers to the aggregate or sum of surrounding things, conditions or influences. It considers the total of all the factors that are outside the control of the individual or group, whether the group be a village, city or business organisation. Environmental factors are not static — they are subject to change.

It should be made clear that this subject is vast and too difficult to treat every aspect, nor treat any one aspect of it from various points of view.[15]

The two areas selected for discussion are 'conurbations' and 'pollution'.

Conurbations/metropolitan areas

The term 'conurbation' means "an area of urban development where a number of separate towns have grown into each other or become linked by such factors as a common industrial or business interest or a common centre for shopping or education".[16]

The movement of population, especially during the latter part of the 19th century, was to move into the big cities — London being a good example. As the area became congested other people moving towards the cities settled as near as possible to it. Others, already in the congested centres began moving out from the centre (land prices and rents rose). This movement continued to take place and, at the same time, others moved into the next surrounding area of the big cities. Thus, we have three classifications of 'urban areas', namely:

'dense urban area' — where 100 or more persons are living to a hectare of land (it take 259 hectares to make one square mile).

14. The Observer, Oct. 27, 1957. Comment made by Lord Beveridge when discussing Peter Townsend's book 'Old People at Home'.

15. The various publications of 'Social Trends' provides statistics under a section called 'Environment'. This will give students an idea of subject matter under this title. Examples: sunshine, rainfall, air pollution, river pollution, radioactivity, population in conurbations, recycling of waste, water supply, etc..

16. Definition provided as footnote at bottom of Table 16 in Annual Abstract of Statistics, 1976, C.S.O., H.M.S.O.

'urban area' — where 25 to 100 persons live per hectare, and

'suburban area' — where 1½ to 25 persons live per hectare.[2]

This movement of population created the conurbation.

Some statistical information about migration that supports the above statement is as follows:

1. Dense urban areas. In 1931 approximately 11 million of the British population lived in these areas compared to almost 3 million in 1971. (British population in 1931 was 44.8 million; in 1971 it was 54 million.)

2. Urban and suburban areas. Almost 46 million of the British population lived in these areas in 1971, but slightly less than 28 million in 1931.

Also in support of the statement is the movement of population in the London area. The exodus from 'Inner London' began around the turn of the 20th century, and during this period 'Greater London' and 'Outer London' were growing in population. Around 1939 there was an increase in the number of people leaving 'Inner London', and at the same population statistics shown the beginning of a decline in 'Greater London'. The outward flow of population from 'Outer London' took place at the beginning of the 1950s. Throughout the whole of the 1900s up to 1975 the area immediately outside these three London sectors steadily increased.

The term 'conurbation' "apparently owes its origin to Professor Patrick Geddes, who wrote many well-known works on Town Planning during the first quarter of the present century."[18] The term was fashionable up to the second world war. Today, we tend to use the term 'metropolitan area', or 'metropolitan counties'.

In the chapter on population we made note of the reorganisation of local government in 1974 and the establishment of 'metropolitan counties'.

The problems, social, economic and strategic, that are associated with large concentrations of population is not new. The Barlow Report made note that it was difficult to separate social and economic factors because they tend to overlap, but they discussed the problems in terms of health, housing, planning, recreation, smoke and noise. Since the Barlow Report many things have changed, for example, health is provided by the government under the National Health Service, housing is a problem but of a different sort, and action has been taken on smoke. Today, two of the worst problems are congestions and pollution. Efforts have been made to reduce pollution and congestion but they are are 'evils' especially in these areas of concentrated population.

Other problems that have to be faced by metropolitan areas that affect the social life of its inhabitants include crime, deterioration of houses, high rise flats, refuse disposal, sewage, traffic, water supply, etc..

As people moved outwards from the centres of large cities there is the problem of encroachment on the 'green belt' area and thereby reducing, usually, valuable agricultural land.

17. Information can be found in Table 10.7 p.166 in Social Trends No. 8, 1977, HMSO.

18. Royal Commission on The Distribution of the Industrial Population Report, Cmd 6153, January 1940, HMSO para 12. (Barlow Report)

Also linked to population concentration is: location of factories and siting of new houses to take the 'overspill population'. This is not only a problem of the 1970s, but has been a major problem of the past. Some interesting developments in town planning took place in the second half of the 1940s. Under the New Towns Act of 1946 Development Corporations were appointed to supervise the expansion of areas which would house the overspill population from the existing centres of concentrated population, especially Greater London.[19] Within four years of the Act fourteen New Towns were designated, eight forming the London 'ring' of Basildon, Bracknell, Crawley, Harlow, Hatfield, Hemel Hempstead, Stevenage and Welwyn, and six in other parts of the country; Corby, Cwmbrun, East Kilbride, Glenrother, Newton Aycliffe and Peterlee.

The Town and Country Planning Act of 1947 laid down the base for controlling the location and expansion of factories. In 1963 the Location of Offices Bureau was established to encourage firms to move their offices out of central London, and in 1964 a curb was put on further office development in the Greater London area.

Early in 1964 the Government published 'The South East Study' — planning for a halt to the population drifting to the South East.

The ramifications of conurbations/metropolitan areas are many — it branches off into many areas in the social, economic, political and strategic arena.

Pollution

Pollution refers to the act of making air, rivers, water, etc. foul or unclean, and these acts are normally associated more with areas of population concentration rather than sparse population areas.

As pollution grew and factories and houses were erected the problem of pollution increased. Although legislation existed before World War II on the pollution of the atmosphere from smoke there was little done to enforce the Acts. In the 1970s the Governments were making greater efforts to attack the problem. The Deposit of Poisonous Waste Act, 1972, made it an offence to create an environmental hazard by depositing poisonous waste. In 1974 the Health and Safety at Work etc. Act made provisions for controlling certain emissions into the atmosphere, and in the same year the Control of Pollution Act contained new and more stringent provisions, which were to be introduced in stages, covering waste disposal, water pollution, noise and air pollution in Great Britain.

Pollution has an effect on the physical environment and this in turn has an effect on social behaviour: people want to work and live in areas that are free from noise of pollution. It has been claimed that efforts to reduce these evils over the past 20 years have been successful. "In general there is less

---

19. New Towns (Amendment) Act 1976 provides for the transfer to the appropriate district councils of ownership of rented dwellings and related assets held by new town development corporations and the Commission for the New Towns.

pollution now than twenty years ago; however, some specific pollutants are more in evidence, and in some local areas there are still very high concentrations."[20]

Since 1960 smoke and sulphur dioxide[21] concentrations have been measured systematically. The trend of these two pollutants has been steadily downwards since 1962-63.

On the other hand, estimates of carbon monoxide from road vehicles (caused mainly by petrol engines) has shown an upward trend until 1973. Since then is appears to be levelling. The effect of fumes from road traffic is greater where the vehicle flows are higher, and the problem is worse in conurbations.[22]

The Barlow Report in 1939 stated that the production of smoke from factories and houses reduces the effective sunshine and that this was one major factor which caused higher mortality rates in the towns of Great Britain compared with the country (para 123 item 4). Since then smoke and sulphur dioxide concentrates in the air have been reduced and the mean hours per day of winter sunshine (at least at the London Weather Centre) has increased.

Emission of smoke has been reduced as the number of smoke control orders (in operations under the Clean Air Act 1956) has increased. In 1970 statistics show that about 90 per cent of smoke was emitted from homes.[23]

River pollution appears to be more a problem of tidal rivers. Almost half of the 1,784 miles of tidal rivers are not polluted, compared to more than threequarters of the 22,317 miles of non-tidal rivers. Recent figures show there has been some improvement in cleaning up the rivers.

Pollution is part of the physical environment but has an effect on the social environment. Removing pollutants from the air and rivers makes for cleanliness, and this is beneficial to the health and happiness of the population of the U.K..

Social cost — economics

Removing the social evils discussed (and those not discussed) requires resources (goods and services). Basically, the amount of resources that can be made available will depend upon the economic situation of the community — viewed by considering the size of the National Income.

20. Social Trends No. 7, 1976, HMSO, p162

21. Sulphur dioxide is released when fuels containing sulphur are burnt. When combined with water in the atmosphere it may oxidise to form dilute sulphuric acid which is corrosive and can damage metals, stone and textiles. Sulphur dioxide, in sufficient concentrations, can irritate the respiratory system and can damage plants.

22. "Road Traffic and the Environment" by F. D. Sando and Miss V. Batty, in Social Trends No. 5, 1974, HMSO, p68.

Assignments

1. Reference the Age Composition of the U.K. table at the top of chapter 10 questions. Explain the effects the changed population will have on the social services?

2. Would you agree that the larger the population the greater the need for more dwellings? Assuming you agree with this, how do you build more dwellings and yet preserve the 'green belt'?

3. From mid-1975 to mid-2011 the elderly population is expected to increase by approximately 410,000. What social problems will this bring?

Chapter 14

Population and Social Implications: Education

Learning objectives:
At the end of your study of this chapter you should be able to:

1. identify and explain the main social implications of major demographic characteristics with reference to education.
2. associate the need for education to remove the social evil 'ignorance'.
3. appreciate the significance that a change in population shape has on establishing education policy.
4. understand the education system existing in the U.K.

Education (ignorance)

Ignorance means the state or fact of being ignorant, and a person who is ignorant lacks knowledge, is unlearned and uninformed. Education is the act or process by which a person can acquire knowledge, and be informed by teaching, instruction or schooling.

Education is one of two main activity phases of the population; the other is employment. This is the reason why both have been singled out and treated in greater depth.

A comprehensive and national education service, like the other remedies to remove the other social evils, is important for the well being of the individual and nation.

Defining and measuring education

What is the meaning of education? How is it measured? First, there is no general agreement about the definition. One thing which most people would agree upon is that there are many definitions and perhaps the variations are more than any other service discussed. Generally, education aims at producing 'character' or 'shaping the development of indivudals' so they can perform or contribute effectively to their own well-being and the well-being of the state. Thus, in education there must be direction towards 'standards'.

As to measurement; there is no general agreement about this. There are many indicators that can be used but they are merely indicators (this is the right procedure or direction), such as the ability to read, ability to perform the three R's, length of time at school, number of degrees, etc. These do not measure the quality of education, nor do they show directly that one person who has achieved these standards are better educated than others. It is probable that they may be better educated and are better trained, but not accurate enough to be certain — measurements do imply a high degree of certainty.

One thing that is certain about education is that it is suppose to provide individuals with knowledge; to remove them from the social evil called 'ignorance'.

Development of education

In the U.K. education has developed along the following lines.

1. Voluntary. Examples being 'Sunday Schools' and 'Charity Schools'.
2. State-aided. The Elementary Education Act, 1870, was aimed at providing a school place for every child. Voluntary school societies were given the option to provide for those they did not have room for. If they could not, then a School Board was elected and funds were obtained from the rates. This Act produced a voluntary system, aided and supervised by the State, which competed with a School Boards system backed by the State.
3. National school system as provided under the Education Act, 1944. This Act was a product of a coalition government.

The 'education scene' therefore is mainly concerned with the life of individuals, from the first time they enter the educational system to the time they normally would take up an economic activity. The education scene of the late 1970's can be viewed in three different phases:

1. Voluntary education. Before the age of 5 young children may attend some form of education (nursery school) but whether they do or do not is left to the decision of the parent(s).
2. Compulsory education. A child at the age of 5 *must* attend school and remain until the age of 16 has been reached.
3. Voluntary education. The decision to continue education beyond 16 is voluntary.

Education is important to the employment phase because it has considerable influence in determining, the occupations of a large number of students.

Recent legislation

During the first half of the 1970s there has been little legislation that has been associated with education in general. There have been Acts relating to handicapped children and supplying milk. Severely mentally handicapped children who were hitherto considered to be unsuitable to be educated and trained at schools has been changed. Education authorities (in England and Wales under the Education (Handicapped Children) Act 1970 and Scotland under the Education (Mentally Handicapped Children) (Scotland) Act 1974) have been made responsible for their education.

In 1971 there were two Acts, one for England and Wales and the other for Scotland, called Education (Milk) Act, which restricted the provision of free milk by the education authorities to primary schools (after their 7th birthday in Scotland, and below the age of 8 in England and Wales), older pupils on health grounds and pupils receiving special education. These Acts did empower the educational authorities to sell milk to pupils.

The supplying of milk to pupils has undergone considerable change. Up to 1967 milk was supplied to all nursery, primary and secondary school pupils. From 1968 free milk supplies were withdrawn from pupils in secondary schools (other than special schools), and from September 1971 the above Acts were put into operation. The selling of milk to pupils by the education authorities was repealed, by the Education (Scotland) Act 1976 and the Education Act 1976 for England and Wales.

The beginning of the second half of the 1970s began with the Education Act 1976 (for England and Wales) which required Local Education Authorities to submit proposals for a comprehensive school system in their area. This is a highly controversial area in education; Labour prefers a comprehensive school system and the Conservatives do not. This has been an on-off situation for the whole of the 1970s. The situation in Scotland, where the educational system differs in many respects, virtually all public sector schools were comprehensive by 1974.

Other educational activities, stimulated by the government, in the period 1970-76 were:

1 September 1972: school leaving age raised from 15 to 16.

13 August 1973: a building programme for nursery schools was announced.

21 August 1975: regulations (The Direct Grant Grammar Schools — Cessation of Grant — Regulations) to phase out direct grant schools over 7 years from September 1976 came into effect.

Various 'Reports' were submitted during the period. Such as:

James Report (Jan 1972) for England and Wales, Lelievre Report (Dec 1973) for Northern Ireland, and a Report for Scotland (Nov 1972) on the training of teachers. A report on the reading and use of English in schools was published (Feb 1975); the Bullock Report. The Alexander Report on adult education in Scotland was published (March 1975).

It can be seen from the above that there are differences in the structure and administration of the educational system in the various countries making up the U.K.. It is difficult to discuss these countries as one.

Basic details on education in U.K. — 1975

The following material, under this heading, comes mainly from the introductory pages of "Education Statistics for the United Kingdom — 1975".[1]

1. Published by HMSO. A detailed outline of the U.K. Education Systems are on page vi to xi.

"In general the education services of the United Kingdom are not subject to detailed central control. Standards are maintained by an Inspectorate with advisory functions having access to all institutions except the universities and related bodies. Within this framework detailed control is exercised by local education authorities or by various forms of independent governing bodies, in association with the teaching staff. In all sectors, such matters as engaging teachers and selection of textbooks and curricula are parts of these detailed local responsibilities."

"There are four central government departments dealing with education:

Department of Education and Science,
   which deals with all sectors of education in England, all sectors in Wales other than schools and with the Government's responsibilities towards universities in Great Britain.

Welsh Office,
   whose Welsh Education Office deals with schools in Wales.

Scottish Education Department:
   Schools and further education in Scotland.

Department of Education, Northern Ireland:
   Schools, further education and universities in Northern Ireland."

"There are three stages of education: primary (including nursery), secondary, and further education, including higher education and teacher training. The first two stages are compulsory for all children between the ages of 5 and 16 years."

Now that we are aware of the educational scene in general, and in the U.K., we can begin considering the link between population and education.

Population and education

The wheels grind slowly in education; for those who had gone through the educational system before the raising of the school-leaving age to 15 in 1947 it ground more slowly than for those going through the sytem in 1947. The younger generation have benefited, compared to their grandparents, from the increased educational opportunity made possible by the Education Act, 1944.

The evidence to support the above statement is borne out by the following:

1. men and women born, in England and Wales, in the year 1917 — approximately 84 out of every 100 left school at age 13 and under, and

2. those born in 1952 (35 years later) — none left school at age 13 and under.[2]

One further piece of evidence, about wheels grinding slowly, relates to the highest educational achievement reached by individuals, in Great Britain, by the year 1971 — namely:

1. men and women, born in Great Britain, and aged approximately 54 in 1971 (born around 1917), on average, approximately 7 out of 10 had no qualifications, and

2. Abstracted from Table XV page 15 in Social Trends No. 4, 1973, HMSO.

2. those aged approximately 19 in 1971 (born around 1952), approximately 5 out of 10 had no qualifications.[3]

It follows from the above that the children of the 1950's, and since the raising of the school leaving age to 16 those in the 1970's, generally speaking, are educationally much better off than their grandparents.

Perhaps the material that follows, keeping the 1970's in the spotlight whenever possible, will give us a better insight into the educational system in this country, and perhaps at the same time enable us to accept or reject the previous statement.

Number of pupils?

The first question to be posed is — what determines the number of pupils (and teachers) in the educational system at various levels? The answer, very simply stated, is:

1. the numbers that make up the population at relevant age levels during the compulsory education years,

2. at the lower (below age 5) and higher level (above age 16), the proportion of the population in those age groups that voluntarily stay on at school, and

3. government policy.

Pupil population — changing scene

Concentrating on (1) and (2) above we will need some details about births in different years. First, we can note the average size of births using 5 year averages to give some idea of the changing potential size of pupil population. This information is found in Exhibit 14.1.

Exhibit 14.1

**U.K. Birth Movements
in 5-Year Periods
1925-29 to 1970-74**

(thousands)

Five Year Periods	Average Number of Births per Year		
	Totals	Boys	Girls
1925-29	798	408	390
1930-34	730	374	356
1935-39	723	371	352
1940-44	772	397	375
1945-49	907	467	440
1950-54	801	412	389
1955-59	843	434	409
1960-64	969	499	470
1965-69	961	495	466
1970-74	831	428	403

Source: Calculated from Table I(1) p.3 in Education Statistics for the United Kingdom 1975, HMSO.

3. Based on graphs shown in Figure VI, page 15 in Social Trends No. 4, 1973, HMSO.

The first thing that can be noted is that the number of births per year (averaging 5 year periods) swing up and down, and therefore the population of pupils, even when planning intakes five years forward, can not be planned with certainty. If a diagram were to be drawn for this 50 year span of time we would find that there were 3 periods of high births (1925-29, 1945-49 and 1960-64), and 3 periods when birth movements reached a low (1935-39, 1950-54, with the 3rd downward movement continuing beyond the 1970-74 period). The range over these years was 723,000 to 969,000 — a difference of 246,000.

The above swings provide us with one of the problems that educational planners must face. More interesting, of course, are the number of births for each year. Exhibit 14.2 provides year by year details of births commencing with the year of the Education Act 1944.

Exhibit 14.2 shows the number of births in the U.K. from 1944 to 1975. The figures are straight forward: two peak years, 1947 and 1964, when births were greater than 1,000,000, and then a continuous fall from the peak of 1964 to 1975. Over the 32 year span (roughly, a generation), the lowest number of births recorded was 1975 (697,000). Comparing 1975 with the peak year of 1947 there was a difference of 328,000.

Of course, looking at the chapter on population there were signs that the birth rate and fertility rate were declining, the annual rate of change of population was moving towards 'zero population' since 1961/62, and total population was increasing but at a decreasing rate. The number of births shown in Exhibit 14.2 is simply another set of figures that fits into the general pattern of events.

A close look at the 1944 to 1975 birth figures shows that the number of boys born exceeds girls in every year.

These figures show the potential education population. When the compulsory school age of 5 is reached the numbers shown will be less because of deaths. In 1974, for example, there were 7,180 males who died before reaching their first birthday, and 5,172 females — a total of 12,352. During this same year, in the U.K., there was a further 2,288 deaths of children aged 1 to 4 (males 1,307 — females 981). Other figures to be taken into consideration would be the net migration of children of pre-school age and their year of birth. The overall figures, once these calculations have been made, will give the more accurate figure of children starting school at age 5.

It might be worth noting that many headmasters of infant schools make contact with the Health Visitor in their area to determine numbers. By law, HV's must keep in contact with children (carrying out various assessments) below school age.

Students might like to take the opportunity of calculating the possible number of school children that start school in 1979 and later years. Also, take the year in which you were born and compare it with the group size in the year before and after — were your class sizes bigger or less?

U.K. Births
1944 to 1975

Calendar Year	Total	Boys	Girls
1944	878,000	453,000	425,000
1945	796,000	410,000	386,000
1946	955,000	491,000	464,000
1947	1,025,000	527,000	498,000
1948	905,000	466,000	439,000
1949	855,000	440,000	415,000
1950	818,000	421,000	397,000
1951	797,000	410,000	387,000
1952	793,000	407,000	386,000
1953	804,000	414,000	390,000
1954	795,000	409,000	386,000
1955	789,000	406,000	383,000
1956	825,000	424,000	401,000
1957	851,000	438,000	413,000
1958	871,000	448,000	423,000
1959	879,000	453,000	426,000
1960	918,000	473,000	445,000
1961	944,000	486,000	458,000
1962	976,000	503,000	473,000
1963	990,000	508,000	482,000
1964	1,015,000	523,000	492,000
1965	997,000	513,000	484,000
1966	980,000	505,000	475,000
1967	962,000	495,000	467,000
1968	947,000	487,000	460,000
1969	920,000	473,000	447,000
1970	904,000	465,000	439,000
1971	902,000	464,000	438,000
1972	834,000	430,000	404,000
1973	779,000	402,000	377,000
1974	737,000	379,000	358,000
1975	697,000	359,000	338,000

Source: Part of Table I(1) page 3 in 'Education Statistics for the United Kingdom, HMSO.

Educating the under 5's

Education is not compulsory until a child is 5, but the demand by parents for some form of pre-school care has been increasing over the years as more females (including mothers with under 5's) enter the employed population. For example, in 1961 the number of places in registered nurseries totalled 18,000, by 1975 this had risen to 370,000.

Pre school facilities are either made available by the public sector in the form of nursery schools and nursery classes in primary schools, or in private nurseries. The main difference between the two, as far as parents are concerned, is that fees are not payable in the public sector establishment.

In 1975, in the U.K., the number of children in nursery schools and nursery classes in the public sector totalled approximately 165,000. The children not fortunate enough to attend these schools had to be cared for in the private sector (self-help play groups, voluntary play groups, child minders, etc.). The number of places *could* be increased in the public sector. As one writer stated "The Department of Education and Science has repeatedly stated that nursery schools should be provided for those who need them. Nearly half the Local Education Authorities have not taken up the grants allocated for this purpose by the Department. It is depressing to read in a parliamentary written reply in Hansard that only 15 per cent of children aged three and four years were attending nursery schools in January of last year." (i.e. January 1977).[4]

In 1975 the ration of full time and part time pupils aged 2, 3 and 4 who were attending schools to all children in the U.K. within each age group was as follows:

2 year olds, ratio of 1 to 200 (4,000 out of 800,000 two year olds),

3 year olds, ratio of 1 to 9   (90,600 to 847,000), and

4 year olds, ratio of 1 to 2   (437,000 to 883,000).

As children approach the age of 5 more and more attend schools. Out of the total 1975 population of 2 to 4 year olds, 1 out of every 5 (531,600 out of 2,530,000) attended schools.

Respective ratios for 1967 were:

1 to 250 for the 2 year olds,

1 to 25   for the 3 year olds, and

1 to 4   for the 4 year olds.

The demand for more pre-school places in schools is steadily increasing. All it needs is for more Local Education Authorities to increase supply.

Compulsory school population

Education is compulsory, since the raising of the minimum school leaving age on 1 September 1972, between the ages of 5 and 16. Pupils may attend:

1. a public sector school (schools that are administered and financed by local education authorities), or

2. an assisted school (schools that are provided with grants from central government funds), or

3. an independent school (schools that are 'private' — administered and financed privately by charitable institutions, companies and individuals).

4. "Jottings" by Janus in "Midwife, Health Visitor and Community Nurse" April 1978, p.99.

In 1975 there were approximately 10,500,000 pupils (from those aged 5 to and including those aged 16)[5] attending schools in these three sectors in the U.K.; this represents almost 19 per cent of the home population.[6]

The break down of total pupils, based on ages at the beginning of January 1975 (actually based on ages at 31 December 1974), into the different school sectors is shown in Exhibit 14.3

Exhibit 14.3

School Sectors	All Pupils[7] Totals	as %	Males Totals	as %	Females Totals	as %
Public	9,902,258	94.7	5,067,779	94.4	4,834,479	94.9
Assisted	160,833	1.5	86,913	1.6	73,920	1.5
Independent	397,995	3.8	214,366	4.0	183,629	3.6
All Sectors	10,461,086	100.0	5,369,058	100.0	5,092,028	100.0

Some points that can be noted from the above table is that roughly 95 out of every 100 pupils in the U.K. go to schools in the public sector. Also, that there are more males than females, in the public sector but the percentage of females is greater than males. The opposite occurs in the independent sector; a greater proportion of males (in absolute terms and as a percentage) go to these schools than to females. The assisted schools have the least number of pupils, and it is possible that these numbers will fall in the 1980s as the government removes its financial assistance to The Direct Grant Grammar Schools (Regulations published in August 1975).

The above table showed the all pupils total at 10,461,086. This was approximately 55,000 more pupils than 1974. As the compulsory school age population increases in size, greater effort and expenditure is needed to maintain 'equality' between one year and the next.

Roughly speaking, the age groups making up the 1975 total would include children born in the years 1958 up to and including 1969; approximately half of those born in 1958 being in the 'all pupil' total.

Now, if we compare the years forward from 1975 for those in these schools, using the births shown in Exhibit 14.2 as a rough guide for change in size, we can say something about the 'expanding or declining' compulsory school age population. First, looking at the 1975 total — if we take into consideration the number of births from the year 1958 to 1969 (but only half the births in 1958) we have a total of approximately 10,963,000. When deducting deaths of the pre 5 year olds (remembering that in 1974 the total was around 14,640) and others that died between the ages 5 to 16, and then consider the net migration figures, the figure of 10½ million for 1975 is closely related to the 'births' totals.

5. It was decided to include the 16 year old group that stayed on at school. The number of 16 year olds in 1975 represented about ½ the 15 year old population of 1974.

6. These figures agree favourably with those calculated and shown in Exhibit 7.3 in the chapter on Population.

7. Information for this table came from Table 4 pages 8 and 9 of Education Statistics for the United Kingdom 1975.

What, then, would be the size of the compulsory school population for the educational year at January 1976? or January 1977?

For 1976 — if we subtract the figures for 1958 and add those for 1970 (not taking into considerations deaths or migration changes) we would expect an expanding school population.[8]

Carrying out similar calculations for the educational years after 1975 we arrive at the following 'expansion or decline' situation of the school population 5 to 16.

> January 1976 — expansion
>
> January 1977 — static
>
> January 1978 — declining
>
> January 1979 — declining
>
> January 1980 — declining
>
> January 1981 — declining

These are rough calculations and should be used only as a rough guide. However, it does indicate that the educational system will have less pupils as we go into the 1980s — about 750,000 less in 1981 compared to 1975. This would indicate a substantial change in government educational policy — use of schools, building programmes, ratio of pupils to teachers, training of teachers, places for nursery classes, etc..

Projections of population (births) show a continued downward trend. The implications for school population is that we can expect a continued decline right up to, at least 1984.

Pupils in the compulsory age groups are educated in schools classified as:

1. primary education, and

2. secondary education.

Primary education

In England, Wales and Northern Ireland, the number of years, normally, that a child stays in primary education is 5 to 10; entering secondary education at the age of 11. In Scotland pupils normally stay 7 years in primary education.

Schools in primary education, and there were 26,924 in the U.K. public sector, are divided into:

1. infant schools (for children aged 5-7), and

2. junior schools (for children aged 7-11 or 7-12 in Scotland).

About 50 per cent of the schools in primary education in England, Wales and Northern Ireland take both infants and juniors; about 20 per cent take infants only; about 17% take juniors only; the remainder (in England and Wales) are schools that make up part of a three-tier system and are called first, first and middle, and middle schools.

8.   Method: subtract ½ the births for 1958 and for 1959 and then add on the 1970 births.

246

The great majority of these schools take both boys and girls in mixed classes. The curriculum is much the same for both sexes, but there is some segregation for sports, for certain boys' subjects, and girls' subjects (such as needlework).

The size of primary education population will depend, to a great extent, upon the number of births in previous years. For example: 1964 totalled over 1 million and 1975 almost 700,000 — 5 years after birth they enter primary education. The size of classes will depend upon the number of schools, the number of class rooms, the number of teachers, and the number of students. For example: the 'pupils per teacher' in primary education in the public sector in 1969 was 28.0, and only 24.2 in 1975.[9]

Secondary education

Schools in the secondary education area cater for pupils from about age 11 (12 in Scotland) until they leave. Generally, these schools are much larger than primary schools (almost ½ take between 400 and 800 pupils whereas more than ½ of primary schools in the public sector had between 100 and 300 pupils).

In most Local Educational Authorities there are comprehensive schools. As stated before, in Scotland in 1974, virtually all public sector schools were comprehensive. The Labour Government introduced the Education Act 1976 to encourage Local Education Authorities to adopt a comprehensive school system but this might be changed if the Conservatives win at the next election.

Alongside comprehensive schools are 'grammar' and 'modern' schools. These schools tend to separate pupils by the level of their academic ability based on some selection system (the most famous and controversial is the '11 plus') when pupils leave primary education.

It is in secondary education that pupils prepare for some qualification, such as General Certificate of Education at Ordinary level or Certificate of Secondary Education in England and Wales,[10] and in Scotland the Scottish Certificate of Education at Ordinary level. As such there is a difference in the subjects that boys and girls tend to take. In Great Britain, in 1972, there were 140,800 entrants for 'home economics' subjects; 2,800 of these were boys. On the other hand there were 96,300 woodwork and metalwork entrants; 300 were girls. Boys tend to concentrate on physics and chemistry, whereas girls tend to study biology. "Such differentiation is only partly a reflection of school structures and organisation and the differences of programme and examination choice of boys and girls is again more largely the outcome of complex and subtle social pressures and expectation."[11]

9. Further details about number of pupils, number of teachers, and pupils per teacher at various stages of education (nursery, primary, secondary, special) can be found in Education Statistics for the United Kingdom, 1975, HMSO, table 9, page 14.

10. Introduced in 1965.

11. "Social commentary: men and women" section II 'Education' page 13 in Social Trends No. 5, 1974, HMSO.

Secondary education for the compulsory school age pupils ends at 16, but many remain to continue their education in secondary schools. Those that stay on do so voluntarily.

The size of pupil population (excluding voluntary students) in secondary education depends upon the birth rates in the relevant years. For example, persons born in the birth explosion year of 1964 would have entered the secondary education system in 1975 thereby swelling the pupil population. On the other hand the much smaller number of births in 1975 enter secondary schools in 1986. The births movements can create considerable problems, as already noted for primary schools, for government policy.

It is in secondary education that pupils prepare themselves for qualifications which will improve their prospects in seeking employment.

Beyond compulsory school age

Education beyond the compulsory school age is voluntary. There are a variety of options open to pupils when they reach the age of 16. They may:

1. leave school and opt out of educational establishments, or
2. stay on at secondary schools seeking further knowledge and qualifications, or
3. continue their education in other educational establishments on a part-time or full-time basis.

Their choice will often depend upon examination results achieved at secondary schools .... such as GCE and SCE 'Ordinary' passes or CSE's. "The interaction between opportunity, achievement, circumstances, and choice produces the patterns or participation in education by young persons ....."[12]

Opting out

The 16 year olds that opt out of full time education, as a proportion of all 16 year olds in Great Britain, has tended to decline. In 1974/75 they consistuted slightly more than 40 per cent.

Why do they leave education? The reasons[13] given for wishing to leave were:

1. to earn a wage and be independent as soon as possible,
2. did not like school work, and
3. they were not good enough to stay on.

Quite a few gave more than one reason.

When asked what the most important aspects of a job were, the two most common answers were that jobs should:

1. involve variety, and
2. should be well paid.

12. 'Fifteen to twenty-five: a decade of transition", page 13, in Social Trends No. 8, 1977, HMSO.
13. Findings of the National Child Development Study, as reported in Social Trends No. 8, 1977. HMSO. p12.

The next two most frequent responses were that jobs should:

3. provide opportunities for helping others, and

4. offer chances of promotion.

It appears that opting out of full time education is closely related to the socio-economic group of the father. More young persons opt out whose fathers are 'unskilled' — the least whose fathers are classified as 'professional'. The proportion of young persons of 'non-manual' fathers opt out of full-time education much less than those whose fathers have 'manual' backgrounds.

Continuing education

The size of student population continuing with their education depends first upon the size of the age population of 16, 17, etc. years of age, and the proportion of these totals that decide voluntarily to carry on with their education. Many of these students are aware that there is a strong association between educational qualifications and occupations, and that further education will have an important influence throughout their working life.

As stated before, young persons who continue their education are probably influenced by the background of their fathers — those with non-manual fathers tend to continue their education.

The opportunity to continue can take place either in secondary schools or some other educational establishment such as Colleges of Further Education, Colleges of Art, or Commerce, or Technology or some combination of these.

Educationally speaking, as noted previously, the young people of the 1970s are more fortunate than their parents and grandparents. They not only have had the opportunity of staying more years in education, but also achieving more examination qualifications.

Opting out or continuing figures

First, using data for England and Wales and looking at the percentages of persons leaving school after reaching 16 years of age, comparing those born in 1922 with those born 30 years later, we find:[14]

1. of those born in 1922 approximately 11 per cent of men and 9 per cent of women stayed on at school beyond the age of 15, whereas

2. those born in 1952 approximately 50 per cent of men and 49 per cent of women stayed on at school beyond the age of 15.

This is strong evidence supporting the statement about staying more years in education than their parents.

In support of the second statement about educational achievement, the following exhibit (Exhibit 14.4) is produced.

14. Based on Table XV p15 in Social Trends No. 4, 1973, HMSO.

Exhibit 14.4   Highest Educational Achievement
by Age
Great Britain — 1971

Percentages

| | Age Group | | | |
| | 15-24 | | 45-54 | |
Educational Achievement	Males	Females	Males	Females
First and higher degree	2.1	1.1	4.1	1.0
Non graduate teachers/ HNC/HND/nursing qualification	1.9	2.3	4.3	4.4
At least 1 GCE 'A' level or SCE 'H' grade	10.6	5.7	2.8	0.5
At least 1 GCE 'O' level or SCE 'O' grade	27.9	24.8	8.1	6.0
Clerical/commerical qualifications/CSE	4.6	9.1	1.0	6.2
Apprenticeship	2.3	0.5	10.2	1.0
Other qualifications	2.5	2.6	3.8	3.0
No qualifications	47.8	53.9	65.7	77.8
	100.0	100.0	100.0	100.0

Source: figures obtained from Appendix Table 1 p.20 in Social Trends No. 4, 1973, HMSO. Original figures are from General Household Survey.

It should be noted that this exhibit considers Great Britain and is for the year 1971. The age group 15-24 was used because persons born in 1952 would be included in this group; the 45-54 age group would include those born in 1922.

Educational achievements

The exhibit clearly shows there were fewer persons in the age group 15-24 having no qualifications compared to the 45-54 age group. It also shows that there were more females, in both age groups, having no qualifications compared to males. On the other hand the younger females have closed the big gap in the 'no qualification' area. There appears to be a greater equality of opportunity for females in education as we move towards the 21st century.

Another point that is brought out by the table is the decline in apprenticeships, and on the other hand, the increase in GCE and SCE examinations. This, one might say, is a sign of the times.

As to the first two educational achievements mentioned, it is only fair to say that the figures for 15-24 relate to the upper ages in the group; this is not so for the 45-54 group. A more favourable situation will be achieved by the 15-24 group as we move farther into the 1970s.

During the rest of the 1970s and the 1980s the younger population are expected to achieve more qualifications than the next higher age groups, or to put it another way, less students in the school leaving age group will leave the educational system with no qualifications. More are continuing their full-time education after leaving, for example:

1965/66 — approximately 2 out of every 5 of 16 to 19 year olds were in full-time education, and ten years later,
1975/76 — 3 out of 5 were in full-time education.

Education — expensive

Education in the public sector may be free in that parents do not have to pay directly to schools, but indirectly it is paid through taxes and rates to central and local authorities. In Great Britain, public expenditure on education for the 1975-76 period, at current prices, was: £6,780,000,000 or approximately £124½ for each person in the population.

Providing knowledge, to remove the social evil 'ignorance' is expensive but worthwhile because, overall, it enhances the well being of the individual and the nation.

Assignments

1. Discuss the effects that an increase in student population will have on the education service.
2. What determines the pupil population and teacher population in the educational system at various levels?
3. In 1964 there were 1,015,000 births in the U.K. compared to 697,000 in 1975. Compare and contrast the likely effects this change will have on the primary education scene.

Chapter 15

Changing Role of Private and Public Services

Learning objectives:

At the end of your study of this chapter you should be able to:

1. outline the changing roles of private and public services and agencies (actions) in relation to changes in the population.

2. distinguish different types of organisation in terms of their function and purpose, with particular reference to those producing goods and services.

3. analyse *some* of the characteristics of organisations in a mixed economy with respect to different types of activities.

4. recognise the increasing importance of the public sector in the U.K. economy.

The development of the 'Welfare State' in the U.K., which has been going on for more than 100 years, was seen as a movement away from private and more towards public services. The reason for this is that it was claimed that the proper function of government is to ward off the strains and stresses among *all* classes of society.

A movement from private to public effort has led the U.K. to become more of a mixed economy in the 1970's relative to the 1870's and 1770's. Basically, the change in the U.K. mixed economy and the growing importance of the public sector might be viewed, roughly, as shown in Exhibit 15.1A and 15.1B.

Exhibit 15.1A

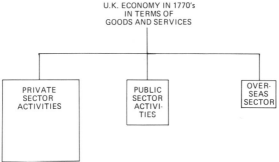

Exhibit 15.1B

It can be seen from the exhibits that the U.K. economy has grown in size, in terms of goods and services made available to the community, over the time span 1770's to 1970's. Also, the exhibits show that the U.K. economy has become more mixed as the public sector has grown considerably at the expense of the private sector, but both have grown over time.

During this time span we can note that the population of the U.K. has also grown — from less than 10,000,000 in the 1770's to more than 55,000,000 in the 1970's.

Population and public sector activities have both moved in the same direction — upwards. However, it does not necessarily follow that one movement is directly caused by the other but evidently there are links between the two. Perhaps the simple diagrams below will make clear that the link is the situation created by population movement. For example:

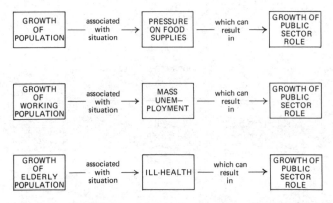

To the above it is possible to add other noticeable changes in population. The consequences (situation arising fom the change in population) may take different forms and each consequence has different impacts on society. The greater the consequences the more important it is for the public sector to take direct action by increasing its activities in controlling the resources (goods and services) of the nation. An example of consequences with great impact:

war—
larger population puts pressure on food supplies and land and more land is sought, or a foreign nation creates war for this purpose. In either case the public sector (central government in this case) takes on a greater role of controlling the nation's resources.

crisis of mass unemployment— public sector takes on an additional role of creating employment.

revolution—
large sector of population becomes dissatisfied with their way of life so the public sector must take on the role of creating services to raise the quality of life.

Other consequences of less impact take longer for the public sector to react. For example:

change in electoral voters— women may be given the right to vote or the voting age may be lowered. These extra votes now enable these sectors of the population to voice their demands to their government representatives.

entrance of new political party— changing attitudes of certain sectors of the population may indicate the need for a new political party to publicly voice their needs.

How about other activities of various population sectors: riots, marches, strikes, petitions, etc? They tend to show discontent with the status quo and invite the public sector to enter situations that may have been strictly private.

It can be seen from the foregoing that to understand the increasing role of the public sector it is necessary to have an appreciation of:

population change,

historical events,

political movements,

changed social attitudes, and

knowledge of economics.

In other words, there are many forces in the community which help to determine the changing role between the private and public sector. Population changes must be viewed as creating stresses and strains which trigger off events which may eventually lead to growth in public sector activities.

Public sector — public services

The public sector refers to the activities of central and local government plus the various agencies controlled by them, such as public corporations.

They provide a regular or continuous supply of goods or services to meet the needs or requirements of the population Supplies may be goods or services and the type and amount supplied will depend upon the intensity of activities of the public sector in their attempt to meet the material and social needs of the nation. In the economic sense goods refer to items that can be seen and physically touched — materials such as food, clothing, shelter. Services are those that can not be seen or touched, such as insurance, education, health.

Public services then refers to services, such as education and health, provided by the various sections in the public sector. For them to provide services it is often necessary to supply goods, but not all these goods come from the public sector. Emphasis is on the services provided — goods being a means to provide the services. A few examples may clarify the previous statements.

1. The armed forces of the U.K. provide a service to the community by providing protection from foreign aggression. Goods, such as ships, tanks and planes are the materials required by the armed forces to afford this services. These military materials are produced mainly by organisations in the private sector, but the defence service is primarily controlled by central government.

2. Schools provide a service called education. Goods required by these institutions take the form of buildings, desks, chairs, books, etc. Again, a large proportion of goods are produced in the private sector to enable the public sector to furnish the education service.

3. Hospitals provide a service associated with health. To help the surgeon to operate there is a need for certain goods such as surgical instruments, sterilised clothing, operating tables, etc.. The surgeon provides the service with the help of these materials.

Public services, therefore, refers to the non-material activities that the public sector provides to enhance the quality of life of everyone in the community.

Private sector — private services

Very simply stated, the private sector and the services they provide refer to the greater part of those activities not covered by the public sector. They could be referred to as 'non-public sector' and 'non public services'.

The services provided by the wholesaler to retailers, and the retailer to individual members of the community are good examples of 'private services'. The professional services of the accountant, barrister, estate agent, solicitor, stock exchange broker are all examples of 'private services'. Private services also include the services of the banks, insurance companies and privately run transport organisations.

Mixture — public and private

The previous information related to the production of services (or goods) that can be clearly classified as being in either the public or private sector. Some activities can be placed in both sectors, such as hospitals and personal social services. There is, however, no mixture of the sectors because the financial and administrative control is purely public or purely private. Even on occasions when a public sector department or agency makes a temporary loan to an enterprise in the private sector there is no mixture.

A mixture exists when both the public and private sector share in the ownership and management of the enterprise and its activities. A good example is the British Petroleum Company.

Background to changing roles

In the 18th century the countries making up the U.K. had a population of approximately 10 million and the majority of these were living off the land — in agriculture. The state was moving gradually in the direction of laissez-faire; a signal that indicates the decline of state power and state interference in the lives of man. This was the century that saw the beginning of the so-called industrial revolution which created new situations as machines and factories were introduced into the lives of the population. In the predominantly agricultural society people led an orderly life made possible by long established social traditions.

During the 18th century public expenditure, based on the budget of central government, was primarily spent on protecting the country against foreign enemies. Approximately 75 per cent of total expenditure in 1760 went towards the up-keep of the army and navy, and 20 per cent to pay for the national debt. Nil or negligible expenditures were made by the state in providing social services. In terms of population the state was spending roughly £2 per person, a total of £20,000,000.

The transition from the predominantly agricultural scene to the new industrial scene created social distress.

At first, during the latter part of the 18th and first two decades of the 19th century, the state did little or nothing to alleviate the new social problems — the greatest social evil being the exploitation of child labour. The state was reluctant to intervene; it was held back by the previously established policies of laissez-faire. Individualism was the trait that set the scene in the country at this time and individuals, notably the entrepreneurs, swayed public opinion in favour of non-intervention by the state. But circumstances and the structure of society was changing quite rapidly relative to the past. A large part of the population moved into towns and were employed in factories, workshops and mines; these activities lacked social tradition and stability that existed in the past. From one decade to another there was an increase in social confusion and there was need for readjustments. The state began intereferring; began moving away from laissez-faire. Interference was necessary to right social evils and bring social confusion into some form of orderliness. During this time public opinion changed and the state was urged to take steps to reform society — to correct the economic scene which tended to lower the quality of life (ill-health, unhappiness) for a large proportion of the population.

State interference can be seen as a movement from individualism towards communalism; a movement from private services to public services, and a movement away from the dogmas of laissez-faire. Communalism developed at the expense of individualism and public services at the expense of private services. Movements were gradual at the beginning of the 19th century but gathered speed as the 20th century was approached. During this time, population was increasing and state expenditure had a positive role to play in the realm of change and in the general working of the economy. As population increased and the state interfered we would expect an increase in public expenditure and more than likely an increase in public expenditure per head of the population.

In 1860 public expenditure was calculated to be approximately £70,000,000 and this amounted to roughly £3 per head of the population. The greater part of the total went towards the up-keep of defence services and paying off the national debt. There was an indication that attention was being paid to the social services; about one per cent of the total (£700,000). The greater part of this included grants to schools set up by voluntary societies. It was also noticeable that larger outlays were being made for law and justice.

The change from private to public effort was taking place but it was still slow relative to changes that took place in the 20th century. Nevertheless change was taking place as shown by the following examples.

Example 1. Home Life

1847— A private society was formed to improve the dwellings of the labouring classes.

1864— model working class houses were being built privately (by Octavia Hill and John Ruskin).

1875— The state passed an act which empowered local authorities to clear slums and provide better housing.

Example 2. Education

1833— the state started to contribute to church schools.

1870— the state compelled local authorities to build schools where church provision was inadequate. This was considered to be an early landmark in the social revolution.

1888— school attendance was compulsory.

1891— education was made 'free'.

Example 3. Child Welfare

1844— the Society for the Prevention of Cruelty to Children was founded.

1890s— Margaret MacMillan founded nursery schools where medical treatment was given.

1907— medical inspection of school children was introduced.

Example 4. Public Health

1848— Public Health Act encouraged local authorities to create local Boards of Health and Medical Officers of Health. Also encouraged towns to provide pure water and decent sanitation.

1886— Sanitary inspectors were to be appointed by local authorities

1875— Public Health Act. An Act of consolidation. Considered to be another early landmark in the social revolution.

In the above areas and in other areas, such as working life, pensions for the elderly, maternal welfare, assistance to the poor, etc., the public sector was taking action to develop public services and in so doing replaced private efforts.

The public sector began introducing new standards. Minimum standards were being set to which everyone was entitled, and these were always higher than those that existed in the past.

During the 19th century the public sector became more and more concerned with the well being of everyone and this trend continued throughout the 20th century up to the present time.

We should note that public sector action was not always complete. Gaps appeared when social problems were not brought under public services. These gaps were plugged primarily by individual reformers and other interested groups. Eventually they were taken over to a great extent by the public sector. It is useful to remember that 'gaps' always seem to appear even when we think it is impossible (because of all the services provided by both the public and private services sectors).

In the 20th century the pace at which the public sector took over the role of private services, especially in the social area, was increasing. The giant step forward in this movement came during and immediately after World War II. Details of these movements are covered in other sections in this book, notably the chapter on the mixed economy and the chapter on social implications of population change.

Evidence of the increase in public sector activities can be shown by noting that in 1959 government expenditure amounted to about £5,500,000,000 or approximately £115 per head.

Comparing 1959 with previous periods mentioned we find that:

1. Total government expenditure in 1959 was more than 78 times that spent in 1860, and 275 times as much as in 1760.

2. Government expenditure per head was only £2 in 1760, £3 in 1860 and £115 in 1959. To put it another way: over the 200 year period from 1760 to 1959 government expenditure per head of population had risen by 5,750 per cent.

Of course these figures are based on money values current to the years mentioned. Prices in 1959 were about 10 times higher than those in 1760 and about 5 times higher than those in 1860. Even allowing for these substantial increases in prices the increase in government expenditure is vast and shows the increased responsibility and much larger role of the government in the economy.

What, in 1959, did the the government spend this money on? Defence took about 28 per cent of the total and paying off the national debt 15 per cent. Expenditures going to the social services represented 36 per cent of the total.

This information by itself may not appear to be meaningful — a comparison over the 200 year period (1760 to 1959) is shown in Exhibit 15.2.

Exhibit 15.2

**Pattern of
Government Expenditure
1760, 1860 and 1959**

Years	How Expenditure has grown (£)	How the money was spent (% of total current expenditure)			
		Defence	National Debt	Civil Government	Social Services
1760	20,000,000	75	20	5	—
1860	70,000,000	40	39	20	1
1959	5,500,000,000	28	15	21	36

Source: "Government Revenue and Expenditure", Broadsheets on Britain, April 1961, No. 94, p.3.

Exhibit 15.2 simply brings together information that has been provided earlier in this chapter. It does show that the level and pattern of government spending has changed radically, and the most prominent development was the big increase in providing for social services. This arose because social problems came to be seen more as a national and not merely a local problem.

Recent figures of public sector expenditure can be found in the National Income and Expenditure 'blue book'. In this case it should be noted that expenditures are those of the public sector, not only central government. Expenditures for 1965 and 1975 are shown in Exhibit 15.3.

Exhibit 15.3 shows expenditure in terms of money spent on the behalf of the community by the public sector and the percentage share that money represents of total public sector expenditure for 1965 and 1975. It should be pointed out that the money figures are current to each year and takes no account of inflation. Nevertheless the sums that are spent by the public sector have increased as a share of the national income, from slightly more than 49 per cent in 1965 to more than 65 per cent in 1975. This is strong evidence of the increasing role of the public sector.

The figures speak for themselves. Students should study the figures, note the changes and make further observations about likely changes in public sector policy. For example, military defence has increased in money terms by approximately 145 per cent but less of total expenditure is directed towards this 'protection service'. On the other hand, expenditures on social services increased by over 300 per cent. Evidently policy has been that of favouring social services, and military defence has been relegated to a much lower priority in 1975 compared to 1965.

Exhibit 15.3

Public Sector Expenditure
1965 and 1975

	1965		1975	
Expenditure on	£m	as %	£m	as %
Military defence	2,105	14.9	5,173	9.5
Social services[1]	5,500	38.9	22,465	41.2
Debt interest	1,456	10.3	4,513	8.3
Environmental services[2]	602	4.3	2,405	4.4
Housing	958	6.8	4,291	7.9
Police	217	1.5	973	1.8
Fire service	53	0.4	241	0.4
Agriculture, forestry, fishing, food	335	2.4	1,702	3.1
Other industry and trade	1,013	7.2	5,285	9.7
Roads and public lighting	436	3.1	1,502	2.8
Transport and communications	598	4.2	2,495	4.6
Other expenditures[3]	864	6.0	3,420	6.3
Total public sector expenditure	14,137	100.0	54,465	100.0
Goods and services	6,041	42.7	22,907	42.1
Subsidies	571	4.0	3,906	7.2
Current grants to personal sector	2,596	18.4	10,208	18.7
Debt interest	1,456	10.3	4,513	8.3
Others	3,473	24.6	12,931	23.7
Total public sector expenditure (TPSE)	14,137	100.0	54,465	100.0
National income	£28,787m		£83,188m	
U.K. home population (mid-years)	54,218,000		55,962,000	
TPSE as percentage of National income	49.1		65.5	
TPSE per head of population	£260.74		£973.25	

Notes:
1. Social services includes: Education; National Health Service; Personal social services; Social security benefits; School meals, milk, and welfare foods.
2. Environmental services includes: Water, sewage and refuse disposal; Public health services; Land drainage and coast protection; Parks, pleasure grounds, etc.; Miscellaneous local government services.
3. Other expenditures include: Civil defence; Employment services; Prisons, Records, registration and surveys; Finance and tax collection; Parliament and Law courts; Research; External relations; other services.

Source: TPSE money figures obtained from National Income and Expenditure 1965-75, HMSO, 1976, Table 10.2, pages 64-68
National income figures from same source, Table 1
U.K. home population from Annual Abstract of Statistics 1976, HMSO, 1976, Table 6.

Overall — the public sector is increasing its role in the community, and this must be at the expense of the private sector. The size and pattern of public sector spending as shown in the last exhibit is a useful indicator of showing the increasing importance of the public sector at the expense of the private sector in the U.K.

Assignments

1. The development of the so-called 'Welfare State' in the United Kingdom can be seen as a movement away from private services towards public services. Discuss.

2. What changes would you expect in the private vs public sectors as a result of the 3 May 1979 elections when Conservatives were swept into power?

3. "Society owes its members a good living." Argue the case that it is necessary for the State to take over more activities in order to satisfy this statement.

4. There is a positive relationship between the increased role of the public sector and a movement towards the planned economy. Discuss.

Chapter 16

Nature and Role of Law

Learning Objectives
At the end of your study of this chapter you should be able to:
1. explain the sources and nature of public and private rights and duties
2. explain the nature and forms of legal liability, for example: criminal and civil, fault, strict and vicarious
3. explain judicial, administrative and other means of conflict resolution.

The contents of this chapter has been divided into three parts to satisfy the objectives listed above.

PUBLIC AND PRIVATE RIGHTS AND DUTIES

In a social context, the rights and duties of organisations in the public and private sector, and of individuals, are governed by the law. Society is organised by the law in such a way as to draw up limits within which everyone must move in their relationships with other organisations and individuals. In our society people possess rights, but they also have duties in relation to each other, and largely it is the law which defines the extent of such rights and duties.

There are many theories of the nature of law and the notion of rights and duties, and doubtless many more will be evolved. We can do no more than consider, in brief, what is involved with two particular theories. All do agree, however, that law is a set of rules forming the basis of behaviour by those who are subject to it in a given society.

The theory of *natural law* is that there is a complete and perfect set of rules for the guidance of human conduct. Man-made laws aspire to reach this goal, and must be judged by these rules. In fact then, all men are born free. What they do in practise, to give society some semblance of order, is to agree that they will surrender some of this freedom and undertake various obligations.

Another notion is that law is imposed by superior beings who emerge as leaders in society. This is the theory of legal positivism: that law is a command imposed by a superior on an inferior, and is backed ultimately by some sort of sanction, that is that some consequence of an unpleasant nature will follow if any commands are broken. An obvious example is imprisonment. In our society, the superior being is the state enacting laws through Parliament, and the inferior being is any individual or organisation which is subject to those rules.

Whatever the nature of our law, in general it is concerned basically with the protection of rights and their enforcement. If one person has a right which is protected by the law, this gives rise to a corresponding duty on the part of someone else. An example might illustrate the point. In common with everyone in our society, I have a right to enjoy possession of my property, for instance my wallet and the money in it. If someone disregards my right by dishonestly taking my wallet, criminal charges can be brought against that person under the Theft Act, 1968.

A legal right, then, consists of some interest which the law is prepared to recognise and accept. The respect for this right by others is termed a duty. If they disregard it then they have committed a wrong in law. Each right is personal to the owner of it, and results in a duty imposed on others who are therefore bound by it and are under an obligation to respect it by doing some act, or refraining from some conduct in such a way as to benefit the person who owns the right.

All rights involve duties, and a right capable of being exercised by one person may be someone else's duty. For example, if X has a right to walk over Y's land, Y has a duty to allow him to do so. If Y then prevents X from exercising that right, X may take action at law for the recognition and enforcement of his right. A legal duty, then, is an obligation recognised by law to carry out or refrain from carrying out some action.

Disregard for another's right results in the commission of a wrong, and this is the concern of the law. A legal wrong is distinct from a moral wrong, and the law generally does not concern itself with moral wrongs. Morality is a code of conduct practised in a society, recognised and obeyed because people agree that it is the correct way to act. It differs from the law in that if a person commits a moral wrong, there will be no legal action taken against him. He has not acted in disregard of a legal right. The only thing such a person is likely to endure is the condemnation of others in the society. A legal wrong, on the other hand, consists of some act or omission (that is a failure to do something) which is contrary to legal rules resulting from disregard for the rights of others. So if a person is walking along a canal bank and sees a young child who has fallen into the canal, he is under no legal duty to rescue that child, unless, perhaps, he is the child's parent or guardian. In law he could watch that child drown, and there would be no legal consequences for his failure to act. On the other hand, an attempted rescue in this situation would be regarded by society as a person's moral obligation, and the moral wrong committed by the failure to act would undoubtedly carry social consequences.

In many cases, however, something which is a moral wrong is also a legal wrong. The two, law and morality, overlap. Common examples would be theft and murder. Here the moral wrongs are recognised as such an interference with the rights of others that they give rise to legal rights which are capable of enforcement.

Legal rules can be classified into main types, public law and private law. These give rise to public and private rights and duties. It will be sufficient for the moment to look at these branches of the law in the context of rights and duties, since this theme will be developed later in the chapter when we consider the nature and forms of certain aspects of legal liability, arising from the failure to respect legal rights resulting in the commission of legal wrongs.

A diagramatical representation appears in the following exhibit, and forms the basis of the discussion which follows in the remainder of the section.

Exhibit 16.1

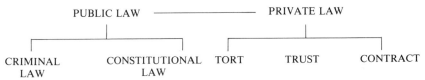

While these categories are in no way exhaustive, they do give indications of the major areas involving rights and duties. Briefly, criminal law is concerned with offences against the state arising from obligations imposed by law. Constitutional law deals with the rights which individuals have within the state, such as the right to vote in general and local authority elections. Tort, which like criminal law consists of obligations imposed by the law, deals with wrongs against individuals as opposed to the state. Trust law deals with duties which are undertaken voluntarily, a trust being the legal relationship existing where one person (a trustee) holds property for the benefit of another called a beneficiary. The duties imposed in this relationship, although governed by law, are undertaken voluntarily by the trustee for the beneficiary's benefit. Finally, contract concerns rights and obligations which arise between the parties to a legally enforceable agreement.

Before examining legal liability a degree of re-capitulation might be valuable.

The role of law is to lay down rules of conduct which will govern the operation of individuals and organisations. These rules are necessary to give society some sort of order so that the affairs of any community can be conducted in a way which is right and peaceable. Legal liability arises whenever the rules are broken. The effect is that the person or organisation concerned is answerable in law for his conduct, either in his actions (that is for something he had actually done) or in his omissions (that is for his failure to do something). The nature and extent of legal liability depends upon the act or omission in question. It is now proposed to examine various forms of legal liability.

THE NATURE AND FORMS OF LEGAL LIABILITY

1. *Criminal and Civil Liability.* Criminal law can be classified as a branch of public law. This term covers those parts of the law which are mainly concerned with the state itself. Certain actions are readily recognisable by most people as constituting criminal offences, for example, murder, treason, theft, assault, and fraud. But it is difficult to define a crime even

though we might recognise it when we read or hear about it. A crime involves some sort of wrongdoing which has a particularly harmful effect on the public and not only on the individual concerned, although, of course, he may be the person who is wronged. Because of this, action is taken on behalf of the public by the state, which takes the initiative in dealing with the offender, that is to say, it is collective action.

For example, if X, intending to murder Y, shoots him but not fatally, then X may be prosecuted for attempted murder. Obviously Y is the one who has suffered injury as a result of X's action, but also X's conduct is of such a nature that the public as a whole must be protected from such actions.

The same principle applies equally to organisations as it does to individuals. So if a company has no assets, but nevertheless still obtains goods on credit from its suppliers when its directors know that it is unlikely that the goods will be paid for, then those who are aware of this may be prosecuted for fraud. Here the suppliers are the people who have suffered injury, but similarly the public must be protected.

Criminal proceedings, as we said, are instituted by the State. In fact, all prosecutions are brought in the name of the Queen. So the Crown prosecutes the Accused (or Defendant), and some form of penalty is imposed, assuming that the prosecution is successful. Once the offender has been sentenced by the court, the state again takes over responsibility for the enforcement of that sentence.

The basic aim of criminal law is the punishment of offenders. These punishments may vary because people's views as to the object or justification of punishment have undergone change. For instance, the penalty for murder used to be death by hanging. Now life imprisonment has been substituted for death under the Murder (Abolition of Death Penalty) Act, 1965. Briefly, the aims of punishment are:-

a) To prevent the offender from committing the offence again. This is achieved by imposing a term of imprisonment;

b) To deter others from committing offences because they have seen the punishment given to offenders;

c) To avenge the wrong done by the criminal to society;

d) A means of reforming the offender.

In criminal law, every accused person or body is presumed to be innocent until proved guilty beyond a reasonable doubt. It is for the prosecution to prove this, and so if, after a consideration of the evidence, there is a reasonable doubt as to guilt, the accused must be acquitted.

As a general rule, criminal liability will arise where the prosecution can successfully prove two constituent elements of a crime.

a) A wrongful act committed by the accused (called the "actus reus"), and

b) A guilty mind (called "mens rea"). This involves, generally, proving a degree of fault.

For instance, if an organisation makes false statements to the Inland

Revenue as to the profits of its business, this constitutes the wrongful act, and doing so with intent to defraud the Revenue constitutes the guilty mind. However, this general rule is subject to qualifications. Firstly, certain statutes have created offences of "strict liability", in that the element of a guilty mind need not be proved. Strict liability will be discussed more fully later. Secondly, a person must always be taken as intending the natural consequences of his action. Thus in the example above, the organisation could not escape liability by claiming that it did not intend to deceive the Revenue. Deception is the natural consequence of concealing the profits of the business.

Civil law, on the other hand, is basically concerned with the rights and duties of individuals towards each other. As such, it is classified as *private* law. The term includes in its scope several aspects of law which we have to consider in detail at a much later stage, but for the present it will be sufficient to know that the following are included, although the list is not exhaustive.

a) The *law of contract,* which deals with the making and breaking of legally enforceable promises.

b) The *law of tort,* which is concerned with compensating for any loss caused to a person due to the breach of a duty imposed by law on someone else. For example, a motorist is under a legal duty to take reasonable care while driving. If he fails to do so, and injures another motorist as a result, he will be liable in damages for the tort of negligence.

c) The *law of property,* which is concerned with rights which can be exercised by people over land or personal property.

Civil liability will arise whenever the legal rules established in the above categories are broken.

It is essential to realise that it is the individual who is important so far as enforcement of his rights is concerned. Someone who, for example, suffers loss as a result of a breach of contract must take action himself to enforce his rights. So civil law depends on individual action, rather than the collective action of criminal law. The person bringing an action is called the plaintiff, a plaint being the old term for a plea, hence a plaintiff was a person pleading his case, He sues a defendant, usually for damages, that is to say, compensation in the form of money. Assuming his case is successful, any damages awarded will go to the plaintiff. The aim of the civil law, then, is basically to compensate, rather than to punish a defendant for his conduct.

Although we have placed the various branches of the law into compartments, really for the sake of convenience, the distinctions between them need not always be so rigid. So, for example, the same situation could give rise to both civil and criminal liability. The illustration was given earlier of a company's directors being criminally responsible for fraud by ordering goods on credit when they know that the company has no assets and no probability of any. For such conduct they can be imprisoned for up to two years and/or fined £500. But in addition to this criminal liability, civil liability also arises, because they will be personally liable without limit for any of the company's debts or other liabilities as the court may direct.

In a similar way, an action could simultaneously amount to a tort and a breach of contract. So if a haulage company makes a contract to carry another firm's goods, but does so without reasonable care so that those goods are damaged, then they will be liable for breach of the contract of carriage *and* for the tort of negligence.

2. *Fault.* The commission of crimes and torts by individuals or organisations normally involves *fault* on their part which gives rise to liability in law. Fault is a state of mind inferred from conduct which falls below the accepted community standard of careful and unintentional conduct. We can see from this definition that the state of mind of the person concerned is relevant when coming to a decision as to whether he is accountable to the law. The problem is that the courts are not mind-readers, so that anyone's state of mind must be seen by reference to his conduct. There are four states of mind to be considered in a descending scale.

a) *Intention.* Where a person means to bring about the consequences of his actions, that is to say, any harm caused was the natural and probable consequence of the defendant's conduct. For example, if a person, hoping to kill someone else, points a loaded gun at him and pulls the trigger, this would be an intentional killing should death result.

b) *Recklessness.* Where the defendant did not necessarily *mean* to bring about the consequences of his actions, but acted in disregard of them. So, in the example above, if the gunman did not know that the gun was loaded, but realised the possibility that it might be, then he was reckless, and it does not matter whether he hoped it was not loaded, or simply did not care whether it was loaded or not. In effect, a person acting recklessly is taking a deliberate unjustifiable risk.

c) *Negligence.* Where consequences undesired by the defendant are brought about through his inadvertent failure to conform to the community standard of reasonable care. The essence of acting negligently, then, is that a reasonable man would have forseen the consequences of his actions and taken steps to avoid them. Again using the gunman as an example, if he pulls the trigger not intending harm and not recklessly, but in circumstances when any reasonable man would have realised the possibility of the gun being loaded, he had acted negligently.

d) *Innocence.* The absence of any degree of fault at all.

Generally speaking, most tort and criminal cases, it has to be proved that the person responsible for the harm caused committed a wrong against another, *and* that one part of the mental elements apart from innocence was present at the relevant time.

Fault and motive

It is perhaps worth commenting on the question of motive in the context of legal liability. A person's motive is the reason why he acted the way he did. We have seen that the presence or absence of fault will be determined by inference from a person's conduct because the courts cannot read minds. To determine a person's motive, however, we would need to know his *actual* state of mind at the time. This is impossible to discover, and because of this motive is largely disregarded by the law. Returning to our gunmen again, the fact that he shoots someone through anger or jealousy for example, is irrelevant to deciding his legal liability, although it certainly would be from the point of view of evidence. People do not usually act without a motive, so if it can be proved that the gunman had a motive for his actions it makes it much more likely that he did commit the crime.

In some instances, however, motive is relevant, and is an ingredient of the type of liability involved. For example, in the offence of malicious prosecution, it is obvious from the title of the offence that malice, that is acting from spite or improper motive, must be established.

3. *Vicarious Liability.* The term *vicarious* means deputed, or something done or suffered by one person on behalf of someone else. In the legal sense, vicarious liability arises where one person is regarded by the law as being liable for the acts or omissions of another. This liability arises most commonly as a result of the legal relationship between employer and employee, principal and agent, partners amongst themselves, and corporations and their officers.

In the law of tort, employers are vicariously responsible for torts committed by their employees in the course of their employment. Even if the employer has not expressly ordered or authorised the tort to be committed, he is still responsible at law. The reason for this dual liability, at least originally, was the likelihood of an employee having insufficient money himself to meet an award of damages to an injured plaintiff, whereas the employer, who controls and manages the organisation giving the employment anyway, is more likely to be financially sound, and may very well be insured in any case. It is true to say, however, that the employee is still himself liable for the harm done, and if an employer is successfully sued he can make good his loss by claiming from the employee. Two matters require further consideration.

Firstly, for an employer to be liable, the person committing the tort must be his employee. This may appear to cause little difficulty, since in most instances it is easy to recognise an employee. For example, an electrician working for the Electricity Board would normally be an employee, as would a sales representative for a company. But in the case of a self-employed electrician called in by a householder to re-wire a house, such a person would be termed an independent contractor and not an employee. Briefly the notion is that an employee is a person who works for another in such a way that the employee is subject to the employer's control so far as the manner in which the work to be done is concerned. That is, then, the employer controls the work to be done and how it is done. An independent contractor, on the other hand, is only controlled as to the work to be done. When it comes to how it is to be done, he is free to select his own method.

Secondly, the wrong committed must have been done by the employee "in the course of his employment". This means that the act must be one which he is expressly or impliedly authorised to do. If, on the other hand, the employee was acting purely on his own behalf, the employer will not be liable. For example, if a sales representative for a company is driving his car between visits to clients and negligently collides with another vehicle, the company will be liable. But if he had intentionally deviated from his route instead of going directly to his destination he is termed to be on a "frolic of his own" and no vicarious liability will arise.

This same principle of vicarious liability also applied in the relationship between principal and agent. An agent is someone authorised by another (the principal) to bring the principal into a contractual relationship with another. A common example would be where a houseowner employs an estate agent to sell his house for him. Again, in a partnership the same notion applies. Under s.5 Partnership Act, 1890, every partner is an agent for his other partners and for the firm for the purpose of the business of the partnership. This means that a contract made by one partner acting in the ordinary course of the firm's business will be binding on the firm as a whole, and all the partners can be liable for the actions of one of them. In tort, the partnership will be liable for the torts of each partner if they are committed in the ordinary course of business or with the authority of the other partners. Liability may also arise for those who are not in fact partners. In Lloyd v Grace, Smith and Co., 1912, a managing clerk was employed by a firm of solicitors to deal with conveyancing, which is basically concerned with the transfer of land between one person and another. The plaintiff had some cottages to sell and consulted the solicitors. The managing clerk fraudulently induced the plaintiff to sign various documents transferring the cottages to him, which he then disposed of for his own benefit. The plaintiff sued the firm. It was held by the court that the solicitors were liable, even though the firm received no benefit from the transaction. They had represented that the clerk had authority to get clients to agree to transfers of property by allowing him to deal with such matters. Since the clerk was acting within the scope of his authority, his employer was vicariously responsible for his actions.

Finally, with corporations and their officers, vicarious liability may arise, if only because in many cases for example directors and to some extent the company secretary act as agents for the company in contractual negotiations. In such cases, provided the corporation is acting "intra vires", that is within the scope of its constitution, then it will be liable for the actions of its officers so long as they in turn have acted within the authority given to them or which appears to have been given to them.

An illustration concerning a company secretary arose in the case of Panorama Developments v. Fidelis Furnishing Fabrics Ltd. The facts were that the plaintiffs ran a car-hire business. The secretary of the defendant company rented cars from them allegedly on the company's behalf in order to convey the company's clients. In fact, he was using the cars for his own purposes. Ultimately, of course, the plaintiffs presented their bill to the company for the hire charges. The company refused to pay on the grounds that the secretary had no actual authority from it to make such contracts. The court, however, decided that the company was liable to pay. Even though the secretary had no actual authority, he had, as the company's chief administrative officer, authority to make contracts concerning the administrative side of its affairs. The renting of cars was something which the secretary might be expected to do because of his position.

4. *Strict Liability.* Certain statutes and decisions of the courts have created situations of strict liability. This means that the commission of certain wrongs in both civil and criminal law gives rise to liability which is absolute. In criminal law an offence is punishable without "mens rea" being present; usually the damage caused to the public in such instances is likely to be extensive, and the guilty mind of the accused when committing the offence is going to be difficult to establish. An organisation which makes false statements to obtain insurance certificates for cars driven by its sales representatives, for example, commits an offence of strict liability under road traffic legislation.

In the civil law, the commission of certain wrongs may give rise to liability and which does not depend on the presence of fault. A classic example is to be found in the case of Rylands v Fletcher, 1868. Here the defendant had a mill on his land and, since he wanted water power to operate it, he employed independent contractors to build a reservoir on the land as well. During the course of construction, the contractors discovered disused mine shafts, but since the shafts were filled with earth they did not tell him about them. The reservoir was duly finished and filled with water. Unfortunately the shafts linked with mine workings on the plaintiff's land. The reservoir water seeped through the shafts on the defendant's land into the plaintiff's workings flooding them and causing damage. The plaintiff sued. Certainly the defendant was not at fault here. He had employed independent contractors to do the jobs, and if anyone had been negligent is must surely have been them. In any case, the defendant had no knowledge that the shafts existed and there was no reason for him to even suspect that they were there. Despite this, though, the defendant was held liable because he had kept something on his land which was not naturally there and which was likely to cause harm if it escaped his control, and it had done so. Liability was strict.

A more modern example of this strict liability would be the case of a company making industrial tools. Factory legislation provides that moving parts and dangerous parts of any machinery should be securely guarded if only to protect employees operating the machines from coming into contact with them and suffering injury. If these rules are not observed and damage is caused as a consequence, the company is strictly liable.

Although strict liability is said to be "absolute", in some instances defences are available to the person committing the wrong. Reverting to the liability imposed under the rule in Rylands v Fletcher as an example, it is a defence to prove that the escape of something dangerous kept on the defendant's land such as sewage or noxious smells was caused by the act of a stranger — a person of whose existence the defendant could not have reasonably been expected to know.

METHODS OF CONFLICT RESOLUTION

When a dispute arises between an organisation and an individual or other organisation, most people would normally think that the courts would be involved to resolve the dispute. Why should a company make contracts if they are not intended to be enforced by law if promises are broken, for example? This is undoubtedly true, but using the courts, as we shall see, is only one method of resolving conflicts. Others may be as effective and suit the circumstances of the parties involved much better.

The Courts

The system of courts in English law is dependant on a hierarchy where some courts are regarded as being higher and therefore more authoritive than others. The idea is that decisions made in higher courts are binding on lower courts — that is that their decisions must be followed. Exhibit 16.2 and 16.3 shows the structure of the main criminal and civil courts in a descending scale.

Basically the court which is used to resolve any dispute depends on what is involved in the dispute itself, since the courts have their jurisdiction fixed by statute, for example the County Courts Act, 1959 (as amended by later provisions) and the Courts Act, 1971. In any event, both criminal and civil systems do make provision for appeals to be lodged from lower courts to higher courts, particularly to the Court of Appeal and the House of Lords. As to the lower courts, the Magistrates Court deals mainly with the less serious criminal offences such as petty theft. The County Court similarly deals with less serious civil wrongs, for example a claim for damages as compensation for breach of contract where the amount claimed does not exceed £2,000. Indictable offences (those tried by judge and jury) such as murder and manslaughter will be heard by the Crown Court. The High Court is divided into three divisions. The Queen's Bench, like the other Divisions, has no financial limit on the actions it can hear and deals for instance with breaches of contract and damage arising from the commission of torts. The Chancery Division, amongst other things, deals with partnership and company matters, and the Family Division with such things as matrimonial matters.

Unfortunate aspects of the courts' system are:

a) The courts have an extremely large number of cases to deal with and so a dispute may take a long time to resolve;

b) They can be expensive, particularly if appeals are made to higher courts.

Exhibit 16.2

CRIMINAL COURTS

House of Lords

|

Court of Appeal (Criminal Division)

|

Crown Courts

|

Magistrates Courts

--- ---

Exhibit 16.3

CIVIL COURTS

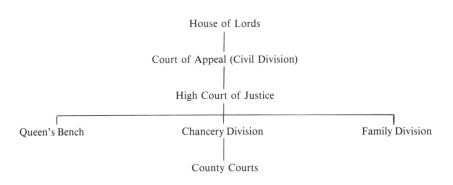

House of Lords

|

Court of Appeal (Civil Division)

|

High Court of Justice

|

Queen's Bench   Chancery Division   Family Division

|

County Courts

c) The procedure is very technical involving, in civil actions for example, the issue of a writ, a statement of defence to the action, a statement of the plaintiff's claim, and hearing the evidence of the parties in the case, to name but a few stages in the action. Procedure is very formal too, involving as it does adherence to rules of evidence. The court is then left with the task of what has cynically been described as deciding which of the parties before it is lying the least, since each side would naturally put forward arguments favouring its own position.

For these reasons the courts might only be used where the parties consider it absolutely necessary. It is much better if possible to settle a dispute "out of court", where those involved resolve their problems without recourse to law.

If the courts are to be used, then conflict between individuals or organisations implies that civil law will be involved. It is therefore appropriate at this stage to consider the main civil rememdies available in an action.

Remedies of the Civil Law

1. *Damages.* The awards of damages has been available as a remedy for centuries. it involves the payment of compensation for loss or damage in the form of money to a successful plaintiff in an action and is the usual remedy which is sought. Most claims involving organisations will be in contract and tort. In tort, the main aim is to compensate for loss inflicted on the defendant. In contract, the aim is to put the person injured by a breach of contract in the position he would have been in if the contract had been performed in the way it should. The assessment of damages is not always an easy task for the courts, particularly where they have to arrive at a figure to compensate someone for pain and suffering arising from physical injury, loss of expectation of life, or loss of the ability to enjoy life. In effect, though, the courts have to specify some figure, if only because that is part of their task and no one else will do it for them. Indeed, newspaper reports often contain details of awards of damages to persons who are permanently incapacitated as a result of, for example, a motor accident. An additional difficulty in granting damages is that, for practical purposes, the defendant must have the money to pay them. It is all very well for a plaintiff to win his case, but it will be no use if they cannot enforce a decision in his favour and recover his compensation. Damages can be classified in various ways.

1. *General damages.* These are damages which are not capable of exact calculation but which will automatically be awarded by the court as soon as the wrong in question has been proved, for example the loss of a finger.

2. *Special damages.* These are awarded, but not automatically, for loss which can be precisely calculated. The court does not presume that the loss is a necessary result of the wrong committed, and must be the subject of a special claim by the plaintiff. Examples would be loss of earnings or profits, and medical expenses.

3. *Nominal damages.* A plaintiff may prove a breach of contract or that some right has been interfered with, but really he has suffered no actual financial loss. In such cases nominal damages, for example £2, can be awarded to him. This simply shows that the courts recognises that the plaintiff was within his rights to bring action.

4. *Ordinary damages.* Also called *substantial damages*. These depend for their amount on the loss actually suffered by the plaintiff however large or small it may be.

5. *Aggravated damages.* These will be awarded where the court considers that more than the usual damages should be awarded as compensation because of the defendant's motive or conduct, such as where he has acted out of spite or in a way which causes greater than normal injury to the plaintiff's feelings.

6. *Exemplary damages.* These are a departure from the basic rule that damages are intended to compensate, and are awarded to punish the defendant and, by that example, to deter anyone else from acting in the same way. They may be awarded where:

a) the plaintiff has suffered loss as a result of arbitrary or unconstitutional action by the government servant's, for example, unjustified false imprisonment.

b) the defendant's conduct was calculated to make himself a profit which might very well exceed any compensation he would have to pay to the plaintiff.

c) the payment of such damages is expressly authorised by statute.

Such damages are not awarded very often.

7. *Contemptuous damages.* The plaintiff may very well win his case, but the court may show its disapproval of his bringing the action if it considers it a waste of the court's time. Disapproval is shown by awarding a really small sum, say one pence, as damages.

8. *Liquidated damages.* These arise in case of breach of contract but not in the case of torts. The damages payable are agreed upon by the parties expressly in the contract itself as payable in the event of breach, and so the plaintiff need not prove any actual loss. The only qualification to the award is that the amount of damages must be a genuine estimate of the loss and not a penalty, that is intended to penalise the defendant for failure to carry out his part of the bargain. For example the payment of a sum which is extravagant.

9. *Unliquidated damages.* Not fixed by a contract itself, and always awarded as the result of the commission of torts, the amount awarded here is fixed by the court when the plaintiff has produced evidence of his loss.

A final difficulty concerning the assessment of damages is that the loss must not be too remote. This means that there must always be some connection between the defendant's conduct and the loss suffered by the plaintiff. If the two are not sufficiently connected, no damages will be awarded. Whether damage is too remote is for the court to decide.

Equitable remedies

Certain remedies have been developed to supplement the only common law remedy of damages. These are the equitable remedies, so called because they were originally developed by the old Court of Chancery which decided cases before it according to what was right and fair according to conscience. The word 'equity' itself comes from the Latin 'aequitas' which means fair. Because the award of a remedy depended upon what the court considered right in conscience, equitable remedies were, and indeed still are only given at the court's discretion. Although at one time they could only be claimed through the Chancery Court (the court of equity), since the Judicature Acts, 1973-75, they are available in any court as are damages. The main two equitable remedies are those of specific performance and injunction, but it should be realised that they would only be awarded where damages would be inadequate or unsuitable to compensate the plaintiff, and failure to comply with the court order amounts to contempt of court.

1. *Specific Performance.* This is a court order which compels a person to carry out obligations which he has agreed to perform. In most cases it is used to enforce contracts for the sale or lease of land, and in some instances where a contract involves the sale of unique goods so that the plaintiff could not obtain a satisfactory substitute article elsewhere.

2. *Injunction.* This is a court order whereby an individual or organisation will be prevented from or continuing with some wrongful act, like committing a tort or a breach of contract. For example, if a company has become registered with a name which is similar to that used by another company which was formed earlier, it can be restrained from using the name as a result of a tort action for "passing off" (attempting to pass off its business as being that of another company so that the public would be misled into thinking there was some connection between the two).

   Injunctions can be classified as follows:

   a) *Mandatory.* This orders the performance of some positive act, such as putting down a building which has been erected unlawfully.

   b) *Prohibitory.* This orders a person not to do some particular act or thing.

   c) *Perpetual.* Such an injunction is granted after a trial where the party claiming some right has established his claim to it. It is intended to settle the dispute once and for all so that the plaintiff need not bring further actions as and when his rights are interfered with. The term *perpetual* would seem to indicate that the court order will remain in force indefinitely. This is not always so, however, the injunction could be granted for a specified period, for example where a person contracts not to compete with his former employer's business for a definite number of years after leaving his employment.

   d) *Interlocutory.* In contrast to the perpetual injunction, this is only a temporary measure granted before the dispute is heard, and intended to prevent any further damage being caused until the case comes before the court.

Administrative conflict

A dispute which arises in the administrative field can be resolved by the issue of the prerogative orders of Mandamus, Prohibition, and Certiorari, and the prerogative writ of Habeas Corpus. These remedies are designed to protect people against the abuse or excess of power by individuals, lower courts, tribunals and enquiries, civil servants, local authorities, and in some instances, the Executive itself. The jurisdiction to issue these remedies is given to the High Court, and is exercised by the Queen's Bench Division. In all cases it is discretionary, and so the court can take all the circumstances of the case into account when deciding whether or not to grant the remedy. Now as to the nature of the remedies themselves.

1. *Mandamus.* The term "mandamus", translated from the Latin, means *"we command"*. The order, then, commands some person or body to perform a public duty which it is bound to do. Thus it may be used to force local authorities to hold an election of aldermen and to make their accounts available for inspection by ratepayers, or to force an administrative tribunal to hear an appeal which it is refusing to deal with.

2. *Prohibition.* Whereas mandamus commands the performance of a duty, prohibition is an order preventing something from being done. Traditionally it was used to prevent lower courts from exceeding their jurisdiction. Now, in addition, it is used to prevent any public body, such as a tribunal, from exceeding its powers. But it is available only against public bodies and not private ones or domestic tribunals such as club committees.

3. *Certiorari.* The term means to certify or inform. So the reason for the issue of this order by the High Court is so that it can be informed of any excess of jurisdiction by a lower court or tribunal which has, is, or is about to decide some issue. If jurisdiction has been exceeded, the decision of that court or tribunal will be quashed. In addition to these instances, certiorari will also be available where the principles of natural justice have been ignored. Briefly, these principles state that no one who has a personal interest in the outcome of a case should take part in deciding it; both parties to the case must be given the opportunity to present their side of it; and the court or tribunal must not show bias or act from any improper motive. Finally, if any error appears on the face of the record of the inferior court or tribunal resolving the dispute, the order can be granted. This means that where the reasons given for the decision in the dispute clearly show that an error of law has been made, certiorari can be issued.

4. *Habeas Corpus.* Meaning literally "you have the body", this is an order granted to secure the release of anyone unlawfully imprisoned.

A further avenue to a remedy in the administrative field is a complaint to the Ombudsman. This is the office of Parliamentary Commissioner established by the Parliamentary Commissioner Act 1967. It is his task under the Act to investigate complaints from members of the public who allege that the administrative functions of government departments and various public authorities have been improperly exercised. But his job is one of investigation only. He himself provides no remedy. Certainly any injustice may be remedied by those responsible for it as a consequence of his investigation, but otherwise all he can do is to report his findings to Parliament. Initially, complaints cannot be made to the Ombudsman direct. They must be produced in writing to an M.P., who will then forward the complaint to the Ombudsman. He then has a discretion whether to investigate or not. Unfortunately for anyone wishing to complain, the scope of the Commissioner's powers is limited. For example, his jurisdiction does not cover local authorities, the police, and public corporations. Nevertheless, on the principle that any protection however small is better than none, the office is useful.

Arbitration

In the earlier part of this section, when discussing conflict resolution by the courts, it was stated that the use of the courts is only one method of resolving conflict. An "out of court" settlement has also been mentioned. Another appropriate method, depending on the type of dispute in which the organisation is involved, is arbitration.

It is not uncommon for business contracts to contain a clause in which the parties agree that any dispute between them should first be referred to arbitration before either of them resorts to the courts to settle a dispute. All an aribtrator is, is a person who is independent and, since he has no personal interest in the outcome of the dispute, will give an unbiased judgement. Recourse to arbitration, then, does not involve the courts necessarily, and has certainly been in favour to deal with trade union disputes over wage claims, for example, with the use of the Arbitration and Conciliation Service.

The procedure involved in arbitration is laid down in the Arbitration Act, 1950, and this provides for certain aspects of normal judicial procedure to be followed. Any excess of jurisdiction can always be dealt with by the granting of prerogative orders by the High Court which, in any case, can be called upon to determine points of law where necessary.

The main advantage of arbitration is that, although judicial procedure may be followed, the hearing of the dispute is much less formal than a hearing in open court. Also the hearing is held in private rather than in open court, and the arbitrator's decision is similarly private. It is more likely to deal with a dispute quickly since the courts generally are over-worked, and above all it is cheap. Court actions, particularly in the High Court are notoriously expensive.

Assignments

1. Why has it been considered necessary in this country to set up special tribunals for the hearing of certain cases instead of leaving them to the ordinary courts?

2. What is understood by 'legal right'? How does a legal rule differ from any other rule of conduct?

3. Distinguish between civil and criminal law.

4. According to the theory of Natural Law, people agree to surender some of their freedom and undertake obligations in exchange. Is the idea of strict liability consistent with this principle?

5. Branch delivers steel girders for Manager and Co. Ltd.. The lorry he drives is not built for speed because of the weight load it has to carry, and so Manager's transport director tells him not to drive above 40 miles per hour. While Branch is out on deliveries one day, however, he decides to test that lorry's performance and reaches 60 miles per hour, but in doing so he runs into and severely injures Miss Twig who is crossing the road at the time.

   You are asked to prepare a report for your board of directors at Manager Ltd. setting out any relevant legal considerations.

Chapter 17

Formation of public and private sector organisations

Learning objectives:
At the end of your study of this chapter you should be able to:
1. list the main reasons why organisations are formed.

By definition an organisation is formed when two or more persons join together and organise themselves to achieve some end or work.

An individual may find that it is not possible to get done what he or she sets out to do. Another person, trying to achieve the same end also finds the task impossible. However, they are made aware of each others purpose and agree to combine their efforts to achieve the common end. Of course the end may be so big (such as a building, bridge, or providing the medical needs of all the community) that two persons or even a small number of persons could not accomplish the task. In such cases, there would be need to bring together and organise a much larger number of persons who are interested in achieving the same end or work.

The end or work is the reason for the formation and existence of an organisation. Interested parties recognise that the combined efforts of individuals, when added together, will be greater than the sum of their individual efforts; in other words the whole is greater than the sum of its parts. As long as the end or work is acceptable to every participant, and this normally ensures full co-operation, it is fairly certain that the end will be achieved.

From the above, it can be seen that organisations can be as small as two persons or extremely large, numbering participants in the thousands. In special cases, when considering a nation and its central organisation the number of members may be counted in the millions.

Small organisations, we might say most of them, probably view their end as serving the local community. As organisations progress in size they probably view their ends more widely — serving national communities. When they reach supra-national size their ends can be viewed as being the world community.

Classifying organisations

If we look at organisations from a broad point of view we can classify them in a variety of ways. This would enable us to give a variety of reasons why they have been formed.

Within a country, such as the U.K., we might classify organisations as operating in either the private or public sector. Organisations are private in the sense that they are owned by individuals and/or groups who are not associated with public control in the form of finance or management. On the other hand, organisations in the public sector attempt to accomplish a common public end or work, such as health and education. They are public in the sense that they are controlled by central government — financed by public funds and managed by persons selected by central government.

In each of these sectors organisations can be further classified according to whether their end is seen as being business, social, political, strategic, etc.. These can be further classified. For example, social organisations can be broken down into health, education, etc.. It is this classification of organisations according to their needs that enable us to be more specific in stating why they have been formed.

Why formed

Let us start this section by considering the reason for the formation of strategic organisations. In this context, in the U.K., we are referring to the major defence organisations; the Royal Navy, Marines, Air Force and Army. These military organisations, when combined, were formed to defend the nation against foreign aggression. This is the overall end. In achieving this common end each of the armed force organisations were formed having other ends. For example, the Royal Navy was formed to protect the country's territorial waters and to keep the sea lanes (so vital to the movement of goods and services to and from the country) open.

Each military organisation, in order to achieve their basic end, have formed organisations within the central organisation. The Royal Navy, we might say, has organised itself into an organisation dealing with ships, and another dealing with aircraft. Each have their own ends. In terms of ships we can note that there are different types of ships — built to difference specifications and organised to carry out its own end. Mine sweepers, for example, are built to keep the sea lanes free from mines. This helps the Royal Navy to achieve its overall end of keeping the sea lanes free. Different ships will have different ends, just as different aircraft have their own ends.

In the social sector we find organisations that were formed to cure or prevent social evils. Organisations that deal with these social evils are called social organisations.

Within the U.K. there are some private health organisations, but the predominant form of organisation in this field is the public social organisation, the National Health Service. To reduce the scale of ill health in the U.K. the state took on the responsibility of providing medical care for every member of the community, and to this end the N.H.S. was formed to bring about improvements in physical and mental health, and to prevent, diagnose and treat illness.

Sometimes a social evil or some aspect of that evil (for example, the health of children) is a problem that faces most countries in the world. When this happens a world wide organisation may be formed, such as the World Health Organisation. This organisation was formed to reduce the incidence of ill health in the world or conversely, we might say, to foster and develop practices leading to better world health conditions.[1]

Illiteracy is another social evil that may be attacked by forming an organisation. Individuals who have similar interests to remove this social evil would have to form a large organisation. Often, small educational organisations in the private sector are not capable of removing this evil from the community. To remove illiteracy on such a vast scale it is necessary, as done in the U.K., to form a public sector organisation.

While state formed educational organisations tend to meet the basic educational needs, private organisations have been formed to provide for the healthy recreation of youth. Two familiar organisations in this field are the scouts and guides.

In the U.K., in the social sector, state organisations exist alongside private organisations. The latter were formed basically to fill 'gaps' — special situations that were not covered by the existing state organisations. For example, the 'meals on wheels' organisation was privately formed to ensure that the elderly, infirm and the disabled get a good cooked meal when they are not capable of preparing one for themselves.

When gaps appear in the services provided by existing organisations individuals who have the same interest combine and form a private organisation to fill the gap.

Business organisations are numbered in the thousands in the U.K. — the majority of them are small. Initially each organisation is formed by two or more individuals who wish to produce and distribute a specific good or provide a specific service to the community or any section of it in return for payment.

At some later stage business organisations in the same field of business may join together and form a larger organisation. For example, in 1901, 13 British tobacco manufacturers joined forces and formed Imperial Tobacco. The end product of this formation was to resist an attack on the home market by American tobacco manufacturers.

Often business organisations, normally in the same field of business, form an organisation to further the interests of their trade. These are called 'Employers' organisations.

Many employers' organisations combine and form a federation and federations combine and form bigger national federations. In the U.K., in 1965, the three giant national federations representing various sectors of

---

1. The World Health Organisation took over many of the activities of the League of Nations Health organisation and other agencies. It began its functioning activities in 1949 adopting a programme of attacking world health problems associated with child health, maternal health, malaria, tuberculosis, etc..

manufacturers (British Employer's Confederation, Federation of British Industries and National Association of British Manufacturers) merged into one organisation, the Confederation of British Industry.[2] The main reason for the formation of the Confederation of British Industry was to have a unified body which could collectively put pressure on other large organisations, such as the Government and the Trades Union Congress, and thus exert influence on their policies.

Workers also have their organisations; trade unions. Trade unions were formed to promote the interests of their member. Also, like the employers, the trade unions have a large representing body called the Trades Union Congress. This organisation was formed to apply collective pressure on the Government and the large employer federations.

Some trade unions are classified as 'occupational organisations'. These would include professional associations, such as accountants, economists, statisticians, etc.; formed to improve the status and conditions of their members.

In the political arena of the U.K. there are different political parties. These have been formed by interested individuals to compete against the ideals and ends of other political party organisations. For example, the labour party was formed to champion the cause of the working man and his family and their needs.

Some organisations go beyond national boundary lines; they are normally referred to as supranational organisations. They are formed when many nations meet and set up an organisation to achieve some end which is in the interest of all member nations. The World Health Organisation, already noted, is an excellent example. Two more examples would be the International Monctary Fund and the International Bank for Reconstruction and Development. The IM.F. and the I.B.R.D. had their origin at a conference[3] held in 1944, a year of war. 44 nations met to hammer our the shape and character of the future international monetary system. They created the IMF and IBRD as economic organisations, and other non-economic organisations, to achieve the common interest of world economic stability in the years after the end of World War II. In the latter 1970's more than one hundred nations are members of these two organisations.

The U.K. is a member nation of the IMF and IBRD, and is also a member of a world regional economic organisation in Europe, the European Economic Community. The EEC was formed to unite European nations so that its members could collectively promote common economic interests over a wide range of economic activities.

---

2.   C.B.I. was formed on 14 September 1965.

3.   Conference was held in the first weeks of July 1944 at Bretton Woods, New Hampshire, U.S.A.

There are organisations in virtually all walks of life. Only a few examples have been given. One thing common to all organisations whether they be religious (church organisations) or cultural (peace organisations) or supranational or others mentioned is that they were formed basically to bring together individuals, groups of individuals or nations who have a like interest in order to develop these interests into a common interest.

Common interest may or may not be achieved. Much will depend upon whether the action taken by an organisation is guided by 'rule of thumb' (based on experience or practice) *or* guided by a plan.

Assignments

1. What is understood by the term 'organisation'? Explain why organisations are formed.
2. Take a telephone directory of your locality (the yellow pages) and classify various organisations:
   a) into private and public sector organisations,
   b) into business, social, political, strategic, etc., and
   c) into those that serve only the local area, and those that are known to serve much wider areas.
3. If the labour party was formed to champion the cause of the working man and his family and their needs, why was the conservative party formed? or the liberal party? or the communist party?

Chapter 18

Organisation planning — objectives and policies

Learning objectives:
At the end of your study of this chapter you should be able to:
1. state *possible* objectives for an organisation.
2. state *possible* policies to meet those objectives.

A plan is a guide to intelligent action, and an organisation carries out the planning process because it is the pre-requisite for its activities and success. An organisation that does not plan must carry out its action based on 'rule by the thumb', and this can lead to waste of time, material and effort.

Small organisations, those that have fewer persons, fewer goods and services to offer, and a less complicated structure of organisation, find it easier to carry out the planning process compared to the larger organisations. Planning programmes may take less time to put into action in small organisations but all organisations, small or large, should plan because planning requires thinking ahead and forecasting the future.

Planning, a thinking process, comprises a series of steps:
1. Find out the facts about the past and about the potentials and problems in the future.
2. Analyze the facts.
3. Determine the objectives.
4. Establish policies.
5. Put policies into operation to achieve the objectives.
6. Review the operations and judge the results.

In this chapter our task is to:
1. State the *possible* objectives for an organisation.
2. State the *possible* policies to meet those objectives.

Because we are considering *an* organisation the objectives and policies to be stated will be general (not specific to any one organisation) but should be relevant to any organisation. It is worth noting that each organisation is unique and there will always be some objectives and policies that are special to their uniqueness — these are not considered here.

Before we state the objectives and policies it is essential to have some understanding about the terms.

Objectives

We already know that an organisation is formed to achieve a common interest but the form or shape it takes is determined by its objectives. The objective of an organisation may be defined as its primary aim, destination or purpose towards which efforts will be directed.[1]

Why are objectives important? The simple answer is that they give direction to the decisions made by individuals in the organisation. In every organisation decisions have to be made about the action that should take place to achieve desired goals. If there were no objectives then the decisions made by decision makers would be pointless — they have nothing to aim their decisions at.

In the paragraph above the words 'objectives' and 'goals' were used as though they were the same thing. There is a subtle difference between the two, and this can best be explained by the use of an example. An objective refers to a broad aim such as 'to increase our share of the market'; a goal gives substance to the objective by stating an element of degree and time such as 'to increase our share of the market by 10 per cent by the year 1985'.

It sounds easy to determine objectives and goals. This may be true here but an organisation must face reality and this makes it difficult to lay down its objectives. It is difficult because objectives must be based on information about the future, and everything in the future is uncertain; details should not be treated as being 100 per cent certain. It is a hazardous business looking into the future.

Objectives are geared to the future and for this reason it is important to stress certain words in the following statement. Objectives indicate *what* an organisation *tries* or *wants* to achieve. Whether they achieve them or not is another matter. Success will depend on decisions being the right decisions, but it should be pointed out that decisions have a better chance of being right if the organisation has control in that area. Organisations have greater control over their internal operations but less control over their environment.

Policies

Objectives indicate *what* an organisation wants to achieve. Decisions made to show the course of action adopted by an organisation to achieve objectives becomes the organisation's policy. In other words, policies refer to decisions which say something about the course of action about *how* objectives will be attained.

In defining 'policies' we may say that they refer to a collection of general laws (or codes or rules or principles) which state the established procedure to be followed by an organisation's members, in their action or conduct, in achieving the objectives of the organisation. The action or conduct refers mainly to those situations that tend to occur again and again in an organisation.

Why are policies important? They are important because they help organisations to achieve their objectives by guiding decision makers and other members to carry out their tasks in the organisation with the minimum of friction. Rules are made to be followed — not broken.

However, laws (the policies) must be flexible to meet 'out of the ordinary' situations, and often they may have to be changed, improved or modified to conform to the discovery of new procedures.

Above all else policies must be enforced if they are to be effective. Most writers would agree that an organisation is a government in itself as long as it stays within the law of the land; they must have authority to enforce policies, give commands and expect replies, and maintain discipline among its members.

Policies, then, say something about the course of action about *how* objectives will be attained.

Possible objectives and policies

The following are but a few of the many possible objectives and policies that can be envisaged for an organisation. The few selected will give an idea of the relationship between objectives and policies in the planning process. The first to be mentioned are those that relate to 'broad' objectives and policies; they relate to the primary purpose of the organisation. For example:

Broad Possible Objectives	Broad Possible Policies
To be of service to society by providing them with 'good' products and/or services.	Make the basic rule that all decisions and action taken must be geared, regardless of cost or benefit, to the making of 'good' products and/or services.
To operate succcessfully in order to fulfil its desires to serve society.	Make available to all members a set of clear and complete rules for each part of the organisation to ensure that each rule is in harmony with the broad objectives, creates unity of action and are acceptable to all members so that they can give their 'wholehearted' support.
To achieve broad objectives	Make use of long range (say, 5, 10 or 15 years) planning and apply this across all major areas in the organisation.

Once an organisation has established its broad objectives and policies it can then concentrate on supporting objectives and policies. These must be in harmony with the broad objectives and policies. They can be classified under different headings, but here we will consider them as being 'major' and 'minor'. First, a few examples of those classified as major.

Major Possible Objectives	*Major Possible Policies*
To operate more effectively and at lower cost.	Establish an 'information system' designed to provide details for long range planning. This must include environmental information to ensure the organisation is producing 'good' products and/or services that are desired by society.
To organise personnel so as to carry out policy decisions to the best advantage	Provide an organisation chart and make it available to all members showing positions of personnel and defining their responsibilities and the chain of command (order down the line and information up the line).
To maximise efficiency. (Efficiency being: $\frac{output}{input} \times 100\%$)	Establish a special committee representing all areas of the organisation to investigate known areas of waste (waste of time, effort and materials), to make reports and recommend methods removing waste to responsible decision makers.
To maintain good relations with people in the environment - social responsibility	Create strict rules which state specifically how smoke from chimneys are to be controlled, how contaminated materials should be treated, etc. with the object of keeping the environment free from pollution.

The above are but a few of the possibilities that could be listed. At this stage there is more room for disagreement about the policies selected. Decision makers will find that there are several alternative courses of action that could be taken. Whatever they may be it is the decision maker's responsibility to select the best. In doing so he must make sure that they conform to the broad objectives and policies.

Down at the lower end of the organisation we can list objectives and policies which might be classified as minor. For example:

Minor possible objectives	*Minor possible policies*
To control negligence and sub-standard work.	Make a rule that the person responsible for the area where these problems occur is responsible to review at any time the problems as they become known and take immediate action to resolve the problem.
To select personnel of the right quality and who can happily work with other people.	Employ the most scientific methods available.
To establish a formal procedure in giving orders.	Produce a principle that no person shall give orders to anyone except those who are his immediate subordinates.
To maintain or increase output per person per given period of time (productivity)	Lay down firm 'manning' requirements for different operations and make a rule that there shall be 'no overmanning'.

To create a standard procedure for promotions.	Make a general rule that the organisation promote from within as long as there are one or more within who fully meet the qualifications for a job.
•	
To maintain a reputation in answering correspondence.	Lay down a rule that mail must be answered, or at least acknowledged, within three days or so of receipt. Telegrams should be answered or acknowledged within 24 hours.
To establish a procedure relating to 'personal criticism'.	State the principal that persons in authority shall not make personal criticism of a subordinate in the presence of others.
To provide for further education of the younger members.	Produce a rule which states that younger members in the organisation shall be given the opportunity of advancing their educational status and that the organisation will provide 'special release' so they can take a 'Business Education Council' or 'Technical Education Council' course.

As stated before, there are alternative policies to those stated above but the 'best' should be selected and it should fit in to the other policies established at higher levels.

Success of an organisation

The above listed objectives and policies are a few of the many possible situations that can be considered for an organisation. However, each organisation is unique. It must decide for itself which aspects of organisational life are most relevant to its own purpose and work out objectives and policy statements towards that end.

Each organisation must realise that stating objectives and policies does not guarantee, but it does go a long way in achieving, success.

Assignments

1. Planning, which involves an organisation in determining its *objectives* and establishing *policies,* does not guarantee success. Define the italicised words and then give reasons supporting the statement.
2. State some of the objectives (or goals if known) of your employing organisation and the action they introduced to say how these objectives will be attained.
3. Formulate for *an* organisation the following:
   a) one broad objective and its associated policy,
   b) four minor objectives and related policies.

Chapter 19

Forms of Organisation

Learning objectives:

At the end of your study of this chapter you should be able to:

1. define and distinguish the different legal forms of organisation, corporate and unincorporated, in commerce, industry and government.

2. analyse *some* of the legal, social and economic consequences of choice between forms of business unit.

3. distinguish different types of organisation in terms of their function and purpose.

The establishment of an organisation depends initially on the purpose which the promoters of such a body have in mind. As soon as these aims have been determined, legal, social and economic considerations arise. These will affect the type of organisation to be formed, the way in which it is to be formed, and ultimately the consequences of formation. It is now proposed to examine different legal forms of organisation, concentrating also on the consequences of choice between forms of business unit.

Organisations in business

The simplest way to approach an understanding of these is to consider that you yourself are about to form a business to undertake a particular project. Either you have the necessary finance to begin such a venture, or you have obtained a loan. The first question to arise for your consideration is: which type of organisation should I choose? Essentially, the choice is between three types:

> A sole trader.
>
> A partnership.
>
> A corporation.

Sole Trader

The word "sole" means single, or one. Hence a sole trader is a person who is trading alone. This is commonly referred to as the 'one-man business'. The term may be slightly misleading, because a person who is a sole trader may not run his business completely on his own. For example, he may be helped by his family and he may employ other people to work for him. In fact the traditional "corner-shop" business may well run on these lines. The way the business is conducted in this respect, however, is not really relevant. The point is that the management and control of the business is entirely in the hands of the person who formed it. So the sole trader *alone* takes the profits of the business if any. Legally, no type of association has been formed in such circumstances. No particular legal rules have to be complied with to form the business itself, except that if you intend to carry on business in a name other than your own, you must register such a name under the Registration of Business Names Act, 1916. The information given to the Registrar of Business Names will include your full name, and the name by which you wish your business to be known. Once it has been formed, however, your organisation will become subject to certain *legal constraints*. For example, you will be subject to taxation, and the Equal Pay Act and Sex Discrimination Act will apply to the employment of staff to assist you in conducting the business. Another factor is that you alone, whilst taking the profits of the business, also bear alone the responsibility of running it. So as regards debts and other liabilities, you are responsible for them to the extent of your personal wealth. If the business should fail drastically, then, your creditors, might take steps under the Bankruptcy Act, 1914, as amended by the Insolvency Act, 1976, to have you adjudged a bankrupt. In such a case, all your property, such as cash, your house, and your car will, with only minor exceptions, may be used to pay off your debts. This then is the real disadvantage of such an organisation.

A second disadvantage arises from the fact that the sole trader is normally handicapped by lack of capital. Once the main source of funds, from family and friends, dries up there are few outside sources interested. For this reason the growth of the organisation is slow.

The third disadvantage arises from the second — lack of capital restricts development of the business. The owner finds that there is little opportunity to apply and receive the advantages associated with 'division of labour'.[1]

The last disadvantage to be noted here relates to the death or retirement of the sole trader. Continued success of the business depends on the successor having the necessary ability to carry on the business.

Some of the advantages of this type of business are provided in the next few paragraphs.

The main advantage is that the sole trade is in full control of the business — he is his own boss. As such, he decides policy and puts policy into operation. He is independent; he is the owner-manager and makes all business decisions.

From the above it follows that the sole trader participates in all aspects of the management of the business (personnel, production, purchasing, selling, etc.) and sets standards for all operations. He is in close contact with his employees, his goods or service, his suppliers and his customers, and this can only help to enhance the business.

The good or service provided will be to the best possible standards reflecting the needs of the customers. Larger businesses (corporations) find it difficult to foster this type of relationship.

1. Division of labour refers to the break down of an operation into parts whereby one man is responsible for one task of the productive process, a second person does the second task, etc. The major advantage is the increase in output of each operator for a given period of time.

Industrial relations within the business is, normally, highly satisfactory. The sole trader knows the personal background of each employee and their idiosyncracies, and they in turn know the 'boss'. This makes it possible for the majority of sole traders and their employees to operate in harmony — no strikes.

These are the type of advantages associated with the sole trader and some of them show a social-economic mix.

The sole trader has an economic role, and he also has a social role. As an individual he recognises his social responsibility towards those that are closely associated with him. Part of his social role can be seen as contributing to the quality of life and happiness of employees and customers to the best of his ability.

Sole traders, collectively, provide the community with a wide range of goods and services and makes these available in a personal way. Families in the suburbs of large cities, towns and villages find their lives made more pleasant by the facilities offered by the sole trader.

In the local community the sole trader can be seen as not only the owner of a business but also a member of the community. They contribute their experience, and some provide their services, to the local community. Whether there is an advantage of having businessmen on community councils, such as parish or district, is debatable — they might consider using the councils to develop their own business and this may not always be to the advantage of the local community.

Sole traders are found in many business activities[2]. They may have different activities but they do *tend* to have common characteristics. These arise principally from:

> their legal status (no particular legal rules have to be complied with to form the business),

> their ownership-managership status (the owner has full control over all operations and he alone bears the losses or benefits from the profits of his decisions),

> their financial structure status (their long term source of finance is restricted usually to the owner, his family and friends)

> their employer status (it is unlikely that their employees will be members of trade unions and they are normally not affected by strikes), and others.

Compare the activities of the sole trader with those of big business organisations and you will see how easy it is to list the characteristics of the sole trader.

Expansion of the sole trader, if it does take place, will change the business from the simplest to a more complex type of organisation; a partnership or private company or public joint stock company. Let us now consider the partnership type of business organisation.

2.   Such as: caterers, chimney sweeps, confectionary retail shops, farmers, greengrocers, tobacconists, window cleaners.

The Partnership

Section 1 of the Partnership Act, 1890 defines a partnership as "the relationship which subsists between persons carrying on a business in common with a view of profit". A partnership then is an association of individuals acting together for a common business purpose. The definition in the Act is not much help in terms of guidance as to what constitutes a partnership. It simply states that:

(a) there must be more than one person;

(b) these must carry on a business in common;

(c) that for its objects there must be a business carried on with a view of profit.

This association is governed by legal rules in certain respects.

As regards its formation, a partnership need not be created by any formal process. Indeed it may arise through a verbal agreement, or even by the conduct of the individuals involved. More usually, however, the partners will govern their various rights, for example the proportions in which they will share any profits, by a written contract in the form of a partnership deed. If they do so, then this contract will govern their relations between themselves, if not, then the Partnership Act itself will regulate the position. So, for example, the Act governs such things as the retirement and expulsion of partners, their *accountability* for private profits, and their duties to the partnership.

One *legal constraint* in the inception of a partnership concerns the number of partners. From the definition stated above, which refers to *"persons"* carrying on a business in common, it is obvious that there must be at least two people to form the organisation. Naturally enough, there may be more than two. Legal rules govern the maximum number of partners. The basic rule is stated in section 434 Companies Act, 1948. This states that the maximum number is twenty for the purpose of carrying on a business for gain. Sections 120 and 121 of the Companies Act, 1967 exempt certain partnerships, those of solicitors, accountants, and members of stock exchanges, from this provision. As to banking partnerships, section 429 Companies Act, 1948 restricted the maximum numbers to ten, although this rule was relaxed under section 119 Companies Act, 1967, which allows a partnership of up to twenty provided they are authorised to be members by the Department of Trade. Certain other partnerships have also been exempted from the general rule by Regulations, such as Estate Agents, Valuers, Surveyors and Patent Agents. However, if a partnership exceeds that maximum number, the business must be incorporated. This is dealt with later in this chapter.

Another *legal constraint* is that a partnership, logically enough, must not be formed for an illegal purpose. If it is, then the whole arrangement is void. The supposed partners have no enforceable rights amongst themselves, although any creditor can enforce their claims if they did not know of the illegal objects. So, in FOSTER v. DRISCOLL, 1929, a partnership was formed in England to smuggle whisky into the United States which was then subject to Prohibition, and the sale and importing of alcohol was banned. It was held that the partnership was illegal, since it was against the interests of a friendly nation, and was therefore void.

Finally, the name of the partnership may be subject to legal rules. A partnership may use the words "and Co" as part of its name. This, however, does not indicate that it is a company in law. It is merely a convenient way of showing that there are other partners in the business apart from those mentioned previously in the name. A partnership can trade under any name it pleases, except that:

(a) The word 'Limited' or any abbreviation of it must not be the last word of its name.

(b) Under the Registration of Business Names Act, 1916, every partnership with a place of business in the U.K. must be registered unless the true surnames of all the partners are used without any addition other than their forenames or initials.

The legal position of partners is not far removed from that of a sole trader, in that all partners are jointly liable for all the firms debts to the extent of their personal wealth and so could be made bankrupt by their creditors if the business failed.

The obvious advantages over being a sole trader which would counteract this, though, are that there are more people to bear responsibility for any loss, and credit may be more easily obtainable; where, for example, one partner is known to be wealthy. On the other hand, there are always more people entitled to a share of the profits than there are if a sole trader carries on business.

One particular type of partnership is worth further consideration, although it might only rarely be met in practise. This is the 'limited partnership' governed by the Limited Partnership Act, 1907.

A limited partner is one who contributes a given amount of capital or property to the firm, and who is not liable for the firm's debts and other obligations beyond that amount. If, for example, he put a capital contribution of £1,000 into the firm, he is only liable up to that amount for its debts and cannot be sued or made bankrupt for any amount beyond that.

It is possible to have more than one limited partner in a particular firm. However, there must always be at least one general partner whose liability is unlimited. So, in the example above, if the firm had two partners, one limited and one general, and it owed £6,000, the limited partner would be liable for his £1,000, leaving the general partner responsible for the other £5,000. Conversely, though, the general partner would normally take the greater share of the profits.

The rules governing the numbers in a limited partnership are the same as for ordinary partnerships, that is to say, they may not generally consist of more than 20 people. The firm must also be registered with the Registrar of Companies, in particular stating that it is limited, giving a description of every limited partner, and giving details of the amount contributed by each limited partner whether in cash or otherwise.

In terms of his activities, however, the limited partner is restricted. Unlike ordinary partners, he has no power to bind the firm by making contracts on its behalf, and may not take part in its management. All he can do is advise the other partners. This is the price he pays for his limited liability — having put money or property into the firm, he has no absolute say in how it is used. In fact, if he does take part in management, he becomes responsible for all liabilities incurred by the firm during that period.

As stated above, limited partnerships are rare, largely because the possibility of forming a private limited company was also introduced by a Companies Act in 1907. A business could then be established in which the liability of all its participants was limited.

Who forms partnerships

Where are we likely to find partnerships? They can exist in any business area but they are normally associated with individuals who provide professional services, such as accountants, dentists, doctors and property agents, to people in local areas. We would also find partnerships operating in stock exchange activities (brokers and jobbers), and in other areas where specialist knowledge is used in serving specialised markets.

Wherever partnerships operate they tend to have, just like any other business organisation, their advantages and disadvantages.

Advantages

The first group to be noted are the obvious advantages that partnerships have over sole traders. One or two of the following have already been briefly noted.

Because partnerships involve more than one person in its operations it is only natural to expect advantages from increased numbers; burdens can be shared. Firstly, there are more persons to provide finance when the partnership is formed, and in the future when there is need to speed up its actvities to keep pace with industrial progress. In addition we can note that increased numbers makes it easier to obtain credit; creditors recognise the fact that there are more persons to bear any loss. Further, an increase in numbers makes it possible for the function of management to be shared. Each active partner may concentrate on specific managerial activities, for example one partner may take over all responsibilities for activities relating to production and personnel, and a second partner on purchasing and selling. The larger the number of active partners the greater the opportunity for each to specialise.

Other advantages have been claimed for partnerships when comparing them to corporations. These advantages arise, mainly, because partnerships normally have less owners, and it can be noted that they tend to be the same as those listed for sole traders.

In a partnership control is very closely linked to ownership. The people who make decisions are the owners (not employed managers), and, as such, there is no 'partial divorce' between ownership and control. The decisions that have to be made can be made quickly and they can be made in such a way as to make the business more flexible to meet changes in the partnership's internal and external environment.

Partnerships are normally of the size that enables partners to keep in close contact with customers, suppliers and others in the *external* environment, and with its own employees, output and other forces in the *internal* environment. As a result they tend to be more flexible. This not only creates an economic advantage — it also brings about 'very good' community and industrial relations.

The last advantage to be noted relates to the beginning and ending of a partnership. The cost of forming a partnership is less than that of forming a corporation, and it is much easier to dissolve and wind-up its affairs.

Partnerships do not normally remain the same size. As they grow we would expect those advantages associated with increased numbers (compared to sole traders) to become more advantageous. But, on the other hand, the last mentioned advantages will tend to become less advantageous. As the latter advantages gradually disappear partners may rethink their position and consider forming a corporation. This latter decision will, of course, take into consideration the disadvantages normally associated with partnerships.

Disadvantages

The first set of disadvantages compares the partnership to the sole trader. One point already raised was that partners in a partnership have the disadvantage of sharing the profits of the business. We can note that this is not the only thing to be shared — ownership is shared, and decisions become joint. This may result in delays in the decision making process if the partners, at times, do not work in harmony.

Obviously many disadvantages arise if one of the partners is not all that he should be. If a partner is dishonest the other partner (or partners) will suffer from his cheating, lying or stealing. On the other hand partners could suffer additional costs of running the business if one of them did not have good business sense.

This next point is a disadvantage of partnerships compared to the sole trader business and the corporation; there is lack of continuity. When a partner is made bankrupt or dies or wishes to withdraw from the partnership the partnership has to be dissolved.

The next group of disadvantages arises when we compare partnerships to a corporation. The prime disadvantage, one already noted but worth repeating, is that all partners are jointly liable for all the firms debts to the extent of their personal wealth should the venture fail. This unlimited liability puts partners at high risk compared to businessmen who form a limited liability company.

Partnerships are limited by law to having a maximum of 'x' members. This can create a disadvantage because it tends to put a limit to the amount of finance partners can raise from their own pockets and this will automatically dampen the growth of the business.

Growth does take place. As a partnership grows and grows the partners will soon realise that this type of business is not *normally* suited to large scale activities.

When the last two mentioned situations materialise the partners should seriously think of dissolving the partnership and continuing the business as a corporation. The reasons for this will become evident when we discuss corporations.

What is the social role of partnerships? Basically the role is similar to that of the sole trade, but the characteristics of a partnership do differ from a sole trader in some cases because they arise from a different set of relations. They arise principally from:

their legal position (forming the business requires no formal process but the relations between partners are governed by contract or Partnership Act),

their ownership-managership position (partners normally share ownership and control, and in most cases they tend to share in the various aspects of management),

their financial structure status (their long term source of finance is restricted to the finance of the partners),

their employer status (this is similar to the sole-trader; there is a close relationship between partners and employees. Industrial relations can be described as good; employees are normally not members of trade unions nor are they prone to strikes),

their market situation (this is also similar to the sole trader; the majority of partnerships have a very small share of the market).

Sole trader and partnership

These two types of business are the predominant form of business organisations in the U.K., and they operate in a wide variety of activities. They are typically small firms. In the words of the Bolton Report, "The majority (60 per cent) of small firms who responded to our inquiry are not incorporated but are either partnerships or sole traders..."[3] Most businesses that we encounter in our daily lives are partnerships and sole traders. This is why we have considered them in considerable depth.

A Corporation

The most likely type of corporation you would form if you were going into business in this form is a 'private company'. But this is only one particular type of corporation as a later diagram illustrates. It is therefore thought appropriate to identify and examine the features of corporations.

A corporation can be defined as: "A legal person distinct from it members, having perpetual succession, a distinctive name, and which is capable of owning property and of suing and being sued." The definition highlights various factors which are of great importance to an understanding of the legal position of corporations.

3.   Report of the Committee of Inquiry on Small Firms, Chairman J. E. Bolton, Cmnd 4811, para 2.2, H.M.S.O..

1. A corporation is a legal person. This shows that a corporation is recognised by the law as a person, but it is artificial and not human. A Mr. Smith would be a human person with, in our society, all normal legal rights and duties. He has a physical existence. Smith and Co. Ltd., on the other hand, has no such physical existence. It is not created by natural birth. Instead it is created by process of law in the ways mentioned later. But although the corporation is non-human, it does, as a person, have rights and duties at law. For example it can make valid contracts, albeit acting through human agents who would normally be its directors. Obviously though there are certain things which an artificial person cannot do, such as commit murder, and great difficulty would be encountered in attempting to imprison a person who lacks a physical make-up! Nevertheless, the notion of legal personality is the essence of corporations.

2. A corporation is distinct from its members. This means that once a corporation has been created by the appropriate legal process it becomes a person which is entirely separate from the human persons who are its members. This idea of separate personality was established in the case of Salomon v Salomon and Co. Ltd.. In this case, Aaron Salomon had carried on business as a sole trader for many years as a boot manufacturer and leather merchant. While the business was still solvent, he decided to convert the business into a corporation — a company limited by shares. The notion here is that the members of the company are only liable, in the event of liquidation of the company, for the amount if any remaining unpaid on the shares which they hold. The company was formed with Salomon, his wife, daughter, and four sons. As the shareholders of it, seven persons being required by law to form a public company validly. He then sold his original business to the company for more than it was worth. This in itself is not unlawful provided all the members agreed, and they duly did. The purchase price of the business was partly satisfied by the company alloting Salomon 20,000 £1 shares all fully paid. His wife and children held one share each. The balance of the purchase price was made up by the company issuing debentures to Salomon, that is to say, documents issued by the company acknowledging that it owed him the money, secured by a charge on the company's assets. Following a depression in the leather trade, the company went into liquidation. As well as Salomon himself, who was a secured creditor because of his debentures, there were also several unsecured trade creditors claiming money due to them from the company. The company's assets were insufficient to pay everyone off, and the rule is that secured creditors are entitled to be paid off in full before unsecured creditors receive anything. So the unsecured creditors stood to receive nothing at all.

They argued, not suprisingly, that since Salomon was carrying on the same business as he did while he was a sole trader, and since he was the majority shareholder most of the profits of the business would have gone to him both before and after the company was formed, he and the company should be regarded as one and the same. In effect, the company was only an agent acting on his behalf. Because of this, they said, he should be compelled to contribute personally to the company's assets the amount required to meet their claims. This would have made him responsible for debts in the same way as a sole trader.

The court decided to reject this argument. They said that for a company to be validly formed it needed seven members: there were. Each member must hold at least one share: they did. Once the company had been registered it became a legal person separate from its members, and was not an agent for them. Therefore Salomon and his company were distinct entities, and he, as a secured creditor, was entitled to the amount of the company's assets and the unsecured creditors got nothing.

3. A corporation has perpetual succession. This means that a corporation cannot die in the same way as a human. It can carry on for ever even though the individuals who are its members may die. A corporation was created by legal process and it can only be ended by legal process. The corporation is said to be liquidated, or wound up.

4. A corporation has a distinctive name and can sue or be sued in that name. Human persons have names, largely to distinguish them one from the other. A corporate name has the same purpose. In the same way as a human person can sue or be sued in his name, so a corporation can bring or defend actions using its own name to do so. As a person, albeit artificial, it can enforce its own rights and be sued if it does not fulfil its own duties.

5. A corporation is capable of owning property. Again, just like a human person of full capacity can own property, so can a corporation because it is regarded as a person by the law. The members of the corporation, then, are not part-owners of it.

Having now discussed the features common to all corporations, we now must examine the various types of corporations. Exhibit 19.1 shows most of the types you may encounter.

Exhibit 19.1

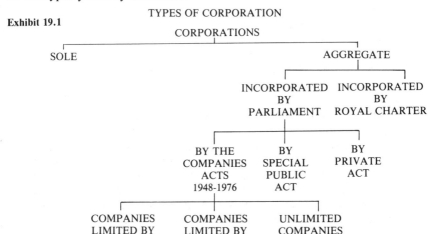

TYPES OF CORPORATION

The initial division is into corporations sole and corporations aggregate. A corporation sole, as its name suggests, is one which is represented by a single person at any one time. Such corporations are not commercial bodies as such, but are merely a legal device ensuring, for example, the continued ownership of property. One example is the Crown. It is customary when one monarch dies for a statement to be made such as "the King is dead, long live the King." At first glance the statement seems ridiculous, until you realise that the purpose behind the exercise is to show that, although one King has died, there is another King (or Queen) to take over the position of monarch. In fact, then, the 'office' of monarch never dies even though the individual holding the office must do at some time. There is perpetual succession.

Corporations aggregate, as their name suggests, are corporations having more than one member. As Exhibit 19.1 shows, they can be divided into various types. These are largely distinguishable by the method of their creation.

1. *Charter corporations.* These are incorporated by Royal Charter. Many original trading corporations were of this type, for example the East India Company and the Hudson Bay Company. The purposes for which such companies are formed (that is their 'objects') are to be found in the charter which was granted. Should they exceed the powers granted to them, there is the possibility that the charter could be withdrawn. Modern examples of charter corporations would be the British Broadcasting Corporation, and certain professional bodies such as the Institute of Cost and Management Accountants (I.C.M.A.). This is not a form of incorpororation used by trading companies today, and you would not use the process to establish your business.

2. *Statutory companies.* These are incorporated by Private Act of Parliament. These are largely historical, and again you would not use this process if you went into business. Such corporations were mainly, for example, the old railway companies or canal companies, needing a Private Act for their creation because they required some powers and privileges which were special to them and which they could not have obtained by incorporation under the Companies Acts, such as the power to acquire land by compulsory purchase. Many of these companies were nationalised after world war II, and their business taken over by public corporations. Local water companies are examples of the few remaining statutory companies today.

3. *Public corporations.* These are incorporated by special Public Act. Nationalised Industries such as the National Coal Board incorporated under the Coal Industry Nationalisation Act, 1946, are examples of this type of corporation, as is the Independent Television Authority. Such corporations are run by members responsible to and appointed by the appropriate government minister, such as the Secretary of State for Energy. We will discuss 'Nationalised Industries' more fully in the next chapter.

4. *Companies registered under the Companies Acts, 1948 to 1976.* It is within this category that you would choose the type of corporation to run a business you had considered forming.

As Exhibit 19.1 shows, registered companies are of three types which must be examined in turn.

4A. *Companies limited by shares.*

These comprise the vast majority of companies registered under the Companies Acts, and examples are abundant. We probably tend to think of these companies only in terms of the giant sized corporations like GKN (Guest, Keene and Nettlefold) or ICI (Imperial Chemical Industries), but these are really the top end of the scale. Indeed it is possible for a company limited by shares to have as few as two members.

Two terms require further explanation. Firstly, we talk of these companies being 'limited'. What this strictly means is that the members of the company (who as we have seen, are separate entities from the legal personality of the company itself) have limited liability; that is their liability to account at law is limited. They are not liable as with partners or sole traders, to account for the company's debts to the extent of their personal wealth. Once the limit of their liability has been reached, they are not liable beyond that limit. In the case of the type of company under discussion, the members are liable to the extent of the amount, if any, unpaid on their shares. So if you take 50 £1 shares in a company, agreeing to pay £1 for each of them, and you pay 75 pence on each share, the most you can be made liable for at law is 50 × 25 pence — the amount unpaid on the shares which you hold. Your liability is limited to £50 in total, but you have already paid 50 × 75 pence. So, even if the company's debts run into hundreds or even thousands of pounds, you as an individual member cannot be called upon to contribute more towards the payments of those debts. But it is worth pausing for a moment to appreciate fully what the legal position is. We have said that the liability of the members of a company for the *company's* debts is limited. The company itself, of course, is a person in law. A human person is always liable for his or her own debts, and a company is no exception to this rule even though it is an artificial person. It is liable for debts which it incurs to the full extent of any assets which it may have. Thus it follows that, while the liability of members is limited, the company itself has unlimited liability. There is always the possibility that the company's assets will not be sufficient to discharge the debts owed to its creditors. In this respect it is no different from a human person who encounters the same difficulty. What will happen then is that the company will be liquidated — a similar idea to that of the bankruptcy of a human person — and any assets which it has will be divided amongst its creditors according to the pattern laid down by law.

It can readily be appreciated, though, that this aspect of the members of a company having limited liability for its debts is a considerable advantage to them. No wonder this type of business organisation is to popular.

Secondly, we talk about these companies being limited by *shares,* so it is important to understand the legal nature of a share in a company. If you were to form a company and take shares in it, the fact of your being a shareholder would be evidenced by your having a share certificate. This is a formal document issued to you by the company showing that, at the time it was issued, you were the holder of the number and type of shares specified in it. A share is a "chose in action", that is a type of property the rights in respect of which can only be enforced by taking legal action. So that granted you might be able to hold your share certificate in your hand and have physical possession of it, but that physical possession in itself does not enable you to enforce any rights you may have as a shareholder. Let us suppose that your shares give you the right to vote at general meetings of the company where you can take part in deciding the business policy to be followed by the company. Although you have this right, your possession of the share certificate will not enable you to enforce it if, for whatever reason, you are prevented from exercising the right to vote. All you can do to enforce your right is to take legal action for a declaration from a court that yours is a valid right, and the company can then be compelled by order of the court to allow you to cast your vote.

By holding shares in a company, a shareholder is not a "part-owner" of that company. This is because, as we have seen, the company is a person in its own right. The company is itself and owns itself. If a shareholder is not a part-owner of the company, then what is he? The answer is that he holds an *interest* in the company. It is the share which shows the extent of that interest. It shows the extent of his monetary liability to the company (and we have just discussed what this means and how it is calculated), and it measures his financial benefits in the company as well, for example his right to receive duly declared dividends on the shares. Other rights may attach too: for example the right to vote at meetings and take part in deliberations of the company's affairs. This is the true position of a shareholder then — not an owner of the company but an owner of a defined interest in it.

4B. *Companies limited by guarantee.*

Again with such companies, the liability of the members is limited. In this case, though, the members' liability is limited to the amount which they have agreed to contribute to the company's assets in the event of it being liquidated. That is then that they undertake to contribute a specified amount if the company is liquidated while they are members of it, or within one year of ceasing to be members, towards payment of the company's debts contracted before they ceased to be members, plus the costs of liquidation as well.

It is most unlikely that anyone forming a business enterprise would choose this form of organisation. Although such companies can have their capital divided into shares and pay dividends to members, they are usually formed without a share capital. Any money which they might need to acquire business premises for example would probably be raised by loans from members. In practice, most companies limited by guarantee are formed to promote the interests of professional bodies, clubs, commerce, or charity, and generally the same legal rules governing companies limited by shares apply to them.

4C. *Unlimited companies*

As their name suggests, unlimited companies are an association of human persons formed as a corporation, but in such a way that there is no limit to the liability of members. Each one is personally liable to the extent of his personal wealth for the debts of the company in exactly the same way as partners are. Unlike the partnership, though, the company does enjoy the benefits of perpetual succession as with all corporations, and there need not necessarily be any limit on the maximum number of members which the company can have. In fact, of course, the major reason most businessmen form companies is to secure the undoubted benefits of limited liability. With the unlimited company there is no such benefit, and as result the number of unlimited companies formed is very small compared with the other types of registered company. The thing to be said in favour of an unlimited company arises because of the aim of successive Companies Acts to secure more and more publication of information about companies. As a general rule, every company is required by s.1 Companies Act, 1976 to deliver a copy of its profit and loss account, balance sheet, auditors' and directors' reports to the Registrar of Companies. This means that such documents then become public information so that, for instance, competitors can guage the company's financial position, and possibly encroach on its business. Unlimited companies, however, are exempt from the obligation to deliver such documents to the Registrar provided, basically, they are not either the holding or subsidiary company of a limited company. It follows then that the greatest advantage of forming an unlimited company is that it can keep its financial position to itself. In this respect it is in the same position as a sole trader or partnership which need not divulge financial information. Whether such an advantage is sufficient to outweight the disadvantage of unlimited liability is one purely for the individuals interest on forming the company to decide.

The formation of any of the above types of company is by the process of registration with the Registrar of Companies as prescribed by the Companies Act, 1948. A company to be registered in England or Wales must register with the Registrar in Cardiff, and for Scotland the Registrar in Edinburgh. To obtain registration certain documents have to be delivered to the appropriate Registrar by the promoters of the company, that is to say those who are engaged in its formation with reference to some particular project and who take the necessary steps to accomplish that purpose. The essential documents are:

(i) *The Memorandum of Association.* This document, which must be signed (or "subscribed") by those persons wishing to be associated together as a company, regulates the company's dealing with the outside world. It must contain, as a minimum, various compulsorily clauses required by the Act:

(a) The name clause, stating the company's name with, where appropriate, the word 'limited' or an abbreviation of it as the last word of the name, so that anyone dealing with the company knows that they are dealing with a body which has limited liability.

(b) The Registered Office clause, stating in which country the company is to be registered.

(c) The objects clause, stating the main purposes which the company is formed to pursue, that is to say the outer limits of its powers. This clause is extremely important because if a company makes contracts which are *ultra vires*, that is beyond the scope of its objects clause, such contracts cannot be enforced by the company. This is of particular interest to creditors and shareholders who naturally want to know the purposes for which their money can be used.

(d) The limited liability clause, containing a statement that the liability of members of the company is limited either by shares or by guarantee as the case may be. Obviously no such clause will appear in the memorandum of an unlimited company.

(e) The share capital clause, if the company does have a share capital, and containing details of the division of its capital into shares of a fixed amount, for example £1,000 divided into 1,000 shares of £1 each.

(ii) *The Articles of Association.* These must also be subscribed by the same people who subscribed to the Memorandum, and govern the company's internal management. Consequently they are chiefly of interest to directors and shareholders. Directors are those appointed to run the company's business because, although a company is a person, it has no physical existence and cannot obviously run the business itself. The Articles usually cover such matters as the conduct of company meetings, the rights of shareholders, and the appointment, retirement, removal, and powers of directors.

(iii) A statement of the company's nominal capital, unless it is to have no share capital. The 'nominal' capital is the amount of share capital which the company is authorised to issue by its memorandum.

(iv) Particulars of the first directors and secretary, containing the signed consents to act in that capacity.

(v) The intended location of the company's registered office.

(vi) A statutory declaration that all the requirements of the Companies Act regarding registration have been complied with. This must be made by a solicitor engaged in the company's formation, or by a person who has been named as director or company secretary.

When all necessary documents have been delivered to the Registrar of Companies, they are examined. If the Registrar is satisfied that all registration requirements have been fulfilled, he issues the company its Certificate of Incorporation. This approximates to a birth certificate in the case of a human person. Once it is issued, the company legally exists. It is then a person so far as the law is concerned, and is a distinct being from its members. It has acquired corporate personality.

The three types of registered company, unlimited, limited by guarantee, and limited by shares, can all, in theory, be either *PUBLIC* or *PRIVATE* companies. Generally, though, only companies limited by shares are ever public. Although the term 'public' company does not appear in the Companies Act, 1948 (which is the main governing statute), the term refers to any company which requires at least seven members of its valid formation. There is no maximum number of members. A private company on the other hand requires only two members for its formation. Further features of a private company are to be found in s.28 Companies Act, 1948, which describes such a company as one which, by its Articles of Association:

(a) limits the number of its members to 50 excluding present and past employees who are shareholders,

(b) restricts the right to transfer its shares, and

(c) prohibits an invitation to the public to subscribe for its shares.

The effect of this provision is to make the private company an ideal form of business organisation for family concerns, and very often is used to incorporate a business which was being run as a sole trader or partnership business so that the members can then enjoy the benefits of limited liability. Because of the limit on the number of members, many of them will have direct involvement in determining company policy, and since the general public cannot subscribe for shares, this means that the members themselves will have to raise the company's capital privately.

A summary of the major distinctions between *private* and *public* companies is shown below.

PRIVATE	PUBLIC
1. Minimum members = 2 Maximum members = 50	1. Minimum members = 7 No maximum.
2. Must restrict the right to transfer shares.	2. Shares generally freely transferable.
3. Must raise its capital privately.	3. Can raise capital by inviting the public to subscribe for shares.
4. Can commence business immediately on issue of Certificate of Incorporation.	4. Must first obtain a Trading Certificate to ensure it has sufficient capital to embark on its business.
5. Need only have one director.	5. Must have at least 2 directors.
6. No age limit on directors.	6. Directors retire at 70 unless members or Articles provide otherwise.
7. Members generally have direct involvement in running the company.	7. Business generally run by directors. Members have little direct involvement with policy except through general meetings.

In essence, then, the *private* company is an attractive form of enterprise for the small family business, whereas the *public* company is ideal for a business which is to be conducted on a large scale and where large capital input is required.

Finally in this part of the chapter it is worthwhile to compare two forms of organisation in commerce which we have mentioned — the Registered Company and the Partnership. The main points of distinction are given together with their advantages and disadvantages.

REGISTERED COMPANIES	PARTNERSHIPS
FORMATION	
Formation is by the registration of documents required by the Companies Acts.	Formation is by agreement between partners. No formalities are required except for limited partnerships.
SEPARATE PERSONALITY	
A registered company is a corporation distinct from the personalities of its members.	No separate personality, merely an association of human persons.
NUMBER OF MEMBERS	
Private company is 2 to 50, and public company has minimum of 7 but no maximum.	No more than 20 members, with exceptions for accountants, solicitors, etc.
LIMITED LIABILITY	
Limited either by shares or by guarantee, unlimited companies being relatively uncommon.	No limited liability except for unlimited partnerships.
CREDITORS	
Creditors have no right to sue individual members for the company's debts, except in unlimited companies.	Creditors can sue partners jointly or individually for the firm's debts.
POWERS	
A company's powers are fixed by its Memorandum and Articles. Powers can only be altered by following the specified procedure under the Companies Act.	Powers are fixed by the partnership agreement, if any, or the Partnership Act, 1890, and can be altered at any time by agreement between the partners.
PUBLIC DOCUMENTS	
The Memorandum, Articles, and certain other documents are open to public inspection.	Any partnership agreement, assuming it is in writing, is not available for public inspection.
AGENCY	
Members are not agents for the company and cannot contract on its behalf.	Each partner is an agent for his other partners and the firm for the purpose of the partnership business, and all are bound by his actions.
TRANSFER OF SHARES	
In public companies shares are usually freely transferable, although a private company has to restrict transferability in some way.	Shares and other rights in the firm cannot be transferred by partners without the consent of the others.
LIQUIDATION	
Companies are wound up according to the procedure in the Companies Act either by the Court or a liquidator.	Partnerships are dissolved as provided in the Partnership Act, 1890, usually by the partners themselves.

ADVANTAGES

It may prove easier to acquire capital, particularly in public companies where shares can be offered to the general public.	(1) Inexpensive to form if indeed any cost is incurred at all. Fewer formalities to be observed.
Members usually have the advantage of limited liability.	(2) Fewer formalities to be complied with in running the business, and so there is less publicity of information about it. For example accounts are never open to public inspection.
Corporate personality — the company can own property, employ servants, and sue and be sued in its own name.	(3) The ultra vires rule does not apply to partnerships, so they can do anything lawful if the partners agree to do it.
Greater facilities for borrowing exist. For example a company can issue debentures and create a charge on its property as security for a loan.	(4) Each partner has a right to manage the firm's business.
	(5) Easier to alter firm's powers.

DISADVANTAGES

Expensive to form. For example registration fees and legal costs.	(1) No limited liability. Each partner being personally liable for the firm's debts in full.
Strict requirements as to publicity of information about the business.	(2) No separate legal personality of the firm.
Company constitution must be complied with strictly and can only be altered as specified by the Act.	(3) It may prove more difficult to acquire capital.
Members, especially in a public company, may take little part in management.	(4)

Students, at this stage, can produce their own but additional set of advantages and disadvantages simply by making use of the knowledge gathered when reading about partnerships (and sole traders) earlier in this chapter. Some points that could be developed might relate to the following type of situations.

achieving economies of scale,
complexity of organisation structure,
contact with customers,
industrial relations,
specialisation of personnel,
speed of decision making,
ownership and control,
winding up the organisation, and
others.

Characteristics of corporations

The characteristics of corporations can be described as arising from:

their legal status (corporation become a legal person and have their own existence apart from its members. They can sue or be sued in their own name. Also, corporations have perpetual succession in that they were created by a legal process and are brought to an end by legal processes) their owner-managership status (the tendency is for shareholders to be divorced from managing the corporation, in other words they have little — if any — control over the operations of the firm)

their financial structure status (there tends to be less restriction, relative to sole traders and partnerships, on where they obtain their long term finance)

their employer status (the majority of corporations tend to be large firms and thus employ more personnel relative to small firms. Many of their employees will be members of trade unions. As a result corporations are likely to be faced with problems associated with trade unions, for example, demarcation disputes and strikes.

their market situation (corporations tend to have a larger share of the market, and the larger the share the greater the opportunity to exert power in affecting its environment).

When comparing the above to those of the sole trader and partnership it can be seen that there are 'big' differences in the situations that give rise to their characteristics.

Now to consider various forms of specialised business organisations.

Specialised business organisations

To date we have only considered the general types of business organisation, which an individual or group of individuals are likely to form to run a business. Nevertheless there are other forms of business organisation similarly governed by legal rules which operate in more specialised fields, and, because they too are organisations the main features of several of them must be considered. Indeed you may come across them, if not actually deal with them, in a day-to-day situation.

Building Societies

A Building Society is a corporation, but it is not a company since it is not governend by the Companies Acts but by particular statutes which relate to it. Many of these were passed from 1874 onwards, and the present rules are contained in the Buildings Societies Act, 1962. Most people are aware that the purpose of forming such an organisation is to raise money from its members by the issue of shares in the Society. Once a fund has been built up, advances may be made to members to help them buy their own houses or other land. The Society lends this money on mortgage, that is that in exchange for a loan to a member for a certain period of time, the Society takes the land to be bought as security, retaining the title deeds to the land in its possession until such time as the loan plus interest has been paid off.

To form a Building Society at least ten people are needed, and they have to register the society's rules with the Registrar of Friendly Societies. Since the Society is a corporation, it will receive a certificate of incorporation from him, and if it should ever be dissolved, the Registrar has powers to deal with this.

We have said that members of a building society are shareholders in it. But the shares which they hold are completely different from shares in a registered company. Here, for example, members receive interest on their paid up shares and do not, like shareholders in, say, a public company, participate in the Society's profits by way of dividend. However they do enjoy the advantages of limited liability. So that if they have received an advance from the Society on their shares, liability is limited by the amount payable on it. If no advance has been made, liability is limited to the amount of their paid-up share.

Industrial and Provident Societies

These Societies are formed for a wide variety of purposes such as the provision of loans, housing and insurance. They can be registered with the Registrar of Friendly Societies by the incorporation procedure specified in the Industrial and Provident Societies Acts, 1965-1975. Any such co-operative society can only be used, by law, to improve the conditions of members of the "working classes" or to provide some other benefit to the community.

Friendly Societies

These Societies, which are unincorporated associations, may be registered under the Friendly Societies Act 1974, and are formed for some beneficial purpose, for example the provision of social, educational, or recreational facilities. A common type of such organisation is the working men's club. Since the society is not a corporation it does not have the ability in law to hold its own property and consequently any property is held by trustees for the benefit of the society. Should the society be dissolved, any members of it at the date of dissolution are entitled to share in the distribution of its assets.

Trustee Savings Banks

Savings Banks are regulated by the Trust Savings Bank Act, 1969. They are formed to receive deposits from customers on which interest is paid, but they do not obtain any benefit from those deposits apart from paying any necessary management expenses. In this way any investor, who can only deposit a maximum of £10,000, can obtain interest on savings while having the advantage of being able to cash them when needed. Current accounts can also be opened for customers who already have savings accounts although interest cannot be paid.

Co-operatives

As we mentioned earlier, some co-operatives carrying on production, loan, retail, and insurance businesses may be registered under the Industrial and Provident Societies Acts. The type of organisation you are sure to be familiar with is the retail co-operative society (C.W.S.) which operates in most areas of the country, and which has the advantage of being able to buy in bulk and pass benefits on to its members. Such co-operatives are consumer oriented. This means that the members are also the customers of the shops. They have voting rights, and can elect a Management Committee to run the business. They may also receive benefits in the form of fixed interest on shares which they hold in the society, and a dividend (often in the form of stamps) on goods which they buy. More modern societies are now more likely to be registered as companies limited by shares.

Another form of co-operative is the co-ownership firm. This takes the form of a company limited by shares and an example would be the John Lewis Partnership which controls such large chain stores as Lewis's. With this type of organisation the employees have some direct involvement with the firm. They may have some say in the appointment and removal of its directors, and the right to participate in its profits.

Recently, and usually with active government backing, another type of co-operative organisation was developed — the worker co-operative; formed as a company limited by shares. The Meriden Motorcycle Co-operative and the Scottish Daily News were examples of such organisations which were brought into existence because otherwise the business would have had to close and jobs would have been lost. The common feature of such a co-operative is that employees control the company's operations since they have the vast majority of representatives, if not all, on the board of directors or whatever the management body may be called. Financial help for these co-operatives has inevitably come from the government since private investors tend to fight shy of putting their money in such an organisation.

Banks

The business of banking is not controlled by any particular legislation, and there is no statutory definition of the term "bank". In fact, of course, everyone readily recognises that the main aspects of the business of banking involve the collection of cheques for customers and the crediting of the accounts with the value, paying out on cheques drawn by customers on their bank, and the keeping of current and deposit accounts. As we have seen previously, a banking partnership may consist of up to 20 members if Department of Trade recognition is given to the partners. Otherwise, under the Companies Act, 1948, a banking parternship or other unincorporated banking association with more than 10 members must register under the Act. It is then obliged to deliver an annual return detailing its financial position in addition to publishing financial details on a half-yearly basis which you may well have seen framed on the wall of your local bank.

A note about characteristics

In previous pages we have been bold to state the characteristics of the *major* forms of business organisations. Naturally we must treat what has been said with care because in stating the characteristics we have been generalising. The danger arises because organisations are made up of diverse groups, for example operating in different industries. As such we can find individual organisations that do not fit one or more of the general characteristics stated. An example here would be that of a sole trader or partnership who has a large share of the market, or who has industrial relations problems. There are, usually, exceptions to general statements. Thus, the general characteristics provided will satisfy most organisations in the group — but not all.

We can now turn to certain organisations that have their own special characteristics — multinationals, mixed enterprise and nationalised industries.

Assignments

1. Before a company is issued with its Certificate of Incorporation by the Registrar of Companies the promoters of the company must submit to the Registrar a number of essential documents. Two of these are: (a) The Memorandum of Association, and (b) The Articles of Association. What matters are contained in these documents?

2. Outline the advantages obtained by a company limited by shares. In view of these advantages, how do your account for the preponderance of sole traders and partnerships in the U.K. economy?

3. What is a public company? What advantages does a private limited company gain in changing itself to a public company?

4. A friend of yours approaches you in the hopes that you can provide him with information about partnerships. He puts so many questions to you that you decide to write an essay to cover the most essential points, such as the legal aspects, advantages, and disadvantages. What points would you include in your essay?

5. Provide information about the type of legal constraints that the following forms of organisations must face:

   a) partnerships, and

   b) public companies.

6. Compare partnerships and registered companies.

Chapter 20

Special Forms of Organisations

Learning objectives:
At the end of your study of this chapter you should be able to:
1. distinguish different types of *special* organisations in terms of their *special* function and purpose.
2. define and distinguish the different forms or *special* organisations in commerce, industry and government.
3. analyse *some* of the consequences of choice between forms of business unit.

In this chapter we will identify three forms of business organisation which merit special attention, namely:

1. Multinationals — operating in the private sector.

2. Mixed enterprise — a mixture of private and public sector.

3. Nationalised industries — operating in the public sector.

Multinationals

The term 'multinational' may be a new term but it represents a movement which has been going on for centuries; since the day the East India and Hudson Bay companies acquired overseas interests. However, since the end of World War II the movement has been speeded up.

What do we mean by the term? First, it should be noted that there is not one definition but several. The following[1] is a useful way of looking at these definitions.

"Lack of statistical information and organisational knowledge has made it difficult to closely define the multinational. Professor J. H. Dunning[2] has loosely described it as "an enterprise which owns or controls production facilities (i.e. factories, mines, oil refineries, offices, etc) in more than one country". Many enterprises in the U.K. would easily satisfy this criterion by the fact that they have small subsidiaries overseas. The title "multinational" would flatter them. Such companies might be better described as simply "international companies". The Economist suggests, however that a truly multinational company is one whose overseas operations are at least as great as its domestic activities. A multinational might also be expected to show centralisation of control with each of its overseas units having little autonomy and being run as part of a group plan.

1.   Taken from Economics for Business Studies, Vol. 1, Ed. N. L. Paulus, pages 242-243.
2.   "The Multinational Enterprise", John H. Dunning, Lloyds Bank Review, July 1970, p.20.

Each subsidiary might also display evidence of interchange of personnel, management information, capital and technical knowledge. Multinationals also tend to create an international as opposed to a national image; the title of some of these companies indicating a desire to shrug off national ties. Examples would include International Business Machines, International Harvester, International Telephone and Telegraph, etc..

The President of one of the largest multinationals, International Business Machines, defined the multinational even more finely by setting out five basic criteria for a multinational company.[3]

1. It must do business in many countries ... it must be in many countries that are in different stages of economic development.

2. It must have foreign subsidiaries with the same Research and Development, manufacturing, sales, services, and so on, that a true industrial entity has.

3. There should be nationals running these local companies.

4. There must be a multinational headquarters, staffed with people from different countries.

5. There should be multinational stock ownership — the stock must be owned by people in different countries.

It should be noted however that having outlined these criteria the President of the company admitted that no multinational company would satisfy it perfectly.''

Some examples of business organisations that have been given the title of multinationals are: Exxon, General Motors, Ford and International Business Machines, all of these have their origin in the U.S.A.. From the U.K. we have British Petroleum and Imperial Chemical Industries. Some of these multinationals, it might be worth noting, have sales figures which are greater than the gross national products of smaller countries in this world. For example, Exxon and General Motors have sales figures greater than the GNP of Ireland.

It can be noted that British Petroleum Company Limited had direct and indirect holdings in about 1,000 subsidiary and associated companies in some 70 countries in 1978.[4]

Many of the previously named organisations operate in the U.K.. For example General Motors owns and controls Vauxhall, and Ford Motor Company owns and controls Ford's of Britain.

Multinationals operating in the U.K. are subject to the laws of the land; Companies Acts, contracts, exchange controls, etc.. Nevertheless some of them are so big that they can, to a large extent, act as their own 'pressure group' to move governments along lines they would like. It is not unknown for them to threaten a country whose policies have been against them by

3. "Multinationalism and the 29th day", G. E. Bradley and E. C. Bursk, in Harvard Business Review, January-February 1972, page 39.

4. Information obtained from BP's Annual Report and Accounts 1978, p.8.

claiming they will refuse to invest further in its organisation in the country, and they might even go so far as to withdraw their company from such a country completely. One thing that is certain is that some of them are so big that they can shield themselves from an individual country's adverse economic fluctuations.

On the other hand, multinationals bring advantages to their host country. Their export efforts can benefit the country's balance of payments, and as we have seen in this country just recently they can plough vast sums of money into exploration (North Sea oil) which helps the balance of payments by cutting down on oil imports and provides industry with work and U.K. population with jobs.

Multinationals are here today and it is expected that we will see many more of them in the future.

Mixed Enterprise in U.K.

Mixed enterprise is a term used to describe a business organisation that involves a partnership between private firms and the State. It, like nationalisation, is another form of public ownership, but in this case the State is not taking over a whole industry nor a whole firm. Mixed enterprises are not common in the U.K., but when they do take place the State may be either a passive or active participant. In several European countries, such as Italy and France, the mixed enterprise is a common business form.

The most important mixed enterprise in the U.K. is 'The British Petroleum Company Limited'; an organisation that employed in the U.K. an average weekly number of 38,550 persons during 1978.[5]

The State's share in BP's total of 'ordinary stock' (£386,500,000) was as follows on 31 December 1978:

Her Majesty's Government owned £119,300,000 or 30.9 per cent of the total, and Bank of England owned £77,800,000 or 20.1 per cent.

The remainder (£189,400,000) was held by approximately 170,000 holders.

As a result of its shareholding the Government has the right to appoint two directors to represent its interests on the Board. The Board operates with a similar freedom to that of private sector business organisations because the Government has not exercised its right to veto certain resolutions made by the Board.

Other private sector business organisations have been brought into the fold of the mixed enterprise banner, from the late 1960's onwards, as the Government acquired financial interests of such businesses as part of its modernisation and rationalisation programme.

Whether the mixed enterprise will grow in importance or not will depend very much upon the political party in power in the U.K.

---

5. Information obtained from BP's Annual Report and Accounts 1978, p.8.

Mixed enterprise and Industrial Reorganisation Corporation

The Labour Government in 1966 set up the Industrial Reorganisation Corporation to promote rationalisation in U.K. industry by encouraging mergers. If necessary the Government would take up ordinary shares (it is these shares which convey ownership upon the holder) and when this happened a mixed enterprise was brought into existence. An example of a notable IRC promoted merger was that which produced British Leyland.

When the Conservatives came into power in the early 1970s they conveniently allowed the IRC to disappear. Conservatives do not encourage the use of public money going into private organisations. They do not believe in helping 'lame duck' businesses that cannot seem to survive in the world of private business.

Mixed Enterprise and National Enterprise Board

The Conservatives lost the elections of February 1974. The Labour Government brought forward the Industry Act of 1975. The introduction of this Act made it possible for them to set up the National Enterprise Board.

The main role of the NEB was to provide new equity (ordinary shares that convey ownership) capital to private sector business organisation in order for them to carry out re-equipment and modernisation schemes. NEB funds were a new source of finance for industrial development. As before, it was considered by the Opposition to be a 'back-door entry to public ownership'. Like the IRC, the NEB was given the task of promoting the restructuring of certain sectors of industry.

The NEB was to act as a holding company for the government — it was to hold the ownerships rights the government acquired through the operations of the IRC. This brought shares of Ferranti Ltd., Leyland Ltd., and Rolls-Royce (1971) Ltd. into the investment portfolio of the NEB.

When the NEB was formed it was given the task of:

1. bringing Government and private industry closer together, and

2. promote industrial democracy.

Industrial democracy is a term used that refers to "a change of atmosphere and relationships in industry, which will give to the workers a better status, more power, more responsibility, and a true sense of participation."[6]

The NEB started carrying out its tasks, under the supervision of a Minister of State. Like the nationalised industries, the NEB is responsible to a Minister of the government; in its case it is the Secretary of State.

By mid 1978 the NEB held shares or equity in a number of business organisations in the private sector. Below are some of the companies they hold shares in:

The Cambridge Instrument Co. Ltd.	I.C.L. Ltd.
Fairey Engineering Holdings Ltd.	Power Dynamics Ltd.
Sinclair Radionics Ltd.	Twinlock Ltd.

These were in addition to those already mentioned.

6. "Socialism and Nationalisation", Hugh Gaitskell, Fabian Tract 300, July 1956, p.5.

As a result of IRC and NEB activities the number of mixed enterprises have tended to increase in the U.K.; the State has increased public ownership.

With the advent of a Conservative government in May 1979 the place of the NEB will change considerably.

Now to turn our attention to public ownership on a big scale — the nationalised industries.

Nationalised Industries

Most writing on the nationalised industries has been written under the heading of 'nationalisation'. This term, according to Hugh Gaitskell,[7] is generally understood to mean the taking over by the State of a *complete* industry so that it is owned by and managed and controlled for the Community. He went on to say that nationalisation is part of a wider subject called *public ownership;* a term that refers to the ownership by the State of any property whether industrial or not, whether embracing the whole of an industry or only part of it.

It follows from the above that nationalised industries are business organisations that operate as part of the public sector of the U.K. economy.

Nationalised industries, as stated early on in chapter 19, are public corporations incorporated by special Acts of Parliament and ultimately are responsible to Parliament. These statutes lay down the duties and powers of the Boards of the nationalised industries and the appropriate government Minister. Normally the Boards are given a considerable degree of independence but they are watched over by their relevant Ministers. The general policy on the running of the nationalised industries were set out in a 1978 White Paper.[8] The basic philosophy was that the Boards should make the day-to-day decisions but the Government should lay down the broad economic and financial framework within which the nationalised industries should work. The reason for the Government laying down broad objectives is that these nationalised industries are very important in the national economy as a whole and they should operate in the national interest.

How important are they? The following exhibit (Exhibit 20.1) high-lights the names of the nationalised industries and provides details of their size and importance.

7.   Hugh Gaitskell was a former Member of Parliament and former leader of the Parliamentary Labour Party. His statement defining nationalisation (and state ownership) can be found in Fabian Tract 300 entitled "Socialism and Nationalisation", July 1956, page 6.

8.   "The Nationalised Industries", Cmnd 7131, April 1978, HMSO.

Exhibit 20.1

Nationalised Industries, 1977-78

Industry	Capital employed* (£ million)	Number of employees (thousand)	Turnover (£ million)
National Coal Board	1,218	303	2,733
Electricity Council and Boards	6,511	159	4,494
North of Scotland Hydroelectric Board	498	4	146
South of Scotland Electricity Board	723	14	408
British Gas Corporation	2,102	100	2,568
British National Oil Corporation	557	1	25
British Steel Corporation	3,723	197	3,154
Post Office	6,881	401	4,183
British Airways Board	829	57	1,355
British Airports Authority	333	6	125
British Railways Board	1,191	178	1,678
British Transport Docks Board	179	12	111
British Waterways Board	14	3	11
National Freight Corporation	85	40	387
National Bus Company	179	65	392
Scottish Transport Group	62	14	94
British Aerospace	287	69	860
British Shipbuilders	89	87	548
TOTAL	25,461	1,710	23,272

Note: * At historical cost

Source: Economic Progress Report No. 107, February 1979, Published by the Treasury.

The above exhibit provides basic facts about the 18 nationalised industries operating in the U.K. in the period 1977-78. It shows that they operate in the strategic areas of communications, energy and public transport, their goods and services are of great importance to all sectors in the community. On the other hand they are important purchasers for many goods supplied by the private sector.

The nationalised industries employ 1,710,000 persons, or to put it another way they employ approximately 7 out of every 100 members of the country's labour force.

The two biggest employers are the Post Office and the National Coal Board. In fact, they rank first and second as top employers of all business organisations in the U.K. The Post Office employs approximately twice as many persons as General Electric or Imperial Chemical Industries; two of the largest organisations in the private sector.

Nationalising industries was seen as an alternative to private monopoly. Quite often one reads that nationalised industries are monopolies. Nothing could be farther from the truth. Perhaps the only one that comes closest to having a pure monopoly is the Post Office. The others invariably meet considerable competition from home and abroad.

One big difference between the nationalised industries and firms operating in the private sector is that the nationalised industries "are not subject to the same market disciplines as the private sector".[9] This it was claimed provided "more scope for argument about their proper role and objectives".

Proper Role?

What is the proper role (or function) of the nationalised industries? What are the nationalised industries appointed or expected to do? The answer is very simple — they are expected to do what the Government tells them to do. This means they are expected to do different things at different times depending on:

(a) who controls Parliament, and

(b) the state of the nation.

A 'Labour Government' we assume would expect the nationalised industries to function in such a way as to make economic planning easier because Labour tends to favour a mixed economy that leans towards the planned economy. On the other hand a 'Conservative Government' tends to favour a mixed economy that leans towards the free enterprise type of economy. They, then, would set the nationalised industries the role of operating to the disciplines of the market.

In the mixed economy which we have in the U.K. we would expect both political parties to lay down the role of the nationalised industries as that of helping the nation achieve its major economic objectives. If unemployment were on the increase we would expect the role of the nationalised industries to be that of maintaining their present employment level (regardless of cost?). On the other hand, if the nation was experiencing moderate or galloping inflation they may be given the role of keeping their prices low.

Nationalised industries may have many roles at one time and many different roles at other times; their roles are subject to change.

Objectives

The objective of nationalised industries refer to their primary aim or purpose; it indicates what the organisation wants to achieve. In this case we must see their primary objective as being what the government wants them to achieve. This is the same as other organisations in the private sector — providing goods and services for the community for which there is a demand. But, unlike business organisations in the private sector who pursue the objective with the desire of making high profits the nationalised industries pursue different and much wider goals.

Naturally it is possible to state some objectives that are common to all nationalised industries such as supplying goods and services of the type, quality and quantity desired by their consumers, but it should be realised that each nationalised industry has its own special objectives. For example, the electricity supply industry provides power to consumers in outlying areas.

9. Report by the National Economic Development Office on the nationalised industries. November 1976.

Nationalised industries had the common objective of serving the national interest in some wider sense — social objectives. For example the objective of making profits may not be as important as that of achieving industrial democracy. They may be given the objectives of avoiding the costs of road congestion, or, they may be given the objective of operating in high cost areas in order to encourage regional development. In other words what we are saying is that nationalised industries would consider social costs and benefits — this must be compared to the private costs and benefits which organisations in the private sector are primarily concerned with.

The White Paper[10] on the nationalised industries explained the Government's views on the running of the industries. The following are worthy of mention.

1. Ministers should be given *powers,* subject to certain safeguards, to give directions specifying how the nationalised industries can help the Government in achieving matters that affect the national interest. In other words the Government will lay down broad objectives and leave the day-to-day decisions to the industries themselves on how they reach these objectives.

2. One broad objective would relate to the *targets* (objectives) for the industries' profits — their financial goals. Targets should be set for 3 to 5 years, and actual targets would vary from industry to industry. The level of the targets will depend on the sectoral and social objectives set for each industry; on the earning power of its existing assets; on the required rate of return for new investment.

3. Financial targets are important in setting *prices* for nationalised industries which are considered to have a monopoly, such as public utilities as opposed to steel whose prices are determined by the market forces of supply and demand. For these monopoly industries, financial targets will determine the general level of prices that they can charge.

4. A certain amount of *profits*, usually referred to as surpluses, is necessary for the continuing well-being of the industries. This will keep them from burdening the economy with their borrowing programmes.

Accountability

The above broad objectives clarify the accountability that Boards of the nationalised industries have to meet to the owners of the industries — the Government. In so far as these industries are concerned there is a considerable degree of control by the owners. The channels through which nationalised industries are accountable to the Government and the public are shown in the following exhibit.

10. "The Nationalised Industries" Cmnd 7131, April 1978, HMSO.

318

Exhibit 20.2   **Channels through which Nationalised**
Industries are accountable to the public

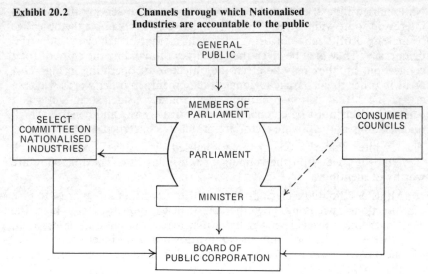

Source: "Economics for Business Studies" Ed. N. L. Paulus, Polytech Publishers, Vol. 1, Aug. 1974, p54.

Advantages and disadvantages of nationalisation

Advantages and disadvantages of nationalisation can be broken down into those that are common to all nationalised industries and another set for those applicable to each industry. The following are a few of each which might be applied *generally* to a policy of nationalisation.

Advantages

The following advantages are briefly noted and are capable of being discussed more fully through group projects. It should be noted that they are not listed in any predetermined order; one advantage is not given a weight against the others.

1. Can bring about greater efficiency in an industry by eliminating waste — for example in supplying householders with gas or electricity.

2. Tends to remove excessive profits that are normally made by business organisations in the private sector.

3. It follows from point 2 that consumers are not exploited by paying abnormal prices.

4. It makes it easier for the Government to implement economic policy when the state has control over the key sectors of the economy.

5. Goods and services which would normally not be provided by the private sector because they are not profitable would be produced by the nationalised industries as long as they would benefit the community.

6. Nationalising an industry removes the conflict caused by private ownership and public accountability.

    Others can be stated — competition, investment, research, etc.

Disadvantages

Disadvantages given are subject to the same notes provided before noting advantages. Some disadvantages might be as follows:

1. Nationalised industries normally have a monopoly or near-monopoly situation and as a result what they produce may be seen as a restriction of consumer choice.

2. Absence of profit motive may create an atmosphere in the nationalised industries that does not provide an incentive to operate at greatest efficiency.

3. Most nationalised industries, especially those that have monopoly situations, are not subject to the disciplines of the market. They are not faced with competition.

4. Nationalised industries are writ 'large scale enterprise' and in such organisations there is little or no room for individuals who are tempermentally unfitted to work in large-sized organisations.

5. There is no fear of losses being made — taxpayers are burdened with these. In other words there is no real incentive to make profits.

6. Because nationalised industries are subject to the control of Parliament they are subject to the inefficiencies associated with red-tape and with changing objectives associated with changing powers in Parliament.

There are other disadvantages. It is suggested that students re-read the chapter on the mixed economy and note the disadvantages associated with the state taking over more and more of the economic activities of the nation.

Nationalised industry versus Joint Stock Company

At this stage it might be useful to make a comparison between the nationalised industries and those organisations in the private sector which have the opportunity to become large-scale organisations (a joint stock company).

The following are but a few of the many differences that can be noted.

Nationalised industries	**Joint Stock Company**
1. Owned by the public who bear the risk.	Owned by shareholders who take varying degrees of risk.
2. Losses are met by owners in full (taxation) – there is no limit.	Losses are met by owners only to the extent of the value of the shares they hold.
3. Run by a Board appointed by a responsible Minister.	Run by a Board appointed by shareholders.
4. Profits, if any, may be used to alleviate rates and taxes.	Profits are paid to owners in the form of dividends.
5. Major aim is to achieve socialist objectives – not high profits.	Main aim is to achieve profits. This may sometimes not be in the interest of the public at large.
6. Industries are accountable to Parliament.	Firms are accountable to their owners – their shareholders.
7. Others.	Others.

Nationalisation must be seen as part of the U.K. way of life — a situation one can expect to find in a mixed economy such as we have in the U.K.

Assignments

1. When the Labour Party win Parliamentary elections they normally have as part of their manifesto that of taking certain industries into public ownership. What are the reasons given to justify such action?

2. In what ways do nationalised industries differ from large scale private enterprise organisations?

3. Public ownership means we must consider ownership on a wider scale than the nationalised industries.

   a) Distinguish between the terms 'public ownership' and 'nationalised industries'.

   b) Identify the major forms of government ownership in the economy.

4. Much comment has been centered on the large sums of public money made available for private enterprise. Examine the forms and extent of such assistance. Would you say that such assistance is justifiable?

5. By the end of the 20th century it has been calculated that multinational companies will control approximately 50 per cent of the world's output. What is a multinational company and what benefits do they bring to the host nation?

Chapter 21

Organisations — accountability and constraints

Learning objectives:
At the end of your study of this chapter you should be able to:
1. identify the groups to which organisations may be accountable.
2. identify the difference in accountability for different types of organisation.
3. identify the main framework of constraints within which different types of organisation operate.

We all know the expression "no man is an island" — likewise no organisation is "an island". Every organisation has to encounter other organisations, as well as other groups of people, with which it maintains a continuous relationship and which affect its functioning in a direct manner.

It is often worthwhile to consider a particular organisation, and then to list all the other organisations which it encounters. If we take as an example a company operating in the private sector, then such an organisation will have to encounter others which are also private sector organisations, for example suppliers and customers. There are other organisations which are in the public sector, which are also encountered, such as the Inland Revenue, and the Department of Employment.

What we must realise is that no organisation is operating in a vacuum, unaffected by other organisations, and indeed, by standards laid down by other organisations.

Groups to which organisations are accountable

There are a number of groups to which organisations are accountable, and in order to identify such groups it is advisable to consider each organisation in turn. It is possible then to compile a comprehensive list of such groups. It will also become apparent that not all organisations are accountable to the same groups. It is nevertheless possible to consider the question of accountability in more general terms, but reminding ourselves of the differences between organisations in the public and private sectors. Public accountability has to be viewed as a very special process, and will be discussed later. The following examples can be given of particular groups to which certain organisations are accountable:

1. *Shareholders* – who have invested money in a company and have therefore agreed to share the profits or losses of the business. The interests of the shareholders have to be regarded by the Board of Directors, and the Board is ultimately accountable for maintaining these interests.

2. *Employees* – whose interests cannot be ignored. A distinction is often made between 'staff' and 'workers'. The staff include managers whose responsibility it is to organise materials, equipment, and manpower, including the workers. Both staff and workers are represented by particular organised groups. Staff belong to various professional bodies or associations which lay down standards which may affect the way organisations function. Workers belong to trade unions which again make particular demands on the organisation, not only on pay, but also on conditions under which people work.

3. *Creditors* – have also to be remembered, the people to whom the company is in debt at any one particular time. The interests of creditors have to be protected against fraud and negligence in the use of the company's assets. There are times when the creditors may become even more important. If there is some doubt about a company's future, the creditors may decide to secure the winding up of that company in order to protect their own financial stake.

4. *Consumers* – whose interests are increasingly important. Many consumers' associations have been established to represent consumer interests collectively. Consumer dissatisfaction can seriously affect an organisations's ability to maintain a favourable share of the market. Faulty products can now be publicised very easily and an organisation's image consequently affected.

5. *Customers* – who have to be distinguished from the consumers, although when we consider members of the general public we realise that they can be both 'customers' and 'consumers'. More specifically, however, we may also view other organisations as customers whose interests cannot be neglected by a company whose goods or services are being bought by those organisations, for example a motor manufacturer may be a customer of a company which makes accessories.

Differences in accountability have to be recognised between different types of organisation. We live in a world where the large scale organisation is ever present. The problems of organisation are likewise more complex and perhaps there may be many more groups to which the organisation is accountable. Certainly it is often said that human relations problems are greater in larger organisations.

In the public sector, organisations are necessarily subject to public accountability — they have to work within a strict legal framework too. Central Government Departments are subject to Parliamentary control through their Minister. Local government authorities are responsible to local elected representatives — the councillors. In both instances, the people have a means of exerting some control over these organisations through their elected representatives.

The existence of independent Commissioners or Ombudsman can also be seen as deriving from the need to exert public accountability over public organisations, such as Central Government Departments, Local authorities, and the National Health Service.

Public accountability is also important when we consider the financial basis of public organisations. They are responsible for spending large amounts of public money, and there must be adequate checks and controls to ensure that such money is being used for the purpose for which it has been authorised. The accounts of public organisations must be subjected to control by independent auditors. Central Government Departments, in particular, have a very rigorous audit procedure to which their accounts are subjected. The Office of Comptroller and Auditor General is of great importance in this respect. The House of Commons has a Select Committee – the Public Accounts Committee – to scrutinise the Departments' financial operations with assistance from this officer. The accounts of the nationalised industries are also subjected to independent audit by auditors appointed by the appropriate Minister. Likewise, the accounts of the local authorities are subject to audit by a district auditor or by an 'approved' auditor, whose appointment by a particular authority has been approved by the Environment Secretary.

Constraints

At this point we should note that different organisations have to consider many different influences which will affect their operations. There is some overlap between the forms of accountability to which organisations are subject and the influences (or constraints) which affect the way organisations operate. The following examples of such constraints can be given:

1. *The 'public interest' and social attitudes.* Organisations in the public sector have to work within a framework where the public interest is necessarily important, and equality of provision and impartiality have to be strictly regarded. All organisations have social responsibilities, but some will pay more attention to such responsibilities than others. Some organisations have constantly to pay attention to the possible effects of their particular operations on the environment at large. Both interest groups, and Government regulations will serve to remind organisations of their responsibilities lest they forget.

2. *The challenge of competitors.* In the private sector, organisations are competing with one another for a share of the market, and no organisation can forget what its competitors are doing. The recognition that such competitors exist and are actively involved in the same, or a similar, field will necessarily affect the way that particular organisation functions. For example, it may be forced to spend more and more money on advertising.

3. *The actual working of the market economy* which can be so unpredictable and uncertain as far as organisations which operate within this sector are concerned. The internal economic system in this country has to be considered from this standpoint and many organisations have also to pay attention to other circumstances which they cannot control in the world at large. This particular dimension has become more apparent this century, and increasingly since the end of the second World War in 1945.

4. *Political constraints* can pose all kinds of problems for organisations and once again these can be both internal (they operate within the U.K.), and external (operate internationally). A change in Government in this country can bring about many other developments since different political parties which control the system may have totally different attitudes and policies which can affect the way other organisations operate. For example, we can expect more government intervention within the economy by a Labour Government. Political problems in other countries can also have a distinct effect upon organisations. In 1979 political disturbances in Iran and the reduction in oil supplies led to an increase in petrol prices in this country. Of course, decisions by the Organisation of Petroleum Exporting Countries (OPEC) to increase the price of oil are also likely to have a direct effect on organisations. Such decisions may, or may not, be 'political'. We should remember that constraints cannot be neatly pigeon-holed and many such constraints overlap.

5. Therefore, by no means completely separated from the above constraints is the question of *legal constraints* which may affect the various organisations which are functioning in a particular type of economic and political system in the U.K. We have to bear in mind the nature of our political system, and what the public expect a Government to do on their behalf. Whatever legal constraints are operating, what is certain is that the Government in office has an overriding interest in such constraints. Whilst it is difficult for "outsiders" to change the law — a constraint in itself — the Government in office is able more or less to monopolise the law making process. Even this factor has to be considered in the light of political circumstances, for example the size of the Government's majority and/or a split in the Cabinet on a particular issue. Government regulations which impose legal restrictions on organisations have to be considered, and important examples concern health and safety at work, industrial training, and employment protection. Of course there are also regulations which have been introduced in an attempt both to reduce and remove monopolies. The protection of the consumer, and the promotion of the "public interests" are both expected from Governments.

6. *Technological developments and changes* have also to be considered. Some of these will benefit the organisation in the long term, but even so there may be problems thrown up in their wake which will have to be

attended to. Many technological developments have occurred which have brought about a reduction in manpower required for the organisation. Inevitably, professional associations and trade unions will seek to preserve the interests of their members and may resist attempts to reduce the number of staff and workers required. Of course, certain technological developments may actually result in a particular organisation being forced to close down, for example a change in materials or processes used. The newspaper industry has been affected by television, and with the further development of information systems associated with television, who knows what the future holds. New technologies, such as the "silicon chip" pose considerable possibilities for certain organisations, but many problems for other organisations.

Assignments

1. Why is public accountability considered to be so important?
2. Make a list of all organisations which your own employing organisation encounters on a regular basis.
3. "All organisations, public and private, must pay attention to the 'public interest'." Discuss.
4. Political constraints can pose considerable problems for an organisations. Elucidate.

Index

NOTES

NOTES

NOTES

NOTES

NOTES

NOTES

NOTES

NOTES

NOTES

NOTES